Mastering iOS
Frameworks

Mastering iOS Frameworks

Beyond the Basics, Second Edition

Kyle Richter
Joe Keeley

✦ Addison-Wesley

Hoboken, NJ • Boston • Indianapolis • San Francisco
New York • Toronto • Montreal • London • Munich • Paris • Madrid
Cape Town • Sydney • Tokyo • Singapore • Mexico City

Library of Congress Control Number: 2015932706

ISBN-13: 978-0-134-05249-6
ISBN-10: 0-134-05249-8
Text printed in the United States on recycled paper at RR Donnelley in Crawfordsville, Indiana.
First printing: April 2015

Editor-in-Chief
Mark Taub

Senior Acquisitions Editor
Trina MacDonald

Development Editor
Sheri Replin

Managing Editor
Kristy Hart

Project Editor
Elaine Wiley

Copy Editor
Cheri Clark

Indexer
Ken Johnson

Proofreader
Kathy Ruiz

Technical Reviewers
Niklas Saers
Justin Williams

Editorial Assistant
Olivia Basegio

Cover Designer
Chuti Prasertsith

Senior Compositor
Gloria Schurick

❖

I would like to dedicate this book to my co-workers who continually drive me to never accept the first solution.

—Kyle Richter

I dedicate this book to my wife, Irene, and two daughters, Audrey and Scarlett. Your boundless energy and love inspire me daily.

—Joe Keeley

❖

Table of Contents

Contents vii

Foreword

I have been working with the iPhone SDK (now iOS SDK) since the first beta released in 2008. At the time, I was focused on writing desktop apps for the Mac and hadn't thought much about mobile app development.

If you chose to be an early adopter, you were on your own. In typical Apple fashion, the documentation was sparse, and since access to the SDK required an NDA—and, apparently, a secret decoder ring—you were on your own. You couldn't search Google or turn to StackOverflow for help, and there sure as hell weren't any books out yet on the SDK.

In the seven years (yes, it really has been only seven years) since Apple unleashed the original iPhone on the world, we've come a long way. The iPhone SDK is now the iOS SDK. There are dozens of books and blogs and podcasts and conferences on iOS development. And ever since 2009, WWDC has been practically impossible to get into, making it even harder for developers—old and new—to learn about the latest features coming to the platform. For iOS developers, there is so much more to learn.

One of the biggest challenges I have as an iOS developer is keeping on top of all the components and frameworks available in the kit. The iOS HIG should help us with that, but it doesn't go far enough—deep enough. Sure, now I can find some answers by searching Google or combing through StackOverflow; but, more often than not, those answers only explain the how and rarely the why, and they never provide the details you really need.

And this is what Kyle and Joe have done with this book—they're providing the detail needed so you can fully understand the key frameworks that make up the iOS SDK.

I've had the pleasure of knowing Kyle and Joe for a number of years. They are two of the brightest developers I have ever met. They have each written some amazing apps over the years, and they continuously contribute to the iOS development community by sharing their knowledge—speaking at conferences and writing other books on iOS development. If you have a question about how to do something in iOS, chances are good that Kyle and Joe have the answer for you.

But what makes these guys so awesome is not just their encyclopedic knowledge of iOS, but their willingness to share what they know with everyone they meet. Kyle and Joe don't have competitors, they have friends.

Kyle and Joe's in-depth knowledge of the iOS SDK comes through in this book. It's one of the things I like about this book. It dives into the details for each component covered at a level that you won't always find when searching online.

I also like the way the book is structured. This is not something that you'll read cover to cover. Instead, you'll pick up the book because you need to learn how to implement a collection view or sort out some aspect of running a task in a background thread that you can't quite wrangle. You'll pick up the book when you need it, find the solution, implement it in your own code, and then toss the book back on the floor until you need it again. This is what makes *Mastering iOS Frameworks* an essential resource for any iOS developer—regardless of your experience level. You might think you're a master with Core Location and MapKit, but I reckon you'll find something here that you never knew before.

Kyle and Joe don't come with egos. They don't brag. And they sure don't act like they are better than any other developer in the room. They instill the very spirit that has made the Mac and iOS developer community one of the friendliest, most helpful in our industry, and this book is another example of their eagerness to share their knowledge.

This book, just like the seminal works from Mark and LaMarche or Sadun, will always be within arm's reach of my desk. This is the book I wish I had when I first started developing iOS apps in 2008. Lucky you, it's here now.

—Kirby Turner

Chief Code Monkey at White Peak Software, author of *Learning iPad Programming: A Hands-On Guide to Building iPad Apps, Second Edition* (Addison-Wesley Professional), and Cocoa developer community organizer and conference junkie

Preface

Welcome to *Mastering iOS Frameworks: Beyond the Basics*!

There are hundreds of "getting started with iOS" books available to choose from, and there are dozens of advanced books in specific topics, such as Core Data or Security. There was, however, a disturbing lack of books that would bridge the gap between beginner and advanced niche topics.

This publication aims to provide development information on the intermediate-to-advanced topics that are otherwise not worthy of standalone books. It's not that the topics are uninteresting or lackluster; it's that they are not large enough topics. From topics such as working with JSON to accessing photo libraries, these are frameworks that professional iOS developers use every day but are not typically covered elsewhere.

Additionally, several advanced topics are covered to the level that many developers need in order to just get started. Picking up a 500-page Core Data book is intimidating, whereas Chapter 15 of this book provides a very quick and easy way to get started with Core Data. Additional introductory chapters are provided for debugging and instruments, TextKit, HomeKit, HealthKit, and CloudKit.

Topics such as Game Center leaderboards and achievements, AirPrint, music libraries, Address Book, and Passbook are covered in their entirety. Whether you just finished your first iOS project or you are an experienced developer, this book has something for you.

The chapters have all been updated to work with iOS 8. Please let us know if you encounter issues and we will release updates and corrections.

If you have suggestions, bug fixes, corrections, or anything else you'd like to contribute to a future edition, please contact us at mastering.ios.frameworks@gmail.com. We are always interested in hearing what would make this book better and are very excited to continue refining it.

—Kyle Richter and Joe Keeley

Prerequisites

Every effort has been made to keep the examples and explanations simple and easy to digest; however, this is to be considered an intermediate to advanced book. To be successful with it, you should have a basic understanding of iOS development, Objective-C, and C. Familiarity with the tools such as Xcode, Developer Portal, iTunes Connect, and Instruments is also assumed. Refer to *Programming in Objective-C,* by Stephen G. Kochan, and *Learning iOS Development,* by Maurice Sharp, Rod Strougo, and Erica Sadun, for basic Objective-C and iOS skills.

What You'll Need

Although you can develop iOS apps in the iOS simulator, it is recommended that you have at least one iOS device available for testing:

- Apple iOS Developer Account: The latest version of the iOS developer tools including Xcode and the iOS SDKs can be downloaded from Apple's Developer Portal (http://developer.apple.com/ios). To ship an app to the App Store or to install and test on a personal device, you will also need a paid developer account at $99 per year.

- **Macintosh Computer:** To develop for iOS and run Xcode, you will need a modern Mac computer capable of running the latest release of OS X.

- **Internet Connection:** Many features of iOS development require a constant Internet connection for your Mac as well as for the device you are building against.

How This Book Is Organized

With few exceptions (Game Center and Core Data), each chapter stands on its own. The book can be read cover to cover but any topic can be skipped to when you find a need for that technology; we wrote it with the goal of being a quick reference for many common iOS development tasks.

Here is a brief overview of the chapters you will encounter:

- **Chapter 1, "UIKit Dynamics":** iOS 7 introduced UI Kit Dynamics to add physics-like animation and behaviors to UIViews. You will learn how to add dynamic animations, physical properties, and behaviors to standard objects. Seven types of behaviors are demonstrated in increasing difficulty from gravity to item properties.

- **Chapter 2, "Core Location, MapKit, and Geofencing":** iOS 6 introduced new, Apple-provided maps and map data. This chapter covers how to interact with Core Location to determine the device's location, how to display maps in an app, and how to customize the map display with annotations, overlays, and callouts. It also covers how to set up regional monitoring (or geofencing) to notify the app when the device has entered or exited a region.

- **Chapter 3, "Leaderboards":** Game Center leaderboards provide an easy way to add social aspects to your iOS game or app. This chapter introduces a fully featured iPad game called Whack-a-Cac, which walks the reader through adding leaderboard support. Users will learn all the required steps necessary for implementing Game Center leaderboards, as well as get a head start on implementing leaderboards with a custom interface.

- **Chapter 4, "Achievements":** This chapter continues on the Whack-a-Cac game introduced in Chapter 3. You will learn how to implement Game Center achievements in a fully featured iPad game. From working with iTunes Connect to displaying achievement progress, this chapter provides all the information you need to quickly get up and running with achievements.

- **Chapter 5, "Getting Started with Address Book":** Integrating a user's contact information is a critical step for many modern projects. Address Book framework is one of the oldest available on iOS; in this chapter you'll learn how to interact with that framework. You will learn how to use the people picker, how to access the raw address book data, and how to modify and save that data.

- **Chapter 6, "Working with Music Libraries":** This chapter covers how to access the user's music collection from a custom app, including how to see informational data about the music in the collection, and how to select and play music from the collection.

- **Chapter 7, "Implementing HealthKit":** HealthKit provides a centralized location for health information that can be shared among apps. This chapter explains how to get started with HealthKit, how to access information available in HealthKit, and how to read and write various types of health data.

- **Chapter 8, "Implementing HomeKit":** This chapter explains how to get started using HomeKit, which enables iOS devices to communicate with home automation technology. It explains how to set up a home in HomeKit, and how to discover, set up, and interact with home automation devices such as lights, locks, and garage door openers.

- **Chapter 9, "Working with and Parsing JSON":** JSON, or JavaScript Object Notation, is a lightweight way to pass data back and forth between different computing platforms and architectures. As such, it has become the preferred way for iOS client apps to communicate complex sets of data with servers. This chapter describes how to create JSON from existing objects, and how to parse JSON into iOS objects.

- **Chapter 10, "Notifications":** Two types of notifications are supported by iOS: local notifications, which function on the device with no network required, and remote notifications, which require a server to send a push notification through Apple's Push Notification Service to the device over the network. This chapter explains the differences between the two types of notifications, and demonstrates how to set them up and get notifications working in an app.

- **Chapter 11, "Cloud Persistence with CloudKit":** CloudKit offers public and private remote data storage, with notifications for changes in data. This chapter explains the basic CloudKit concepts, and illustrates how to build an app that uses CloudKit for storing and syncing both private and public data remotely.

- **Chapter 12, "Extensions":** Extensions provide a way to access an app's functionality outside the app's sandbox. This chapter explains the different types of extensions that are available, and illustrates how to create a Today extension and an Apple Watch extension.

- **Chapter 13, "Handoff":** Handoff is one of the Continuity features introduced with iOS 8 and Yosemite. It enables the user to switch between devices and have an activity seamlessly move from one device to another. This chapter explains the basic Handoff mechanisms, and how to implement Handoff for developer-defined activities and document-based activities.

- **Chapter 14, "AirPrint":** An often-underappreciated feature of the iOS, AirPrint enables the user to print documents and media to any wireless-enabled AirPrint-compatible printer. Learn how to quickly and effortlessly add AirPrint support to your apps. By the end of this chapter you will be fully equipped to enable users to print views, images, PDFs, and even rendered HTML.

- **Chapter 15, "Getting Up and Running with Core Data":** This chapter demonstrates how to set up an app to use Core Data, how to set up a Core Data data model, and how to implement many of the most commonly used Core Data tools in an app. If you want to start using Core Data without digging through a 500-page book, this chapter is for you.

- **Chapter 16, "Integrating Twitter and Facebook Using Social Framework":** Social integration is the future of computing, and it is accepted that all apps have social features built in. This chapter walks you through adding support for Facebook and Twitter to your app using the Social Framework. You will learn how to use the built-in composer to create new Twitter and Facebook posts. You will also learn how to pull down feed information from both services and how to parse and interact with that data. Finally, using the frameworks to send messages from custom user interfaces is covered. By the end of this chapter, you will have a strong background in Social Framework as well as working with Twitter and Facebook to add social aspects to your apps.

- **Chapter 17, "Working with Background Tasks":** Being able to perform tasks when the app is not the foreground app was a big new feature introduced in iOS 4, and more capabilities have been added since. This chapter explains how to perform tasks in the background after an app has moved from the foreground, and how to perform specific background activities allowed by iOS.

- **Chapter 18, "Grand Central Dispatch for Performance":** Performing resource-intensive activities on the main thread can make an app's performance suffer with stutters and lags. This chapter explains several techniques provided by Grand Central Dispatch for doing the heavy lifting concurrently without affecting the performance of the main thread.

- **Chapter 19, "Using Keychain and TouchID to Secure and Access Data":** Securing user data is important and an often-overlooked stage of app development. Even large public companies have been called out in the news over the past few years for storing user credit card info and passwords in plain text. This chapter provides an introduction to not only using the Keychain to secure user data but developmental security as a whole. By the end of the chapter, you will be able to use Keychain to secure any type of small data on users' devices and provide them with peace of mind.

- **Chapter 20, "Working with Images and Filters":** This chapter covers some basic image-handling techniques, and then dives into some advanced Core Image techniques to apply filters to images. The sample app provides a way to explore all the options that Core Image provides and build filter chains interactively in real time.

- **Chapter 21, "Collection Views":** Collection views, a powerful new API introduced in iOS 6, give the developer flexible tools for laying out scrollable, cell-based content. In addition to new content layout options, collection views provide exciting new animation capabilities, both for animating content in and out of a collection view and for switching between collection view layouts. The sample app demonstrates setting up a basic collection view, a customized flow layout collection view, and a highly custom, nonlinear collection view layout.

- **Chapter 22, "Introduction to TextKit":** iOS 7 introduced TextKit as an easier-to-use and greatly expanded update to Core Text. TextKit enables developers to provide rich and interactive text formatting to their apps. Although TextKit is a very large subject, this chapter provides the basic groundwork to accomplish several common tasks, from adding text wrapping around an image to inline custom font attributes. By the end of this chapter, you will have a strong background in TextKit and have the groundwork laid to explore it more in depth.

- **Chapter 23, "Gesture Recognizers":** This chapter explains how to make use of gesture recognizers in an app. Rather than dealing with and interpreting touch data directly, gesture recognizers provide a simple and clean way to recognize common gestures and respond to them. In addition, custom gestures can be defined and recognized using gesture recognizers.

- **Chapter 24, "Accessing the Photo Library":** The iPhone has actually become a very popular camera, as evidenced by the number of photos that people upload to sites such as Flickr. This chapter explains how to access the user's photo library, and handle photos and videos in a custom app. The sample app demonstrates building some of the concepts from the iOS 8 version of Photos.app.

- **Chapter 25, "Passbook and PassKit":** With iOS 6, Apple introduced Passbook, a standalone app that can store "passes," or such things as plane tickets, coupons, loyalty cards, or concert tickets. This chapter explains how to set up passes, how to create and distribute them, and how to interact with them in an app.

- **Chapter 26, "Debugging and Instruments":** One of the most important aspects of development is to be able to debug and profile your software. Rarely is this topic covered even in a cursory fashion. This chapter introduces you to debugging in Xcode and performance analysis using Instruments. Starting with a brief history of computer bugs, the chapter walks you through common debugging tips and tricks. Topics of breakpoints and debugger commands are briefly covered, and the chapter concludes with a look into profiling apps using the Time Profiler and memory analysis using Leaks. By the end of this chapter, you will have a clear foundation on how to troubleshoot and debug iOS apps on both the simulator and the device.

About the Sample Code

Each chapter of this book is designed to stand by itself; therefore, each chapter with the exception of Chapter 26, "Debugging and Instruments," has its own sample project. Chapter 3, "Leaderboards," and Chapter 4, "Achievements," share a base sample project, but each expands on that base project in unique ways. Each chapter provides a brief introduction to the sample project and walks the reader through any complex sections of the sample project not relating directly to the material in the chapter.

Every effort has been made to create simple-to-understand sample code, which often results in code that is otherwise not well optimized or not specifically the best way of approaching a problem. In these circumstances the chapter denotes where things are being done inappropriately for a real-world app. The sample projects are not designed to be standalone or finished apps; they are designed to demonstrate the functionality being discussed in the chapter. The sample projects are generic with intention; the reader should be able to focus on the material in the chapter and not the unrelated sample code materials. A considerable amount of work has been put into removing unnecessary components from the sample code and condensing subjects into as few lines as possible.

Many readers will be surprised to see that the sample code in the projects is built with Objective-C instead of Swift; this is by design as well. Since all the APIs illustrated are built with Objective-C, it is easier to interact with them using Objective-C, rather than add an additional layer of complexity by using Swift. The concepts illustrated are easily portable to Swift after the reader is comfortable with developing in Swift. The sample code is prefixed with "ICF" and most, but not all, sample projects are named after the chapter title.

When you're working with the Game Center chapters, the bundle ID is linked to a real app, which is in our personal Apple account; this ensures that examples continue to work. It also has the small additional benefit of populating multiple users' data as developers interact with the sample project. For chapters dealing with iCloud, Push Notifications, and Passbook, the setup required for the apps is thoroughly described in the chapter, and must be completed using a new App ID in the reader's developer account in order to work.

Getting the Sample Code

You will be able to find the most up-to-date version of the source code at any moment at https://github.com/dfsw/icf, in the Mastering folder. The code is publicly available and open source. Each chapter is broken down into its own zip file containing an Xcode project; there are no chapters with multiple projects. We encourage readers to provide feedback on the source code and make recommendations so that we can continue to refine and improve it long after this book has gone to print.

Installing Git and Working with GitHub

Git is a version control system that has been growing in popularity for several years. To clone and work with the code on GitHub, you will want to first install Git on your Mac. A command-line version Git is included in the Xcode command-line tool installation, or a current installer for Git can be found at http://git-scm.com/downloads. Additionally, there are several GUI front ends for Git, even one written by GitHub, which might be more appealing to developers who avoid command-line interfaces. If you do not want to install Git, GitHub also allows for downloading the source files as a zip.

GitHub enables users to sign up for a free account at https://github.com/signup/free. After Git has been installed, from the terminal's command line $git clone git@github.com:dfsw/ icf.git will download a copy of the source code into the current working directory. The sample code for this version of the book is in the Mastering folder. You are welcome to fork and open pull requests with the sample code projects.

Contacting the Authors

If you have any comments or questions about this book, please drop us an e-mail message at mastering.ios.frameworks@gmail.com, or on Twitter at @kylerichter and @jwkeeley.

Acknowledgments

This book could not have existed without a great deal of effort from far too many behind-the-scenes people; although there are only two authors on the cover, dozens of people were responsible for bringing this book to completion. We would like to thank Trina MacDonald first and foremost; without her leadership and her driving us to meet deadlines, we would never have been able to finish. The editors at Pearson have been exceptionally helpful; their continual efforts show on every page, from catching our typos to pointing out technical concerns. The dedicated work of Niklas Saers, Olivia Basegio, Justin Williams, Sheri Replin, Elaine Wiley, Cheri Clark, Chuti Prasertsith, and Gloria Shurick made the following pages possible.

We would also like to thank Jordan Langille of Langille Design (http://jordanlangille.com) for providing the designs for the Whack-a-Cac game featured in Chapters 3 and 4. His efforts have made the Game Center sample projects much more compelling.

The considerable amount of time spent working on this book was shouldered not only by us but also by our families and co-workers. We would like to thank everyone who surrounds us in our daily lives for taking a considerable amount of work off of our plates, as well as understanding the demands that a project like this brings.

Finally, we would like to thank the community at large. All too often we consulted developer forums, blog posts, and associates to ask questions or provide feedback. Without the hard efforts of everyone involved in the iOS community, this book would not be nearly as complete.

About the Authors

Kyle Richter is the Chief Executive Officer at MartianCraft, an award-winning Mobile Development Studio. Kyle began developing software in the early 1990s and has always been dedicated to the Apple ecosystem. He has authored and coauthored several books on iOS development, including *Beginning iOS Game Center Development, Beginning Social Game Development,* and *iOS Components and Frameworks*. Between running day-to-day operations at MartianCraft, Kyle travels the world speaking on development and entrepreneurship. He currently calls the Florida Keys home, where he spends his time with his border collie. He can be found on Twitter at @kylerichter.

Joe Keeley is a Partner and Lead Engineer at MartianCraft. Joe provides technical leadership on iOS projects for clients, and has led a number of successful client projects to completion. He has liked writing code since first keying on an Apple II, and has worked on a wide variety of technology and systems projects in his career. Joe has presented several technical topics at iOS and Mac conferences around the U.S. Joe lives in Denver, Colorado, with his wife and two daughters, and hopes to get back into competitive fencing again in his spare time. He can be reached on Twitter at @jwkeeley.

1

UIKit Dynamics

Apple introduced UIKit Dynamics with iOS 7, which enables developers to easily provide realistic physics simulations that can be applied to UIViews. For many years, developers have incorporated realistic-feeling effects into sections of their apps, such as swipeable cells and pull-to-refresh animations. Apple has taken a big steps in iOS 7 and iOS 8 to bring these animations into the core OS, as well as to encourage developers to implement them at an aggressive rate.

The `UIDynamicItem` protocol, along with the dynamic items that support it, is a giant leap forward in user experience. It is incredibly easy to add effects such as gravity, collisions, springs, and snaps to interfaces to provide a polished feel to an app. The APIs introduced for dynamic items are simple and easy to implement, providing very low-hanging fruit to increase the user experience of an app.

The Sample App

The sample app (shown in Figure 1.1) is a basic table demoing the various functions of UIKit Dynamics. Seven demos are presented in the app, from gravity to properties. Each demo is covered in order with a dedicated section. Besides the table view and basic navigation, the sample app does not contain any functionality not specific to UIKit Dynamics.

Although the sample app will run and perform in the iOS Simulator running iOS 8, the best performance is seen on physical devices. It is recommended that UIKit Dynamic code be thoroughly tested on physical devices before shipping.

> **Note**
>
> Having UIKit Dynamics and autolayout enabled on the same view can cause layout issues. Often this is presented as autolayout and UIKit Dynamics fighting over the correct position of a view and causing it to jump around wildly and unpredictably. If the view is not behaving as expected, check the autolayout settings to ensure that they are not in conflict.

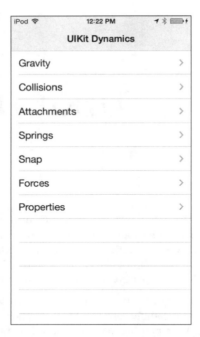

Figure 1.1   First glance at the sample app for UIKit Dynamics showing the list of demos available.

Introduction to UIKit Dynamics

UIKit Dynamics is a new set of classes and methods that was first introduced to iDevices starting with iOS 7. In short, it provides an easy-to-implement method to improve the user experience of apps by incorporating real-world behaviors and characteristics attached to UIViews. UIKit Dynamics is, in the simplest terms, a basic physics engine for UIKit; however, it is not designed for game development like most traditional physics engines. Apple provides several game frameworks, such as SpriteKit, that include a build in the physics engine.

Dynamic behavior becomes active when a new UIDynamicAnimator is created and added to a UIView. Each animator item can be customized with various properties and behaviors, such as gravity, collision detection, density, friction, and additional properties detailed in the following sections.

There are six additional classes that support the customization of a UIDynamicAnimator item: UIAttachmentBehavior, UICollisionBehavior, UIDynamicItemBehavior, UIGravityBehavior, UIPushBehavior, and UISnapBehavior. Each of these items allows for specific customization and will result in realistic behavior and animation of the UIView to which they are attached.

Implementing UIKit Dynamics

Creating a new animation and attaching it to a view is accomplished using two lines of code. In this example `self.view` is now set up to use UIKit Dynamic behavior. Each specific dynamic item must be added to the animator using the `addBehavior:` method.

```
UIDynamicAnimator *animator = [[UIDynamicAnimator alloc]
initWithReferenceView:self.view];

[animator addBehavior:aDynamicBehavior];
```

Each `UIDynamicAnimator` is independent and multiple animators can be run at the same time. For an animator to continue to run, a reference to it must be kept valid. When all items associated with an animator are at rest, the animator is not executing any calculations and will pause; however, best practices recommend removing unused animators.

Lessons from Game Developers

Physics simulations are something that game developers have been working with for many years, and some hard lessons have been learned. Now that physics is spreading into the application world, there are some basic truths every developer can benefit from.

When adding physics to a game or an app, do so in small increments. Writing a dozen interacting pieces and trying to figure out where the bug lies is next to impossible. The smaller the steps that are taken toward the end result, the easier the process will be to polish and debug.

In the physical world there are limits and boundaries often not addressed in computer simulations. In the classic computer game Carmageddon, released in 1997, the physics were based on an uncapped frame rate. When computers became faster, the frame rates increased significantly, creating variables in formulas that produced unexpected results. When applying any type of calculation into a physics engine, ensure that both min and max values are enforced and tested.

Expect the unexpected; when dealing with collisions, shoving 30 objects into an overlapping setup, things can go awry. UIKit Dynamics has some great catches in place to ensure that you cannot push objects through boundaries with tremendous applications of force, and collisions are handled rather gracefully. However, there will most certainly be edge cases and bugs when you're dealing with many objects with complex interactions. The more that is going on with a physics engine, the more it needs to be tested and debugged; expect to see the laws of the universe toyed with in unexpected and unusual fashions.

Gravity

Gravity is arguably the easiest `UIDynamicItem` to implement, as well as one of the most practical. Apple makes heavy use of the gravity item in iOS 8, and a user does not need to go further than the lock screen to interact with gravity. Dragging up on the camera icon from the iOS 8 lock screen and releasing it under the halfway point will drop the home screen back into place using `UIGravityBehavior`. This functionality, even before the introduction of UIKit Dynamics in iOS 7, was often cloned and implemented by hand using timers and traditional animations.

The following code snippet will set up a gravity effect on `frogImageView` that is a subview of `self.view`. First a new `UIDynamicAnimator` is created for the enclosing view that the animated view will appear in, in this example `self.view`. A new `UIGravityBehavior` object is created and initialized with an array of views that should have the gravity effect applied to them. The gravity behavior is then set; the example will apply a downward y-axis force of 0.1. When the behavior is configured, it is added to the `UIDynamicAnimator` using the `addBehavior:` method.

```
animator = [[UIDynamicAnimator alloc] initWithReferenceView:self.view];

UIGravityBehavior* gravityBehavior = [[UIGravityBehavior alloc]
➥initWithItems:@[frogImageView]];


[gravityBeahvior setXComponent:0.0f yComponent:0.1f];
[animator addBehavior:gravityBehavior];
```

> **Note**
> The dynamic item must be a subview of the reference view; if the item is not a subview, the animator will simply not provide any movement.

UIKit Dynamics uses their own physics system, jokingly referred to by Apple Engineers as UIKit Newtons. Although there is no direct correlation to standard formulas, Apple does provide a close approximation. A force of 1.0 equals roughly 9.80655 m/s^2, which is the force of gravity on earth. To apply gravity roughly one-tenth of that found on earth, 0.1 would be used. Gravity in UIKit Dynamics does not need to be specified as only a downward force; if a negative value is provided for the `yComponent`, gravity will pull up. Likewise, gravity can be specified for the x-axis in the same fashion. Items also have a density property, which is discussed in more detail in the "Item Properties" section.

Running the sample code for gravity results in the `imageView` simply falling at roughly one-tenth the rate of earth gravity (shown in Figure 1.2) and completely sliding off the screen. Because no boundaries or collisions are set, the object isn't aware that it hit something that should cause it to stop falling, so it falls in essence forever.

Collisions

In the preceding section, gravity was covered; however, the object that the gravity was applied to fell through the bottom of the screen and continued on its way into infinity. This is because no collision points were defined and the object had nothing to stop its descent.

The previous example will be modified to add collision boundaries to the enclosing view, as well as adding a secondary image object. The collision example begins the same way as gravity; however, two image views are now used.

Figure 1.2   An image view with the force of gravity applied to it falling down the screen in the gravity example from the sample app.

Creating a `UICollisionBehavior` object is very similar to creating a `UIGravityBehavior` object. The object is initialized with the UIViews that should be affected, in this case two `UIImageViews`. In addition to the views, collision behavior also needs to be specified with one of three possible values. `UICollisionBehaviorModeItems` will cause the items to collide with each other. `UICollisionBehaviorModeBoundaries` will cause the items not to collide with each other but to collide with boundaries. Finally, `UICollisionBehaviorModeEverything` will cause the items to collide both with each other and with the boundaries.

For objects to interact with boundaries, those boundaries first need to be defined. The easiest boundary to define is set through a Boolean property on the `UICollisionBehavior` object called `translatesReferenceBoundsIntoBoundary`. In the example this will use the bounds of `self.view`. Boundaries can also be set to follow an `NSBezierPath` using the method `addBoundaryWithIdentifier:forPath:` or based on two points using `addBoundaryWith-Identifier:fromPoint:toPoint:`.

```objc
animator = [[UIDynamicAnimator alloc] initWithReferenceView:self.view];

UIGravityBehavior* gravityBehavior = [[UIGravityBehavior alloc]
➥initWithItems:@[frogImageView, dragonImageView]];

[gravityBehavior setXComponent:0.0f yComponent:1.0f];


UICollisionBehavior* collisionBehavior = [[UICollisionBehavior alloc]
➥initWithItems:@[frogImageView, dragonImageView]];

[collisionBehavior setCollisionMode: UICollisionBehaviorModeBoundaries];

collisionBehavior.translatesReferenceBoundsIntoBoundary = YES;

[animator addBehavior:gravityBehavior];
[animator addBehavior:collisionBehavior];
```

UICollisionBehavior also provides a delegate callback that conforms to the UICollisionBehaviorDelegate protocol.

```objc
collisionBehavior.collisionDelegate = self;
```

The UICollisionBehaviorDelegate has four callback methods, two for beginning collisions and two for ended collisions. Each set of callbacks has one method that will identify the boundary hit and one that will not. All methods provide a reference to the object that has caused the callback method to fire. The collision begun methods also provide a CGPoint to reference the exact area of contact. The sample code will update a label after it has detected that an object has been hit.

```objc
-(void)collisionBehavior:(UICollisionBehavior *)behavior
➥beganContactForItem:(id<UIDynamicItem>)item
➥withBoundaryIdentifier:(id<NSCopying>)identifier atPoint:(CGPoint)p
{
    if([item isEqual:frogImageView])
        collisionOneLabel.text = @"Frog Collided";
    if([item isEqual:dragonImageView])
        collisionTwoLabel.text = @"Dragon Collided";
}


-(void)collisionBehavior:(UICollisionBehavior *)behavior
➥endedContactForItem:(id<UIDynamicItem>)item
➥withBoundaryIdentifier:(id<NSCopying>)identifier
{

    NSLog(@"Collision did end");
}
```

Attachments

An attachment specifies a dynamic connection between two objects. This allows for the behavior and movement of one object to be tied to the movement of another object. By default, UIAttachmentBehaviors are fixed to the center of an object, although any point can be defined as the attachment point.

The sample app builds on the work done in the "Collisions" section. Once again, two image views are used. A boundary collision is created and applied to the UIDynamicAnimator. A new CGPoint is created and set to the reference point of the center of the frog image view. A new UIAttachmentBehavior object is created and initialized using initWithItem:attachedTo-Anchor:. There are also additional initialization methods on UICollisionBehavior that allow specification of points or other objects. The collision and the attachment behavior are both added to the animator object.

```
animator = [[UIDynamicAnimator alloc] initWithReferenceView:self.view];

UICollisionBehavior* collisionBehavior = [[UICollisionBehavior alloc]
➥initWithItems:@[dragonImageView, frogImageView]];

[collisionBehavior setCollisionMode: UICollisionBehaviorModeBoundaries];

collisionBehavior.translatesReferenceBoundsIntoBoundary = YES;

CGPoint frogCenter = CGPointMake(frogImageView.center.x,
➥frogImageView.center.y);

self.attachmentBehavior = [[UIAttachmentBehavior alloc]
➥initWithItem:dragonImageView attachedToAnchor:frogCenter];

[animator addBehavior:collisionBehavior];
[animator addBehavior:self.attachmentBehavior];
```

These objects are now bound by an invisible connector the length equal to their initial distance. If the frog image view moves, the dragon image view will move with it holding onto the center point. However, the frog image view has no capability to move; to solve this, the sample app implements a simple pan gesture. As the frog image view is moved around the view, the center point is updated and the updated anchor point is set.

```
- (IBAction)handleAttachmentGesture:(UIPanGestureRecognizer*)gesture
{
    CGPoint gesturePoint = [gesture locationInView:self.view];

    frogImageView.center = gesturePoint;
    [self.attachmentBehavior setAnchorPoint:gesturePoint];
}
```

During the movement, the collision boundaries are still in effect and override the desired behavior of the attachment. This can be demonstrated by pushing the dragon image into the boundaries of the view.

It is also possible to update the length property of the attachment view in order to change the distance the attachment gives to the two objects. The attachment point itself does not need to be the center of the attached object and can be updated to any offset desired using the `setAnchorPoint` call.

Springs

Springs (shown in Figure 1.3) are an extension of the behavior of attachments. UIKit Dynamics allows for additional properties to be set on `UIAttachmentBehavior`, frequency and damping.

Figure 1.3   A spring effect attaching the dragon image to the frog, which demonstrates using the effects of gravity as well as `UIAttachmentBehavior` damping and frequency.

The following section of the sample app adds three new UIKit Dynamic properties after creating the `UIAttachmentBehavior`. The first, `setFrequency`, sets the oscillation or swing for the object. Next, `setDamping` evens out the animation peaks. The length is also adjusted for this example from its initial position. To better demonstrate these behaviors, gravity is added to this example.

```
animator = [[UIDynamicAnimator alloc] initWithReferenceView:self.view];

UICollisionBehavior* collisionBehavior = [[UICollisionBehavior alloc]
➥initWithItems:@[dragonImageView, frogImageView]];

UIGravityBehavior* gravityBeahvior = [[UIGravityBehavior alloc]
➥initWithItems:@[dragonImageView]];

CGPoint frogCenter = CGPointMake(frogImageView.center.x,
➥frogImageView.center.y);

self.attachmentBehavior = [[UIAttachmentBehavior alloc]
➥initWithItem:dragonImageView attachedToAnchor:frogCenter];

[self.attachmentBehavior setFrequency:1.0f];
[self.attachmentBehavior setDamping:0.1f];
[self.attachmentBehavior setLength: 100.0f];

[collisionBehavior setCollisionMode: UICollisionBehaviorModeBoundaries];

collisionBehavior.translatesReferenceBoundsIntoBoundary = YES;

[animator addBehavior:gravityBeahvior];
[animator addBehavior:collisionBehavior];
[animator addBehavior:self.attachmentBehavior];
```

Moving the frog around the screen now results in the dragon hanging 100 points from the bottom and swinging from the effect of the attachment and gravity combined.

Snap

An item can be dynamically moved to another point in a view with a snapping motion. Snapping is a very simple behavior to implement. In the sample app the action is tied to a tap gesture, and tapping anywhere on the screen causes the image to jump to that spot. Each UISnapBehavior is linked to a single item at a time, and during initialization an end point where the item should end up is specified. A damping property can also be specified to affect the amount of bounce in the snap.

```
CGPoint point = [gesture locationInView:self.view];
animator = [[UIDynamicAnimator alloc] initWithReferenceView:self.view];

UISnapBehavior* snapBehavior = [[UISnapBehavior alloc]
➥initWithItem:frogImageView snapToPoint:point];

snapBehavior.damping = 0.75f;
[animator addBehavior:snapBehavior];
```

Push Forces

UIKit Dynamics also allows for the application of force, referred to as pushing. UIPushBehavior is slightly more complex to use than the previously covered behaviors, but it remains fairly easy compared to other physics engines. The sample also uses a UICollisionBehavior object seen in the previous demos. This ensures that the image view stays on the screen while push effects are applied.

A new UIPushBehavior behavior is created and initialized with a reference to an image view. For the time being, the properties for angle and magnitude are set to 0.0.

The sample app also features a reference in the form of a small black square in the center of the screen.

```
animator = [[UIDynamicAnimator alloc] initWithReferenceView:self.view];

UICollisionBehavior* collisionBehavior = [[UICollisionBehavior alloc]
➥initWithItems:@[dragonImageView]];

collisionBehavior.translatesReferenceBoundsIntoBoundary = YES;
[animator addBehavior:collisionBehavior];

UIPushBehavior *pushBehavior = [[UIPushBehavior alloc]
➥initWithItems:@[dragonImageView]
➥mode:UIPushBehaviorModeInstantaneous];

pushBehavior.angle = 0.0;
pushBehavior.magnitude = 0.0;

self.pushBehavior = pushBehavior;
[animator addBehavior:self.pushBehavior];
```

If the project were to be run now, the image view would stay fixed on the screen since the push effect has no values associated with it. A new pan gesture is created and in its associated action a new value for magnitude and angle are calculated and applied. In the example an angle is calculated to determine where the push force is coming from. This is based on the angle from the center reference point. A distance is also calculated to apply increasing force. The result is that tapping outside of the black square will apply an amount of force in that direction to the image view. The farther away from the square, the more force is applied.

```
CGPoint point = [gesture locationInView:self.view];

CGPoint origin = CGPointMake(CGRectGetMidX(self.view.bounds),
➥CGRectGetMidY(self.view.bounds));

CGFloat distance = sqrtf(powf(point.x-origin.x, 2.0)+powf(point.y-
➥origin.y, 2.0));

CGFloat angle = atan2(point.y-origin.y, point.x-origin.x);
distance = MIN(distance, 100.0f);
```

```
[self.pushBehavior setMagnitude:distance / 100.0];
[self.pushBehavior setAngle:angle];

[self.pushBehavior setActive:YES];
```

In addition to setting an angle and a magnitude by hand, you can have them be calculated and applied automatically by using `setTargetPoint:forItem:` to specify a target point. It might also become necessary to apply force to a part of the view that is not the center, in which case `setXComponent:yComponent:` can be used to specify a `CGPoint` to which the focus of the force will be applied.

There are two types of push force that can be applied, `UIPushBehaviorModeContinuous` and `UIPushBehaviorModeInstantaneous`. With continuous push the object accelerates under the force, whereas with instantaneous the force is immediately applied.

Item Properties

Dynamic items have a number of default properties preset on, and these properties can be heavily configured to customize their reactions to the physics engine. The sample app (shown in Figure 1.4) demonstrates modifying these properties for one image view while leaving the defaults in place for the other image view.

Figure 1.4   Modifying properties on dynamic items to create a unique physics reaction applied under identical forces.

To modify the properties on an object, create a new `UIDynamicItemBehavior` initialized with the views that the properties should be applied to. The result is that one object acts like a rubber ball and becomes much more prone to bounce when gravity and collisions are applied to it. The properties and their descriptions are presented in Table 1.1.

```
animator = [[UIDynamicAnimator alloc] initWithReferenceView:self.view];

UIGravityBehavior* gravityBeahvior = [[UIGravityBehavior alloc]
➥initWithItems:@[dragonImageView, frogImageView]];

UICollisionBehavior* collisionBehavior = [[UICollisionBehavior alloc]
➥initWithItems:@[dragonImageView, frogImageView]];

collisionBehavior.translatesReferenceBoundsIntoBoundary = YES;

UIDynamicItemBehavior* propertiesBehavior = [[UIDynamicItemBehavior
➥alloc] initWithItems:@[frogImageView]];

propertiesBehavior.elasticity = 1.0f;
propertiesBehavior.allowsRotation = NO;
propertiesBehavior.angularResistance = 0.0f;
propertiesBehavior.density = 3.0f;
propertiesBehavior.friction = 0.5f;
propertiesBehavior.resistance = 0.5f;

[animator addBehavior:propertiesBehavior];
[animator addBehavior:gravityBehavior];
[animator addBehavior:collisionBehavior];
```

Table 1.1   **UIDynamicItem Properties and Their Descriptions**

Property	Description
allowsRotation	A Boolean value that specifies whether the item will rotate as the result of forces applied; defaults to YES.
angularResistance	A CGFloat from 0.0 to CGFLOAT_MAX that indicates angular damping; the higher the number, the faster rotation will slow down.
density	A representation of density. Density is defaulted to 1.0 for a 100x100 object, or 2.0 for a 100x200 object. Adjustments to density affect the reactions of gravity and collisions.
elasticity	Valid for ranges of 0.0 to 1.0, indicating the amount of bounce an object has when colliding with other objects. 0.0 indicates no bounce, whereas 1.0 indicates that the entire force will be applied back into the bounce.

Property	Description
friction	The linear resistance applied when two items slide across each other. 0.0 indicates no friction and 1.0 indicates strong friction; however, values greater than 1.0 can be applied for additional friction.
resistance	A linear resistance encountered in open space. Values of 0.0 to `CGFLOAT_MAX` are accepted. 0.0 indicates no resistance, whereas 1.0 indicates that the item should stop as soon as no force is applied to it.

In-Depth `UIDynamicAnimator` and `UIDynamicAnimatorDelegate`

The beginning of this chapter introduced `UIDynamicAnimator`, and the samples have all used `addBehavior`; however, this class has much more power that can be leveraged. In addition to dynamic effects being added, they can also be removed either one at a time or as a group using `removeBehavior:` and `removeAllBehaviors`. To get a list of all behaviors currently attached to a `UIDynamicAnimator`, the behaviors property can be used to return an array of behaviors.

It is also possible not only to poll whether the animator is running using the running property but also to determine the length of time using `elapsedTime`. The `UIDynamicAnimator` also has an associated delegate, `UIDynamicAnimatorDelegate`. The delegate provides two methods to handle pausing and resuming. `UIDynamicAnimator` cannot be explicitly paused by the developer. The animation effects are automatically paused when all items have come to a rest and are no longer moving. Any new effect that is applied will cause the items to begin moving and they will be moved back into the active state.

```
- (void)dynamicAnimatorDidPause:(UIDynamicAnimator *)animator
{
    NSLog(@"Animator did pause");
}


- (void)dynamicAnimatorWillResume:(UIDynamicAnimator *)animator
{
    NSLog(@"Animator will resume");
}
```

Summary

UIKit Dynamics is an interesting topic not only from a development standpoint but also as to what it means for the direction of iOS. Apple is making a strong push to bring software into the real world. Interacting with an app should feel like interacting with the physical world. Users expect to see apps respond in the same way the world around them does. This is not new for Apple; one of the main selling features of the original iPhone was momentum scrolling, and they are now giving the tools to add that type of functionality to developers.

This chapter covered the basics of UIKit Dynamics and its basic components; however, the real power of these methods will be in what developers create with them. There are endless possibilities and combinations for the effects that have been described, and what developers will create with these tools will surprise even Apple. The one definite in the redefined mobile user experience world, though, is that realistic physical reactions in software are no longer optional, and users will be expecting them.

2

Core Location, MapKit, and Geofencing

Maps and location information are some of the most useful features of iOS. They give apps the capability to help users find their way with relevant, local information. Apps exist today to help users find locations for very specific needs, find roads and directions, and use specialized transportation services, and even to bring an element of fun to visiting the same locations over and over. With the addition of Apple's new maps, some powerful new features have been added that developers can take advantage of to take their apps to the next level.

iOS offers two frameworks to assist with locations and maps. The Core Location framework provides classes that help the device determine its location and heading, and work with location-based information. The MapKit framework provides the user interface aspect of location awareness. It includes Apple Maps, which provides map views, satellite views, and hybrid views in normal 2D and a new 3D view. MapKit offers the capability to manage map annotations like pins, and map overlays for highlighting locations, routes, or other features on a map.

The Sample App

The sample app for this chapter is called FavoritePlaces. It enables users to collect favorite places and view them on a map, along with the device's current location. Users can use Core Location to geocode, or find the latitude and longitude, for an address. In addition, it can notify users when they go within a radius that they set around a favorite location. The app also provides a special location (signified with a green arrow) that can be dragged around the map to pinpoint a desired next destination; when that arrow is dropped at a location, it will automatically reverse-geocode the location to display the name and address of the location.

Obtaining User Location

To use Core Location to obtain the current location, several steps need to take place. The app must obtain permission from the user to access the current location. In addition, the app needs to ensure that location services are enabled for the device before attempting to acquire a location. After those requirements are met, the app can start a location request and parse the result for usage after the location has been provided by Core Location. This section describes all these steps in detail.

Requirements and Permissions

To use Core Location in an app, import `CoreLocation` as needed:

```
@import CoreLocation;
```

To use MapKit in an app, import MapKit in any classes that need it:

```
@import MapKit;
```

Core Location respects the privacy of the user, and requires the user to provide permission to have access to the current location of the device. Location Services can be turned on or off for all apps on the device in the Settings app under the Privacy section, and can be set to Always, While Using, or Never for each app individually, as shown in Figure 2.1.

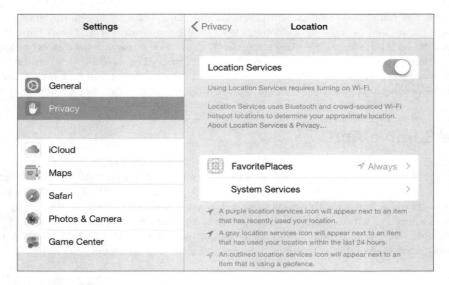

Figure 2.1   Settings app, Location Services privacy settings.

Always indicates that the app is allowed access to the user's location even when the app is not active. While Using indicates that the app is allowed access to the user's location only while the app is active in the foreground. "Never" means that no access to the user's location is granted to the app. To request permission to use Location Services, the app needs to ask `CLLocationManager` for the correct type of permission (either While Using or Always). For the sample app, the location is needed while the app is active and for geofencing, so Always is requested:

```
[appLocationManager.locationManager requestAlwaysAuthorization];
```

If Location Services are turned off for the device, Core Location will prompt the user to turn on Location Services in Settings.app to allow the app to access the current location, as shown in Figure 2.2.

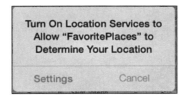

Figure 2.2   FavoritePlaces sample app location services disabled alert.

If the location manager has not requested permission previously to get the device's location, it will present an alert view to ask the user's permission, as shown in Figure 2.3. Note that you must add an entry in the `.plist` file for the app with some text explaining to the user what the app will do with the user's location. Use the key `NSLocationWhenInUseUsageDescription` or `NSLocationAlwaysUsageDescription`. If the key for the permission type is not found, the permission dialog will not be presented by the call.

Figure 2.3   FavoritePlaces sample app location permission request alert.

If the user taps Allow, permission will be granted and the location manager will be able to acquire the current location. If the user taps Don't Allow, permission for the current location will be denied, and the CLLocationManager's delegate method for authorization status changes will be called in ICFLocationManager.

```
- (void)locationManager:(CLLocationManager *)manager
➥didChangeAuthorizationStatus:(CLAuthorizationStatus)status
{
    if (status == kCLAuthorizationStatusDenied)
    {
        [self.locationManager stopUpdatingLocation];

        NSString *errorMessage =
        ➥@"Location Services Permission Denied for this app.";

        NSDictionary *errorInfo =
        ➥@{NSLocalizedDescriptionKey : errorMessage};

        NSError *deniedError =
        ➥[NSError errorWithDomain:@"ICFLocationErrorDomain"
                             code:1
                         userInfo:errorInfo];

        [self setLocationError:deniedError];
        [self getLocationWithCompletionBlock:nil];
    }
    if (status == kCLAuthorizationStatusAuthorizedWhenInUse)
    {
        [self.locationManager startUpdatingLocation];
        [self setLocationError:nil];
    }
}
```

The sample app's ICFLocationManager class uses completion blocks for location requests from the rest of the app to be able to easily handle multiple requests for the current location. The getLocationWithCompletionBlock: method will process any completion blocks after a location is available or an error has occurred so that the calling logic can use the location or handle the error as appropriate in the local context. In this case, the caller will present an alert view to display the location permission-denied error, as shown in Figure 2.4.

Figure 2.4   FavoritePlaces sample app location permission denied alert.

If the user later changes the authorization status for location services, either for the app specifically or for the device overall (refer to Figure 2.1), that same delegate method will be called and can respond appropriately. In ICFLocationManager the delegate method is implemented to display an error alert if the permission is denied, or to restart updating the current location and clear the last error if permission is granted.

Checking for Services

To directly determine whether location services are enabled for the device, there is a class method available on the CLLocationManager called locationServicesEnabled.

```
if ([CLLocationManager locationServicesEnabled])
{
    ICFLocationManager *appLocationManager =
    ➥[ICFLocationManager sharedLocationManager];

    [appLocationManager.locationManager startUpdatingLocation];
}
else
{
    NSLog(@"Location Services disabled.");
}
```

This can be used to customize how the app deals with having or not having the current location available. An app that deals with locations should gracefully handle when the user does not grant access to the current location, and give the user clear instructions for enabling access to the current location if desired.

Starting Location Request

When permission for location services has been granted, an instance of CLLocationManager can be used to find the current location. In the sample app, ICFLocationManager provides a central class to manage location functionality, so it manages one instance of CLLocationManager for the app. In the init method of ICFLocationManager, a CLLocationManager is created and customized for the desired location-searching approach.

```
[self setLocationManager:[[CLLocationManager alloc] init]];

[self.locationManager
➥setDesiredAccuracy:kCLLocationAccuracyBest];

[self.locationManager setDistanceFilter:100.0f];
[self.locationManager setDelegate:self];
```

A CLLocationManager has several parameters that can be set to dictate how it manages
the current location. By specifying the desired accuracy parameter, the app can tell the
CLLocationManager whether it is worthwhile to achieve the best accuracy possible at the
expense of the battery, or whether a lower-level accuracy is preferred to preserve battery life.
Using lower accuracy also reduces the amount of time necessary to acquire a location. Setting
the distance filter indicates to the CLLocationManager how much distance must be traveled
before new location events are generated; this is useful to fine-tune functionality based on
changing locations. Lastly, setting the delegate for the CLLocationManager provides a place for
custom functionality in response to location events and permission changes. When the app is
ready to get a location, it asks the location manager to start updating the location.

```
ICFLocationManager *appLocationManager =
➥[ICFLocationManager sharedLocationManager];

[appLocationManager.locationManager startUpdatingLocation];
```

The CLLocationManager will engage the GPS and/or Wi-Fi as needed to determine the current
location according to the parameters specified. There are two delegate methods that should be
implemented to handle when the location manager has updated the current location or has
failed to update the current location. When a location is acquired, the locationManager:
didUpdateLocations: method will be called.

```
- (void)locationManager:(CLLocationManager *)manager
     ➥didUpdateLocations:(NSArray *)locations
{
    //Filter out inaccurate points
    CLLocation *lastLocation = [locations lastObject];
    if(lastLocation.horizontalAccuracy < 0)
    {
        return;
    }

    [self setLocation:lastLocation];
    [self setHasLocation:YES];
    [self setLocationError:nil];

    [self getLocationWithCompletionBlock:nil];
}
```

The location manager can deliver multiple locations in the array of locations provided. The last object in the array is the most recently updated location. The location manager can also return the last location the GPS was aware of very quickly before actually starting to acquire a location; in that case, if the GPS has been off and the device has moved, the location might be very inaccurate. The method will check the accuracy of the location and ignore it if the value is negative. If a reasonably accurate location has been found, the method will store it and execute completion blocks. Note that the location manager might call this method multiple times as the location is refined, and any logic here should work with that in mind.

```
- (void)locationManager:(CLLocationManager *)manager
    ➥didFailWithError:(NSError *)error
{
    [self.locationManager stopUpdatingLocation];
    [self setLocationError:error];
    [self getLocationWithCompletionBlock:nil];
}
```

If the location manager failed to acquire a location, it will call the `locationManager:didFailWithError:` method. The error might be due to lack of authorization, or might be due to GPS or Wi-Fi not being available (in Airplane Mode, for example). The sample app implementation will tell the location manager to stop updating the current location if an error is encountered, will capture the location error, and will execute the completion blocks so that the code requesting the current location can handle the error appropriately.

A location manager delegate can monitor for course changes. This could be useful, for example, to update a map indicator to display what direction the user is going relative to the direction of the map. To receive course or heading information, the location manager needs to start monitoring for it. A filter can optionally be set to prevent getting updates when changes are smaller than the number of degrees provided.

```
CLLocationDegrees degreesFilter = 2.0;
if ([CLLocationManager headingAvailable])
{
    [self.locationManager setHeadingFilter:degreesFilter];
    [self.locationManager startUpdatingHeading];
}
```

Heading change events are then delivered to the `locationManager:didUpdateHeading:` delegate method.

```
- (void)locationManager:(CLLocationManager *)manager
    ➥didUpdateHeading:(CLHeading *)newHeading
{
    NSLog(@"New heading, magnetic: %f",
    newHeading.magneticHeading);

    NSLog(@"New heading, true: %f",newHeading.trueHeading);
    NSLog(@"Accuracy: %f",newHeading.headingAccuracy);
    NSLog(@"Timestamp: %@",newHeading.timestamp);
}
```

The new heading provides several pieces of useful information. It includes both a magnetic and a true heading, expressed in degrees from north. It provides an accuracy reading, expressed as the number of degrees by which the magnetic heading might be off. A lower, positive value indicates a more accurate heading, and a negative number means that the heading is invalid and there might be magnetic interference preventing a reading. The time stamp reflects when the reading was taken, and should be checked to prevent using an old heading.

Parsing and Understanding Location Data

When the location manager returns a location, it will be an instance of CLLocation. The CLLocation contains several pieces of useful information about the location. First is the latitude and longitude, expressed as a CLLocationCoordinate2D.

```
CLLocationCoordinate2D coord = lastLocation.coordinate;

NSLog(@"Location lat/long: %f,%f",coord.latitude, coord.longitude);
```

Latitude is represented as a number of degrees north or south of the equator, where the equator is zero degrees, the North Pole is 90 degrees, and South Pole is –90 degrees. Longitude is represented as a number of degrees east or west of the prime meridian, which is an imaginary line (or meridian) running from the North Pole to the South Pole, going through the Royal Observatory in Greenwich, England. Going west from the prime meridian gives negative longitude values to –180 degrees, whereas going east gives positive longitude values up to 180 degrees.

Complementary to the coordinate is a horizontal accuracy. The accuracy is expressed as a CLLocationDistance, or meters. The horizontal accuracy means that the actual location is within the number of meters specified from the coordinate.

```
CLLocationAccuracy horizontalAccuracy =
➥lastLocation.horizontalAccuracy;

NSLog(@"Horizontal accuracy: %f meters",horizontalAccuracy);
```

The location also provides the altitude of the current location and vertical accuracy in meters, if the device has a GPS capability. If the device does not have GPS, the altitude is returned as the value zero and the accuracy will be –1.

```
CLLocationDistance altitude = lastLocation.altitude;
➥NSLog(@"Location altitude: %f meters",altitude);

CLLocationAccuracy verticalAccuracy =
lastLocation.verticalAccuracy;

NSLog(@"Vertical accuracy: %f meters",verticalAccuracy);
```

The location contains a time stamp that indicates when the location was determined by the location manager. This can be useful to determine whether the location is old and should be ignored, or for comparing time stamps between location checks.

```
NSDate *timestamp = lastLocation.timestamp;
NSLog(@"Timestamp: %@",timestamp);
```

Lastly, the location provides the speed, expressed in meters per second, and course, expressed in degrees from true north.

```
CLLocationSpeed speed = lastLocation.speed;
NSLog(@"Speed: %f meters per second",speed);

CLLocationDirection direction = lastLocation.course;
NSLog(@"Course: %f degrees from true north",direction);
```

Significant Change Notifications

After a location has been acquired by the app, Apple strongly recommends stopping location updates to preserve battery life. If the app does not require a constant, accurate location, monitoring for significant location changes can provide an efficient way of informing the app when the device has moved without consuming a lot of power to keep the GPS and Wi-Fi monitoring the current location.

```
[self.locationManager startMonitoringSignificantLocationChanges];
```

Typically, a notification is generated when the device has moved at least 500 meters, or has changed cell towers. Notifications are not sent unless at least five minutes has elapsed since the last notification. Location update events are delivered to the locationManager: didUpdateLocations: delegate method.

Using GPX Files to Test Specific Locations

Testing location-based apps can be daunting, especially when specific locations need to be tested that are not convenient to test from. Fortunately, there is robust support for testing locations provided by Xcode using GPX files. A GPX file is a GPS Exchange Format document, which can be used to communicate GPS information between devices using XML. In debugging mode, Xcode can use a "waypoint" defined in a GPX file to set the current location for the iOS Simulator or device.

In the sample app, the current location is set with the file DMNS.gpx, or the location of the Denver Museum of Nature and Science.

```
<?xml version="1.0"?>
<gpx version="1.1" creator="Xcode">

    <wpt lat="39.748039" lon="-104.94000">
        <name>Denver Museum of Nature and Science</name>
    </wpt>

</gpx>
```

To tell Xcode to use a GPX file in debugging, select Edit Scheme from the Scheme selection drop-down in the upper-left corner of a project window, select the Options tab, and check the Allow Location Simulation check box, as shown in Figure 2.5. When this is checked, a location can be selected from the drop-down next to Default Location. This drop-down includes some built-in locations, and any GPX files that have been added to the project.

When the app is run in debug mode, Core Location will return the location specified in the GPX file as the current location of the device or simulator. To change the location while debugging, select Debug, Simulate Location from the menu in Xcode and select a location (as shown in Figure 2.6). Core Location will change the location to the selected location and will fire the locationManager:didUpdateLocations: delegate method.

Figure 2.5   Xcode FavoritePlaces scheme.

Figure 2.6   Xcode Product, Debug, Simulate Location.

Displaying Maps

MapKit provides mapping user-interface capabilities for iOS. The base class used is an MKMapView, which displays a map, handles user interactions with the map, and manages annotations (like pins) and overlays (like routing graphics or region highlights). To better understand how maps in iOS work, it is important to understand the coordinate systems at work.

Understanding the Coordinate Systems

There are two coordinate systems at work in MapKit: the coordinate system for the map, and the coordinate system for the view. The map uses a Mercator Projection, which takes the 3D map of the world and flattens it into a 2D coordinate system. Coordinates can be specified using latitude and longitude. The map view represents the portion of the map displayed on the screen using standard UIKit view coordinates. The map view then determines where in the view to display points determined by map coordinates.

MKMapKit Configuration and Customization

In ICFMainViewController in the sample app, the map view is configured in Interface Builder to default to the standard map type, to display the user location on the map, and to allow scrolling and zooming. ICFMainViewController has a segmented control to enable the user to adjust the type of map displayed.

```
- (IBAction)mapTypeSelectionChanged:(id)sender
{
    UISegmentedControl *mapSelection =
    ➥(UISegmentedControl *)sender;

    switch (mapSelection.selectedSegmentIndex)
    {
        case 0:
            [self.mapView setMapType:MKMapTypeStandard];
            break;
        case 1:
            [self.mapView setMapType:MKMapTypeSatellite];
            break;
        case 2:
            [self.mapView setMapType:MKMapTypeHybrid];
            break;

        default:
            break;
    }
}
```

Beyond setting the map type, another common customization is to set the region displayed by the map. In ICFMainViewController, a method called zoomMapToFitAnnotations will examine the current favorite places, and will size and center the map to fit them all. The method starts by setting default maximum and minimum coordinates.

```
CLLocationCoordinate2D maxCoordinate =
➥CLLocationCoordinate2DMake(-90.0, -180.0);

CLLocationCoordinate2D minCoordinate =
➥CLLocationCoordinate2DMake(90.0, 180.0);
```

Looking at the existing annotations on the map (described in more detail in the next main section, "Map Annotations and Overlays"), the method calculates the maximum and minimum latitude and longitude values for all the coordinates represented in the annotations.

```
NSArray *currentPlaces = [self.mapView annotations];

maxCoordinate.latitude =
➥[[currentPlaces valueForKeyPath:@"@max.latitude"] doubleValue];

minCoordinate.latitude =
➥[[currentPlaces valueForKeyPath:@"@min.latitude"] doubleValue];

maxCoordinate.longitude =
➥[[currentPlaces valueForKeyPath:@"@max.longitude"] doubleValue];
```

```
minCoordinate.longitude =
➡[[currentPlaces valueForKeyPath:@"@min.longitude"] doubleValue];
```

The method then calculates the center coordinate from the maximum and minimum latitude and longitude coordinates.

```
CLLocationCoordinate2D centerCoordinate;

centerCoordinate.longitude =
➡(minCoordinate.longitude + maxCoordinate.longitude) / 2.0;

centerCoordinate.latitude =
➡(minCoordinate.latitude + maxCoordinate.latitude) / 2.0;
```

Next, the method calculates the span needed to display all the coordinates from the calculated center coordinate. The calculated span for each dimension is multiplied by 1.2 to create a margin between the farthest-out points and the edge of the view.

```
MKCoordinateSpan span;

span.longitudeDelta =
➡(maxCoordinate.longitude - minCoordinate.longitude) * 1.2;

span.latitudeDelta =
➡(maxCoordinate.latitude - minCoordinate.latitude) * 1.2;
```

After the center point and span have been calculated, a map region can be created and used to set the map view's displayed region.

```
MKCoordinateRegion newRegion =
➡MKCoordinateRegionMake(centerCoordinate, span);

[self.mapView setRegion:newRegion
              animated:YES];
```

Setting `animated:` to `YES` will zoom the map in as if the user had zoomed to it; setting it to `NO` will instantaneously change the region with no animation.

Responding to User Interactions

An `MKMapViewDelegate` can be specified to react to user interactions with the map. Typical user interactions with a map include responding to panning and zooming, handling draggable annotations, and responding when the user taps a callout.

When the map is being panned and zoomed, the `mapView:regionWillChangeAnimated:` and `mapView:regionDidChangeAnimated:` delegate methods are called. In the sample app no additional action is required for the map to resize and adjust the annotations; however, in an app with a large number of potential items to display on the map or an app that shows different information at different zoom levels, these delegate methods are useful for removing map annotations that are no longer visible and for adding annotations that are newly visible. The delegate method in the sample app demonstrates how one would get the newly displayed map region, which could be used to query items for display on the map.

```
- (void)mapView:(MKMapView *)mapView
➡regionDidChangeAnimated:(BOOL)animated
{
    MKCoordinateRegion newRegion = [mapView region];
    CLLocationCoordinate2D center = newRegion.center;
    MKCoordinateSpan span = newRegion.span;

    NSLog(@"New map region center: <%f/%f>, span: <%f/%f>",
    ➡center.latitude,center.longitude,span.latitudeDelta,
    ➡span.longitudeDelta);
}
```

Handling draggable annotations and callout taps is described in the next section.

Map Annotations and Overlays

A map view (MKMapView) is a scroll view that behaves specially; adding a subview to it in the standard way will not add the subview to the scrollable part of the map view, but rather the subview will remain static relative to the frame of the map view. Although that might be a feature for items like hovering buttons or labels, being able to identify and mark points and details on the map is a key feature. Map annotations and overlays are a way to mark items or areas of interest in a map view. Annotations and overlays maintain their position on a map as the map is scrolled and zoomed. Map annotations are defined by a single coordinate point on the map, and map overlays can be lines, polygons, or complex shapes. MapKit draws a distinction between the logical annotation or overlay and the associated view. Annotations and overlays are data that represent where on the map they should be displayed, and are added to the map view directly. The map view will then request a view for an annotation or overlay when it needs to be displayed, much like a table view will request cells for index paths as needed.

Adding Annotations

Any object can be an annotation in a map view. To become an annotation, the object needs to implement the MKAnnotation protocol. Apple recommends that the annotation objects should be lightweight, since the map view will keep a reference to all the annotations added to it, and map scrolling and zooming performance can suffer if there are too many annotations. If the requirements for the annotation are very simple and basic, an MKPointAnnotation can be used. In the sample app the ICFFavoritePlace class, which implements the MKAnnotation protocol, is a subclass of NSManagedObject so that it can be persisted using Core Data. Refer to Chapter 15, "Getting Up and Running with Core Data," for more information on using Core Data and NSManagedObject subclasses.

To implement the `MKAnnotation` protocol, a class must implement the `coordinate` property. This is used by the map view to determine where the annotation should be placed on the map. The coordinate needs to be returned as a `CLLocationCoordinate2D`.

```
- (CLLocationCoordinate2D)coordinate
{
    CLLocationDegrees lat =
    ➡[[self valueForKeyPath:@"latitude"] doubleValue];

    CLLocationDegrees lon =
    ➡[[self valueForKeyPath:@"longitude"] doubleValue];

    CLLocationCoordinate2D coord =
    ➡CLLocationCoordinate2DMake(lat, lon);

    return coord;
}
```

Because the `ICFFavoritePlace` class stores the latitude and longitude for the place individually, the `coordinate` property method creates a `CLLocationCoordinate2D` from the latitude and longitude using the `CLLocationCoordinate2DMake` function provided by Core Location. `ICFFavoritePlace` will break apart a `CLLocationCoordinate2D` in the setter method for the `coordinate` property to store the latitude and longitude.

```
- (void)setCoordinate:(CLLocationCoordinate2D)newCoordinate
{
    [self setValue:@(newCoordinate.latitude)
        forKeyPath:@"latitude"];

    [self setValue:@(newCoordinate.longitude)
        forKeyPath:@"longitude"];
}
```

Two other properties for the `MKAnnotation` protocol can optionally be implemented: `title` and `subtitle`. These are used by the map view to display the callout when the user taps an annotation view, as shown in Figure 2.7.

Figure 2.7 FavoritePlaces sample app: displaying map annotation view callout.

The `title` property is used for the top line of the callout, and the `subtitle` property is used for the bottom line of the callout.

```
- (NSString *)title
{
    return [self valueForKeyPath:@"placeName"];
}

- (NSString *)subtitle
{
    NSString *subtitleString = @"";

    NSString *addressString =
    ➥[self valueForKeyPath:@"placeStreetAddress"];

    if ([addressString length] > 0)
    {
        NSString *addr =
        ➥[self valueForKeyPath:@"placeStreetAddress"];

        NSString *city = [self valueForKeyPath:@"placeCity"];
        NSString *state = [self valueForKeyPath:@"placeState"];
        NSString *zip = [self valueForKeyPath:@"placePostal"];

        subtitleString =
        ➥[NSString stringWithFormat:@"%@, %@, %@ %@",
          ➥addr,city,state,zip];
    }
    return subtitleString;
}
```

In `ICFMainViewController`, the `updateMapAnnotations` method is called from `viewDidLoad:` to populate the map annotations initially, and again after the favorite place detail editing view is dismissed. The method starts by removing all the annotations from the map view. Although this approach works fine for a small number of annotations, with more annotations a more intelligent approach should be developed to efficiently remove unneeded annotations and add new ones.

```
[self.mapView removeAnnotations:self.mapView.annotations];
```

Next, the method performs a Core Data fetch request to get an `NSArray` of the stored favorite places, and adds that array to the map view's annotations.

```
NSFetchRequest *placesRequest =
➥[[NSFetchRequest alloc] initWithEntityName:@"FavoritePlace"];

NSManagedObjectContext *moc = kAppDelegate.managedObjectContext;

NSError *error = nil;

NSArray *places = [moc executeFetchRequest:placesRequest
                                     error:&error];
```

```
if (error)
{
    NSLog(@"Core Data fetch error %@, %@", error,
    ➥[error userInfo]);
}
[self.mapView addAnnotations:places];
```

The map view will then manage displaying the added annotations on the map.

Displaying Standard and Custom Annotation Views

An annotation view is the representation of the annotation on the map. Two types of standard annotation views are provided with MapKit, the pin for searched locations and the pulsing blue dot for the current location. Annotation views can be customized with a static image, or can be completely customized with a subclass of MKAnnotationView. The sample app uses standard pins for favorite places, the standard blue dot for the current location, and a green arrow for a draggable annotation example, as shown in Figure 2.8.

Figure 2.8   FavoritePlaces sample app: displaying map annotation views.

To allow a map view to display annotation views for annotations, the map view delegate needs to implement the mapView:viewForAnnotation method. In the sample app, the mapView:viewForAnnotation method is implemented in the ICFMainViewController. The method first checks whether the annotation is the current location.

```
if (annotation == mapView.userLocation)
{
    return nil;
}
```

For the current location, returning `nil` for an annotation view will tell the map view to use the standard blue dot. The method then examines the `ICFFavoritePlace` annotation to determine what type of annotation it is. If the annotation represents the "going next" location, then a custom annotation view will be returned; otherwise, a standard pin annotation view will be returned.

```
MKAnnotationView *view = nil;

ICFFavoritePlace *place = (ICFFavoritePlace *)annotation;

if ([[place valueForKeyPath:@"goingNext"] boolValue])
{
    ...
}
else
{
    ...
}

return view;
```

To return a standard pin annotation view, the method first attempts to dequeue an existing, but no longer used, annotation view. If one is not available, the method will create an instance of `MKPinAnnotationView`.

```
MKPinAnnotationView *pinView = (MKPinAnnotationView *)
➡[mapView dequeueReusableAnnotationViewWithIdentifier:@"pin"];

if (pinView == nil)
{
    pinView = [[MKPinAnnotationView alloc]
    ➡initWithAnnotation:annotation reuseIdentifier:@"pin"];
}
```

After the pin annotation is created, it can be customized by setting the pin color (choices are red, green, and purple), indicating whether the callout can be displayed when the user taps the annotation view, and indicating whether the annotation view can be dragged.

```
[pinView setPinColor:MKPinAnnotationColorRed];
[pinView setCanShowCallout:YES];
[pinView setDraggable:NO];
```

The callout view that appears when the annotation view is tapped has left and right accessory views that can be customized. The left accessory view is set to a custom image, and the right accessory view is set to a standard detail disclosure button. If the left or right accessory views are customized with objects that descend from `UIControl`, the delegate method `mapView:annotationView:calloutAccessoryControlTapped:` will be called when they are tapped. Otherwise, the objects should be configured by the developer to handle the tap as desired. Note that Apple states that the maximum height for the accessory views is 32 pixels.

```
UIImageView *leftView = [[UIImageView alloc]
➥initWithImage:[UIImage imageNamed:@"annotation_view_star"]];

[pinView setLeftCalloutAccessoryView:leftView];

UIButton* rightButton = [UIButton buttonWithType:
                            ➥UIButtonTypeDetailDisclosure];

[pinView setRightCalloutAccessoryView:rightButton];
view = pinView;
```

To return a custom pin annotation view, the method will attempt to dequeue an existing but no longer used annotation view by a string identifier. If one is not available, the method will create an instance of `MKAnnotationView`.

```
view = (MKAnnotationView *)
➥ [mapView dequeueReusableAnnotationViewWithIdentifier:@"arrow"];

if (view == nil)
{
    view = [[MKAnnotationView alloc]
    ➥initWithAnnotation:annotation reuseIdentifier:@"arrow"];
}
```

The annotation can be customized much like a standard pin annotation, indicating whether the callout can be displayed when the user taps the annotation view, and indicating whether the annotation view can be dragged. The main difference is that the image for the annotation can be set directly using the `setImage:` method.

```
[view setCanShowCallout:YES];
[view setDraggable:YES];

[view setImage:[UIImage imageNamed:@"next_arrow"]];

UIImageView *leftView = [[UIImageView alloc]
➥initWithImage:[UIImage imageNamed:@"annotation_view_arrow"]];

[view setLeftCalloutAccessoryView:leftView];
[view setRightCalloutAccessoryView:nil];
```

The annotation view will display with a green arrow instead of a standard pin, as shown previously in Figure 2.8.

Draggable Annotation Views

Draggable annotation views can be useful to enable the user to mark a place on a map. In the sample app, there is one special favorite place to indicate where the user is going next, represented by a green arrow. An annotation view can be made draggable by setting the `draggable` property when the annotation view is being configured for presentation.

```
[view setDraggable:YES];
```

The user can then drag the annotation view anywhere on the map. To get more information about the dragging performed on an annotation view, the map view delegate implements the `mapView:annotationView:didChangeDragState:fromOldState:` method. That method will fire anytime the dragging state changes for a draggable annotation view, and indicates whether the dragging state is none, starting, dragging, canceling, or ending. By examining the new dragging state and old dragging state, custom logic can handle a number of different use cases presented by dragging.

When the user stops dragging the arrow in the sample app, it will reverse-geocode the new location indicated by the arrow (described in more detail in the later section "Geocoding and Reverse-Geocoding") to get the name and address of the new location. To do this, the method needs to check whether dragging is completed.

```
if (newState == MKAnnotationViewDragStateEnding)
{
    ....
}
```

If dragging is complete, the method will get the annotation associated with the annotation view to figure out the new coordinates that need to be reverse-geocoded.

```
ICFFavoritePlace *draggedPlace =
➡(ICFFavoritePlace *)[annotationView annotation];
```

The method adds a standard spinner to the callout view so that the user knows it is being updated, and then calls the method to reverse-geocode the new place, described later in the chapter in the geocoding section.

```
UIActivityIndicatorViewStyle whiteStyle =
➡UIActivityIndicatorViewStyleWhite;

UIActivityIndicatorView *activityView =
➡[[UIActivityIndicatorView alloc]
➡initWithActivityIndicatorStyle:whiteStyle];

[activityView startAnimating];
[annotationView setLeftCalloutAccessoryView:activityView];

[self reverseGeocodeDraggedAnnotation:draggedPlace
                   forAnnotationView:annotationView];
```

Working with Map Overlays

Map overlays are similar to map annotations, in that any object can implement the MKOverlay protocol, and the map view delegate is asked to provide the associated view for a map overlay. Map overlays are different from annotations in that they can represent more than just a point. They can represent lines and shapes, so they are very useful for representing routes or areas of interest on a map. To demonstrate map overlays, the sample app provides a feature to add a geofence (described in detail later in the section "Geofencing") with a user-defined radius for a favorite place. When a geofence is added for a favorite place, the user's selected radius will be displayed on the map with a circle around the place's coordinate, as shown in Figure 2.9.

Figure 2.9   FavoritePlaces sample app: displaying map overlay view.

As mentioned previously in the "Adding Annotations" section, the updateMapAnnotations method adds annotations to the map. This method also adds overlays to the map at the same time. The method starts by clearing all existing overlays from the map view.

```
[self.mapView removeOverlays:self.mapView.overlays];
```

Since overlays are displayed only for places that have the geofence feature enabled, the method iterates over the places, and adds an overlay to the map only for those places.

```
for (ICFFavoritePlace *favPlace in places)
{

    BOOL displayOverlay =
➥[[favPlace valueForKeyPath:@"displayProximity"] boolValue];

    if (displayOverlay)
    {
        [self.mapView addOverlay:favPlace];
        ...
    }
}
```

When the map needs to display a map overlay, the map view will call the delegate method
`mapView:viewForOverlay`. This method will create an overlay view for the map to display.
Three options are provided by MapKit: circle, polygon, and polyline; custom shapes and overlays can also be created if the MapKit options are insufficient. The sample app creates a circle
around the location, using the radius and map coordinate from the favorite place.

```
ICFFavoritePlace *place = (ICFFavoritePlace *)overlay;

CLLocationDistance radius =
➥[[place valueForKeyPath:@"displayRadius"] floatValue];

MKCircle *circle =
➥[MKCircle circleWithCenterCoordinate:[overlay coordinate]
                                 radius:radius];
```

After the map kit circle is ready, the method creates a map kit circle view, and customizes the
stroke and fill colors and the line width. This circle view is then returned, and the map will
display it.

```
MKCircleRenderer *circleView =
➥[[MKCircleRenderer alloc] initWithCircle:circle];

circleView.fillColor =
➥[[UIColor redColor] colorWithAlphaComponent:0.2];

circleView.strokeColor =
➥[[UIColor redColor] colorWithAlphaComponent:0.7];

circleView.lineWidth = 3;

return circleView;
```

Geocoding and Reverse-Geocoding

Geocoding is the process of finding latitude and longitude coordinates from a human-readable
address. Reverse-geocoding is the process of finding a human readable address from coordinates. As of iOS 5.0, Core Location supports both, with no special terms or limitations (as with
MapKit in iOS 5.1 and earlier).

Geocoding an Address

The sample app enables the user to add a new favorite place by entering an address in
`ICFFavoritePlaceViewController`. The user can tap Geocode Location Now to get the latitude and longitude, as shown in Figure 2.10.

Figure 2.10   FavoritePlaces sample app: adding a new favorite place.

When the user taps the Geocode Location Now button, the geocodeLocationTouched: method is called. That method begins by concatenating the address information provided by the user into a single string, like 2100 York St, Denver, CO 80205, to provide to the geocoder.

```
NSString *geocodeString = @"";
if ([self.addressTextField.text length] > 0)
{
    geocodeString = self.addressTextField.text;
}
if ([self.cityTextField.text length] > 0)
{
    if ([geocodeString length] > 0)
    {

        geocodeString =
        ➥[geocodeString stringByAppendingFormat:@", %@",
        ➥self.cityTextField.text];

    }
    else
    {
        geocodeString = self.cityTextField.text;
    }
}
if ([self.stateTextField.text length] > 0)
    {
    if ([geocodeString length] > 0)
```

```
        {

            geocodeString =
        ➥[geocodeString stringByAppendingFormat:@", %@",
        ➥self.stateTextField.text];

        }
        else
        {
            geocodeString = self.stateTextField.text;
        }
    }
    if ([self.postalTextField.text length] > 0)
        {
        if ([geocodeString length] > 0)
        {

            geocodeString =
        ➥[geocodeString stringByAppendingFormat:@" %@",
        ➥self.postalTextField.text];

        }
        else
        {
            geocodeString = self.postalTextField.text;
        }
    }
}
```

The method will then disable the Geocode Location Now button to prevent additional requests from getting started by multiple taps. Apple explicitly states that the geocoder should process only one request at a time. The method also updates the fields and button to indicate that geocoding is in process.

```
[self.latitudeTextField setText:@"Geocoding..."];
[self.longitudeTextField setText:@"Geocoding..."];

[self.geocodeNowButton setTitle:@"Geocoding now..."
                    forState:UIControlStateDisabled];

[self.geocodeNowButton setEnabled:NO];
```

The method gets a reference to an instance of CLGeocoder.

```
CLGeocoder *geocoder =
➥[[ICFLocationManager sharedLocationManager] geocoder];
```

The geocoder is then asked to geocode the address string, with a completion handler block, which is called on the main queue. The completion handler will first reenable the button so that it can be tapped again, and will then check to see whether an error was encountered with geocoding or whether the geocoder completed successfully.

```
[geocoder geocodeAddressString:geocodeString
➥completionHandler:^(NSArray *placemarks, NSError *error) {

    [self.geocodeNowButton setEnabled:YES];
    if (error)
    {
        ...
    }
    else
    {
        ...
    }
}];
```

If the geocoder encountered an error, the latitude and longitude fields are populated with Not found and an alert view is presented with the localized description of the error. The geocoder will fail without an Internet connection, or if the address is not well formed or cannot be found.

```
[self.latitudeTextField setText:@"Not found"];
[self.longitudeTextField setText:@"Not found"];

UIAlertController *alertController =
➥[UIAlertController alertControllerWithTitle:@"Geocoding Error"
                                      message:error.localizedDescription
                               preferredStyle:UIAlertControllerStyleAlert];

[alertController addAction:
➥[UIAlertAction actionWithTitle:@"OK"
                          style:UIAlertActionStyleCancel
                        handler:nil]];

[self presentViewController:alertController
                   animated:YES
                 completion:nil];
```

If geocoding succeeded, an array called placemarks will be provided to the completion handler. This array will contain instances of CLPlacemark, which each contain information about a potential match. A placemark has a latitude/longitude coordinate and address information.

```
if ([placemarks count] > 0)
{
    CLPlacemark *placemark = [placemarks lastObject];
```

```
    NSString *latString =
    ➥[NSString stringWithFormat:@"%f",
    ➥placemark.location.coordinate.latitude];

    [self.latitudeTextField setText:latString];

    NSString *longString =
    ➥[NSString stringWithFormat:@"%f",
    ➥placemark.location.coordinate.longitude];

    [self.longitudeTextField setText:longString];
}
```

If more than one placemark is returned, the user interface could allow the user to select the one that most closely matches his intention (Maps.app uses this approach). For simplicity the sample app selects the last placemark in the array and updates the user interface with the coordinate information.

Reverse-Geocoding a Location

The sample app enables users to drag the green arrow to indicate where they would like to go next, as shown in Figure 2.11.

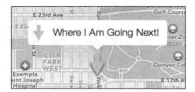

Figure 2.11   FavoritePlaces sample app: Where I Am Going Next.

When the user drags the green arrow, the map view delegate method `mapView:annotation View:didChangeDragState:fromOldState:` in `ICFMainViewController` gets called. That method checks the drag state as described earlier in the "Draggable Annotation Views" section, and, if the green arrow has stopped being dragged, updates the callout view with a spinner and starts the reverse-geocoding.

```
ICFFavoritePlace *draggedPlace =
➥(ICFFavoritePlace *)[annotationView annotation];

UIActivityIndicatorViewStyle whiteStyle =
➥UIActivityIndicatorViewStyleWhite;

UIActivityIndicatorView *activityView =
➥[[UIActivityIndicatorView alloc]
➥initWithActivityIndicatorStyle:whiteStyle];
```

```
[activityView startAnimating];
[annotationView setLeftCalloutAccessoryView:activityView];

[self reverseGeocodeDraggedAnnotation:draggedPlace
                  forAnnotationView:annotationView];
```

The `reverseGeocodeDraggedAnnotation:forAnnotationView:` method gets a reference to an instance of `CLGeocoder`.

```
CLGeocoder *geocoder =
➥[[ICFLocationManager sharedLocationManager] geocoder];
```

An instance of `CLLocation` is created for use by the geocoder from the coordinate of the moved arrow.

```
CLLocationCoordinate2D draggedCoord = [place coordinate];

CLLocation *draggedLocation =
➥[[CLLocation alloc] initWithLatitude:draggedCoord.latitude
                        longitude:draggedCoord.longitude];
```

The geocoder is then asked to reverse-geocode the location from which the annotation has been dragged with a completion handler block, which is called on the main queue. The completion handler will replace the spinner in the callout with the green arrow, and will then check to see whether an error was encountered with geocoding or whether the geocoder completed successfully.

```
[geocoder reverseGeocodeLocation:draggedLocation
➥completionHandler:^(NSArray *placemarks, NSError *error) {

    UIImage *arrowImage =
    ➥[UIImage imageNamed:@"annotation_view_arrow"];

    UIImageView *leftView =
    ➥[[UIImageView alloc] initWithImage:arrowImage];

    [annotationView setLeftCalloutAccessoryView:leftView];

    if (error)
    {
        ...
    }
    else
    {
        ...
    }
}];
```

If the geocoder encountered an error, an alert view is presented with the localized description of the error. The geocoder will fail without an Internet connection.

```
UIAlertController *alertController =
➡[UIAlertController alertControllerWithTitle:@"Geocoding Error"
                                      message:error.localizedDescription
                               preferredStyle:UIAlertControllerStyleAlert];

[alertController addAction:
➡[UIAlertAction actionWithTitle:@"OK"
                          style:UIAlertActionStyleCancel
                        handler:nil]];

[self presentViewController:alertController
                   animated:YES
                 completion:nil];
```

If the reverse-geocoding process completes successfully, an array of CLPlacemark instances will be passed to the completion handler. The sample app will use the last placemark to update the name and address of the next place.

```
if ([placemarks count] > 0)
{
    CLPlacemark *placemark = [placemarks lastObject];
    [self updateFavoritePlace:place withPlacemark:placemark];
}
```

The placemark contains detailed location information with internationalized terms. For example, a street address is represented by the number (or subThoroughfare) and a street (or thoroughfare), and the city and state are subAdministrativeArea and administrativeArea.

```
[kAppDelegate.managedObjectContext performBlock:^{
    NSString *newName =
    ➡[NSString stringWithFormat:@"Next: %@",placemark.name];

    [place setValue:newName forKey:@"placeName"];

    NSString *newStreetAddress =
    ➡[NSString stringWithFormat:@"%@ %@",
    ➡placemark.subThoroughfare, placemark.thoroughfare];

    [place setValue:newStreetAddress
            forKey:@"placeStreetAddress"];

    [place setValue:placemark.subAdministrativeArea
            forKey:@"placeCity"];
```

```
    [place setValue:placemark.postalCode
            forKey:@"placePostal"];

    [place setValue:placemark.administrativeArea
            forKey:@"placeState"];

    NSError *saveError = nil;
    [kAppDelegate.managedObjectContext save:&saveError];
    if (saveError) {
        NSLog(@"Save Error: %@",saveError.localizedDescription);
    }
}];
```

> **Tip**
>
> `CLPlacemark` instances provided by the geocoder include an `addressDictionary` property, which is formatted for easy insertion into the Address Book (see Chapter 5, "Getting Started with Address Book," for more information).

The place is then saved using Core Data so that it will survive app restarts. Now when the user taps the green arrow annotation view, it will reflect the name and address of the location it was dragged to, as shown in Figure 2.12.

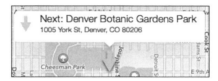

Figure 2.12   FavoritePlaces sample app: Where I Am Going Next after reverse-geocode.

Geofencing

Geofencing, also called regional monitoring, is the capability to track when a device enters or exits a specified map region. iOS uses this to great effect with Siri to accomplish things like, "Remind me to pick up bread when I leave the office," or, "Remind me to put the roast in the oven when I get home." iOS also uses geofencing in Passbook, to help users see the passes that are relevant to them on the home screen (see Chapter 25, "Passbook and PassKit," for more details).

Checking for Regional Monitoring Capability

The Core Location location manager has a class method that indicates whether regional monitoring is available for the device. This can be used to customize whether an app performs regional monitoring tasks. For example, the sample app will conditionally display a switch to enable geofencing for a favorite location in the `ICFFavoritePlaceViewController`.

```
BOOL hideGeofence =
➡![CLLocationManager isMonitoringAvailableForClass:[CLRegion class]];

[self.displayProximitySwitch setHidden:hideGeofence];

if (hideGeofence)
{
    [self.geofenceLabel setText:@"Geofence N/A"];
}
```

Defining Boundaries

Core Location's location manager (`CLLocationManager`) keeps a set of regions being monitored for an app. In `ICFMainViewController`, the `updateMapAnnotations:` method clears out the set of monitored regions when a change has been made.

```
CLLocationManager *locManager =
➡[[ICFLocationManager sharedLocationManager] locationManager];

NSSet *monitoredRegions = [locManager monitoredRegions];

for (CLRegion *region in monitoredRegions)
{
    [locManager stopMonitoringForRegion:region];
}
```

Next, the method iterates over the user's list of favorite places to determine which places the user has set to geofence. For each such place, the method will add the overlay view as described in the previous section, and will then tell the location manager to start monitoring that region. A region to be monitored needs a center coordinate, a radius, and an identifier so that the region can be tracked in the app. The sample app uses the Core Data universal resource ID representation as an identifier for the region so that the same place can be quickly retrieved when a regional monitoring event is generated for the region.

```
NSString *placeObjectID =
➡[[[favPlace objectID] URIRepresentation] absoluteString];


CLLocationDistance monitorRadius =
➡[[favPlace valueForKeyPath:@"displayRadius"] floatValue];

CLCircularRegion *region =
➡[[CLCircularRegion alloc] initWithCenter:[favPlace coordinate]
```

```
                              radius:monitorRadius
                          identifier:placeObjectID];

[locManager startMonitoringForRegion:region];
```

Note that currently only circular regions are supported for regional monitoring.

Monitoring Changes

When the device either enters or exits a monitored region, the location manager will inform its delegate of the event by calling either the locationManager:didEnterRegion: or the locationManager:didExitRegion: method.

In locationManager:didEnterRegion: the method first gets the identifier associated with the monitored region. This identifier was assigned when the location manager was told to monitor the region, and is the Core Data URI of the saved favorite place. This URI is used to get the managed object ID, which is used to retrieve the favorite place from the managed object context.

```
NSString *placeIdentifier = [region identifier];
NSURL *placeIDURL = [NSURL URLWithString:placeIdentifier];

NSManagedObjectID *placeObjectID =
➥[kAppDelegate.persistentStoreCoordinator
➥managedObjectIDForURIRepresentation:placeIDURL];
```

The method gets details from the favorite place and presents them in an alert to the user.

```
[kAppDelegate.managedObjectContext performBlock:^{

    ICFFavoritePlace *place =
    ➥(ICFFavoritePlace *)[kAppDelegate.managedObjectContext
    ➥objectWithID:placeObjectID];

    NSNumber *distance = [place valueForKey:@"displayRadius"];
    NSString *placeName = [place valueForKey:@"placeName"];

    NSString *baseMessage =
    ➥@"Favorite Place %@ nearby - within %@ meters.";

    NSString *proximityMessage =
    ➥[NSString stringWithFormat:baseMessage,placeName,distance];

    UIAlertController *nearbyAlertController =
    ➥[UIAlertController alertControllerWithTitle:@"Favorite Nearby!"
                                        message:proximityMessage
                                  preferredStyle:UIAlertControllerStyleAlert];
```

```
[nearbyAlertController addAction:
➧[UIAlertAction actionWithTitle:@"OK"
                           style:UIAlertActionStyleCancel
                         handler:nil]];

ICFAppDelegate *appDelegate =
➧(ICFAppDelegate *)[[UIApplication sharedApplication] delegate];

[appDelegate.window.rootViewController presentViewController:nearbyAlertController
                                              animated:YES
                                            completion:nil];
}];
```

To test this using the sample app, start the app in debug mode using the included GPX file for the Denver Museum of Nature and Science (DMNS), as described previously in the chapter in the section "Using GPX Files to Test Specific Locations." Ensure that the Denver Art Museum is set to Geofence, as shown in Figure 2.9 in the section "Working with Map Overlays." After the app is running, use Xcode to change the location using the debug location menu from DMNS (as shown in Figure 2.6) to the Denver Art Museum. This should trigger the geofence and display the alert as shown in Figure 2.13.

Figure 2.13   FavoritePlaces sample app: favorite place nearby alert.

The `locationManager:didExitRegion:` method also gets the Core Data identifier from the region, uses Core Data to get the managed object ID, looks up the favorite place, and presents an alert when the user exits the region. To test this using the sample app, start from the Favorite Nearby alert just shown in Figure 2.13. Tap the OK button, and then select Debug, Location, Apple from the iOS Simulator menu. After a few seconds, the simulator will change locations and present the user with an alert, as shown in Figure 2.14.

The location manager intentionally delays calling the delegate methods until a cushion distance has been crossed for at least 20 seconds to prevent spurious messages when the device is close to the boundary of a region.

Figure 2.14   FavoritePlaces sample app: favorite place geofence exited alert.

Getting Directions

As of iOS 6, the standard Maps.app was enhanced to provide turn-by-turn navigation in addition to directions. Maps.app was also enhanced to allow other apps to open it with specific instructions on what to display. Apps can request that Maps.app display an array of map items, provide directions between two locations, or provide directions from the current location. Maps.app can be configured with a center point and span, and a type of map (standard, satellite, or hybrid). As of iOS 7, MapKit offers a directions request, which can provide directions to be used directly in an app. The directions request can return an array of polylines representing route options, with accompanying route steps that can be presented in a table view. Both approaches are demonstrated in the sample app.

To open Maps.app, the class method `openMapsWithItems:launchOptions:` on the `MKMapItem` class can be used, or the instance method `openInMapsWithlaunchOptions:`. In the sample app, there is a button on `ICFFavoritePlaceViewController` to get directions to a favorite place. When that button is tapped, the `getDirectionsButtonTouched:` method is called. In that method, an instance of `MKMapItem` is created for the favorite place.

```
CLLocationCoordinate2D destination =
➥[self.favoritePlace coordinate];

MKPlacemark *destinationPlacemark =
➥[[MKPlacemark alloc] initWithCoordinate:destination
                    addressDictionary:nil];
```

```
MKMapItem *destinationItem =
➡[[MKMapItem alloc] initWithPlacemark:destinationPlacemark];

destinationItem.name =
➡[self.favoritePlace valueForKey:@"placeName"];
```

A dictionary of launch options is set up to instruct Maps.app how to configure itself when opened.

```
NSDictionary *launchOptions = @{
    MKLaunchOptionsDirectionsModeKey :
    MKLaunchOptionsDirectionsModeDriving,
    MKLaunchOptionsMapTypeKey :
    [NSNumber numberWithInt:MKMapTypeStandard]
};
```

Then, an array of map items is created with the favorite place to pass to Maps.app with the dictionary of launch options. If two map items are passed in the array with a directions launch option, the map will provide directions from the first item to the second item.

```
NSArray *mapItems = @[destinationItem];

BOOL success = [MKMapItem openMapsWithItems:mapItems
                              launchOptions:launchOptions];

if (!success)
{
    NSLog(@"Failed to open Maps.app.");
}
```

Maps.app will be opened and will provide directions to the favorite place. If an error is encountered, the openMapsWithItems:launchOptions: will return NO.

To request directions to be displayed in the app, instantiate an MKDirections object with an MKDirectionsRequest instance, specifying a source (or starting point) and destination map item expressed as MKMapItem instances.

```
CLLocationCoordinate2D destination =
➡[self.favoritePlace coordinate];

MKPlacemark *destinationPlacemark =
➡[[MKPlacemark alloc] initWithCoordinate:destination
                         addressDictionary:nil];

MKMapItem *destinationItem =
➡[[MKMapItem alloc] initWithPlacemark:destinationPlacemark];

MKMapItem *currentMapItem =
➡[self.delegate currentLocationMapItem];
```

```
MKDirectionsRequest *directionsRequest =
➥[[MKDirectionsRequest alloc] init];

[directionsRequest setDestination:destinationItem];
[directionsRequest setSource:currentMapItem];

MKDirections *directions =
➥[[MKDirections alloc] initWithRequest:directionsRequest];
```

Then call the `calculateDirectionsWithCompletionHandler:` method, specifying a completion block. The completion block should handle any errors, and inspect the `MKDirectionsResponse` provided. For this example the method ensures that at least one route (which is an instance of `MKRoute`) was returned, and then performs actions with the first route. The method iterates over the `steps` property of the first route, which contains instances of `MKRouteStep`, and logs strings to display the distance and instructions for each route step. Then the method calls the delegate to add the route to the map.

```
[directions calculateDirectionsWithCompletionHandler:
➥^(MKDirectionsResponse *response, NSError *error){
    if (error) {

        NSString *dirMessage =
        ➥[NSString stringWithFormat:@"Failed to get directions: %@",
        ➥error.localizedDescription];

        UIAlertController *dirAlertController =
        ➥[UIAlertController alertControllerWithTitle:@"Directions Error"
                                            message:dirMessage
                                     preferredStyle:UIAlertControllerStyleAlert];

        [dirAlertController addAction:
        ➥[UIAlertAction actionWithTitle:@"OK"
                                  style:UIAlertActionStyleCancel
                                handler:nil]];

        [self presentViewController:dirAlertController
                          animated:YES
                        completion:nil];
    }
    else
    {
        if ([response.routes count] > 0) {
            MKRoute *firstRoute = response.routes[0];
            NSLog(@"Directions received.  Steps for route 1 are: ");
            NSInteger stepNumber = 1;
            for (MKRouteStep *step in firstRoute.steps) {
```

```
            NSLog(@"Step %d, %f meters: %@",stepNumber,
            ➥step.distance,step.instructions);

            stepNumber++;
        }
        [self.delegate displayDirectionsForRoute:firstRoute];
    }
    else
    {
        NSString *dirMessage = @"No directions available";

        UIAlertController *dirAlertController =
        ➥[UIAlertController alertControllerWithTitle:@"No Directions"
                                             message:dirMessage
                                      preferredStyle:UIAlertControllerStyleAlert];

        [dirAlertController addAction:
        ➥[UIAlertAction actionWithTitle:@"OK"
                                  style:UIAlertActionStyleCancel
                                handler:nil]];

        [self presentViewController:dirAlertController
                           animated:YES
                         completion:nil];
    }
  }
}];
```

In the delegate method, the polyline for the route is added to the map's overlays, and the dialog is dismissed.

```
- (void)displayDirectionsForRoute:(MKRoute *)route
{
    [self.mapView addOverlay:route.polyline];

    if (self.favoritePlacePopoverController)
    {
        [self.favoritePlacePopoverController
        ➥dismissPopoverAnimated:YES];

        self.favoritePlacePopoverController = nil;
    } else
    {
        [self dismissViewControllerAnimated:YES
                                 completion:nil];
    }
}
```

Since the polyline has been added as an overlay, the map delegate method to return overlay views must now handle polylines instead of just the custom geofence radius overlays.

```
- (MKOverlayRenderer *)mapView:(MKMapView *)mapView
              viewForOverlay:(id < MKOverlay >)overlay
{
    MKOverlayRenderer *returnView = nil;

    if ([overlay isKindOfClass:[ICFFavoritePlace class]]) {
        ...
    }
    if ([overlay isKindOfClass:[MKPolyline class]]) {
        MKPolyline *line = (MKPolyline *)overlay;

        MKPolylineRenderer *polylineRenderer =
        ➥[[MKPolylineRenderer alloc] initWithPolyline:line];

        [polylineRenderer setLineWidth:3.0];
        [polylineRenderer setFillColor:[UIColor blueColor]];
        [polylineRenderer setStrokeColor:[UIColor blueColor]];
        returnView = polylineRenderer;
    }

    return returnView;
}
```

The mapView:viewForOverlay: method will now check which class the overlay belongs to, and build the correct type of view for it. For the polyline, the method will create an instance of MKPolylineRenderer using the polyline from the overlay, and customize it with a line width and blue fill and stroke color, which will show a directions line on the map between the starting location and the destination location, as shown in Figure 2.15.

Figure 2.15   FavoritePlaces sample app: displaying a direction polyline on the map.

Summary

This chapter covered Core Location and MapKit. It described how to set up Core Location, how to check for available services, how to deal with user permissions, and how to acquire the device's current location.

Next, this chapter explained how to use MapKit to display locations on a map using standard and custom annotations. The chapter covered how to display more detail about an annotation in a callout, and how to respond to the user tapping the callout or dragging the annotation on the map. It also explained how to add overlays to a map to highlight map features.

This chapter then described how to use the geocoder to get latitude and longitude information from a street address, or to get address information from a latitude and longitude coordinate.

Geofencing, or regional monitoring, was demonstrated. The sample app showed how to specify and monitor when the user enters or exits map regions.

Finally, this chapter demonstrated two techniques for providing directions to a favorite place: using Maps.app to provide directions and using a directions request to get information to display directly in the user interface.

3

Leaderboards

Leaderboards have become an important component of nearly every mobile game, as well as having numerous applications outside of gaming. Leveraging Game Center to add leaderboards makes it easier than ever to include them in an iOS app. Although leaderboards have been around almost as long as video games themselves—the first high-score list appeared in 1976—they have more recently become critical parts of a social gaming experience. In this chapter, you'll learn how to add a full-featured leaderboard to a real-world game, from setting up the required information in iTunes Connect to displaying the leaderboard using `GKLeaderboardViewController`.

The Sample App

In both this chapter and Chapter 4, "Achievements," the same sample app is used. It is important to be familiar with the game itself so that you can remove the complexity of it from the process of integrating Game Center. Whack-a-Cac was designed to use minimal code and be simple to learn, so the game can act as a generic placeholder for whatever app you are integrating Game Center into. If you already have an app that you are ready to work with, skip this section and follow along with your existing project.

Whack-a-Cac, as shown in Figure 3.1, is a simple Whack-a-Mole style game. Cacti will pop up and the user must tap them before the timer fires and they disappear behind the sand dunes. As the game progresses, it continues to get more difficult; after you have missed five cacti, the game ends and you are left with a score. The gameplay behavior itself is controlled through the `ICFGameViewController` class. Cacti can appear anywhere along the x-axis and on one of three possible rows on the y-axis. The player will have two seconds from the time a cactus appears to tap it before it goes back down and the player is deducted a life point. Up until a score of 50, every ten cacti that are hit will increase the maximum number shown at one time by one. The game also supports pausing and resuming during gameplay.

Figure 3.1   A first look at Whack-a-Cac, the game that is used for both of the Game Center chapters.

Before we dig into the game-specific code, attention must first be paid to the home screen menu of the game. IFCViewController.m will not only handle launching the gameplay but also enable the user to access the leaderboards and achievements, which are covered in Chapter 4. The Game Center–specific functionality of this class is discussed in detail later in this chapter, but for the time being the focus should be on the play: method. When a new game is created, IFCViewController simply calls alloc and init on IFCGameViewController and pushes it onto the navigation stack. The remainder of the game will be handled by that class.

Whack-a-Cac is a simplified example of an iOS game. It is based on a state engine containing three states: playing, paused, and game over. While the game is in the playing state, the engine will continue to spawn cacti until the user runs out of life and enters the game-over state. The user can pause the game at any time by tapping the pause button in the upper-left corner of the screen. To begin to understand the engine, direct your attention to the viewDidLoad: method.

```
- (void)viewDidLoad
{
    [[ICFGameCenterManager sharedManager] setDelegate: self];

    score = 0;
    life = 5;
```

```
    gameOver = NO;
    paused = NO;

    [super viewDidLoad];

    [self updateLife];

    [self spawnCactus];
    [self performSelector:@selector(spawnCactus) withObject:nil
    ➥afterDelay:1.0];
}
```

On the first line, the ICFGameCenterManager has its delegate set to self, which is covered in depth later in this section. During the viewDidLoad execution, a few state variables need to be set. First the score is reset to zero along with the life integer being set to five. The next requirement is setting two Booleans that represent the current state of the game; since the game starts with gameplay on launch, both gameOver and paused are set to NO. A method named updateLife is then called. Although this method is discussed later in this section, for now just note that it handles rendering the player's lives to the upper right of the screen, as shown in Figure 3.1. The final initialization step is to spawn two cacti at the start of the game. One is spawned instantly and the other is spawned after a delay of one second.

Spawning a Cactus

One of the more important functions in IFCGameViewController is spawning the actual cacti to the screen. In the viewDidLoad method spawnCactus was called twice; turn your attention to that method now. In a state-based game the first thing that should be done is to check to make sure you are in the correct state. The first test that is run is a gameOver check; if the game has ended, the cactus should stop spawning. The next check is a pause test; if the game is paused, you don't want to spawn a new cactus either, but when the game is resumed, you want to start spawning again. The test performed on the paused state will retry spawning every second until the game is resumed or quit.

```
if(gameOver)
{
    return;
}

if(paused)
{
    [self performSelector:@selector(spawnCactus) withObject:nil
    ➥afterDelay:1];

    return;
}
```

If the method has passed both of the state checks, it is time to spawn a new cactus. First the game must determine where to randomly place the object. To randomly place the cactus in the game, two random numbers are generated, the first for the row to be spawned in, followed by the x-axis location.

```
NSInteger rowToSpawnIn = arc4random()%3;
NSInteger horizontalLocation = arc4random()%1024;
```

To create a more interesting gaming experience, there are three different images for the cactus. With each new cactus spawned, one image is randomly selected through the following code snippet:

```
NSInteger cactusSize = arc4random()%3;
UIImage *cactusImage = nil;

switch (cactusSize)
{
        case 0:
            cactusImage = [UIImage imageNamed:
            @"CactusLarge.png"];
            break;
        case 1:
            cactusImage = [UIImage imageNamed: @"CactusMedium.png"];
            break;
        case 2:
            cactusImage = [UIImage imageNamed:
            @"CactusSmall.png"];
            break;
        default:
            break;
}
```

A simple check is performed next to make sure that the cactus is not being drawn off the right side of the view. Because the x-axis is calculated randomly and the widths of the cacti are variable, a simple `if` statement tests to see whether the image is being drawn too far right and if so moves it back to the edge.

```
if(horizontalLocation > 1024 - cactusImage.size.width)
     horizontalLocation = 1024 - cactusImage.size.width;
```

Whack-a-Cac is a depth- and layer-based game. There are three dunes, and a cactus should appear behind the dune for the row it is spawned in but in front of dunes that fall behind it. The first step in making this work is to determine which view the new cactus needs to fall behind. This is done using the following code snippet:

```
UIImageView *duneToSpawnBehind = nil;

switch (rowToSpawnIn)
{
```

```
    case 0:
        duneToSpawnBehind = duneOne;
        break;
    case 1:
        duneToSpawnBehind = duneTwo;
        break;
    case 2:
        duneToSpawnBehind = duneThree;
        break;
    default:
        break;
}
```

Now that the game knows where it needs to layer the new cactus, a couple of convenience variables are created to increase the readability of the code.

```
CGFloat cactusHeight = cactusImage.size.height;
CGFloat cactusWidth = cactusImage.size.width;
```

All the important groundwork has now been laid, and a new cactus can finally be placed into the game view. Since the cactus will act as a touchable item, it makes sense to create it as a type of UIButton. The frame variables are inserted, which cause the cactus to be inserted behind the dune and thus be invisible. An action is added to the cactus that calls the method cactusHit:, which is discussed later in this section.

```
UIButton *cactus = [[UIButton alloc]
➥initWithFrame:CGRectMake(horizontalLocation,
➥(duneToSpawnBehind.frame.origin.y), cactusWidth, cactusHeight)];

[cactus setImage:cactusImage forState: UIControlStateNormal];

[cactus addTarget:self action:@selector(cactusHit:)
➥forControlEvents:UIControlEventTouchDown];

[self.view insertSubview:cactus belowSubview:duneToSpawnBehind];
```

Now that a cactus has been spawned, it is ready to be animated up from behind the dunes and have its timer started to inform the game when the user has failed to hit it within the two-second window. The cactus will slide up from behind the dune in a one-fourth-second animation using information about the height of the cactus to make sure that it ends up in the proper spot. A two-second timer is also begun that will fire cactusMissed:, which is discussed in the "Cactus Interaction" section.

```
[UIView beginAnimations: @"slideInCactus" context:nil];
[UIView setAnimationCurve: UIViewAnimationCurveEaseInOut];
[UIView setAnimationDuration: 0.25];

cactus.frame = CGRectMake(horizontalLocation,
➥(duneToSpawnBehind.frame.origin.y)-cactusHeight/2, cactusWidth,
➥cactusHeight);
```

```
[UIView commitAnimations];

[self performSelector:@selector(cactusMissed:) withObject:cactus
➥afterDelay:2.0];

[UIView animateWithDuration:0.25f
                    delay:0.f
                  options:UIViewAnimationOptionCurveEaseInOut
               animations:^{
                   cactus.frame = CGRectMake(horizontalLocation,
                              (duneToSpawnBehind.frame.origin.y)-
                              ➥cactusHeight/2.f,
                              ➥cactusWidth, cactusHeight);
               } completion:nil];
```

Cactus Interaction

There are two possible outcomes of a cactus spawning: Either the user has hit the cactus within the two-second limit or the user has failed to hit it. In the first scenario cactusHit: is called in response to a UIControlEventTouchDown on the cactus button. When this happens, the cactus is quickly faded off the screen and then removed from the superView. Using the option UIViewAnimationOptionsBeginFromCurrentState will ensure that any existing animations on this cactus are cancelled. The score is incremented by one and displayNewScore: is called to update the score on the screen; more on score updating later in this section. After a cactus has been hit, a key step is spawning the next cactus. This is done in the same fashion as in viewDidLoad but with a randomized time to create a more engaging experience.

```
- (IBAction)cactusHit:(id)sender;
{
    [UIView animateWithDuration:0.1f
                    delay:0.0f
                  options: UIViewAnimationCurveLinear |
                  UIViewAnimationOptionBeginFromCurrentState
               animations:^
      {
              [sender setAlpha: 0];
      }
      completion:^(BOOL finished)
      {
              [sender removeFromSuperview];
    }];

    score++;

    [self displayNewScore: score];
```

```
    [self performSelector:@selector(spawnCactus) withObject:nil
➥afterDelay:(arc4random()%3) + .5f];
}
```

Two seconds after any cacti are spawned, the `cactusMissed:` method will be called, even on cacti that have been hit. Since this method is called regardless of whether it has been hit already, it is important to provide a state check. The cactus was removed from the `superView` when it was hit, and therefore it will no longer have a `superView`. A simple `nil` check and a quick return prevent the user from losing points for cacti that were successfully hit.

You also don't want to penalize the player for pausing the game, so while the game is in the pause state, the user should not lose any life. If the method has gotten this far without returning, you know that the user has missed a cactus and needs to be penalized. As with the `cactusHit:` method, the game still needs to remove this missed cactus from the `superView` and start a timer to spawn a replacement. In addition, instead of incrementing the score, you need to decrement the user's life, and a call to `updateLife` is performed to update the display.

> **Note**
>
> The pause-state approach here creates an interesting usability bug. If you pause the game, the cactus that would have disappeared while paused will remain on the screen forever. Although there are ways to resolve this bug, for the sake of example simplicity, this weakened experience was left in the game.

```
- (void)cactusMissed:(UIButton *)sender;
{
    if([sender superview] == nil)
    {
        return;
    }

    if(paused)
    {
        return;
    }

    CGRect frame = sender.frame;
    frame.origin.y += sender.frame.size.height;


    [UIView animateWithDuration:0.1f
                          delay:0.0f
                        options:UIViewAnimationCurveLinear |
                        UIViewAnimationOptionBeginFromCurrentState
                     animations:^
    {
        sender.frame = frame;
```

```
        }
        completion:^(BOOL finished)
    {
            [sender removeFromSuperview];
            [self performSelector:@selector(spawnCactus)
            withObject:nil afterDelay:(arc4random()%3) + .5f];

            life--;
            [self updateLife];
    }];
}
```

Displaying Life and Score

What fun would Whack-a-Cac be with no penalties for missing and no way to keep track of how well you are doing? Displaying the user's score and life are crucial game-play elements in the sample game, and both methods have been called from methods that have been looked at earlier in this section.

Turn your focus now to displayNewScore: in IFCGameViewController.m. Anytime the score is updated, a call to displayNewScore: is necessary to update the score display in the game. In addition to displaying the score, every time the score reaches a multiple of 10 while less than or equal to 50, a new cactus is spawned. This new cactus spawning has the effect of increasing the difficulty of the game as the player progresses.

```
- (void)displayNewScore:(CGFloat)updatedScore;
{
    NSInteger scoreInt = score;

    if(scoreInt % 10 == 0 && score <= 50)
    {
        [self spawnCactus];
    }

    scoreLabel.text = [NSString stringWithFormat: @"%06.0f",
    updatedScore];
}
```

Displaying life is similar to displaying the user's score but with some minor additional complexity. Instead of a text field being used to display a score, the user's life is represented with images. After a UIImage is created to represent each life, the first thing that must be done is to remove the existing life icons off the view. This is done with a simple tag search among the subviews. Next, a loop is performed for the number of lives the user has left, and each life icon is drawn in a row in the upper right of the game view. Finally, the game needs to check that the user still has some life left. If the user has reached zero life, a UIAlert informs him that the game has ended and what his final score was.

```
-(void)updateLife
{
    UIImage *lifeImage = [UIImage imageNamed:@"heart.png"];

    for(UIView *view in [self.view subviews])
    {
        if(view.tag == kLifeImageTag)
        {
            [view removeFromSuperview];
        }
    }


    for (int x = 0; x < life; x++)
    {
        UIImageView *lifeImageView = [[UIImageView alloc]
        initWithImage: lifeImage];

        lifeImageView.tag = kLifeImageTag;

        CGRect frame = lifeImageView.frame;
        frame.origin.x = 985 - (x * 30);
        frame.origin.y = 20;
        lifeImageView.frame = frame;

        [self.view addSubview: lifeImageView];
    }

    if(life == 0)
    {
        gameOver = YES;
        UIAlertView *alert = [[UIAlertView alloc]
                initWithTitle:@"Game Over!"
                    message: [NSString stringWithFormat: @"You
                    ➥scored %0.0f points!", score]
                    delegate:self
            cancelButtonTitle:@"Dismiss"
            otherButtonTitles:nil];

        alert.tag = kGameOverAlert;
        [alert show];
    }
}
```

Pausing and Resuming

Whack-a-Cac enables the user to pause and resume the game using the pause button in the upper-left corner of the game view. Tapping that button calls the pause: action. This method is very simple: The state variable for paused is set to YES and an alert asking the user to exit or resume is presented.

```objc
- (IBAction)pause:(id)sender
{
    paused = YES;

    UIAlertView *alert = [[UIAlertView alloc] initWithTitle:@""
        message:@"Game Paused!"
        delegate:self
        cancelButtonTitle:@"Exit"
        otherButtonTitles:@"Resume", nil];

    alert.tag = kPauseAlert;
    [alert show];
}
```

Game over and pause both use a UIAlert to handle user responses. In the event of game over or the exit option in pause, the navigation stack is popped back to the menu screen. If the user has resumed the game, all that needs to be done is to set the pause state back to NO.

```objc
- (void)alertView:(UIAlertView *)alertView
➥clickedButtonAtIndex:(NSInteger)buttonIndex
{
    if(alertView.tag == kGameOverAlert)
    {
        [self.navigationController popViewControllerAnimated: YES];
    }

    else if (alertView.tag == kPauseAlert)
    {
        if(buttonIndex == 0)
        {
            [self.navigationController popViewControllerAnimated: YES];
        }
        else
        {
            paused = NO;
        }
    }
}
```

Final Thoughts on Whack-a-Cac

You should now be familiar and confident with the gameplay and functionality of the Whack-a-Cac sample game. However, some additional cleanup methods might warrant a look in the source code. In the following sections, you will learn how to add leaderboards into Whack-a-Cac.

iTunes Connect

Leaderboard data is stored on Apple's Game Center servers. To configure your app to interact with leaderboards, you must first properly configure Game Center in iTunes Connect. Using the iTunes Connect Portal (http://itunesconnect.apple.com), create a new app as you would when submitting an app for sale. If you already have an existing app, you can substitute that as well. After you populate the basic information, your app page should look similar to the one shown in Figure 3.2.

Figure 3.2   A basic app page as seen through iTunes Connect.

Warning

From the time that you create a new app in iTunes Connect, you have 90 days to submit it for approval. This policy was enacted to prevent people from name squatting app names. Although you can work around this by creating fake test apps to hook the Game Center to for testing, it is an important limitation to keep in mind.

Direct your attention to the upper-right corner of the app page, where you will find a button called Manage Game Center. This is where you will configure all the Game Center behavior for your app. Inside the Game Center configuration page, the first thing you will notice is a slider to enable Game Center, as shown in Figure 3.3. Additionally, there is the option of using shared leaderboards across multiple apps, such as free and paid versions. To set up shared group leaderboards, you will need to create a reference name that then can be shared across multiple apps associated with your iTunes Connect account. This configuration is done under the Move to Group option after a leaderboard has been created.

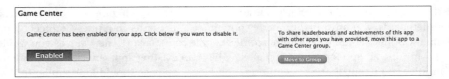

Figure 3.3   Enabling Game Center behavior in your app.

After you have enabled Game Center functionality for your app, you will need to set up the first leaderboard, as shown in Figure 3.4. It is important to note that after an app has been approved and becomes live on the App Store, you cannot delete a leaderboard. Apple has also recently provided an option to delete test data for your leaderboards. It is recommended to wipe your test data that was generated during testing before shipping your app.

Figure 3.4   Setting up a new leaderboard.

After you have selected Add Leaderboard from the portal, you will be presented with two options. The first, Single Leaderboard, is for a standalone leaderboard, like the type used in Whack-a-Cac. The Single Leaderboard will store a set of scores for your app or a game mode within your app. The second option is for a Combined Leaderboard; this option enables you to combine two or more Single Leaderboards to create an ultimate combined style high-score list. For example, if you have a leaderboard for each level of your game, you can create a combined leaderboard to see the top score across all levels at once. For the purpose of this chapter, you will be working only with a Single Leaderboard.

> **Note**
>
> Apple currently limits the number of leaderboards allowed per app to 500 as of iOS 7. This represents a significant increase from the previous limit of 25.

When setting up a leaderboard, you will be required to enter several fields of information, as shown in Figure 3.5. The first entry is the Leaderboard Reference Name. This field is entirely used by you within iTunes Connect to be able to quickly locate and identify the leaderboard. Leaderboard ID is the attribute that will be used to query the leaderboard within the actual project. Apple recommends using a reverse DNS system. The Leaderboard ID used for Whack-a-Cac was `com.dragonforged.whackacac.leaderboard`; if you are working with your own app, be sure to substitute whatever entry you have here in all following code examples as well.

Figure 3.5   Configuring a standard single leaderboard in iTunes Connect for Whack-a-Cac.

Apple has provided several preset options for formatting the score data in the leaderboard list. Table 3.1 provides examples for each type of formatting.

Table 3.1   **Detailed Breakdown of Available Score Formatting Options and Associated Sample Output**

Score Format Type	Output
Integer	123456789
Fixed Point—1 decimal	123456789.0
Fixed Point—2 decimals	123456789.01
Fixed Point—3 decimals	123456789.012

Score Format Type	Output
Elapsed Time—minutes	3:20
Elapsed Time—seconds	3:20:59
Elapsed Time—1/100th seconds	3:20:58.99
Money—whole numbers	$497,776
Money—2 decimals	$497,766.98

> **Note**
>
> If your score doesn't conform to one of the formats shown in Table 3.1, all is not lost; however, you will be required to work with custom leaderboard presentation. Retrieving raw score values is discussed in the section "Going Further with Leaderboards."

The sort-order option controls whether Game Center shows the highest score at the top of the chart or the lowest score. Additionally, you can specify a score range that will automatically drop scores that are too high or too low from being accepted by Game Center.

The final step when creating a new leaderboard is to add the localization information. This is required information, and you will want to provide at a minimum localized data for the app's primary language; however, you can also provide information for additional languages that you would like to support. In addition to the localized name, you have the option to fine-tune the score format, associate an image with this leaderboard, and enter the suffix to be used. When you're entering the score suffix, it is important to note that you might need a space before the entry because Game Center will print whatever is here directly after the score. For example, if you enter "Points" your score output will look like "123Points" instead of "123 Points."

After you finish entering all the required data, you will need to tap the Save button for the changes to take effect. Even after you save, it might take several hours for the leaderboard information to become available for use on Apple's servers. Now that you have a properly configured Game Center leaderboard, you can return to your Xcode project and begin to set up the required code to interact with it.

Game Center Manager

When you are working with Game Center, it is very likely that you will have multiple classes that need to directly interact with a single shared manager. In addition to the benefits of isolating Game Center into its own manager class, it makes it very easy to drop all the required Game Center support into new projects to quickly get up and running. In the Whack-a-Cac project turn your attention to the IFCGameCenterManager class. The first thing you might notice in this class is that it is formed around a singleton; this means that you will have only one instance of it in your app at any given time. The first thing that needs to be done is to create the foundation of the Game Center manager that you will be building on top of. The Game Center manager will handle all the direct Game Center interaction and will use a protocol to send the delegate information regarding the successes and failures of these calls. Since Game Center calls are not background thread safe, the manager will need to direct all delegate callbacks onto the main thread. To accomplish this, you have two new methods. The first method will ensure that it is using the main thread to create callbacks with.

```
- (void)callDelegateOnMainThread:(SEL)selector withArg:(id)arg
error:(NSError*)error
{
    dispatch_async(dispatch_get_main_queue(), ^(void)
    {
        [self callDelegate: selector withArg: arg error: error];
    });
}
```

The callDelegateOnMainThread: method will pass along all arguments and errors into the callDelegate: method. The first thing the callDelegate method does is ensure that it is being called from the main thread, which it will be if it is never called directly. Since the callDelegate method does not function correctly without a delegate being set, this is the next check that is performed. At this point it is clear that we are on the main thread and have a delegate. Using respondsToSelector: you can test whether the proper delegate method has been implemented; if it has not, some helpful information is logged as shown in this example:

```
2012-07-28 17:12:41.816 WhackACac[10121:c07] Unable to find delegate
method 'gameCenterLoggedIn:' in class ICFViewController
```

When all the safety and sanity tests have been performed, the delegate method is called with the required arguments and error information. Now that a basic delegate callback system is in place, you can begin working with actual Game Center functionality.

```
- (void)callDelegate: (SEL)selector withArg: (id)arg
error:(NSError*)error
{
    assert([NSThread isMainThread]);

    if(delegate == nil)
    {
        NSLog(@"Game Center Manager Delegate has not been set");
        return;
    }

    if([delegate respondsToSelector: selector])
    {
        if(arg != NULL)
        {
            [delegate performSelector: selector withObject:
            arg withObject: error];
        }
```

```
    else
    {
        [delegate performSelector: selector withObject:
        error];
    }
}

else
{
    NSLog(@"Unable to find delegate method '%s' in class
    ➥%@", sel_getName(selector), [delegate class]);
}
}
```

Authenticating

Game Center is an authenticated service, which means that you cannot successfully do anything besides authenticate when you are not currently logged in. With this in mind you must first authenticate before being able to proceed with any of the leaderboard relevant code. Authenticating with Game Center is handled mostly by iOS for you. The following code will present a UIAlert enabling the user to log in to Game Center or create a new Game Center account.

> **Note**
>
> Do not forget to include the GameKit.framework and import GameKit/GameKit.h whenever you are working with Game Center.

```
- (void) authenticateLocalUser
{
    if([GKLocalPlayer localPlayer].authenticated == NO)
    {
        [[GKLocalPlayer localPlayer]
        ➥authenticateWithCompletionHandler: ^(NSError *error)
        {
            if(error != nil)
            {
                NSLog(@"An error occurred: %@", [error
                ➥localizedDescription]);

                return;
            }

            [self callDelegateOnMainThread:
            ➥@selector(gameCenterLoggedIn:) withArg: NULL
            ➥error: error];
```

```
        }];
    }
}
```

In the event that an error occurs it is logged to the console. If the login completes without error, a delegate method is called. You can see how these delegate methods are set up in the `ICFGameCenterManager.h` file.

Common Authentication Errors

There are several common cases that can be helpful to catch when dealing with authentication errors. The following method is a modified version of `authenticateLocalUser` with additional error handling built in.

> **Note**
>
> If you are receiving an alert that says your game is not recognized by Game Center, check to make sure that the bundle ID of your app matches the one configured in iTunes Connect. A new app might take a few hours to have Game Center fully enabled. A lot of Game Center problems can be resolved by waiting a little while and retrying.

```
- (void) authenticateLocalUser
{
    if([GKLocalPlayer localPlayer].authenticated == NO)
    {
        [[GKLocalPlayer localPlayer]
        ⮕authenticateWithCompletionHandler:^(NSError *error)
        {
            if(error != nil)
            {
                if([error code] == GKErrorNotSupported)
                {
                    UIAlertView *alert = [[UIAlertView
                    ⮕alloc] initWithTitle:@"Error"
                    ⮕message:@"This device does not support
                    ⮕Game Center" delegate:nil
                    ⮕cancelButtonTitle:@"Dismiss"
                    ⮕otherButtonTitles:nil];

                    [alert show];
                }

                else if([error code] == GKErrorCancelled)
                {
```

```
                    UIAlertView *alert = [[UIAlertView
                 ➥alloc] initWithTitle:@"Error"
                 ➥message:@"This device has failed login
                 ➥too many times from the app; you will
                 ➥need to log in from the Game
                 ➥Center.app" delegate:nil
                 ➥cancelButtonTitle:@"Dismiss"
                 ➥otherButtonTitles:nil];

                    [alert show];
                }

                else
                {
                    UIAlertView *alert = [[UIAlertView
                 ➥alloc] initWithTitle:@"Error" message:
                 ➥[error localizedDescription]
                 ➥delegate:nil
                 ➥cancelButtonTitle:@"Dismiss"
                 ➥otherButtonTitles:nil];

                    [alert show];
                }

                return;
            }

        [self callDelegateOnMainThread:
        ➥@selector(gameCenterLoggedIn:) withArg: NULL
        ➥error: error];
        }];
    }
}
```

In the preceding example, three additional error cases are handled. The first error that is caught is when a device does not support Game Center for any reason. In this event a UIAlert is presented to the user informing her that she is unable to access Game Center. The second error rarely appears in shipping apps but can be a real headache when debugging; if your app has failed to log in to Game Center three times in a row, Apple disables its capability to log in. In this case, you must log in from the Game Center app. The third error case is a catchall for any additional errors to provide information to the user.

Upon successful login, your user is shown a login message from Game Center. This message will also inform you of whether you are currently in a Sandbox environment, as shown in Figure 3.6.

Figure 3.6   A successful login to Game Center from the Whack-a-Cac sample game.

> **Note**
>
> Any non-shipping app will be in the Sandbox environment. After your app is downloaded from the App Store, it will be in a normal production environment. There is no way to test an app outside of the Sandbox without first shipping it to the App Store.

iOS 6 and Newer Authentication

Although the preceding method of authentication continues to work on iOS 8, Apple has introduced a new streamlined approach to handling authentication on apps that do not need to support iOS 5 or older.

With the new approach, an `authenticateHandler` block is now used. Errors are captured in the same manner as in the previous examples, but now a `viewController` can be passed back to your application by Game Center. In the case in which the `viewController` parameter of the `authenticateHandler` block is not `nil`, you are expected to display the `viewController` to the user.

The first time a new `authenticateHandler` is set, the app will automatically authenticate. Additionally, the app will automatically reauthenticate on return to the foreground. If you do need to call `authenticate` manually, you can use the `authenticate` method.

```
-(void)authenticateLocalUseriOSSix
{
    if([GKLocalPlayer localPlayer].authenticateHandler == nil)
    {
        [[GKLocalPlayer localPlayer]
        ➥setAuthenticateHandler:^(UIViewController
        ➥*viewController, NSError *error)
        {
            if(error != nil)
            {
                if([error code] == GKErrorNotSupported)
                {
                    UIAlertView *alert = [[UIAlertView alloc]
                    ➥initWithTitle:@"Error" message:@"This
                    ➥device does not support Game Center"
                    ➥delegate:nil cancelButtonTitle:@"Dismiss"
                    ➥otherButtonTitles:nil];

                    [alert show];
                }

                else if([error code] == GKErrorCancelled)
                {
                    UIAlertView *alert = [[UIAlertView alloc]
                    ➥initWithTitle:@"Error" message:@"This
                    ➥device has failed login too many times from
                    ➥the app; you will need to log in from the
                    ➥Game Center.app" delegate:nil
                    ➥cancelButtonTitle:@"Dismiss"
                    ➥otherButtonTitles:nil];

                    [alert show];
                }

                else
                {
                    UIAlertView *alert = [[UIAlertView alloc]
                    ➥initWithTitle:@"Error" message:[error
                    ➥localizedDescription] delegate:nil
                    ➥cancelButtonTitle:@"Dismiss"
                    ➥otherButtonTitles:nil];

                    [alert show];
                }
            }
```

```
        else
        {
            if(viewController != nil)
            {
                [(UIViewController *)delegate
                ➥presentViewController:viewController
                ➥animated:YES completion: nil];
            }
        }
    }];
}

else
{
    [[GKLocalPlayer localPlayer] authenticate];
}
}
```

Submitting Scores

When authenticated with Game Center, you are ready to begin submitting scores. In the
IFCGameCenterManager class there is a method called reportScore:forCategory. This
enables you to post a new score for the Leaderboard ID that was configured in iTunes Connect.
All new scores are submitted by creating a new GKScore object; this object holds onto several
values such as the score value, playerID, date, rank, formattedValue, category, and context.

When a new score is submitted, most of this data is automatically populated. The value and
category are the only two required fields. An optional context can be provided that is an arbitrary 64-bit unsigned integer (int64_t). A context can be used to store additional information
about the score, such as game settings or flags that were on when the score was achieved; it
can be set and retrieved using the context property. The date, playerID, formattedValue,
and rank are read-only and are populated automatically when the GKScore object is created or
retrieved.

> **Note**
>
> Leaderboards support default categories when being set in iTunes Connect. If a score is being
> submitted to a default leaderboard, the category parameter can be left blank. It is best practice
> to always include a category argument to prevent hard-to-track-down bugs.

After a new GKScore object has been created using the specified category for the leaderboard,
you can assign a raw score value. When you're dealing with integers or floats, the score is
simply the number of the score. When you're dealing with elapsed time, however, the value
should be submitted in seconds or seconds with decimal places if tracking that level of
accuracy.

When a score has been successfully submitted, it will call `gameCenterScoreReported:` on the `GameCenterManager` delegate. This is discussed in more detail in the next section, "Adding Scores to Whack-a-Cac."

```objc
- (void)reportScore:(int64_t)score forCategory:(NSString*)category
{
    GKScore *scoreReporter = [[GKScore alloc]
    initWithCategory:category];

    scoreReporter.value = score;

    [scoreReporter reportScoreWithCompletionHandler: ^(NSError *error)
    {
        if (error != nil)
        {
            NSData* savedScoreData = [NSKeyedArchiver
            ➥archivedDataWithRootObject:scoreReporter];

            [self storeScoreForLater: savedScoreData];
        }

        [self callDelegateOnMainThread:@selector
        ➥(gameCenterScoreReported:) withArg: NULL error:
        ➥error];
    }];
}
```

It is important to look at the failure block of `reportScoreWithCompletionHandler`. If a score fails to successfully transmit to Game Center, it is your responsibility as the developer to attempt to resubmit this score later. There are few things more frustrating to a user than losing a high score due to a bug or network failure. In the preceding code example, when a score has failed, `NSKeyedArchiver` is used to create a copy of the object as `NSData` and passed to `storeScoreForLater:`. It is critical that the `GKScore` object itself is used, and not just the score value. Game Center ranks scores by date if the scores match; since the date is populated automatically when a new `GKScore` is created, the only way to not lose the player's info is to archive the entire `GKScore` object.

When the score data is being saved, the sample app uses the `NSUserDefaults`; this data could also be easily stored into Core Data or any other storage system. After the score is saved, it is important to retry sending that data when possible. A good time to do this is when Game Center successfully authenticates.

```objc
- (void)storeScoreForLater:(NSData *)scoreData;
{
    NSMutableArray *savedScoresArray = [[NSMutableArray alloc]
    ➥initWithArray: [[NSUserDefaults standardUserDefaults]
    objectForKey:@"savedScores"]];
```

```
    [savedScoresArray addObject: scoreData];

    [[NSUserDefaults standardUserDefaults]
    ➥setObject:savedScoresArray forKey:@"savedScores"];
}
```

The attempt to resubmit the saved scores is no different than submitting a score initially. First the scores need to be retrieved from the NSUserDefaults, and since the object was stored in NSData, that data needs to be converted back into a GKScore object. Once again, it is important to catch failed submissions and try them again later.

```
-(void)submitAllSavedScores
{
    NSMutableArray *savedScoreArray = [[NSMutableArray alloc]
    ➥initWithArray: [[NSUserDefaults standardUserDefaults]
    ➥objectForKey:@"savedScores"]];

    [[NSUserDefaults standardUserDefaults] removeObjectForKey:
    ➥@"savedScores"];

    for(NSData *scoreData in savedScoreArray)
    {
        GKScore *scoreReporter = [NSKeyedUnarchiver
        ➥unarchiveObjectWithData: scoreData];

        [scoreReporter reportScoreWithCompletionHandler:
        ➥^(NSError *error)
        {
            if (error != nil)
            {
                NSData* savedScoreData = [NSKeyedArchiver
                ➥archivedDataWithRootObject: scoreReporter];

                [self storeScoreForLater: savedScoreData];
            }

            else
            {
                NSLog(@"Successfully submitted scores that
                ➥were pending submission");

                [self callDelegateOnMainThread:
                ➥@selector(gameCenterScroreReported:)
                ➥withArg:NULL error:error];
            }
        }];
    }
}
```

> **Tip**
>
> If a score does fail to submit, it is always a good idea to inform the user that the app will try to submit again later; otherwise, it might seem as though the app has failed to submit the score and lost the data for the user.

Adding Scores to Whack-a-Cac

In the preceding section the Game Center Manager component of adding scores to an app was explored. In this section you will learn how to put these additions into practice in Whack-a-Cac. Before proceeding, Game Center must first authenticate a user and specify a delegate. Modify the `viewDidLoad` method of `IFCViewController.m` to complete this process.

```
- (void)viewDidLoad
{
    [super viewDidLoad];

    [[ICFGameCenterManager sharedManager] setDelegate: self];
    [[ICFGameCenterManager sharedManager] authenticateLocalUser];
}
```

`IFCViewController` will also need to respond to the `GameCenterManagerDelegate`. The first delegate method that needs to be handled is `gameCenterLoggedIn:`. Since the `GameCenterManager` is handling all the `UIAlerts` associated with informing the user of failures, any errors here are simply logged for debugging purposes.

```
- (void)gameCenterLoggedIn:(NSError*)error
{
    if(error != nil)
    {
        NSLog(@"An error occurred trying to log into Game
        ➥Center: %@", [error localizedDescription]);
    }

    else
    {
        NSLog(@"Successfully logged into Game Center!");
    }
}
```

After the user has decided to begin a new game of Whack-a-Cac, it is important to update the `GameCenterManager`'s delegate to the `IFCGameViewController` class. In Whack-a-Cac the delegate will always be set to the front-most view to simplify providing user feedback and errors. This is done by adding the following line of code to the `viewDidLoad:` method of `IFCGameViewController`. Don't forget to declare this class as conforming to `GameCenterManagerDelegate`.

```
[[ICFGameCenterManager sharedManager] setDelegate: self];
```

The game will need to submit a score under two scenarios: when the user loses a game, and when the user quits from the pause menu. Using the IFCGameCenterManager, submitting a score is very easy. Add the following line of code to both the test for zero life in the updateLife method and the exit button action on the pause UIAlert:

```
[[ICFGameCenterManager sharedManager]reportScore:
➡(int64_t)scoreforCategory:
➡@"com.dragonforged.whackacac.leaderboard"];
```

> **Note**
>
> The category ID you set for your leaderboard might differ from the one used in these examples. Be sure that the one used matches the ID that appears in iTunes Connect.

Although the GameCenterManager reportScore: method will handle submitting the scores and all error recovery, it is important to add the delegate method gameCenterScoreReported: to watch for potential errors and successes.

```
-(void)gameCenterScoreReported:(NSError *)error;
{
    if(error != nil)
    {
        NSLog(@"An error occurred trying to report a score to
        ➡Game Center: %@", [error localizedDescription]);
    }

    else
    {
        NSLog(@"Successfully submitted score");
    }
}
```

> **Note**
>
> Scores should be submitted only when finalized; sending scores to Game Center at every increment can create a poor user experience.

When a user is exiting the game, the delegate for GameCenterManager will disappear while the network operations for submitting the score are still taking place. It is important to have IFCViewController reset the GameCenterManagerDelegate to SELF and implement the gameCenterScoreReported: delegate as well.

Presenting Leaderboards

A new high score is not of much use to your users if they are unable to view their high scores. In this section you will learn how to use Apple's built-in view controllers to present the

leaderboards. The leaderboard view controllers saw significant improvements with the introduction of iOS 6 and maintained through iOS 8, as shown in Figure 3.7. In previous versions
of iOS, leaderboards and achievements were handled by two separate view controllers; these
have now been combined. In addition, a new section for Game Center challenges and Facebook
liking have been added.

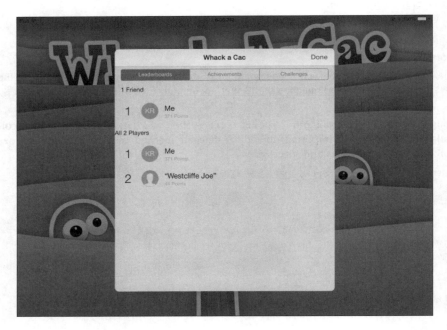

Figure 3.7   The GKLeaderboardViewController saw major improvements and changes in
iOS 6.

In ICFViewController, there is a method called leaderboards: that handles presenting the
leaderboard view controllers. When a new GKLeaderboardViewController is being created,
there are a couple of properties that need to be addressed. First set the category. This is the
same category that is used for submitting scores and refers to which leaderboard should be
presented to the user. A timeScope can also be provided, which will default the user onto the
correct tab, as shown in Figure 3.7. In the following example, the time scope for all time is
supplied. Additionally, a required leaderboardDelegate must be provided; this delegate will
handle dismissing the leaderboard modal.

```
- (IBAction)leaderboards:(id)sender
{
    GKLeaderboardViewController *leaderboardViewController =
    [[GKLeaderboardViewController alloc] init];

    if(leaderboardViewController == nil)
```

```
    {
        NSLog(@"Unable to create leaderboard view controller");
        return;
    }

    leaderboardViewController.category =
    ➥@"com.dragonforged.whackacac.leaderboard";

    leaderboardViewController.timeScope =
    ➥GKLeaderboardTimeScopeAllTime;

    leaderboardViewController.leaderboardDelegate = self;

    [self presentViewController:leaderboardViewController
    ➥animated:YES completion: nil];

    [leaderboardViewController release];
}
```

For a `GKLeaderboardViewController` to be fully functional, a delegate method must also be provided. When this method is invoked, it is required that the view controller be dismissed, as shown in this code snippet:

```
- (void)leaderboardViewControllerDidFinish:(GKLeaderboardViewController
➥*) viewController
{
    [self dismissModalViewControllerAnimated: YES completion: nil];
}
```

There is also a new delegate method to be used with this view controller. It is implemented in the following fashion:

```
- (void)gameCenterViewControllerDidFinish:(GKGameCenterViewController
➥*)gameCenterViewController
{
    [self dismissModalViewControllerAnimated: YES completion: nil];
}
```

It is also possible to work with the raw leaderboard data and create customized leaderboards. For more information on this, see the later section "Going Further with Leaderboards."

Score Challenges

Game Center Challenges enable your users to dare their Game Center friends to beat their high scores or achievements. They provide a great avenue for your users to socially spread your game to their friends. All the work with Challenges is handled for you by Game Center using the new `GameCenterViewController`, as shown in the previous example and Figure 3.8. However, it is also possible to create challenges in code. Calling `issueChallengeToPlayers:withMessage:`

on a `GKScore` object will initiate the challenge. When a player beats a challenge, it automatically rechallenges the person who initiated the original challenge.

Figure 3.8   Challenging a friend to beat a score using the built-in Game Center challenges.

```
[(GKScore *)score issueChallengeToPlayers: (NSArray *)players
➥message:@"Can you beat me?"];
```

It is also possible to retrieve an array of all pending `GKChallenges` for the authenticated user by implementing the following code:

```
[GKChallenge loadReceivedChallengesWithCompletionHandler:^(NSArray
➥*challenges, NSError *error)
{
    if (error != nil)
    {
        NSLog(@"An error occurred: %@", [error localizedDescription]);
    }

    else
    {
        NSLog(@"Challenges: %@", challenges);
    }
}];
```

A challenge exists in one of four states: invalid, pending, completed, and declined.

```
if(challenge.state == GKChallengeStateCompleted)
    NSLog(@"Challenge Completed");
```

Finally, it is possible to decline an incoming challenge by simply calling `decline` on it as shown here:

```
[challenge decline];
```

Challenges create a great opportunity to have your users do your marketing for you. If a user challenges someone who has not yet downloaded your game, that person will be prompted to buy it. Challenges are provided for you for no effort by Game Center using the default GUI, and using the earlier examples, it is fairly easy to implement your own challenge system.

> **Note**
>
> Whack-a-Cac does not implement or demonstrate code-based challenges.

Going Further with Leaderboards

The focus of this chapter has been implementing leaderboards using Apple's standard Game Center GUI; however, it is entirely possible to implement a customized leaderboard system within your app. In this section, a brief introduction is given to working with raw `GKScore` values, as well as retrieving specific information from the Game Center servers.

The following method can be added to the `ICFGameCenterManager`. This method accepts four different arguments. The first, `category`, is the leaderboard ID set in iTunes Connect for the leaderboard that this request will pertain to. This is followed by `withPlayerScore:`, which accepts `GKLeaderboardPlayerScopeGlobal` or `GKLeaderboardPlayerScopeFriendsOnly`. `TimeScope` will retrieve scores for today, this week, or all time. The last argument required is for range. Here you can specify receiving scores that match a certain range. For example, `NSMakeRange(1, 50)` will retrieve the top 50 scores.

```
- (void)retrieveScoresForCategory:(NSString *)category
➥withPlayerScope:(GKLeaderboardPlayerScope)playerScope
➥timeScope:(GKLeaderboardTimeScope)timeScope
➥withRange:(NSRange)range
{
    GKLeaderboard *leaderboardRequest = [[GKLeaderboard alloc] init];

    leaderboardRequest.playerScope = playerScope;
    leaderboardRequest.timeScope = timeScope;
    leaderboardRequest.range = range;
    leaderboardRequest.category = category;

    [leaderboardRequest loadScoresWithCompletionHandler: ^(NSArray
    ➥*scores,NSError *error)
```

```
    {
        [self callDelegateOnMainThread:@selector
        (scoreDataUpdated:error:) withArg:scores error: error];
    }];
}
```

There will also be a newly associated delegate callback for this request called
scoreDataUpdated:error:.

```
- (void)scoreDataUpdated:(NSArray *)scores error:(NSError *)error
{
    if(error != nil)
    {
        NSLog(@"An error occurred: %@", [error localizedDescription]);
    }
    else
    {
        NSLog(@"The following scores were retrieved: %@", scores);
    }
}
```

If this example were to be introduced into Whack-a-Cac, it could look like the following:

```
- (void)fetchScore
{
    [[ICFGameCenterManager sharedManager]
    retrieveScoresForCategory:
    ➥@"com.dragonforged.whackacac.leaderboard"
    ➥withPlayerScope:GKLeaderboardPlayerScopeGlobal
    ➥timeScope:GKLeaderboardTimeScopeAllTime
    ➥withRange:NSMakeRange(1, 50)];
}
```

The delegate method will print something similar to the following:

```
2012-07-29 14:38:03.874 WhackACac[14437:c07] The following scores were
➥retrieved: (

"<GKScore: 0x83c5010>player:G:94768768 rank:1 date:2012-07-28 23:54:19
➥+0000 value:201 formattedValue:201 Points context:0x0"
)
```

> **Tip**
>
> To find the displayName for the GKPlayer associated with a GKScore, use [(GKPlayer *)
> player displayName]. Don't forget to cache this data because it requires a network call.

Summary

Game Center leaderboards are an easy and fun way to increase the social factor of your game or app. Users love to compete, and with Game Center Challenge system it is easier than ever for users to share apps that they love. In this chapter, you learned how to fully integrate Game Center's leaderboards into your game or app. You should now have a strong understanding of not only Game Center authenticating but also submitting scores and error recovery. Chapter 4 continues to expand on the capabilities of Game Center by adding social achievements to the Whack-a-Cac game.

4

Achievements

Like leaderboards, achievements are quickly becoming a vital component of modern gaming. Although the history of achievements isn't as clearly cemented into gaming history as that of leaderboards, today it could be argued that they are even more important to the social success of a game.

An achievement is, in short, an unlockable accomplishment that, although not necessary to the completion of a game, tracks the user's competition of additional aspects of the game. Commonly, achievements are issued for additional side tasks or extended play, such as beating a game on hard difficulty, exploring areas, or collecting items. One of the core features of Game Center is the achievement system, which makes adding your own achievements to your game much simpler than it had previously been.

Unlike most other chapters, this chapter shares its sample app, Whack-a-Cac, with Chapter 3, "Leaderboards." Although it is not necessary to complete that chapter before beginning this one, there are several instances of overlap. For the sake of the environment and trees, that information is not reprinted here; it is recommended that you read the "The Sample App," "iTunes Connect," "Game Center Manager," and "Authenticating" sections of Chapter 3 before proceeding with this chapter. These sections provide the background required to interact with the sample app as well as the basic task of setting up Game Center and authenticating the local user. This chapter also expands on the already existing Game Center Manager sample code provided in Chapter 3.

iTunes Connect

Before beginning writing code within Xcode for achievements, first visit iTunes Connect (http://itunesconnect.apple.com) to set up the achievements. For an introduction to working with Game Center in iTunes Connect, see the "iTunes Connect" section of Chapter 3.

When you are entering the Manage Game Center section of iTunes Connect, there are two configuration options: one to set up leaderboards and the other to set up achievements. In the sample app, Whack-a-Cac, there will be six demonstrated achievements.

To create a new achievement, click the Add Achievement button, as shown in Figure 4.1.

Figure 4.1   A view of the Achievements section before any achievements have been added in iTunes Connect.

As with the leaderboards from Chapter 3, several fields are required to set up a new achievement, as shown in Figure 4.2. The Achievement Reference Name is simply a reference to your achievement in iTunes Connect; it is not seen anywhere outside of the Web portal. Achievement ID, on the other hand, is what will be referenced from the code in order to interact with the achievement. Apple recommends the use of a reverse DNS type of system for the Achievement ID, such as com.dragonforged.whackacac.100whacks.

Figure 4.2   Adding a new achievement in iTunes Connect.

The Point Value attribute is unique to achievements in Game Center. Achievements can have an assigned point value from 1 to 100. Each app can have a maximum of 1,000 achievement points. Points can be used to denote difficulty or value of an achievement. Achievement points are not required, nor are they required to add up to exactly 1,000.

Also unique to achievements is the Hidden property, which keeps the achievement hidden from the user until it has been achieved or the user has made any progress toward achieving it. The Achievable More Than Once setting allows the user to accept Game Center challenges based on achievements that they have previously earned.

As with leaderboards, at least one localized description needs to be set up for each achievement. This information consists of four attributes. The title will appear above the achievement description. Each achievement will have two descriptions, one that will be displayed before the user unlocks it and one that is displayed after it has been completed. Additionally, an image will need to be supplied for each achievement; the image must be at least 512×512 in size. To see how this information is laid out, see Figure 4.3.

> **Note**
>
> As with leaderboards, after an achievement has gone live in a shipping app, it cannot be removed.

See the section "Adding Achievements into Whack-a-Cac" for a walk-through of adding several achievements into the sample game.

Displaying Achievement Progress

If you can't display the current progress of achievements to the user, they are next to useless. If required to present a custom interface for achievements, refer to the section "Going Further with Achievements." The following method launches the combined Game Center View, as shown in Figure 4.3:

```
- (void)showAchievements
{
    [[GKGameCenterViewController sharedController] setDelegate:self];


[[GKGameCenterViewController sharedController]
➥setViewState:GKGameCenterViewControllerStateAchievements];

    [self presentViewController:[GKGameCenterViewController
    ➥sharedController] animated:YES completion: nil];
}
```

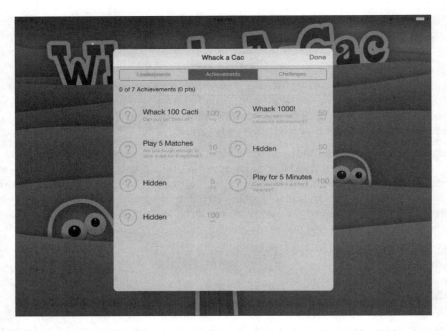

Figure 4.3   The new combined Game Center View Controller, launching to the Achievement section.

In the preceding method, used to launch the Game Center View Controller, you will notice that a delegate was set. There is also a new required delegate method to be used with this view controller, and it is implemented in the following fashion:

```
- (void)gameCenterViewControllerDidFinish:(GKGameCenterViewController
➥*)gameCenterViewController
{
    [self dismissModalViewControllerAnimated: YES completion: nil];
}
```

Game Center Manager and Authentication

In Chapter 3, a new reusable class called Game Center Manager was introduced. This class provides the groundwork for quickly implementing Game Center into your apps. That information is not reprinted in this chapter. Reference the sections "Game Center Manager" and "Authenticating" in Chapter 3 before continuing the material in this chapter.

The Achievement Cache

When a score is being submitted to Game Center, it's simply a matter of sending in the score and having Game Center determine its value compared to previously submitted scores. However, achievements are a bit tricky; all achievements have a percentage complete value, and users can work toward completing an achievement over many days or even months. It is important to make sure that users don't lose the progress they have already earned and that they continue to make steady progress toward their goals. This is solved by using an achievement cache to store all the cloud achievement data locally and refresh it with each new session.

A new convenience method will need to be added to the `ICFGameCenterManager` class, as well as a new classwide `NSMutableDictionary`, which will be called `achievementDictionary`. The first thing that is done in this method is to post an alert if it is being run after an achievement cache has already been established. Although you should not attempt to populate the cache more than once, it will not cause anything to stop functioning as expected. If the `achievementDictionary` does not yet exist, a new `NSMutableDictionary` will need to be allocated and initialized.

After the `achievementDictionary` is created, it can be populated with the data from the Game Center servers. This is accomplished by calling the `loadAchievementsWithCompletion-Handler` class method on `GKAchievement`. The resulting block will return the user's progress for all achievements. If no errors are returned, an array of `GKAchievements` will be returned. These are then inserted into the `achievementDictionary` using the achievement identifier as the key.

> **Note**
>
> The `loadAchievementsWithCompletionHandler` method does not return GKAchievement objects for achievements that do not have progress stored on them yet.

```
- (void)populateAchievementCache
{
    if(achievementDictionary != nil)
    {
        NSLog(@"Repopulating achievement cache: %@",
        achievementDictionary);
    }

    else
    {
        achievementDictionary = [[NSMutableDictionary alloc] init];
    }

    [GKAchievement loadAchievementsWithCompletionHandler:^(NSArray
    ➥*achievements, NSError *error)
    {

        if(error != nil)
```

```
        {
            NSLog(@"An error occurred while populating the
            ➥achievement cache: %@", [error localizedDescription]);
        }

        else
        {
            for(GKAchievement *achievement in achievements)
            {
                [achievementDictionary setObject:achievement
                ➥forKey:[achievement identifier]];
            }
        }
    }];
}
```

> **Note**
>
> You cannot make any Game Center calls until a local user has been successfully authenticated.

Reporting Achievements

After an achievement cache has been implemented, it is safe to submit progress on an achievement. A new method `reportAchievement:withPercentageComplete:` will need to be added to the `ICFGameManager` class to accomplish this task. When this method is called, the achievement ID and percentage complete are used as arguments. For information on how to determine the current percentage of an achievement, see the section "Adding Achievement Hooks."

When you're submitting achievement progress, the first thing you need to do is make sure that the `achievementDictionary` has already been populated. Making sure to check Game Center for the current progress of any achievements prevents users from losing progress when switching devices or reinstalling the app. In this example the app will fail out with a log message if `achievementDictionary` is nil; however, a more complex system of initializing and populating the achievement cache and retrying can be implemented as well.

After it has been determined that the `achievementDictionary` is initialized, a new `GKAchievement` object is created. When created, the `GKAchievement` object is stored in the `achievementDictionary` using the achievement identifier. If this achievement has not yet been progressed, it will not appear in the `achievementDictionary` and the achievement object will be nil. In this case a new instance of `GKAchievement` is allocated and initialized using the achievement identifier.

If the achievement object is non-nil, it can be assumed that the achievement has previously had some sort of progress made. A safety check is performed to make sure that the percentage complete that is being submitted isn't lower than the percentage complete that was found on Game Center. Additionally, a check is performed to make sure that the achievement isn't already fully completed. In either case, an NSLog is printed to the console and the method returns.

> **Note**
>
> It is possible to submit a lower percentage complete on an achievement and decrease the user's progressed value.

At this point, a valid GKAchievement object has been created or retrieved and the percentage complete is greater than the one that is in the cache. A call on the achievement object with setPercentComplete: is used to update the percentage-complete value. At this point the achievement object is also stored back into the achievementDictionary so that the local achievement cache is up-to-date.

To report the actual achievement value to Game Center, reportAchievementWith-CompletionHandler: is called on the achievement object. When it is finished checking for errors, a new delegate callback is used to inform the GameCenterManager delegate of the success or failure.

```
-(void)reportAchievement:(NSString *)identifier
 withPercentageComplete:(double)percentComplete
{
    if(achievementDictionary == nil)
    {
        NSLog(@"An achievement cache must be populated before
        ➥submitting achievement progress");

        return;
    }

    GKAchievement *achievement = [achievementDictionary objectForKey: identifier];

    if(achievement == nil)
    {
        achievement = [[GKAchievement alloc]
        ➥initWithIdentifier: identifier];

        [achievement setPercentComplete: percentComplete];

        [achievementDictionary setObject: achievement forKey:identifier];
    }

    else
    {
        if([achievement percentComplete] >= 100.0 || [achievement
        ➥percentComplete] >= percentComplete)
```

```
      {
            NSLog(@"Attempting to update achievement %@ which is either
            ➥already completed or is decreasing percentage complete
            ➥(%f)", identifier, percentComplete);

          return;
      }

            [achievement setPercentComplete: percentComplete];

            [achievementDictionary setObject: achievement forKey:identifier];

    }

    [achievement reportAchievementWithCompletionHandler:^(NSError *error)
    {
          if(error != nil)
          {
              NSLog(@"There was an error submitting achievement
              ➥%@:%@", identifier, [error localizedDescription]);
          }

          [self callDelegateOnMainThread:
          ➥@selector (gameCenterAchievementReported:)
          ➥withArg: NULL error:error];
    }];
}
```

> **Note**
>
> Achievements, like leaderboards in Chapter 3, will not attempt to resubmit if they fail to suc-
> cessfully reach the Game Center servers. The developer is solely responsible for catching errors
> and resubmitting achievements later. However, unlike with leaderboards, there is no stored
> date property so it isn't necessary to store the actual GKAchievement object.

Adding Achievement Hooks

Arguably, the most difficult aspect of incorporating achievements into your iOS game is
hooking them into the workflow. For example, the player might earn an achievement after
collecting 100 coins in a role-playing game. Every time a coin is collected, the app will need to
update the achievement value.

A more difficult example is an achievement such as play one match a week for six months.
This requires a number of hooks and checks to make sure that the user is meeting the requirements of the achievement. Although attempting to document every single possible hook is a

bit ambitious, the section "Adding Achievements into Whack-a-Cac" has several common types of hooks that will be demonstrated.

Before an achievement can be progressed, first your app must determine its current progress. Because Game Center achievements don't take progressive arguments (for example, add 1% completion to existing completion), this legwork is left up to the developer. Following is a convenience for quickly getting back a GKAchievement object for any identifier. After a GKAchievement object has been returned, a query to percentageComplete can be made to determine the current progress.

```
-(GKAchievement *)achievementForIdentifier:(NSString *)identifier
{
    GKAchievement *achievement = nil;

    achievement = [achievementDictionary objectForKey:identifier];

    if(achievement == nil)
    {
        achievement = [[GKAchievement alloc]
        ➡initWithIdentifier:identifier];

        [achievementDictionary setObject: achievement forKey:identifier];
    }

    return achievement;
}
```

If the achievement requires more precision than 1%, the true completion value cannot be retrieved from Game Center. Game Center will return and accept only whole numbers for percentage complete. In this case you have two possible options. The easy path is to round off to the nearest percentage. A slightly more difficult approach would be to store the true value locally and use that to calculate the percentage. Keep in mind that a player might be using more than one device, and storing a true achievement progress locally can be problematic in these cases; see Chapter 11, "Cloud Persistence with CloudKit," for additional solutions.

Completion Banners

Game Center has the capability to use an automatic message to let the user know that an achievement has been successfully earned. Alternatively, you can also implement a custom system to display nonstandard notifications. There is no functional requirement to inform users that they have completed an achievement beyond providing a good user experience.

To automatically show achievement completion, set the showsCompletionBanner property to YES before submitting the achievement to Game Center, as shown in Figure 4.4. A good place to add this line of code is in the reportAchievement: withPercentageComplete: method.

```
achievement.showsCompletionBanner = YES;
```

Figure 4.4   A Game Center automatic achievement completion banner shown on an iPad with the achievement title and earned description.

Achievement Challenges

Game Center supports Achievement Challenges similar to those found with scores, in which users can challenge a Game Center friend to beat their score or match their achievements, as shown in Figure 4.5.

> **Note**
>
> Game Center allows the user to challenge a friend to beat an unearned achievement as long as it is visible to the user.

```
- (void)showChallenges
{
    [[GKGameCenterViewController sharedController]setDelegate:self];

    [[GKGameCenterViewController sharedController] setViewState:
    ➥GKGameCenterViewControllerStateAchievements];
```

```
    [self presentViewController:[GKGameCenterViewController
    ➡sharedController] animated:YES completion: nil];
}
```

The gameCenterViewControllerDidFinish delegate method will also need to be implemented if that was not already done for the previous examples in this chapter.

```
- (void)gameCenterViewControllerDidFinish:(GKGameCenterViewController
➡*)gameCenterViewController
{
    [self dismissModalViewControllerAnimated: YES completion: nil];
}
```

Figure 4.5   Challenging a friend to complete an achievement that is still being progressed.

> **Note**
>
> If users need to be able to accept achievement challenges for achievements that they have already earned, you will need to select the Achievable More Than Once option when creating the achievement in iTunes Connect.

A challenge can also be created pragmatically using the following approach:

```
[(GKAchievement *)achievement issueChallengeToPlayers: (NSArray
➡*)players message:@"I earned this achievement, can you?"];
```

If it is required to get a list of users that can receive an achievement challenge for a particular achievement (if you do not have the Achievable More Than Once property set to on), use the following snippet to get a list of those users:

```
[achievement selectChallengeablePlayerIDs:arrayOfPlayersToCheck
➥withCompletionHandler:^(NSArray *challengeablePlayerIDs, NSError
➥*error)
{
    if(error != nil)
    {
        NSLog(@"An error occurred while retrieving a list of
        ➥challengeable players: %@", [error localizedDescription]);
    }

    NSLog(@"The following players can be challenged: %@",
    challengeablePlayerIDs);
}];
```

It is also possible to retrieve an array of all pending GKChallenges for the authenticated user by implementing the following code:

```
[GKChallenge loadReceivedChallengesWithCompletionHandler:^(NSArray
➥*challenges, NSError *error)
{
    if (error != nil)
    {
        NSLog(@"An error occurred: %@", [error
        ➥localizedDescription]);
    }

    else
    {
        NSLog(@"Challenges: %@", challenges);
    }

}];
```

Challenges have states associated with them that can be queried on the current state of the challenge. The SDK provides the states invalid, pending, completed, and declined.

```
if(challenge.state == GKChallengeStateCompleted)
    NSLog(@"Challenge Completed");
```

Finally, it is possible to decline an incoming challenge by simply calling decline on it, as shown here:

```
[challenge decline];
```

By leveraging challenges and encouraging users to challenge their friends, you will increase the retention rates and play times of the game. If using the built-in GUI for Game Center, you don't even have to write any additional code to support challenges.

 Note

Whack-a-Cac does not contain sample code for creating programmatic achievement challenges.

Adding Achievements into Whack-a-Cac

Whack-a-Cac will be using six different achievements using various hook methods. Table 4.1 describes the achievements that will be implemented.

Table 4.1   **Achievements Used in Whack-a-Cac with Details on Required Objectives to Earn**

Achievement ID	Description
com.dragonforged.whackacac.killone	Achieved after whacking your first cactus. This is also a hidden achievement and it is not visible to the user until it is earned.
com.dragonforged.whackacac.score100	Achieved after reaching a score of 100 in a single game. This achievement is hidden and is not visible until the user has begun to progress it.
com.dragonforged.whackacac.100whacks	Achieved after hitting 100 whacks; can be across multiple games.
com.dragonforged.whackacac.1000whacks	Achieved after hitting 1,000 whacks; can be across multiple games.
com.dragonforged.whackacac.play5	Achieved after playing five games.
com.dragonforged.whackacac.play5Mins	Achieved after spending five combined minutes in game play.

Assuming that all the ICFGameCenterManager changes detailed earlier in this chapter have been implemented already, you can begin adding in the hooks for the achievements. You will need to add the delegate callback method for achievements into ICFGameViewController. This will allow the delegate to receive success messages as well as any errors that are encountered.

```
-(void)gameCenterAchievementReported:(NSError *)error;
{
    if(error != nil)
    {
```

```
            NSLog(@"An error occurred trying to report an achievement to
            ➥Game Center: %@", [error localizedDescription]);
    }

    else
    {
        NSLog(@"Achievement successfully updated");
    }
}
```

> **Note**
>
> In Whack-a-Cac the `populateAchievementCache` method is called as soon as the local
> user is successfully authenticated.

Earned or Unearned Achievements

The easiest achievement from Table 4.1 to implement is the `com.dragonforged.whackacac.`
`killone` achievement. Whenever you're working with adding a hook for an achievement, the
first step is to retrieve a copy of the `GKAchievement` that will be incremented. Use the method
discussed in the section "Adding Achievement Hooks" to grab an up-to-date copy of the
achievement.

```
GKAchievement *killOneAchievement = [[ICFGameCenterManager
➥sharedManager] achievementForIdentifier:
➥@"com.dragonforged.whackacac.killone"];
```

Next, a query is performed to see whether this achievement has already been completed. If it
has, there is no need to update it again.

```
if(![killOneAchievement isCompleted])
```

Because the Kill One achievement cannot be partially achieved because it is impossible to
kill less than one cactus, it is incremented to 100% at once. This is done using the
`reportAchievement:withPercentageComplete:` method that was added to the
`ICFGameCenterManager` class earlier in this chapter.

```
[[ICFGameCenterManager sharedManager]
➥reportAchievement:@"com.dragonforged.whackacac.killone"
➥withPercentageComplete:100.00];
```

Because this achievement is tested and submitted when a cactus is whacked, an appropriate
place for it is within the `cactusHit:` method. The updated `cactusHit:` method is presented
for clarity.

```
- (IBAction)cactusHit:(id)sender;
{
    [UIView animateWithDuration:0.1
                          delay:0.0
```

```
                    options: UIViewAnimationCurveLinear |
                      ➥UIViewAnimationOptionBeginFromCurrentState
                 animations:^
                 {
                     [sender setAlpha: 0];
                 }
                 completion:^(BOOL finished)
                 {
                     [sender removeFromSuperview];
                 }];

    score++;

    [self displayNewScore: score];

    GKAchievement *killOneAchievement = [[ICFGameCenterManager
    ➥sharedManager] achievementForIdentifier:
    ➥@"com.dragonforged.whackacac.killone"];

    if(![killOneAchievement isCompleted])
    {
        [[ICFGameCenterManager sharedManager]reportAchievement:
        ➥@"com.dragonforged.whackacac.killone"
        ➥withPercentageComplete:100.00];
    }

    [self performSelector:@selector(spawnCactus) withObject:nil
    ➥afterDelay:(arc4random()%3) + .5];
}
```

Partially Earned Achievements

In the preceding example, the achievement was either fully earned or not earned at all. The next achievement that will be implemented into Whack-a-Cac is com.dragonforged. whackacac.score100. Unlike the Kill One achievement, this one can be partially progressed, although it is nonstackable between games. The user is required to score 100 points in a single game. The process begins the same way as the preceding example, in that a reference to the GKAchievement object is created.

```
GKAchievement *score100Achievement = [[ICFGameCenterManager
sharedManager] achievementForIdentifier:
@"com.dragonforged.whackacac.score100"];
```

A quick test is performed to ensure that the achievement is not already completed.

```
if(![score100Achievement isCompleted])
```

After the achievement has been verified as not yet completed, it can be incremented by the appropriate amount. Because this achievement is completed at 100% and is for 100 points tied to the score, there is a 1%–to–1 point ratio. The score can be used to substitute for a percentage complete when this achievement is populated.

```
[[ICFGameCenterManager sharedManager]
reportAchievement:@"com.dragonforged.whackacac.score100"
withPercentageComplete:score];
```

Although this hook could be placed into the `cactusHit:` method again, it makes more sense to place it into the `displayNewScore:` method since it is dealing with the score. The entire updated `displayNewScore:` method with the new achievement hook follows for clarity.

```
- (void)displayNewScore:(float)updatedScore;
{
    int scoreInt = score;

    if(scoreInt % 10 == 0 && score <= 50)
    {
        [self spawnCactus];
    }

    scoreLabel.text = [NSString stringWithFormat: @"%06.0f",
    ➥updatedScore];

    GKAchievement *score100Achievement = [[ICFGameCenterManager
    ➥sharedManager] achievementForIdentifier:
    ➥@"com.dragonforged.whackacac.score100"];

    if(![score100Achievement isCompleted])
    {
        [[ICFGameCenterManager sharedManager] reportAchievement:
        ➥@"com.dragonforged.whackacac.score100"
        ➥withPercentageComplete:score];
    }
}
```

Because the Score 100 achievement is hidden, it will not appear to the user until the user has completed progress toward it (at least one point). At any time after beginning to work on this achievement, the user can see the progress in the Game Center View Controllers, as shown in Figure 4.6.

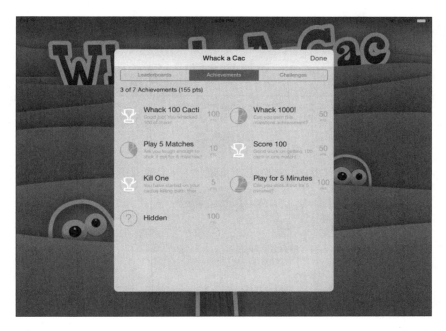

Figure 4.6   Viewing the partially progressed Score 100 achievement after scoring 43 points in a game; note the completion of the Kill One achievement.

Multiple Session Achievements

In the preceding example, the Score 100 achievement required the player to earn the entire 100 points while in a single match. However, there often will be times when it will be required to track a user across multiple matches and even app launches as they progress toward an achievement. The first of the multiple session achievements that will be implemented is the com.dragonforged.whackacac.play5 achievement.

Each time the player completes a round of game play, the com.dragonforged.whackacac.play5 achievement will be progressed. Because the achievement is completed at five games played, each game increments the progress by 20%. This hook will be added to the viewWillDisappear method of ICFGameViewController. As with the previous examples, first a reference to the GKAchievement object is created. After making sure that the achievement isn't already completed, it can be incremented. A new variable is created to determine the number of matches played, which is the percentage complete divided by 20. The matchesPlayed is then incremented by 1, and submitted using reportAchievement: withPercentageComplete: by multiplying matchesPlayed by 20.

```
-(void)viewWillDisappear:(BOOL)animated
{
```

```
GKAchievement *play5MatchesAchievement = [[ICFGameCenterManager
➥sharedManager] achievementForIdentifier:
➥@"com.dragonforged.whackacac.play5"];

if(![play5MatchesAchievement isCompleted])
{
    double matchesPlayed = [play5MatchesAchievement
    ➥percentComplete]/20.0f;

    matchesPlayed++;

    [[ICFGameCenterManager sharedManager]
    ➥reportAchievement: @"com.dragonforged.whackacac.play5"
    ➥withPercentageComplete: matchesPlayed*20.0f];
}

[super viewWillDisappear: animated];
}
```

Piggybacked Achievements and Storing Achievement Precision

Sometimes, it is possible to piggyback two achievements off of each other, such as the next case when dealing with the Whack 100 and Whack 1000 achievements. Because both of these achievements are tracking the same type of objective (whacks), a more streamlined approach can be taken.

As with the other achievement hooks that have been implemented in this chapter, the first thing to do is to create a reference to a GKAchievement. In the following example, a reference to the larger of the two achievements is used. Since the largest achievement has more objectives to complete than it does percentage, it will be rounded down to the nearest multiple of 10. To help combat this problem, a localKills variable is populated from NSUserDefaults. This system falls apart when the achievement exists on two different devices, but can be further polished using iCloud to store the data (see Chapter 11).

A calculation is also made to determine how many kills Game Center reports (with loss of accuracy). If remoteKills is greater than localKills, we know that the player either has reinstalled the game or has progressed it on another device. In this event the system will default to the Game Center's values as to not progress the user backward; otherwise, the local information is used.

This code example can be placed inside the cactusHit: method following the Kill One achievement from earlier in this section. After each hit, the localKills value is increased by one. Two checks are performed to make sure that each achievement is not already completed. Because references to both GKAchievements are not available here, a check of the kills number can be used to substitute the standard isComplete check. After the achievements are submitted, the new local value is stored into the NSUserDefaults for future reference.

```
GKAchievement *killOneThousandAchievement = [[ICFGameCenterManager
➥sharedManager] achievementForIdentifier:
➥@"com.dragonforged.whackacac.1000whacks"];

double localKills = [[[NSUserDefaults standardUserDefaults]
➥objectForKey:@"kills"] doubleValue];

double remoteKills = [killOneThousandAchievement percentComplete] *
➥10.0;

if(remoteKills > localKills)
{
    localKills = remoteKills;
}

localKills++;

if(localKills <= 1000)
{
    if(localKills <= 100)
    {
        [[ICFGameCenterManager sharedManager]
        ➥reportAchievement: @"com.dragonforged.whackacac.100whacks"
        ➥withPercentageComplete:localKills];
    }

    [[ICFGameCenterManager sharedManager]
    ➥reportAchievement:@"com.dragonforged.whackacac.1000whacks"
    ➥withPercentageComplete:(localKills/10.0)];
}

[[NSUserDefaults standardUserDefaults] setObject:[NSNumber
➥numberWithDouble: localKills] forKey:@"kills"];
```

Timer-Based Achievements

One of the most popular achievements in iOS gaming is to play for a certain amount of time. In Whack-a-Cac, com.dragonforged.whackacac.play5Mins is used to track the user's progress toward five minutes of total gameplay. This particular example exists for the loss-of-accuracy problem that was faced in the Whack 1000 example from earlier in this section, and it can be overcome in the same manner.

To track time, an NSTimer will be created. To determine how often the timer should fire, you will need to determine what 1% of five minutes is.

```
play5MinTimer = [NSTimer scheduledTimerWithTimeInterval:3.0 target:self
➥selector:@selector(play5MinTick) userInfo:nil repeats:YES];
```

When the timer fires, a new call to a new `play5MinTick` method is called. If the game is paused or in a `gameOver` state, the achievement progress is ignored and the method returns. As with the other examples, a reference to the `GKAchievement` object is created, and a check is performed to see whether it has completed. If this achievement is completed, the timer is invalidated to prevent wasted CPU time. Otherwise, since the timer is firing every three seconds (1% of five minutes), the achievement is progressed by 1%.

```
- (void)play5MinTick;
{
    if(paused || gameOver)
    {
        return;
    }

    GKAchievement *play5MinAchievement = [[ICFGameCenterManager
    ➥sharedManager] achievementForIdentifier:
    ➥@"com.dragonforged.whackacac.play5Mins"];

    if([play5MinAchievement isCompleted])
    {
        [play5MinTimer invalidate];
        play5MinTimer = nil;
        return;
    }

    double percentageComplete =    play5MinAchievement.percentComplete
    ➥+ 1.0;

    [[ICFGameCenterManager sharedManager] reportAchievement:
    ➥@"com.dragonforged.whackacac.play5Mins" withPercentageComplete:
    ➥percentageComplete];
}
```

Resetting Achievements

There is often a need to reset all achievement progress for a user, more so in development than in production. Sometimes, it is helpful to provide users with a chance to take a fresh run at a game or even some sort of prestige mode that starts everything over, but at a harder difficulty. Resetting achievement progress is simple; the following code snippet can be added into the `IFCGameCenterManager` class to completely reset all achievements to the unearned state. If you are providing this functionality to users, it is a good idea to have several steps of confirmation to prevent accidental resetting.

```
- (void)resetAchievements
{
    [achievementDictionary removeAllObjects];
```

```
   [GKAchievement resetAchievementsWithCompletionHandler:
 ^(NSError *error)
 {
        if(error == nil)
        {
              NSLog(@"All achievements have been successfully
              ➥reset");
        }

        else
        {
              NSLog(@"Unable to reset achievements: %@",
              ➥[error localizedDescription]);
        }
   }];
}
```

Tip

While the app is in development and during debugging, it can be helpful to keep a
call to reset achievements in the authentication successfully completed block of the
ICFGameCenterManager class that can easily be commented out to assist with testing
and implementing achievements.

Going Further with Achievements

Apple provides a lot for free in regard to displaying and progressing achievements. However,
Apple does not allow the customization of the provided interface for viewing achievements.
The look and feel of Apple's achievement view controllers might simply not fit into the app's
design. In cases like this, the raw achievement information can be accessed for display in a
customized interface. Although fully setting up custom achievements is beyond the scope of
this chapter, this section contains information that will assist you.

Earlier, you learned about creating a local cache of GKAchievements. However, GKAchievement
objects are missing critical data that will be needed in order to display achievement data to the
user, such as the description, title, name, and number of points it is worth. Additionally, when
the achievement cache is used, if an achievement has not been progressed, it will not appear in
the cache. To retrieve all achievements and the required information needed to present them to
the user, a new class is required.

Using the GKAchievementDescription class and the class method loadAchievement-
DescriptionsWithCompletionHandler:, you can gain access to an array of
GKAchievementDescriptions. A GKAchievementDescription object contains prop-
erties for the titles, descriptions, images, and other critical information. However, the

GKAchievementDescription does not contain any information about the current progress of the achievement for the local user; in order to determine progress, the identifier will need to be compared to the local achievement cache.

```
[GKAchievementDescription
➥loadAchievementDescriptionsWithCompletionHandler:^(NSArray
➥*descriptions, NSError *error)
{
    if(error != nil)
    {
        NSLog(@"An error occurred loading achievement
        ➥descriptions: %@", [error localizedDescription]);
    }

    for(GKAchievementDescription *achievementDescription in
    ➥descriptions)
    {
        NSLog(@"%@\n", achievementDescription);
    }

}];
```

When the preceding code is executed on Whack-a-Cac, the console will display the following information:

```
WhackACac[48552:c07] <GKAchievementDescription:
0x1185f810>id: com.dragonforged.whackacac.100whacks Whack 100 Cacti
visible Good job! You whacked 100 of them!

WhackACac[48552:c07] <GKAchievementDescription:
0x1185f980>id: com.dragonforged.whackacac.1000whacks Whack 1000!
visible You are a master at killing those cacti.

WhackACac[48552:c07] <GKAchievementDescription:
0x1185f820>id: com.dragonforged.whackacac.play5 Play 5 Matches visible
Your dedication to cactus whacking is unmatched.

WhackACac[48552:c07] <GKAchievementDescription:
0x1185eae0>id: com.dragonforged.whackacac.score100 Score 100 hidden
Good work on getting 100 cacti in one match!

WhackACac[48552:c07] <GKAchievementDescription:
0x1185eaf0>id: com.dragonforged.whackacac.killone Kill One  hidden You
have started on your cactus killing path; there is no turning back now.

WhackACac[48552:c07] <GKAchievementDescription:
0x1185eb30>id: com.dragonforged.whackacac.play5Mins Play for 5 Minutes
visible Good work! Your dedication continues to impress your peers.
```

```
WhackACac[48552:c07] <GKAchievementDescription:
0x1185eb40>id: com.dragonforged.whackacac.hit5Fast Hit 5 Quick hidden
You are truly a quick gun.
```

A list of all the achievements has now been retrieved and can be compared to the local achievement cache to determine percentages completed. You have everything that is needed to create a customized GUI for presenting the achievement data to the user.

Summary

In this chapter, you learned about integrating Game Center Achievements into an iOS project. You continued to build up the sample game Whack-a-Cac that was introduced in Chapter 3. This chapter also continued to expand on the reusable Game Center Manager class.

You should now have a firm understanding of how to create achievements, set up your app to interact with them, post and show progress, and reset all achievement progress. Additionally, a brief look at going beyond the standard behavior was provided. With the knowledge gained in this chapter, you now have the ability to fully integrate achievements into any app.

5

Getting Started with
Address Book

The iOS Address Book frameworks have existed largely unchanged from their introduction in iOS 2.0 (then called iPhone OS 2.0). These frameworks were largely ported unchanged from their OS X counterparts, which have existed since OS X 10.2, making Address Book one of the oldest frameworks available on iOS. This legacy will become evident as you begin working with Address Book technology. It is largely seated on Core Foundation framework, which might seem unfamiliar to developers who have come over to Objective-C and Cocoa development after the introduction of the iPhone SDKs.

Why Address Book Support Is Important

When developing iOS software, you are running in an environment alongside your user's mobile life. Users carry their mobile devices everywhere, and with these devices a considerable amount of their personal lives is intertwined with each device, from their daily calendar to personal photo albums. Paramount to this mobile life is the user's contact information. This data has been collected over long periods, often on several devices, by a user and contains information about the user's family, business, and social life.

An app can use a contact database to determine whether the user already has friends signed up for a service by parsing through a list of their email addresses or phone numbers to automatically add them as friends. Your app can also use a contact list for autopopulating emails or phone numbers or allow users to share their contact info with friends over Bluetooth. The reasons an app might need access to the user's contacts are virtually endless.

> **Note**
>
> It is important to access the contact database only if your app has a legitimate reason to do so; nothing will turn a user off from your app more quickly than a breach of privacy.

Limitations of Address Book Programming

Although the Address Book frameworks remain fairly open, there are some important limitations to consider. The most notable, especially for those coming from the Mac development world, is that there's no "me" card. Essentially, there is no way to identify your user in the list of contacts. Although there are some hacks that attempt to do this, nothing developed so far has proven to be reliable or is sanctioned by Apple.

A newer and welcome limitation—especially by privacy-concerned users—is the addition of Core Location–type authorization to access the contact database. This means that a user will be prompted to allow an app to access his contacts before being able to do so. When writing Address Book software, make an effort to ensure that your software continues to function even if a user has declined to let the app access his contact information.

Starting with iOS 6, a new privacy section exists in the Settings.app. From here, users are able to toggle on and off permissions to access Contacts, Locations, Calendars, Reminders, Photos, and Bluetooth.

The Sample App

The sample app for this chapter is a simple address book viewer and editor. When launched, it will retrieve and display a list of all the contacts on your device. There is a plus button in the navigation bar for adding a new contact via the built-in interface, as well as a toggle button to change between showing either phone numbers or street addresses in the list. Additionally, the app has the capability to add a new contact programmatically and an example of using the built-in people picker.

Because the sample app, shown in Figure 5.1, is merely a base navigation controller project and does not have any overhead that is unrelated to Address Book programming, it is prudent to dive right into the functional code in the next section.

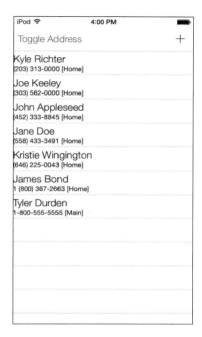

Figure 5.1   A first look at the sample app.

Getting Address Book Up and Running

The first thing you need to do before working with the Address Book frameworks is to link both frameworks in your project. You need to be concerned with two frameworks: AddressBookUI.framework and AddressBook.framework. The first of these frameworks handles the graphical user interface for picking, editing, or displaying contacts, and the second handles all the interaction layers to work with that data. You need to import two headers, as shown here:

```
#import <AddressBook/AddressBook.h>
#import <AddressBookUI/AddressBookUI.h>
```

In the sample app, the headers are imported in RootViewController.h because the class will need to conform to several delegates, which is discussed later. You will also want to create a classwide instance of ABAddressBookRef, which in the sample app is called addressBook. The sample app also has an NSArray that will be used to store an array of the contact entries. It is a fairly expensive operation to copy the address book into memory, so you will want to minimize the number of times you will need to run that operation.

```
ABAddressBookRef addressBook;
NSArray *addressBookEntryArray;
```

To populate this new NSArray, you need to call ABAddressBookCreate. This will create a new instance of the address book data based on the current global address book database. In the sample app, this is done as part of the viewDidLoad method.

```
if(addressBook == NULL)
{
    NSLog(@"Error loading address book: %@",  CFErrorCopyDescription(creationError));
}


ABAddressBookRequestAccessWithCompletion(addressBook, ^(bool granted,
➥CFErrorRef error)
{
    if(!granted)
    {
        NSLog(@"No permission!");
    }
});
```

You will also want to catch the event if our address book has no contacts, which will be the default behavior on the iOS Simulator. The sample app displays a UIAlert in this situation to let the user know that the app isn't broken, but that it has no data available to it. You can query the size of an ABAddressBookRef with the function ABAddressBookGetPersonCount.

```
if(ABAddressBookGetPersonCount(addressBook) == 0)
{
    UIAlertView *alertView = [[UIAlertView alloc]initWithTitle:@""
    message:@"Address book is empty!"
    delegate:nil
    cancelButtonTitle:@"Dismiss"
    otherButtonTitles: nil];

    [alertView show];
}
```

Now you have a reference to the address book, but you will want to translate that into a more manageable dataset. The sample app copies these objects into an NSArray since it will be using the data to populate a table view.

You have access to three functions for copying the address book data that will return a CFArrayRef:

- ABAddressBookCopyArrayOfAllPeople will return an array of all people in the referenced address book (this method is shown in the next code snippet).

- ABAddressBookCopyArrayOfAllPeopleInSource will return all the address book items that are found in a particular source.

- ABAddressBookCopyArrayOfAllPeopleInSourceWithSortOrdering will allow you to sort the list of address book entries while retrieving it.

The sample app does not need to worry about sorting right now, so it simply retrieves the contacts with a call to `ABAddressBookCopyArrayOfAllPeople`. Since a `CFArrayRef` is a toll-free bridge to `NSArray`, it can be typecast and left with an `NSArray`. Now that you have an array of all the address book entries, it is just a simple task to get them displayed in a table.

```
addressBookEntryArray = (NSArray *) ABAddressBookCopyArrayOfAllPeople(addressBook);
```

> **Note**
>
> Sources in this context amount to where the contact was retrieved from; possible values can be `kABSourceTypeLocal`, `kABSourceTypeExchange`, `kABSourceTypeMobileMe`, and `kABSourceTypeCardDAV`. To get a list of all the sources found within the referenced address book, use `ABAddressBookCopyArrayOfAllSources(addressBook)`. From there, you can query the sources that are of interest to your app.

Reading Data from the Address Book

The preceding section demonstrated how to populate an `NSArray` with entries from the user's address book—each of these objects is an `ABRecordRef`. This section covers pulling information back out of an `ABRecordRef`.

The sample app will be displaying the user data through a `UITableView`. There will be two types of values contained within the `ABRecordRef`: The first type is a single value used for objects for which there can be only one, such as a first and last name, and the second type is a multivalue used when dealing with values that a user might have more than one of, such as a phone number or a street address.

The following code snippet pulls an `ABRecordRef` from the address book array that was created in the preceding section and then retrieves the contact's first and last name and sets `NSString` values accordingly. A full listing of available properties is shown in Table 5.1.

```
ABRecordRef record = [addressBookEntryArrayobjectAtIndex:indexPath.row];
NSString *firstName = (NSString *)ABRecordCopyValue(record,
➥kABPersonFirstNameProperty);

NSString *lastName = (NSString *)ABRecordCopyValue(record,
➥kABPersonLastNameProperty);

//...

    if(firstName)
        CFRelease(firstName);
    if(lastName)
        CFRelease(lastName);
```

Table 5.1   **Complete Listing of All Available Single-Value Constants in an `ABRecordRef`**

Property Name	Description
kABPersonFirstNameProperty	First name
kABPersonLastNameProperty	Last name
kABPersonMiddleNameProperty	Middle name or initial
kABPersonPrefixProperty	Name prefix (Mr., Ms., Dr.)
kABPersonSuffixProperty	Name suffix (MD, Jr., Sr.)
kABPersonNicknameProperty	Nickname
kABPersonFirstNamePhoneticProperty	Phonetically spelled first name
kABPersonLastNamePhoneticProperty	Phonetically spelled last name
kABPersonMiddleNamePhoneticProperty	Phonetically spelled middle name
kABPersonOrganizationProperty	Company or organization
kABPersonJobTitleProperty	Job title
kABPersonDepartmentProperty	Department title
kABPersonBirthdayProperty	Birthday `CFDate` format, which is a toll-free bridge to `NSDate`
kABPersonNoteProperty	Personal notes
kABPersonCreationDateProperty	Creation `CFDate`
kABPersonModificationDateProperty	Last modified `CFDate`

> **Note**
>
> NARC (New, Alloc, Retain, Copy) is how I was taught memory management in the early days of Mac OS X programming, and the same holds true today for manual memory management. New advancements to memory management such as ARC are forever changing the way we handle manual memory management. However, Core Foundation is not compliant with ARC. When you perform operations on Address Book with "copy" in the name, you must release that memory using a `CFRelease()` call.

Reading Multivalues from the Address Book

Often, you will encounter Address Book objects that can store multiple values, such as phone numbers, email addresses, or street addresses. These are all accessed using `ABMultiValueRefs`. The process is similar to that for single values with one additional level of complexity.

The first thing you need to do when working with multivalues, such as phone numbers, is copy the value of the multivalue property. In the following code example, use `kABPerson-PhoneProperty` from the record that was set in the previous section. This provides you with an `ABMultiValueRef` called `phoneNumbers`.

A check is then needed to make sure that the contact has at least one phone number using the ABMultiValueGetCount function. Here, you can either loop through all the phone numbers or pull the first one you find (as in the example). Additionally, you will want to handle the "no phone number found" case. From here, you need to create a new string and store the value of the phone number into it. This is done using the ABMultiValueCopyValueAtIndex call, the first parameter of the ABMultiValueRef followed by the index number.

```
ABMultiValueRef phoneNumbers = ABRecordCopyValue(record,
➥kABPersonPhoneProperty);

if (ABMultiValueGetCount(phoneNumbers) > 0)
{
    CFStringRef phoneNumber =
    ➥ABMultiValueCopyValueAtIndex(phoneNumbers, 0);

    NSLog(@"Phone Number: %@", phoneNumber);

    CFRelease(phoneNumber);
}

CFRelease(phoneNumbers);
```

Understanding Address Book Labels

In the preceding section, you retrieved a phone number from the contact database; however, you know it only by its index number. Although this is helpful to developers, it is next to useless for users. You will want to retrieve the label that was used in the contact database. In the next code snippet, the example from the preceding section is expanded on.

The first step to obtaining a label for a multivalue reference is to call ABMultiValueCopyLabelAtIndex. Call this function with the same parameters you used to get the value of the multivalue object. This function will return a nonlocalized string, such as "_$!<Mobile>!$_". Although this is much more helpful than a raw index number, it is still not ready for user presentation.

You will need to run the returned label through a localizer to get a human-readable string. Do so using the ABAddressBookCopyLocalizedLabel using the raw value CFStringRef that was just set. In the example this will now return Mobile or the appropriate value for the device's selected language.

```
ABMultiValueRef phoneNumbers = ABRecordCopyValue(record,
➥kABPersonPhoneProperty);

if (ABMultiValueGetCount(phoneNumbers) > 0)
{
    CFStringRef phoneNumber =
    ➥ABMultiValueCopyValueAtIndex(phoneNumbers, 0);
```

```
    CFStringRef phoneTypeRawString =
    ➥ABMultiValueCopyLabelAtIndex(phoneNumbers, 0);

    NSString *localizedPhoneTypeString =  (NSString
    ➥*)ABAddressBookCopyLocalizedLabel(phoneTypeRawString);

    NSLog(@"Phone %@ [%@]", phoneNumber, localizedPhoneTypeString);

    CFRelease(phoneNumber);
    CFRelease(phoneTypeRawString);
    CFRelease(localizedPhoneTypeString);
}
```

Look back at the example in Figure 5.1—you now have the skill set to fully implement this functionality.

Working with Addresses

In the preceding two sections, you saw how to access single-value information and then how to access multivalue data. In this section, you will work with a bit of both as you learn how to handle street addresses that you encounter in the contact database. If you launch the sample app and tap the toggle button in the navigation bar, you will see that the addresses are now shown instead of phone numbers in the table cells (see Figure 5.2).

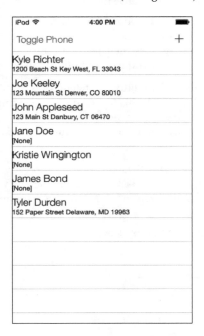

Figure 5.2   The sample app showing addresses pulled from the contact database.

You will begin working with addresses in the same manner as you did for the phone multi-values. First obtain an ABMultiValueRef for the kABPersonAddressProperty. Then you will need to make sure that at least one valid address was found. When you query the multivalue object with an index value, instead of getting back a single CFStringRef, you are returned a dictionary containing the address components. After you have the dictionary, you can pull out specific information using the address constants shown in Table 5.2.

```
ABMultiValueRef streetAddresses = ABRecordCopyValue(record,
kABPersonAddressProperty);

if (ABMultiValueGetCount(streetAddresses) > 0)
{
    NSDictionary *streetAddressDictionary = (NSDictionary
    ➡*)ABMultiValueCopyValueAtIndex(streetAddresses, 0);

    NSString *street = [streetAddressDictionary objectForKey:
    ➡(NSString *)kABPersonAddressStreetKey];

    NSString *city = [streetAddressDictionary objectForKey:
    ➡NSString *)kABPersonAddressCityKey];

    NSString *state = [streetAddressDictionary objectForKey:
    ➡(NSString *)kABPersonAddressStateKey];

    NSString *zip = [streetAddressDictionary objectForKey:
    ➡(NSString *)kABPersonAddressZIPKey];

    NSLog(@"Address: %@ %@, %@ %@", street, city, state, zip);

    CFRelease(streetAddressDictionary);
}
```

Table 5.2 **Address Components**

Property	Description
kABPersonAddressStreetKey	Street name and number, including any apartment numbers
kABPersonAddressCityKey	City name
kABPersonAddressStateKey	Two-character or full state name
kABPersonAddressZIPKey	ZIP code, five or nine digits
kABPersonAddressCountryKey	Full country name
kABPersonAddressCountryCodeKey	Two-character country code

Address Book Graphical User Interface

A standard user interface is provided as part of the Address Book framework. This section looks at those interfaces and how they can save an incredible amount of implementation time. Whether it is editing an existing contact, creating a new contact, or allowing your user to pick a contact from a list, Apple has you covered.

People Picker

You will undoubtedly want your user to be able to simply select a contact from a list. For example, let's say you are writing an app that enables you to send a vCard over Bluetooth to another user; you will need to let your user select which contact card she wants to send. This task is easily accomplished using ABPeoplePickerNavigationController. You can turn on this functionality in the sample app by uncommenting line 63 ([self showPicker: nil];) in the RootViewController.m class.

Your class will first need to implement ABPeoplePickerNavigationControllerDelegate. You can then create a new picker controller using the following code snippet:

```
ABPeoplePickerNavigationController *picker =
[[ABPeoplePickerNavigationController alloc] init];

picker.peoplePickerDelegate = self;
➥[self presentViewController:picker animated:YES completion:nil];
```

This displays a people picker to the user (see Figure 5.3).

You will also need to implement three delegate methods to handle callbacks from the user interacting with the people picker. The first method you need handles the Cancel button being tapped by a user; if you do not dismiss the modal in this method, the user has no way to dismiss the view.

```
- (void)peoplePickerNavigationControllerDidCancel:(ABPeoplePickerNavigationController
➥*)peoplePicker
{
    [self dismissViewControllerAnimated:YES completion:nil];
}
```

When you are picking people, there are two sets of data you might be concerned with. The first is the contact itself, and by extension all the contact information. The second is a specific property, such as a specific phone number or email address from a contact. You can handle both of these cases. The first step will look at selecting the entirety of a person's contact information.

```
- (BOOL)peoplePickerNavigationController:
➥(ABPeoplePickerNavigationController *)peoplePicker
➥shouldContinueAfterSelectingPerson: (ABRecordRef)person
{
    NSLog(@"You have selected: %@", person);
```

```
    [self dismissViewControllerAnimated:YES completion:nil];

    return NO;
}
```

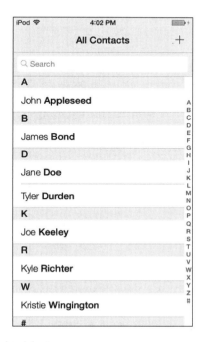

Figure 5.3   The built-in people picker.

In this code snippet, NO is returned for peoplePickerNavigationController: shouldContinueAfterSelectingPerson:. This informs the picker that you do not intend to drill deeper into the contact and you only want to select an ABRecordRef for a person. As with the previous example, you must dismiss the modal view controller when you are done with it. If you do want to dive deeper, you will need to return YES here and implement the following delegate method. Do not forget to remove the dismissModalViewControllerAnimated: completion call from the previous method if you intend to drill deeper.

```
- (BOOL)peoplePickerNavigationController:
➥(ABPeoplePickerNavigationController *)peoplePicker
➥shouldContinueAfterSelectingPerson:(ABRecordRef)person
➥property:(ABPropertyID)property
➥identifier:(ABMultiValueIdentifier)identifier
{
```

```
    NSLog(@"Person: %@\nProperty:%i\nIdentifier:%i", person,property,
➥identifier);

    [self dismissViewControllerAnimated:YES completion:nil];

    return NO;
}
```

Customizing the People Picker

There might be times when you want to allow the picker to choose only from phone numbers or street addresses and ignore the other information. You can do so by modifying the previous method of creating the people picker to match the following example, which will show only phone numbers:

```
ABPeoplePickerNavigationController *picker =
➥[[ABPeoplePickerNavigationController alloc] init];

picker.displayedProperties = [NSArray arrayWithObject:[NSNumber
➥numberWithInt:kABPersonPhoneProperty]];

picker.peoplePickerDelegate = self;
[self presentViewController:picker animated:YES completion:nil];
```

You also can specify an address book for the picker using the addressBook property. If you do not set this, a new address book is created for you when the people picker is presented.

Editing and Viewing Existing Contacts Using ABPersonViewController

Most of the time, you will want to simply display or edit an existing contact using the built-in Address Book user interfaces. In the sample app, this is the default action when a table cell is selected. You first create a new instance of ABPersonViewController and set the delegate and the person to be displayed, which is an instance of ABRecordRef. This approach will display the contact, as shown in Figure 5.4.

```
ABPersonViewController *personViewController = [[ABPersonViewController
➥alloc] init];

personViewController.personViewDelegate = self;

personViewController.displayedPerson = personToDisplay;

[self.navigationController pushViewController:personViewController
➥animated:YES];
```

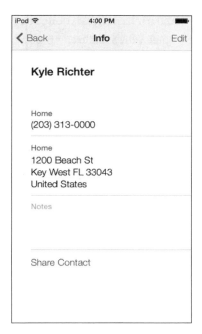

Figure 5.4   The built-in contact viewer.

If you want to allow editing of the contact, you simply add another property to the code snippet.

```
personViewController.allowsEditing = YES;
```

If you want to allow actions in the contact, such as Send Text Message or FaceTime buttons, you can add an additional allowsActions property.

```
personViewController.allowsActions = YES;
```

In addition to the steps you have already implemented, you need to be aware of one required delegate method, personViewController:shouldPerformDefaultActionForPerson: property:identifier. This is called when the user taps on a row such as a street address or a phone number. If you would like the app to perform the default action, such as call or open Maps.app, return YES; if you would like to override these behaviors, return NO.

```
- (BOOL)personViewController:(ABPersonViewController
➡*)personViewController
➡shouldPerformDefaultActionForPerson:(ABRecordRef)person
➡property:(ABPropertyID)property
➡identifier:(ABMultiValueIdentifier)identifierForValue
{

    return YES;
}
```

Creating New Contacts Using `ABNewPersonViewController`

When you want to create a new contact, the sample app has a plus button in the navigation bar that enables you to create a new contact using the built-in user interfaces, shown in Figure 5.5. The next code snippet is straightforward with one caveat: The `ABNewPersonViewController` must be wrapped inside of a `UINavigationController` to function properly.

```
ABNewPersonViewController *newPersonViewController =
➥[[ABNewPersonViewController alloc] init];

UINavigationController *newPersonNavigationController =
➥[[UINavigationController alloc]
➥initWithRootViewController:newPersonViewController];

[newPersonViewController setNewPersonViewDelegate: self];

[self presentViewController:newPersonNavigationController animated:YES
➥completion:nil];
```

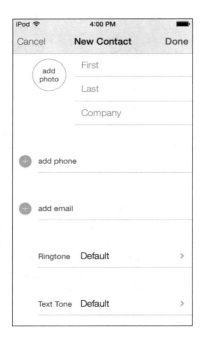

Figure 5.5   The built-in new-person view controller.

There is also a single delegate method that is called when the user saves the contact. After you verify that you have a valid person object being returned, you need to call ABAddressBookAddRecord with the address book you want to add the person into, followed by ABAddressBookSave. If you have an array populated with the address book entries like the sample app, you will need to repopulate that array to see the changes.

```
- (void)newPersonViewController:(ABNewPersonViewController
➥*)newPersonViewController didCompleteWithNewPerson:(ABRecordRef)person
{
    if(person)
    {
        CFErrorRef error = NULL;

        ABAddressBookAddRecord(addressBook, person, &error);
        ABAddressBookSave(addressBook, &error);
        if (error != NULL)
        {
            NSLog(@"An error occurred");
        }
    }

    [self dismissViewControllerAnimated:YES completion:nil];

}
```

Programmatically Creating Contacts

What if you want to programmatically create a new contact instead of using the built-in graphical interface? Think about a contact-sharing app again. You don't want to have to put the user through an interface when you can have the contact information entered programmatically.

In the sample project, uncomment line 66 ([self programmaticallyCreatePerson];) of the RootViewController.m and run it; you will notice that a new person appears in the contact list. The first step you will need to take in creating a new person is to generate a new empty ABRecordRef. You do this with the ABPersonCreate() method. You will also want to create a new NULL pointed CFErrorRef.

```
ABRecordRef newPersonRecord = ABPersonCreate();

CFErrorRef error = NULL;
```

Setting single-value properties is very straightforward, achieved by calling ABRecordSetValue with the new ABRecordRef as the first parameter, followed by the property constant, then the value, followed by the address of the CFErrorRef.

```
ABRecordSetValue(newPersonRecord, kABPersonFirstNameProperty, @"Tyler",
➥&error);

ABRecordSetValue(newPersonRecord, kABPersonLastNameProperty, @"Durden",
➥&error);

ABRecordSetValue(newPersonRecord, kABPersonOrganizationProperty,
➥@"Paperstreet Soap Company", &error);

ABRecordSetValue(newPersonRecord, kABPersonJobTitleProperty,
➥@"Salesman", &error);
```

Setting the phone number multivalue is slightly more complex than with a single-value object. You first need to create a new ABMutableMultiValueRef using the ABMultiValueCreateMutable() method with the type of multivalue property you are creating, in this instance, the phone property.

In the sample app, three different phone numbers are created, each with a different label property. After you finish adding new phone number values, you need to call ABRecordSetValue with the new person record, the multivalue constant you are setting, and the mutable multivalue reference you just populated. Don't forget to release the Core Foundation memory when done.

```
ABMutableMultiValueRef multiPhoneRef =
ABMultiValueCreateMutable(kABMultiStringPropertyType);

ABMultiValueAddValueAndLabel(multiPhoneRef, @"1-800-555-5555",
➥kABPersonPhoneMainLabel, NULL);

ABMultiValueAddValueAndLabel(multiPhoneRef, @"1-203-426-1234",
➥kABPersonPhoneMobileLabel, NULL);

ABMultiValueAddValueAndLabel(multiPhoneRef, @"1-555-555-0123",
➥kABPersonPhoneIPhoneLabel, NULL);

ABRecordSetValue(newPersonRecord, kABPersonPhoneProperty,
➥multiPhoneRef, nil);

CFRelease(multiPhoneRef);
```

Email addresses are handled in the same manner as phone numbers. An example of an email entry is shown in the sample app. Street addresses are handled slightly differently, however.

You will still create a new mutable multivalue reference, but in this step, you also create a new mutable NSDictionary. Set an object for each key of the address that you want to set (refer to Table 5.2 for a complete list of values). Next, you need to add a label for this street address. In the code sample that follows, kABWorkLabel is used. When done, save the data in the same fashion as the phone or email entry.

```
ABMutableMultiValueRef multiAddressRef =
➥ABMultiValueCreateMutable(kABMultiDictionaryPropertyType);

NSMutableDictionary *addressDictionary = [[NSMutableDictionary alloc]
➥init];

[addressDictionary setObject:@"152 Paper Street" forKey:(NSString *)
➥kABPersonAddressStreetKey];

[addressDictionary setObject:@"Delaware" forKey:(NSString
➥*)kABPersonAddressCityKey];

[addressDictionary setObject:@"MD" forKey:(NSString
➥*)kABPersonAddressStateKey];

[addressDictionary setObject:@"19963" forKey:(NSString
➥*)kABPersonAddressZIPKey];

ABMultiValueAddValueAndLabel(multiAddressRef, addressDictionary,
➥kABWorkLabel, NULL);

ABRecordSetValue(newPersonRecord, kABPersonAddressProperty,
➥multiAddressRef, &error);

CFRelease(multiAddressRef);
```

After you set up the new contact with all the information you want to enter, you need to save it and check for any errors that occurred during the process. In the sample app, the array and the table are reloaded to display the new entry.

```
ABAddressBookAddRecord(addressBook, newPersonRecord, &error);
ABAddressBookSave(addressBook, &error);

if(error != NULL)
{
    NSLog(@"An error occurred");
}
```

Summary

This chapter covered the Address Book frameworks and how to leverage them into your iOS apps. You learned about the limitations and privacy concerns of the Address Book, as well as the importance of implementing it into appropriate apps.

Exploring the included sample app, you gained insightful and practical knowledge on how to get the Address Book frameworks quickly up and running. Additionally, you learned how to work with both retrieving and inserting new data into an address book both using Apple's provided graphical user interface and programmatically. You should now have a strong understanding of the Address Book frameworks and be comfortable adding them into your iOS apps.

6

Working with Music Libraries

When Steve Jobs first introduced the iPhone onstage at Macworld in 2007, it was touted as a phone, an iPod, and a revolutionary Internet communicator. Several years later, and partially due to a lot of hard work by third-party developers, the iPhone has grown into something much more than those three core concepts. That original marketing message has not changed, however; the iPhone itself remains primarily a phone, an iPod, and an Internet communication device. Users did not add an iPhone to their collection of devices they already carried every day; they replaced their existing phones and iPods with a single device.

Music is what gave the iPhone its humble start when Apple began planning the device in 2004; the iPhone was always an evolutionary step forward from an iPod. Music inspired the iPod, which, it could be argued, brought the company back from the brink. Music is universally loved. It brings people together and it enables them to express themselves. Although day-to-day iPhone users might not even think of their iPhone as a music playback device, most of them will use it almost absentmindedly to listen to their favorite songs.

This chapter discusses how to add access to the user's music library inside of an iOS app. Whether building a full-featured music player or enabling users to play their music as the soundtrack to a game, this chapter demonstrates how to provide music playback from the user's own library.

The Sample App

The sample app for this chapter is simply called Player (see Figure 6.1). The sample app is a full-featured music player for the iPhone. It enables the user to pick songs to be played via the Media Picker, play random songs, or play artist-specific songs. In addition, it features functionality for pause, resume, previous, next, volume, playback counter, and plus or minus 30 seconds to the playhead. The app also displays the album art for the current track being played, if it is available.

Figure 6.1   A first look at the sample app, Player, a fully functional music player running on an iPod.

Because the iOS Simulator that comes bundled with Xcode does not include a copy of the Music.app, nor does it have an easy method of transferring music into its file system, the app can be run only on actual devices. When the app is launched on a simulator, a number of errors will appear.

```
player[80633:c07] MPMusicPlayer: Unable to
➥launch iPod music player server: application not found
player[80633:c07] MPMusicPlayer: Unable to
➥launch iPod music player server: application not found
player[80633:c07] MPMusicPlayer: Unable to
➥launch iPod music player server: application not found
```

Any attempt to access the media library will result in a crash on the simulator with the following error:

```
*** Terminating app due to uncaught exception
➥'NSInternalInconsistencyException', reason: 'Unable to load
➥iPodUI.framework'
```

Building a Playback Engine

Before it makes sense to pull in any audio data, an in-depth understanding of the playback controls is required. To play music from within an app, a new instance of MPMusicPlayerController needs to first be created. This is done in the header file ICFViewController.h, and the new object is called player. The MPMusicPlayerController will be referenced throughout this chapter to control the playback as well as retrieve information about the items being played.

```
@interface ICFViewController : UIViewController
{
    MPMusicPlayerController *player;
}
```

Inside the viewDidLoad method, the MPMusicPlayerController player can be initialized using a MPMusicPlayerController class method. There are two possible options when a new MPMusicPlayerController is created. In the first option, an applicationMusicPlayer will play music within an app; it will not affect the iPod state and will end playback when the app is exited. The second option, iPodMusicPlayer, will control the iPod app itself. It will pick up where the user has left the iPod playhead and track selection, and will continue to play after the app has entered the background. The sample app uses applicationMusicPlayer; however, this can easily be changed without the need to change any other code or behavior.

```
- (void)viewDidLoad
{
    [super viewDidLoad];

    player = [MPMusicPlayerController applicationMusicPlayer];
}
```

Registering for Playback Notifications

To efficiently work with music playback, it is important to be aware of the state of the music player. When you are dealing with the music player, there are two notifications to watch. The "now playing" item has changed and the playback state has changed. These states can be monitored by using NSNotificationCenter to subscribe to the aforementioned events. The sample app uses a new convenience method, registerMediaPlayerNotifications, to keep the sample app's code clean and readable. After the new observers have been added to NSNotificationCenter, the beginGeneratingPlaybackNotifications needs to be invoked on the player object.

```
- (void)registerMediaPlayerNotifications
{
    NSNotificationCenter *notificationCenter = [NSNotificationCenter
    ➥defaultCenter];

    [notificationCenter addObserver: self
```

```
                          selector: @selector
                              (nowPlayingItemChanged:)
                              name:
➡MPMusicPlayerControllerNowPlayingItemDidChangeNotification
                              object: player];

    [notificationCenter addObserver: self
                          selector: @selector
                              (playbackStateChanged:)
                              name:
➡MPMusicPlayerControllerPlaybackStateDidChangeNotification
                              object: player];

    [player beginGeneratingPlaybackNotifications];
}
```

When registering for notifications, it is important to make sure that they are properly dereg-istered during memory and view cleanup; failing to do so can cause crashes and other unex-pected behavior. A call to endGeneratingPlaybackNotifications is also performed during the viewDidUnload routine.

```
- (void)viewWillDisappear: (BOOL)animated
{
    [[NSNotificationCenter defaultCenter] removeObserver: self
                                          name:
➡MPMusicPlayerControllerNowPlayingItemDidChangeNotification
                                                  object: player];

    [[NSNotificationCenter defaultCenter] removeObserver: self
                                          name:
➡MPMusicPlayerControllerPlaybackStateDidChangeNotification
                                                  object: player];

    [player endGeneratingPlaybackNotifications];

    [super viewWillDisappear: animated];
}
```

In addition to registering for callbacks from the music player, a new NSTimer will be created to handle updating the playback progress and playhead time label. In the sample app, the NSTimer is simply called playbackTimer. For the time being, the notification callback selec-tors and the NSTimer behavior will be left uncompleted. These are discussed in the section "Handling State Changes."

User Controls

The sample app provides the user with several buttons designed to enable them to interact with the music, such as play, pause, skip, and previous, as well as jumping forward and backward by 30 seconds. The first action that needs to be implemented is the play and pause method. The button functions as a simple toggle: If the music is already playing, it is paused; if it is paused or stopped, it resumes playing. The code to update the text of the button from play to pause and vice versa is discussed as part of the state change notification callback in the section "Handling State Changes."

```
- (IBAction)playButtonAction:(id)sender
{
    if ([player playbackState] == MPMusicPlaybackStatePlaying)
    {
        [player pause];
    }

    else
    {
        [player play];
    }
}
```

The user should also have the ability to skip to the previous or next track while listening to music. This is done through two additional calls on the `player` object.

```
- (IBAction)previousButtonAction:(id)sender
{
    [player skipToPreviousItem];
}

- (IBAction)nextButtonAction:(id)sender
{
    [player skipToNextItem];
}
```

Users can also be provided with actions that enable them to skip 30 seconds forward or backward in a song. If the user hits the end of the track, the following code will skip to the next track; likewise, if they hit further than the start of a song, the audio track will start over. Both of these methods make use of the `currentPlaybackTime` property of the player object. This property can be used to change the current playhead, as well as determine what the current playback time is.

```
- (IBAction)skipBack30Seconds:(id)sender
{
    int newPlayHead = player.currentPlaybackTime - 30;

    if(newPlayHead < 0)
    {
```

```
            newPlayHead = 0;
    }

    player.currentPlaybackTime = newPlayHead;
}

- (IBAction)skipForward30Seconds:(id)sender
{
    int newPlayHead = player.currentPlaybackTime + 30;

    if(newPlayHead > currentSongDuration)
    {
        [player skipToNextItem];
    }

    else
    {
        player.currentPlaybackTime = newPlayHead;
    }
}
```

In addition to these standard controls to give the user control over the item playing, the sample app enables the user to change the volume of the audio. An MPVolumeView is created to control the playback volume. The MPVolumeView will provide a slider to control the volume and will also display the Airplay controls when appropriate.

```
-(void) createAndDisplayMPVolumeViews
{
    UIView *volumeHolder = [[UIView alloc] initWithFrame: CGRectMake(125, 115, 185,
    ➥20)];
    [volumeHolder setBackgroundColor: [UIColor clearColor]];
    [self.view addSubview: volumeHolder];

    MPVolumeView *myVolumeView = [[MPVolumeView alloc] initWithFrame: volumeHolder.
    ➥bounds]
    [volumeHolder addSubview: myVolumeView];
}
```

Handling State Changes

Earlier in this section, three notifications were registered to receive callbacks. These notifications allow the app to determine the current state and behavior of the MPMusicPlayerController. The first method that is being watched will be called whenever the currently playing item changes. This method contains two parts. The first part updates the album artwork, and the second updates the labels that indicate the artist, song title, and album being played.

Every audio or video item being played through the `MPMusicPlayerController` is represented by an `MPMediaItem` object. This object can be retrieved by invoking the method `nowPlayingItem` on an instance of `MPMusicPlayerController`. This functionality is seen in the `nowPlayingItemChanged` method.

A new `UIImage` is created to represent the album artwork and is initially set to a placeholder that will be used in the event that the user does not have album artwork for the `MPMediaItem`. `MPMediaItem` uses key value properties for stored data; a full list is shown in Table 6.1. A new `MPMediaItemArtwork` is created and set with the artwork data. Although the documentation specifies that if no artwork is available this will return `nil`, in practice this is not the case as of iOS 8. A workaround is to load the artwork into a `UIImage` and check the resulting value. If it is `nil`, the assumption is that there is no album artwork and the placeholder is loaded. The code used in the sample app will continue to function in the event that `MPMediaItemArtwork` begins returning `nil` when no album artwork is available.

Table 6.1 **Available `MPMediaItem` Constants**

Keys for `MPMediaItem` Properties	Available for Predicate Searching
MPMediaItemPropertyPersistentID	YES
MPMediaItemPropertyAlbumPersistentID	YES
MPMediaItemPropertyArtistPersistentID	YES
MPMediaItemPropertyAlbumArtistPersistentID	YES
MPMediaItemPropertyGenrePersistentID	YES
MPMediaItemPropertyComposerPersistentID	YES
MPMediaItemPropertyPodcastPersistentID	YES
MPMediaItemPropertyMediaType	YES
MPMediaItemPropertyTitle	YES
MPMediaItemPropertyAlbumTitle	YES
MPMediaItemPropertyArtist	YES
MPMediaItemPropertyAlbumArtist	YES
MPMediaItemPropertyGenre	YES
MPMediaItemPropertyComposer	YES
MPMediaItemPropertyPlaybackDuration	NO
MPMediaItemPropertyAlbumTrackNumber	NO
MPMediaItemPropertyAlbumTrackCount	NO
MPMediaItemPropertyDiscNumber	NO
MPMediaItemPropertyDiscCount	NO

Keys for MPMediaItem Properties	Available for Predicate Searching
MPMediaItemPropertyArtwork	NO
MPMediaItemPropertyLyrics	NO
MPMediaItemPropertyIsCompilation	YES
MPMediaItemPropertyReleaseDate	NO
MPMediaItemPropertyBeatsPerMinute	NO
MPMediaItemPropertyComments	NO
MPMediaItemPropertyAssetURL	NO
MPMediaItemPropertyIsCloudItem	YES

The second part of the nowPlayingItemChanged: method handles updating the song title, artist info, and album name, as shown earlier in Figure 6.1. In the event that any of these properties returns nil, a placeholder string is set. A complete list of accessible properties on an MPMediaItem can be found in Table 6.1. When referencing the table, note that if the media item is a podcast, additional keys will be available, which are available in Apple's documentation for MPMediaItem. Also indicated is whether the key can be used for predicate searching when programmatically finding MPMediaItems.

```
- (void) nowPlayingItemChanged: (id) notification
{
    MPMediaItem *currentItem = [player nowPlayingItem];

    UIImage *artworkImage = [UIImage imageNamed:@"noArt.png"];

    MPMediaItemArtwork *artwork = [currentItem valueForProperty:
    ➥MPMediaItemPropertyArtwork];

    if (artwork)
    {
        artworkImage = [artwork imageWithSize: CGSizeMake (120,120)];

        if(artworkImage == nil)
        {
            artworkImage = [UIImage imageNamed:@"noArt.png"];
        }
    }

    [albumImageView setImage:artworkImage];

    NSString *titleString = [currentItem
    ➥valueForProperty:MPMediaItemPropertyTitle];

    if (titleString)
```

```
    {
        songLabel.text = titleString;
    }

    else
    {
        songLabel.text = @"Unknown Song";
    }

    NSString *artistString = [currentItem
    ➥valueForProperty:MPMediaItemPropertyArtist];

    if (artistString)
    {
            artistLabel.text = artistString;

    }

    else
    {
        artistLabel.text = @"Unknown artist";
    }

    NSString *albumString = [currentItem
    ➥valueForProperty:MPMediaItemPropertyAlbumTitle];

    if (albumString)
    {
            recordLabel.text = albumString;
    }

    else
    {
        recordLabel.text = @"Unknown Record";
    }
}
```

Monitoring the state of the music player is a crucial step, especially since this value can be affected by input outside the control of the app. In the event that the state is updated, the playbackStateChanged: method is fired. A new variable playbackState is created to hold onto the current state of the player. This method performs several important tasks, the first of which is updating the text on the play/pause button to reflect the current state. In addition, the NSTimer that was mentioned in the "Registering for Playback Notifications" section is both created and torn down. While the app is playing audio, the timer is set to fire every 0.3 seconds; this is used to update the playback duration labels as well as the UIProgressIndicator that informs the user of the placement of the playhead. The method that the timer fires, updateCurrentPlaybackTime, is discussed in the next subsection.

In addition to the states that are shown in the sample app, there are three additional states. The first, MPMusicPlaybackStateInterrupted, is used whenever the audio is being interrupted, such as by an incoming phone call. The other two states, MPMusicPlaybackStateSeekingForward and MPMusicPlaybackStateSeekingBackward, are used to indicate that the music player is seeking either forward or backward.

```
- (void) playbackStateChanged: (id) notification
{
    MPMusicPlaybackState playbackState = [player playbackState];

    if (playbackState == MPMusicPlaybackStatePaused)
    {
        [playButton setTitle:@"Play"
        ➥forState:UIControlStateNormal];

      if([playbackTimer isValid])
      {
          [playbackTimer invalidate];
      }
    }

    else if (playbackState == MPMusicPlaybackStatePlaying)
    {
        [playButton setTitle:@"Pause" forState:
        ➥UIControlStateNormal];

        playbackTimer = [NSTimer
        scheduledTimerWithTimeInterval:0.3
        target:self
        selector:@selector(updateCurrentPlaybackTime)
        userInfo:nil
        repeats:YES];
    }

    else if (playbackState == MPMusicPlaybackStateStopped)
    {
        [playButton setTitle:@"Play"
        ➥forState:UIControlStateNormal];

        [player stop];

        if([playbackTimer isValid])
        {
            [playbackTimer invalidate];
        }
    }
}
```

In the event that the volume has changed, it is also important to reflect that change on the volume slider found in the app. This is done by watching for the `volumeChanged:` notification callback. From inside this method the current volume of the player can be polled and the `volumeSlider` can be set accordingly.

```
- (void) volumeChanged: (id) notification
{
    [volumeSlider setValue:[player volume]];
}
```

Duration and Timers

Under most circumstances, users will want to have information available to them about the current status of their song, such as how much time has been played and how much time is left in the track. The sample app features two methods for generating this data. The first `updateSongDuration` is called whenever the song changes or when the app is launched. A reference to the current track being played is created, and the song duration expressed in seconds is retrieved through the key `playbackDuration`. The total hours, minutes, and seconds are derived from this data, and the song duration is displayed in a label next to the `UIProgressIndicator`.

```
-(void)updateSongDuration;
{
    currentSongPlaybackTime = 0;

    currentSongDuration = [[[player nowPlayingItem] valueForProperty:
    ➥@"playbackDuration"] floatValue];

    NSInteger tHours = (currentSongDuration / 3600);
    NSInteger tMins = ((currentSongDuration / 60) - tHours*60);
    NSInteger tSecs = (currentSongDuration) - (tMins*60) - (tHours *3600);

    songDurationLabel.text = [NSString stringWithFormat:@"%zd:
    ➥%02d:%02d", tHours, tMins, tSecs ];

    currentTimeLabel.text = @"0:00:00";
}
```

The second method, `updateCurrentPlaybackTime`, is called every 0.3 seconds via an `NSTimer` that is controlled from the `playbackStateChanged:` method discussed in the "Handling State Changes" section. The same math is used to derive the hours, minutes, and seconds as in the `updateSongDuration` method. A `percentagePlayed` is also calculated based on the previously determined song duration and is used to update the `playbackProgressIndicator`. Because the `currentPlaybackTime` is accurate only to one second, this method does not need to be called more often. However, the more regularly it is called, the better precision to the actual second it will be.

```
-(void)updateCurrentPlaybackTime;
{
    currentSongPlaybackTime = player.currentPlaybackTime;

    int tHours = (currentSongPlaybackTime / 3600);
    int tMins = ((currentSongPlaybackTime / 60) - tHours*60);
    int tSecs = (currentSongPlaybackTime) - (tMins*60) - (tHours*3600);

    currentTimeLabel.text = [NSString stringWithFormat:@"%zd:
    ➥%02d:%02d", tHours, tMins, tSecs ];

    float percentagePlayed = currentSongPlaybackTime/
    currentSongDuration;

    [playbackProgressIndicator setProgress:percentagePlayed];
}
```

Shuffle and Repeat

In addition to the properties and controls mentioned previously, an
MPMusicPlayerController also enables the user to specify the repeat and shuffle properties.
Although the sample app does not implement functionality for these two properties, they are
fairly easy to implement.

```
player.repeatMode = MPMusicRepeatModeAll;
player.shuffleMode = MPMusicShuffleModeSongs;
```

The available repeat modes are MPMusicRepeatModeDefault, which is the user's predefined
preference, MPMusicRepeatModeNone, MPMusicRepeatModeOne, and MPMusicRepeatModeAll.
The available modes for shuffle are MPMusicShuffleModeDefault, MPMusicShuffleModeOff,
MPMusicShuffleModeSongs, and MPMusicShuffleModeAlbums, where the
MPMusicShuffleModeDefault mode represents the user's predefined preference.

Media Picker

The simplest way to enable a user to specify which song he wants to hear is to
provide him access to an MPMediaPickerController, as shown in Figure 6.2. The
MPMediaPickerController enables the user to browse his artists, songs, playlists, and
albums to specify one or more songs that should be considered for playback. To use an
MPMediaPickerController, the class first needs to specify that it handles the delegate
MPMediaPickerControllerDelegate, which has two required methods. The first media-
Picker:didPickMediaItems: is called when the user has completed selecting the songs she
would like to hear. Those songs are returned as an MPMediaItemCollection object, and the
MPMusicPlayerController can directly take this object as a parameter of setQueueWith-
ItemCollection:. After a new queue has been set for the MPMusicPlayerController, it can
begin playing the new items. The MPMediaPickerController does not dismiss itself after

completing a selection and requires explicit use of `dismissViewControllerAnimated:`
`completion:`.

```
- (void) mediaPicker: (MPMediaPickerController *) mediaPicker
➥didPickMediaItems: (MPMediaItemCollection *) mediaItemCollection
{
    if (mediaItemCollection)
    {
        [player setQueueWithItemCollection: mediaItemCollection];
        [player play];
    }

    [self dismissViewControllerAnimated:YES completion:nil];
}
```

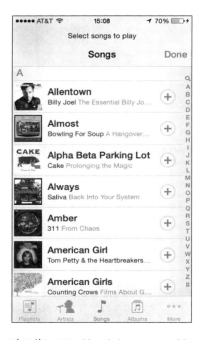

Figure 6.2   Selecting songs using the `MPMediaPickerController` in iOS 8.

In the event that the user cancels or dismisses the `MPMediaPickerController` without making
a selection, the delegate method `mediaPickerDidCancel:` is called. The developer is required
to dismiss the `MPMediaPickerController` as part of this method.

```
- (void) mediaPickerDidCancel: (MPMediaPickerController *) mediaPicker
{
    [self dismissViewControllerAnimated:YES completion:nil];
}
```

After the delegate methods have been implemented, an instance of MPMediaPickerController can be created. During allocation and initialization of a MPMediaPickerController, a parameter for supported media types is required. A full list of the available options is shown in Table 6.2. Note that each media item can be associated with multiple media types. Additional optional parameters for the MPMediaPickerController include specifying the selection of multiple items, and a prompt to be shown during selection, shown in Figure 6.2. An additional Boolean property also exists for setting whether iCloud items are shown; this is defaulted to YES.

```objc
- (IBAction)mediaPickerButtonAction:(id)sender
{
    MPMediaPickerController *mediaPicker =
    ➥[[MPMediaPickerController alloc] initWithMediaTypes:
    ➥MPMediaTypeAny];

    mediaPicker.delegate = self;
    mediaPicker.allowsPickingMultipleItems = YES;
    mediaPicker.prompt = @"Select songs to play";

    [self presentViewController:mediaPicker animated:YES completion:
    ➥nil];
}
```

Table 6.2 **Available Constant Accepted During the Specification of Media Types When a New MPMediaPickerController Is Created**

Constant	Definition
MPMediaTypeMusic	Any type of music media item
MPMediaTypePodcast	An audio podcast media item
MPMediaTypeAudioBook	An audiobook media item
MPMediaTypeAudioITunesU	Audio media type associated with iTunes U
MPMediaTypeAnyAudio	Any audio media type
MPMediaTypeMovie	A media item that contains a movie
MPMediaTypeTVShow	A media item that contains a TV show
MPMediaTypeVideoPodcast	A video podcast, not to be confused with audio podcast (MPMediaTypePodcast)
MPMediaTypeMusicVideo	A music video media item
MPMediaTypeVideoITunesU	Video media from iTunes U, not to be confused with an audio iTunes U item (MPMediaTypeAudioITunesU)
MPMediaTypeAnyVideo	Any video media item
MPMediaTypeAny	Any media item both video and audio

These are all the steps required to enable a user to pick songs for playback using the MPMediaPickerController; however, in many circumstances it might be necessary to provide a custom user interface or select songs with no interface at all. The next section covers these topics.

Programmatic Picker

Often, it might be required to provide a more customized music selection option to a user. This might include creating a custom music selection interface or automatically searching for an artist or album. In this section the steps necessary to provide programmatic music selection are discussed.

To retrieve songs without using the MPMediaPickerController, a new instance of MPMediaQuery needs to be allocated and initialized. The MPMediaQuery functions as a store that references a number of MPMediaItems, each of which represents a single song or audio track to be played.

The sample app provides two methods that implement an MPMediaQuery. The first method, playRandomSongAction:, will find a single random track from the user's music library and play it using the existing MPMusicPlayerController. Finding music programmatically begins by allocating and initializing a new instance of MPMediaQuery.

Playing a Random Song

Without providing any predicate parameters, the MPMediaQuery will contain all the items found within the music library. A new NSArray is created to hold onto these items, which are retrieved using the item's method on the MPMediaQuery. Each item is represented by an MPMediaItem. The random song functionality of the sample app will play a single song at a time. If no songs were found in the query, a UIAlert is presented to the user; however, if multiple songs are found, a single one is randomly selected.

After a single (or multiple) MPMediaItem has been found, a new MPMediaItemCollection is created by passing an array of MPMediaItems into it. This collection will serve as a playlist for the MPMusicPlayerController. After the collection has been created, it is passed to the player object using setQueueWithItemCollection. At this point the player now knows which songs the user intends to listen to, and a call of play on the player object will begin playing the MPMediaItemCollection in the order of the array that was used to create the MPMediaItemCollection.

```
- (IBAction)playRandomSongAction:(id)sender
{
    MPMediaItem *itemToPlay = nil;
    MPMediaQuery *allSongQuery = [MPMediaQuery songsQuery];
    NSArray *allTracks = [allSongQuery items];

    if([allTracks count] == 0)
```

```
{
    UIAlertView *alert = [[UIAlertView alloc]
        initWithTitle:@"Error"
             message:@"No music found!"
            delegate:nil
    cancelButtonTitle:@"Dismiss"
    otherButtonTitles:nil];

    [alert show];
    return;
}

if ([allTracks count] == 1)
{
    itemToPlay = [allTracks lastObject];
}

int trackNumber = arc4random() % [allTracks count];
itemToPlay = [allTracks objectAtIndex:trackNumber];

MPMediaItemCollection * collection = [[MPMediaItemCollection
alloc] initWithItems:[NSArray arrayWithObject:itemToPlay]];

[player setQueueWithItemCollection:collection];
[player play];

[self updateSongDuration];
[self updateCurrentPlaybackTime];
}
```

Note

arc4random() is a member of the standard C library and can be used to generate a random number in Objective-C projects. Unlike most random-number-generation functions, arc4random is seeded automatically the first time it is called.

Predicate Song Matching

Often, an app won't just want to play random tracks and will want to perform a more advanced search. This is done using predicates. The following example uses a predicate to find music library items that have an artist property equal to "Bob Dylan", as shown in Figure 6.3. This method functions very similarly to the previous random song example, except that addFilterPredicate is used to add the filter to the MPMediaQuery. In addition, the results are not filtered down to a single item, and the player is passed an array of all the matching songs. For a complete list of available predicate constants, refer to the second column of Table 6.1 in the "Handling State Changes" section. Multiple predicates can be used with supplemental calls to addFilterPredicate on the MPMediaQuery.

```objc
- (IBAction)playDylan:(id)sender
{
    MPMediaPropertyPredicate *artistNamePredicate =
    [MPMediaPropertyPredicate predicateWithValue: @"Bob Dylan"
                                forProperty:
                    MPMediaItemPropertyArtist];

    MPMediaQuery *artistQuery = [[MPMediaQuery alloc] init];

    [artistQuery addFilterPredicate: artistNamePredicate];

    NSArray *tracks = [artistQuery items];

    if([tracks count] == 0)
    {
        UIAlertView *alert = [[UIAlertView alloc]
        initWithTitle:@"Error"
        message:@"No music found!"
        delegate:nil
        cancelButtonTitle:@"Dismiss"
        otherButtonTitles:nil];

        [alert show];
        return;
    }

    MPMediaItemCollection * collection = [[MPMediaItemCollection
    ➡alloc] initWithItems:tracks];

    [player setQueueWithItemCollection:collection];

    [player play];

    [self updateSongDuration];
    [self updateCurrentPlaybackTime];
}
```

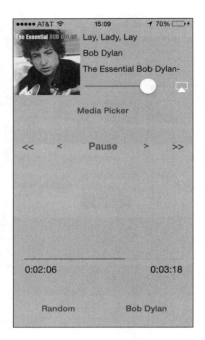

Figure 6.3   Using a predicate search to play tracks by the artist Bob Dylan.

Summary

This chapter covered accessing and working with a user's music library. The first topic covered was building a playback engine to enable a user to interact with the song playback, such as pausing, resuming, controlling the volume, and skipping. The next two sections covered accessing and selecting songs from the library. The media picker demonstrated using the built-in GUI to enable the user to select a song or group of songs, and the "Programmatic Picker" section dealt with finding and searching for songs using predicates.

The sample app demonstrated how to build a fully functional albeit simplified music player for iOS. The knowledge demonstrated in this chapter can be applied to creating a fully featured music player or adding a user's music library as background audio into any app.

7

Implementing HealthKit

People all over the world are becoming increasingly interested and concerned about their personal health, and they are leveraging technology to gain valuable insight. The rise of smartphones enabled common consumers to carry a computer with them wherever they went, and it wasn't long before a rush of third-party fitness and health apps followed.

Health-focused mobile apps were a $2.4 billion industry in 2013, and this is projected to grow to more than $20 billion by 2017. Each quarter more than 100,000 new health apps are published to the iTunes App Store, and until HealthKit it was complete chaos. Due to the sandboxing nature of the iOS platform, these apps haven't been able to share data with other third-party apps. This does not allow a user's sleep-tracking app to monitor his weight loss or exercise routines, or even allow his running app to track his nutritional intake.

HealthKit fixes this problem by providing a secure centralized location for the user's health information, from body measurements to workout data, and even food intake. This not only allows third-party apps to share data with each other, but, more important, makes it easy for a user to switch apps. Up until now, users were easily locked into a particular app since their data was all stored there; now they are free to switch to new and better solutions without the risk of losing their historical records. This is fantastic news for developers, because it removes a giant barrier to entry that was preventing new fitness and health apps to flourish.

Introduction to HealthKit

HealthKit was introduced with the rest of iOS 8 at Apple's WWDC 2014. At its core, HealthKit is a framework that allows apps to share and access health and fitness data. HealthKit also provides a system app that will be bundled with all new iOS 8 devices. This new Health app allows a user to see a consolidated dataset of all their health data taken from all compliant apps.

Specially designed HealthKit hardware devices also allow the direct storage of biometric data as well as directly interacting with newer iOS devices, which feature the M7 motion coprocessor chip. These hardware interactions are outside of the scope of this chapter; however, more information can be found in the HealthKit framework guide located at https://developer.apple.com/library/ios/documentation/HealthKit/Reference/HealthKit_Framework/index.html#//apple_ref/doc/uid/TP40014707.

It is important to remember that when working with HealthKit, the developer has access to personal and private information about the user. HealthKit is a permission-based service, and the user will need to grant the app permission to access each requested piece of information. After the app has access to the information, it is the developer's responsibility to treat that information as highly confidential and sensitive. A good guideline is to treat any health data as you would someone's credit card or Social Security information.

Introduction to Health.app

Before you can write a HealthKit-enabled app, you must first understand Health.app (see Figure 7.1), which comes bundled with iOS 8. Health.app provides the centralized access point to all the user's health data. Users are able to configure their Dashboard to see the metrics that they are interested in; for example, in Figure 7.1, the user is viewing steps, walking and running distance, and sleep analysis. The Health Data section further allows the users to see the individual stored data for every point of entry as well as letting them delete entries they no longer want to retain. The Sources tab allows users to configure which apps have access to which data, which is covered in the section "Requesting Permission for Health Data." Finally, the Medical ID tab allows the user to enter information that might be useful to first responders, such as allergies, emergency contact info, blood type, and medications. This Medical ID information is accessible from the lock screen without the user's passcode.

Figure 7.1   Dashboard section of the iOS Health.app.

The Sample App

The sample app that accompanies this chapter is called ICFFever. ICFFever is a simple HealthKit app that demonstrates the storage and retrieval of basic user info, such as age, height, and weight (see Figure 7.2). Additionally, the app showcases storing, retrieving, sorting, and working with body temperature data (see Figure 7.3). Although the functionality of the app has been kept simple to avoid overcomplication, it will showcase all the required key functionality of interacting with HealthKit data.

Figure 7.2   ICFFever Profile information entry screen.

Figure 7.3   ICFFever entering and viewing body temperature information.

Adding HealthKit to a Project

HealthKit is a standalone framework, and a new project must first be configured to work with HealthKit. This includes adding the proper entitlements, adding a key in your info plist to flag the app as HealthKit enabled, and linking to the HealthKit framework. Apple makes it easy to correctly enable all the proper settings in Xcode 6. While your project is open, select the project icon item from the project navigator and then navigate to the Capabilities section. Toggling the switch next to the HealthKit item will automatically configure your project.

In each class that will be working with HealthKit, the proper header will need to be first imported.

```
@import HealthKit;
```

HealthKit is a permission-based service; before the app can access or write any information, the user will need to grant his permission. To help facilitate this process, a single instance of an HKHealthStore is created in the sample app's app delegate. Each view controller will reference back to this object.

```
@property (nonatomic) HKHealthStore *healthStore;
```

ICFFever is a tab bar-based app and each tab will need to have access to the `HKHealthStore`. Inside the app delegate a method is provided which will populate that shared object to each of the view controllers. Depending on the nature and setup of each unique app, approaches to this might vary. Each view controller will need to create its own property for `healthStore`, which is demonstrated in the sample app.

```
(BOOL)application:(UIApplication *)application didFinishLaunchingWithOptions:
➡(NSDictionary *)launchOptions
{
            self.healthStore = [[HKHealthStore alloc] init];

            UITabBarController *tabBarController = (UITabBarController *)
        ➡[self.window rootViewController];

            for (UINavigationController *navigationController in
        ➡tabBarController.viewControllers)
            {
                id viewController = navigationController;

                if ([viewController respondsToSelector:@
            ➡selector(setHealthStore:)])
                {
                    [viewController setHealthStore:self.healthStore];
                }
            }

            return YES;
}
```

Requesting Permission for Health Data

After the groundwork has been laid to begin working with HealthKit, the app can request permission to access specific health data. This is a multiple-stage process, beginning with a simple check to make sure that HealthKit is available on the current device.

```
if ([HKHealthStore isHealthDataAvailable])
```

The next step is to generate a list of all the datasets the app will need to read and write to. Each point of information must be specifically requested and the user can opt to approve some but not all the data points. The sample app breaks this list generation into two convenience methods that will each return an `NSSet`.

```
// Returns the types of data that the app wants to write to HealthKit.
- (NSSet *)dataTypesToWrite
{
        HKQuantityType *heightType = [HKObjectType
    ➡quantityTypeForIdentifier:HKQuantityTypeIdentifierHeight];
```

```
    HKQuantityType *weightType = [HKObjectType
➥ quantityTypeForIdentifier:HKQuantityTypeIdentifierBodyMass];

    HKQuantityType *tempType = [HKObjectType
➥ quantityTypeForIdentifier:HKQuantityTypeIdentifierBodyTemperature];

    return [NSSet setWithObjects:tempType, heightType, weightType, nil];
}

// Returns the types of data that the app wants wishes to read from HealthKit.
- (NSSet *)dataTypesToRead
{
    HKQuantityType *heightType = [HKObjectType
➥ quantityTypeForIdentifier:HKQuantityTypeIdentifierHeight];

    HKQuantityType *weightType = [HKObjectType
➥ quantityTypeForIdentifier:HKQuantityTypeIdentifierBodyMass];

    HKQuantityType *tempType = [HKObjectType
➥ quantityTypeForIdentifier:HKQuantityTypeIdentifierBodyTemperature];

    HKCharacteristicType *birthdayType = [HKObjectType
➥ characteristicTypeForIdentifier:HKCharacteristicTypeIdentifierDateOfBirth];

    return [NSSet setWithObjects:heightType, weightType,
➥ birthdayType, tempType, nil];
}
```

ICFFever will request permission to write height, weight, and body temperature data. It will also be asking for permission to read height, weight, body temperature, and birthdate information. Keep in mind that it is possible for the app to be allowed to write data it doesn't have access to read, and to read data it doesn't have access to write.

> **Note**
>
> HealthKit contains a type of data point called a characteristic (`HKCharacteristicType`); these characteristics include gender, blood type, and birthday. HealthKit does not allow a third-party app to enter changes to these data points; changes and initial entry to them must be made within the Health.app, although third-party apps may read the data with the user's permission.

More than 70 types of data are currently available from HealthKit, ranging from items as common as weight to more detailed items such as inhaler usage and oxygen saturation. These items are readily available in the HealthKit documentation and in an effort to save trees (or bytes for e-books); they are not listed in this chapter.

After the app has built two `NSSet`s, one for reading data and one for writing, the app is ready to prompt the user for permission. The user is presented with a HealthKit permission request screen (see Figure 7.4) and will then select the permission set the user wants to grant. A user can make further changes to these permissions from within the Health.app at any time.

```
if ([HKHealthStore isHealthDataAvailable])
{
        NSSet *writeDataTypes = [self dataTypesToWrite];
        NSSet *readDataTypes = [self dataTypesToRead];

    [self.healthStore requestAuthorizationToShareTypes:writeDataTypes
➥readTypes:readDataTypes completion:^(BOOL success, NSError *error) {
        if (!success)
        {
            NSLog(@"HealthKit was not properly authorized to be added, check
          ➥ entitlements and permissions. Error: %@", error);

            return;
        }
    }];
}
```

Figure 7.4   A HealthKit permission request for writing body temperature, height, and weight, as well as reading body temperature, date of birth, height, and weight.

Reading Characteristic HealthKit Data

Assuming that the user has granted permission to read the data from the Health.app, the app can now begin to work with data that is already stored. The first tab of the sample app shows the user basic profile information. Because the date of birth cannot be modified from within a third-party app, that is a logical place to start with simple data reading. A new method called updateAge is created in the sample app. HealthKit provides a convenience method for quickly retrieving the user's date of birth named dateOfBirthWithError. Likewise, methods for the other characteristics data gender and blood type exist. The method follows basic error checking flow and, if no entry is found, lets the user know to enter her birthdate into the Health.app. After the data is retrieved as an NSDate, the year is stripped out of it and displayed to the user.

```
- (void)updateAge
{
    NSError *error = nil;
    NSDate *dateOfBirth = [self.healthStore dateOfBirthWithError:&error];

    if (!dateOfBirth)
    {
        NSLog(@"No age was found");
        dispatch_async(dispatch_get_main_queue(), ^{
                self.ageTextField.placeholder = @"Enter in HealthKit App";
        });
    }

    else
    {
        NSDate *now = [NSDate date];

        NSDateComponents *ageComponents = [[NSCalendar currentCalendar]
        components:NSCalendarUnitYear fromDate:dateOfBirth toDate:now
        options:NSCalendarWrapComponents];

        NSUInteger usersAge = [ageComponents year];

        self.ageTextField.text = [NSNumberFormatter localizedStringFromNumber:
    ➡ @(usersAge) numberStyle:NSNumberFormatterNoStyle];
    }
}
```

Reading and Writing Basic HealthKit Data

The sample app also enables the user to not only read in height and weight data but also provide updates to that data from within the app itself. ICFFever breaks this down into two separate steps; the first step is reading the data and the second is writing new data. To retrieve a new data point, first an `HKQuanyityType` object is created using the data point that will be retrieved, in the following example `HKQuantityTypeIdentifierBodyMass`.

Apple has graciously provided a convenience method for retrieving the most recent sample of an entry type; this method is included in the class `HKHealthStore+AAPLExtensions.m`. Assuming that there is weight data in the HealthKit data store, an `HKQuantity` object will be returned. The sample app specifies the units it would like to display. Here an `HKUnit` for a `poundUnit` is created, though the data could also be returned in grams, ounces, stones, or even molar mass. A double value is taken from the `HKQuantity` object after it has been specified what the data should be in pounds. That data is then displayed through a main thread dispatch, since HealthKit runs on a background thread.

```
- (void)updateWeight
{
        HKQuantityType *weightType = [HKQuantityType
    ➡ quantityTypeForIdentifier:HKQuantityTypeIdentifierBodyMass];

        [self.healthStore aapl_mostRecentQuantitySampleOfType:weightType
        ➡predicate:nil
        ➡completion:^(HKQuantity *mostRecentQuantity, NSError *error)
        {
                if (!mostRecentQuantity)
                {
                        NSLog(@"No weight was found");

                        dispatch_async(dispatch_get_main_queue(), ^{
                                self.weightTextField.placeholder = @"Enter in lbs";
                        });
                }
        else
        {
                HKUnit *weightUnit = [HKUnit poundUnit];
                double usersWeight = [mostRecentQuantity
                ➡doubleValueForUnit:weightUnit];

                dispatch_async(dispatch_get_main_queue(), ^{
                    self.weightTextField.text = [NSNumberFormatter
                    ➡localizedStringFromNumber:@(usersWeight)
                    ➡numberStyle:NSNumberFormatterNoStyle];
                });
        }
    }];
}
```

It is likely that the user does not have data saved for his weight yet; the ICFFever app also enables the user to save new weight data. Saving data is very similar to retrieving data; first an `HKUnit` needs to be defined to indicate what type of unit the data is being saved in. In the sample app the user will enter his weight in pounds.

A new `HKQuantity` is created with the type of unit and the value that is being saved. Next an `HKQuanityType` is created specifying which type of data point is being stored. Since the data is a type of weight, the `HKQuantityTypeIdentifierBodyMass` constant is used. Each data point is saved with a time stamp so that information can be charted and compared in the future; the assumption with the ICFFever app is that entered weight and height data is current. A new `HKQuantitySample` is created using the type, quantity, and date range. The health store object then calls `saveObject` and specifies a completion block. The method then can call the earlier method to display the newly entered weight.

```
(void)saveWeightIntoHealthStore:(double)weight
{
        HKUnit *poundUnit = [HKUnit poundUnit];

        HKQuantity *weightQuantity = [HKQuantity quantityWithUnit:poundUnit
        ➥doubleValue:weight];

        HKQuantityType *weightType = [HKQuantityType
        ➥quantityTypeForIdentifier:HKQuantityTypeIdentifierBodyMass];

        NSDate *now = [NSDate date];

         HKQuantitySample *weightSample = [HKQuantitySample
        ➥quantitySampleWithType:weightType quantity:weightQuantity
        ➥startDate:now endDate:now];

         [self.healthStore saveObject:weightSample withCompletion:
        ➥^(BOOL success, NSError *error)
         {
                if (!success)
                {
                    NSLog(@"An error occurred saving weight
                    ➥(%@): %@.", weightSample, error);
                }

                [self updateWeight];
        }];
}
```

The profile screen also enables the user to save and retrieve height information. The process is almost identical to the approach for weight, with a few differences. For height the app specifies an inch unit instead of a pound unit, and the `HKQuantity` type is `HKQuantityTypeIdentifierHeight` instead of `HKQuantityTypeIdentifierBodyMass`.

Reading and Writing Complex HealthKit Data

The preceding section discussed reading and writing very basic profile data such as height and weight information from or to HealthKit. This section dives deeper into data types and working with a more complex dataset, body temperature. The second tab of the ICFFever app enables the user to store current body temperature in either Celsius or Fahrenheit. The app will output not only the most recent body temperature but also the highest, lowest, and average over the past seven days.

HealthKit provides three unit types for working with body temperature, Kelvin, Fahrenheit, and Celsius. Since the app will be switching between Celsius and Fahrenheit, the data will be stored in Kelvin and then converted to the user's selection to display. Specifying a new data type each time the information is stored or retrieved can also solve this problem. There are merits to either system but working in a single unit should be less confusing when this new technology is being learned. A new method is provided to allow for quickly converting units from Kelvin for display.

```
-(double)convertUnitsFromKelvin:(double)kelvinUnits
{
    double adjustedTemp = 0;

    //Kelvin to F
    if([self.unitSegmentedController selectedSegmentIndex] == 0)
    {
        adjustedTemp = ((kelvinUnits-273.15)*1.8)+32;
    }

    //Kelvin to C
    if([self.unitSegmentedController selectedSegmentIndex] == 1)
    {
        adjustedTemp = kelvinUnits-273.15;
    }

    return adjustedTemp;
}
```

The first method will save the most recent temperature data; it is very similar to the methods that were used to save height and weight information. The method starts with converting the entered temperature from whatever units the user has selected to Kelvin. A new HKUnit is specified and set to kelvinUnit. The HKQuantity is created with the Kelvin temperature value, and the type is set to HKQuantityTypeIdentifierBodyTemperature. The current time is once again used for the data entry and the data is then saved into HealthKit.

```
-(void)updateMostRecentTemp:(double)temp
{
        double adjustedTemp = 0;
```

```objc
        //F to Kelvin
        if([self.unitSegmentedController selectedSegmentIndex] == 0)
        {
            adjustedTemp = ((temp-32)/1.8)+273.15;
        }

        //C to Kelvin
        if([self.unitSegmentedController selectedSegmentIndex] == 1)
        {
            adjustedTemp = temp+273.15;
        }

        // Save the user's height into HealthKit.
        HKUnit *kelvinUnit = [HKUnit kelvinUnit];

        HKQuantity *tempQuainity = [HKQuantity quantityWithUnit:kelvinUnit
        doubleValue:adjustedTemp];

        HKQuantityType *tempType = [HKQuantityType
➥ quantityTypeForIdentifier:HKQuantityTypeIdentifierBodyTemperature];

        NSDate *now = [NSDate date];

        HKQuantitySample *tempSample = [HKQuantitySample
➥ quantitySampleWithType:tempType

        quantity:tempQuainity startDate:now endDate:now];

     [self.healthStore saveObject:tempSample withCompletion:
➥^(BOOL success, NSError *error)
        {
            if (!success)
            {
                NSLog(@"An error occurred saving temp (%@): %@.",
               ➥ tempSample, error);
            }

               [self updateTemp];
    }];

}
```

> **Note**
>
> When a `HKQuantitySample` is being created, the option to attach metadata is also provided via the call `quantitySampleWithType:quantity:startDate:endDate:metadata:`. This metadata conforms to a number of predefined keys such as `HKMetadataKeyTimeZone`, `HKMetadataKeyWasTakenInLab`, `HKMetadataKeyBodyTemperatureSensorLocation`, or almost 20 other options. Custom keys can also be created that are specific to the need of each unique app.

Although the app allows for storing only the current body temperature, it also provides the user with insight into historical body temperatures. This process starts in the `updateTemp` method, which begins in the same fashion as retrieving height and weight information from the preceding section. A new `HKQuantityType` is created and set to `HKQuantityTypeIdentifierBodyTemperature`. Apple's convenience method for returning the most recent entry item is used again. If the call returns data, it is converted from Kelvin into the user's selected preference and displayed to the interface.

```
-(void)updateTemp
{
    HKQuantityType *recentTempType = [HKQuantityType
 ➥ quantityTypeForIdentifier:HKQuantityTypeIdentifierBodyTemperature];

    [self.healthStore aapl_mostRecentQuantitySampleOfType:recentTempType
 ➥predicate:nil completion:^(HKQuantity *mostRecentQuantity, NSError *error)
        {
            if (!mostRecentQuantity)
            {
                NSLog(@"No temp was found");

                dispatch_async(dispatch_get_main_queue(), ^{
                    self.recentTempLabel.text =
                    ➥@"Most Recent Temp: None Found";
                });
            }

            else
            {
                HKUnit *kelvinUnit = [HKUnit kelvinUnit];
                double temp = [mostRecentQuantity
                ➥ doubleValueForUnit:kelvinUnit];

                dispatch_async(dispatch_get_main_queue(), ^{
                    self.recentTempLabel.text = [NSString stringWithFormat:
                    ➥@"Most Recent Temp: %0.2f",
                    ➥[self convertUnitsFromKelvin:temp]];
                });
            }
        }];
```

This result, however, provides only a single entry for the most recent temperature; the app will need access to all the temperature data in order to compile the average as well as the lowest and highest entry points. To do this, a new method is created and added to the Apple extensions file. The heart of this new method is the `HKSampleQuery`. A new query is created with the passed-in `quantityType`. The limit is set to `0`, which indicates that all records for the specified type should be returned. The results will not be sorted since no sort descriptor is passed in; in addition, no predicate is supplied so items will not be filtered down. The result will return an `NSArray` of `HKQuantitySample` objects, each representing a body temperature entry.

```
-(void)allQuantitySampleOfType:(HKQuantityType *)quantityType
➥predicate:(NSPredicate *)predicate completion:
➥(void (^)(NSArray *, NSError *))completion
{
    HKSampleQuery *query = [[HKSampleQuery alloc]
  ➥initWithSampleType:quantityType predicate:nil
  ➥limit:0 sortDescriptors:nil resultsHandler:^(HKSampleQuery *query,
  ➥NSArray *results, NSError *error) {

if (!results)
      {
          if (completion)
          {
              completion(nil, error);
          }

          return;
      }

      if (completion)
      {
          completion(results, error);
      }
  }];

      [self executeQuery:query];
}
```

The existing `updateTemp` method can now be expanded. Since all the results will be in Kelvin, a new `HKUnit` is set up specifying that unit type. Some variables are also created to store values for max, min, item count, sum, and the average temperature. The method then loops through the entire result entry array. Each `HKQuantitySample` object contains a start date, an end date, and a quantity. These are compared for min and max against the other items and each value is stored. Additionally, all entries that occurred within the past 604,800 seconds (7 days) are summed and later averaged. After all the data is processed, the labels are updated on the main thread.

```
[self.healthStore allQuantitySampleOfType:recentTempType predicate:nil
➥completion:^(NSArray *results, NSError *error)
{
        if (!results)
        {
                NSLog(@"No temp was found");
        }

        else
        {
                HKUnit *kelvinUnit = [HKUnit kelvinUnit];

                double max = 0;
                double min = 1000;

                double sum  = 0;
                int numberOfSamples = 0;
                double averageTemp = 0;

                for(int x = 0; x < [results count]; x++)
                {
                        HKQuantitySample *sample = [results objectAtIndex: x];

                        if([[sample quantity] doubleValueForUnit:kelvinUnit] > max)
                        {
                                max = [[sample quantity]
                                ➥doubleValueForUnit:kelvinUnit];
                        }

                        if([[sample quantity] doubleValueForUnit:kelvinUnit] < min)
                        {
                                min = [[sample quantity]
                                ➥ doubleValueForUnit:kelvinUnit];
                        }

                        //7 days' worth of seconds
                        if ([[sample startDate] timeIntervalSinceNow] < 604800.0)
                        {
                                sum += [[sample quantity]
                                ➥ doubleValueForUnit:kelvinUnit];
                                numberOfSamples++;
                        }

                }

                averageTemp = sum/numberOfSamples;
```

```
            dispatch_async(dispatch_get_main_queue(), ^{
                self.highestTempLabel.text = [NSString stringWithFormat:
            ➡ @"Highest Temp: %0.2f", [self convertUnitsFromKelvin:max]];

                self.lowestTempLabel.text = [NSString stringWithFormat:
            ➡ @"Lowest Temp: %0.2f", [self convertUnitsFromKelvin:min]];

                self.avgTempLabel.text = [NSString stringWithFormat:
            ➡ @"Average Temp (7 Days): %0.2f", [self convertUnitsFromKelvin:
            ➡ averageTemp]];

        });
    }
}];
```

Summary

HealthKit is a fairly large topic, which can encompass a tremendous amount of data; however, the basic principles described in this chapter, such as reading and writing, hold true for even the most complex use cases. Despite the possibility of dozens of apps storing hundreds of data points into HealthKit each day, that data can be easy to parse and work with.

There are more than 70 unique data types in HealthKit today, and it is likely those will continue to expand with each major iOS revision. There is already a large amount of public outcry that certain data is not standard yet. The information provided in this chapter, as in the rest of this book, is designed to provide you with a kick start to development. Although this is not a definitive guide to HealthKit, it should be more than enough to get traction with the technology to create new apps that far exceed anything Apple had in mind when they created this technology.

Implementing HomeKit

HomeKit, introduced with iOS 8, offers a consistent way for apps to integrate with home automation technology. Instead of needing a separate app to interact with each type of home automation hardware, HomeKit-certified devices (even from different manufacturers, using different communication standards) can all be managed from a HomeKit app. In addition, HomeKit information set up on an iOS device in one app can be used by any other HomeKit app on the same device. That way, the user has to set up information about the home and home automation devices only once, and the information is available in a consistent way.

HomeKit offers remote access so that the user can interact with home automation technology from any connected location, with secure communication between the app and the home automation devices.

HomeKit also offers advanced techniques for organizing and managing home automation devices. For example, rooms can be organized into zones (like Upstairs Rooms and Downstairs Rooms), and then operations can be performed on all the accessories in a zone (like, Turn On Lights in the Upstairs Rooms). In addition, HomeKit offers triggers. Triggers can fire a set of actions at a set time or on a repeatable schedule.

HomeKit interactions can take place only in the foreground, except for triggers that are managed by iOS. This way, the user experience is preserved by ensuring that home automation actions are not taking place by competing background apps with potentially unexpected results.

The Sample App

The sample app for this chapter is called HomeNav. It supports adding homes to HomeKit, adding rooms to homes, adding accessories to homes, and associating accessories to rooms. Accessories can be inspected to see what services they offer, what characteristics are available for each service, and the values for each characteristic. HomeNav can also update characteristics for power settings and lock status, to turn devices on or off and to lock or unlock a door.

Introduction to HomeKit

HomeKit offers a consistent API for apps to set up and communicate with home automation devices. It bears repeating that the data which HomeKit stores about a home and associated devices is independent of any individual app; rather, it is available to all apps that use HomeKit. HomeKit APIs can be accessed only while an app is in the foreground, which prevents potential errors that could come from multiple apps updating HomeKit simultaneously in the background.

HomeKit provides access to home information through the `HMHomeManager` class. Through this class, an app can get access to information about home data available (instances of `HMHome`), and can be notified when homes are added or removed via delegate methods.

Homes in HomeKit can contain rooms (instances of `HMRoom`), which can then be organized into zones (`HMZone`). Rooms can belong to more than one zone; for example, a bathroom could belong to the Upstairs Rooms zone and the Bathrooms zone.

Home automation devices are represented by accessories (instances of `HMAccessory`), which must be discovered through an `HMAccessoryBrowser`. The browser can search locally for Wi-Fi and Bluetooth-capable devices that HomeKit can interact with, and return a list of accessories for display and selection. After an accessory has been added to a house, an app can inspect and update it. Accessories provide services (`HMService`), which are made up of characteristics (`HMCharacteristic`). For example, a coffeemaker accessory might have a coffeemaking service, a light service, and a clock service. The coffeemaker service might have a read-only characteristic that includes whether it is currently brewing, not brewing with heater on, or not brewing with heater off. It might then have a readable and writable characteristic that includes the desired state of the coffeemaker that an app can write in order to change the state of the coffeemaker.

Changes to characteristics can be grouped into action sets (`HMActionSet`), which can be executed all at once, or can be scheduled on a timer (`HMTimerTrigger`). Scheduled updates are the one exception to the rule that all HomeKit APIs must be called by a foreground app; because the schedule is maintained and executed by iOS, the app does not need to be in the foreground for scheduled updates to happen.

When a HomeKit-enabled app accesses HomeKit for the first time (meaning there is no home information set up in HomeKit currently), the app should be able to walk a user through the home setup process. This means that the app should prompt the user to set up a home, add rooms, and add accessories to rooms. The sample app takes a minimal approach to this by just prompting the user to add a home or room when none exists; an app in the store should walk the user through the process and make it simple and clear.

Setting Up HomeKit Components

To set up an app to use HomeKit, first enable the HomeKit capability in the project. Enabling the HomeKit capability requires a valid, paid developer account so that the needed entitlement can be added to the app identifier.

Developer Account Setup

Xcode needs iOS developer account information in order to connect to the Member Center and perform all the setup necessary for HomeKit on the developer's behalf. Select Xcode, Preferences from the Xcode menu, and then select the Accounts tab. To add a new account, click the plus sign in the lower left of the Accounts tab and select Apple ID. Enter the account credentials in the dialog shown in Figure 8.1 and click the Add button.

Figure 8.1   Xcode Accounts tab.

Xcode will validate the credentials and gather account information if valid. After a valid developer account is configured, Xcode will be able to perform the HomeKit capability setup steps.

Enabling HomeKit Capability

To set up the HomeKit capability, view the HomeNav Target in Xcode, click the Capabilities tab, and find the HomeKit section. Change the HomeKit switch to On, and Xcode will automatically create an entitlements file for the project and will configure the app identifier with the HomeKit entitlement, as shown in Figure 8.2. (Note that the app identifier will need to be changed from the sample app's app identifier to something unique before this will work.)

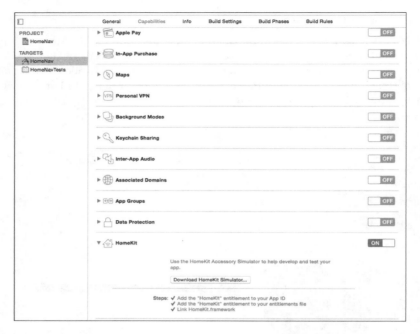

Figure 8.2   Xcode target capabilities—HomeKit.

After the HomeKit capability is enabled, Xcode will present a link to download the HomeKit Simulator, and will note the steps that were completed to enable the HomeKit capability. The HomeKit Simulator will be explained in the section "Testing with HomeKit Accessory Simulator," later in this chapter.

After the HomeKit capability is enabled, and there are checkmarks by all the listed steps, the app is ready to use HomeKit.

Home Manager

The Home Manager (instance of `HMHomeManager`) is the only way to get and update home information in HomeKit. An instance of `HMHomeManager` is needed to get the current homes that have been set up, to add a new home, or to remove an existing home. In addition, the `HMHomeManagerDelegate` protocol should be implemented when home information has been updated in HomeKit. In the sample app, this is done in `ICFHomeTableViewController`, in the `viewDidLoad` method.

```
self.homeManager = [[HMHomeManager alloc] init];
[self.homeManager setDelegate:self];
```

The home manager will update the list of available homes, and call the delegate method
homeManagerDidUpdateHomes: when the list of homes is available. The sample app will reload
the table view to display the most up-to-date home information. If no homes are set up, the
sample app will prompt the user to create a new home.

```
- (void)homeManagerDidUpdateHomes:(HMHomeManager *)manager {
    [self.tableView reloadData];

    if ([manager.homes count] == 0)
    {
        [self addHomeButtonTapped:nil];
    }
}
```

If the home manager has been called for the first time on the device, it will trigger a permission
check, as shown in Figure 8.3.

Figure 8.3   Sample app HomeKit permissions request.

Specifying Don't Allow will prevent HomeKit from providing any information to the app. This
setting can be changed in Settings.app in the Privacy, HomeKit section.

If the user is signed into an iCloud account on the device but has not turned on iCloud Keychain, HomeKit will prompt the user to turn on iCloud Keychain to allow access to HomeKit from all the user's iOS devices, as shown in Figure 8.4. If iCloud Keychain is not enabled, HomeKit will not function correctly and will receive an error for any HomeKit operations.

Figure 8.4   Sample app HomeKit Setup alert for iCloud Keychain.

Tip

In case other errors are encountered with HomeKit, the HomeKit Constants Reference on Apple's Developer Web site is available with a bit more detail about each error code.

Home

The sample app will prompt the user to add a home, as shown in Figure 8.5, if no homes have been set up in HomeKit. The user can also tap the Add (+) button at any time to add a new home.

Figure 8.5   Sample app Add Home dialog.

Tapping Add Home will grab the home name text from the text field, and request that the home manager add a new home with the name provided. The home name must be unique.

```
UITextField *homeNameTextField = addHomeAlertController.textFields.firstObject;
NSString *newHomeName = homeNameTextField.text;
__weak ICFHomeTableViewController *weakSelf = self;
[self.homeManager addHomeWithName:newHomeName
                completionHandler:^(HMHome *home, NSError *error)
{
    if (error)
    {
        NSLog(@"Error adding home: %@",error.localizedDescription);
    } else
    {
        NSInteger rowForAddedHome = [weakSelf.homeManager.homes indexOfObject:home];

        NSIndexPath *indexPathForAddedHome =
        ➥[NSIndexPath indexPathForRow:rowForAddedHome inSection:0];

        [weakSelf.tableView insertRowsAtIndexPaths:@[indexPathForAddedHome]
                            withRowAnimation:UITableViewRowAnimationAutomatic];
    }
}];
```

The home manager will call the completion handler with either an error or a new instance of HMHome. The logic will determine an index path for the new home, and animate it into the table view. The home can now be used to set up rooms and accessories.

If the user has set up a home by mistake or does not want to maintain the home any longer, the user can delete the home from the table view. The table view is set up to allow editing mode. When a delete edit action is received in the tableView:commitEditingStyle:forRowAtIndexPath: method, the home corresponding to the row will be deleted using the removeHome:completionHandler: method on the homeManager.

```
HMHome *homeToRemove = [self.homeManager.homes objectAtIndex:indexPath.row];
__weak ICFHomeTableViewController *weakSelf = self;

[self.homeManager removeHome:homeToRemove completionHandler:^(NSError *error) {

    [weakSelf.tableView deleteRowsAtIndexPaths:@[indexPath]
                            withRowAnimation:UITableViewRowAnimationAutomatic];

}];
```

After the home has been deleted, the completion handler block is used to delete the corresponding row from the table view. Note that deleting a home will delete all other related HomeKit objects, such as rooms and accessories tied to the home.

Rooms and Zones

Rooms in HomeKit (instances of HMRoom) represent a physical room in a home, such as kitchen, master bedroom, or living room. Rooms are also used to organize accessories; for example, the "front door lock" accessory might be in the foyer. To edit rooms for a home, the user can tap on the row for the home in the sample app. If the user is visiting the rooms view and no rooms have been set up for the home, the user will be prompted to add a room. The user will need to provide a room name that is unique within the home, and the method will add the room to the home using the addRoomWithName:completionHandler: method.

```
__weak ICFRoomTableViewController *weakSelf = self;
[self.home addRoomWithName:newRoomName completionHandler:
➡ ^(HMRoom *room, NSError *error)
{
    if (error)
    {
        NSLog(@"Error adding home: %@",error.localizedDescription);
    } else
    {
        NSInteger row = [weakSelf.home.rooms indexOfObject:room];

        NSIndexPath *addedRoomIndexPath =
        ➡ [NSIndexPath indexPathForRow:(row + 1) inSection:0];
```

```
    [weakSelf.tableView insertRowsAtIndexPaths:@[addedRoomIndexPath]
    ➥ withRowAnimation:UITableViewRowAnimationAutomatic];
    }
}];
```

After the room has been added, the completion handler will insert a new row in the table to display it. The table view will use the `rooms` property on the `self.home` instance to determine how many rows are in the table (an extra row is added for the "Tap to add new room" row):

```
- (NSInteger)tableView:(UITableView *)tableView
    ➥ numberOfRowsInSection:(NSInteger)section {
    return [self.home.rooms count] + 1;
}
```

The `rooms` property is an array of `HMRoom` instances. The table view will get the associated `HMRoom` instance for each row, and display the `name` property for it in the table cell.

```
- (UITableViewCell *)tableView:(UITableView *)tableView
        cellForRowAtIndexPath:(NSIndexPath *)indexPath {

    UITableViewCell *cell =
    ➥ [tableView dequeueReusableCellWithIdentifier:@"roomNameCell"
                                    forIndexPath:indexPath];

    if (indexPath.row == 0)
    {
        [cell.textLabel setText:@"Tap to add new room"];
    } else
    {
        NSInteger row = indexPath.row - 1;
        HMRoom *room = [self.home.rooms objectAtIndex:row];
        [cell.textLabel setText:room.name];
    }
    return cell;
}
```

To remove a room, the user can tap the Edit button to change the table view to editing mode, and tap the delete control for any existing room. In the `tableView:commitEditingStyle:forRowAtIndexPath:` method the selected room will be removed from the home:

```
HMRoom *roomToDelete = [self.home.rooms objectAtIndex:(indexPath.row - 1)];
[self.home removeRoom:roomToDelete completionHandler:^(NSError *error) {
    [tableView deleteRowsAtIndexPaths:@[indexPath]
                    withRowAnimation:UITableViewRowAnimationAutomatic];
}];
```

Zones (instances of `HMZone`) are logical groupings of rooms; no physical relationship is necessary between rooms in a zone. A zone can be used to organize rooms for convenient handling;
for example, a zone might be "upstairs" or "downstairs," or a zone might be "bedrooms" or
"bathrooms." The zone can be used to interact with all the rooms and accessories in the zone
together, such as "turn off the lights downstairs."

Zones are maintained on a home in much the same way that rooms are; they can be added to
and removed from a home, and there is a `zones` property on an `HMHome` instance. An `HMZone`
instance will have a `rooms` property that is an array of `HMRooms`; there are methods on `HMZone`
to add and remove an `HMRoom`.

Accessories

An accessory is a physical device that provides services. Examples include lights, switch
controls, coffeemakers, door locks, security system components such as motion sensors and
door sensors, and more. Accessory providers must complete a certification process for their
devices with Apple to work with HomeKit.

> ### Note
>
> In addition to individual devices, there is a special type of device in HomeKit called a *bridge*.
> A bridge is a HomeKit-compliant controller for other devices that are not HomeKit-compliant.
> HomeKit can communicate with the bridge to find out what devices are offered by the bridge,
> and then can use the bridge to communicate with those devices in a way that looks seamless
> to the user.

To add accessories to a home, an instance of `HMAccessoryBrowser` needs to be used to
scan the local environment for HomeKit-compliant accessories that have not been added.
In the sample app, the user can tap on a home, and then tap on accessories to see the
list of accessories currently associated with the home. To search for new accessories, the
user can tap Edit, then Search for New Accessories, which will present an instance of
`ICFAccessoryBrowserTableViewController`. This view controller will create an empty array
to be populated with accessories, and will instantiate an `HMAccessoryBrowser`.

```
self.accessoriesList = [[NSMutableArray alloc] init];
[self.tableView reloadData];

self.accessoryBrowser = [[HMAccessoryBrowser alloc] init];
[self.accessoryBrowser setDelegate:self];
[self.accessoryBrowser startSearchingForNewAccessories];
```

The `accessoryBrowser`'s delegate is set to handle when the accessory browser finds new
accessories:

```
- (void)accessoryBrowser:(HMAccessoryBrowser *)browser
    didFindNewAccessory:(HMAccessory *)accessory {
```

```
    [self.accessoriesList addObject:accessory];
    NSInteger rowAdded = [self.accessoriesList indexOfObject:accessory];
    NSIndexPath *addedIndexPath = [NSIndexPath indexPathForRow:rowAdded inSection:0];

    [self.tableView insertRowsAtIndexPaths:@[addedIndexPath]
    ➥withRowAnimation:UITableViewRowAnimationAutomatic];
}
```

Each new accessory found by the browser is added to the `accessoriesList` array, and then inserted into the table view for display, as shown in Figure 8.6.

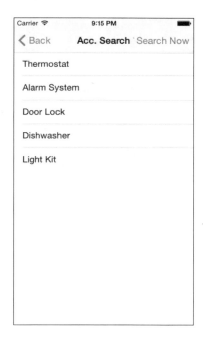

Figure 8.6   Sample app: list of accessories found by the accessory browser.

When the user taps on one of the accessories, an alert controller will be presented to request a name for the accessory that is meaningful to the user. For example, the user might want to add the Door Lock accessory, and give it a more specific name, such as Front Door Lock, as shown in Figure 8.7.

Figure 8.7   Sample app: adding an accessory.

When the user has provided a name, the action block for the alert controller will attempt to add the accessory to the home.

```
UITextField *accNameTextField = addAccAlertController.textFields.firstObject;
NSString *newAccName = accNameTextField.text;
[self.home addAccessory:selectedAccessory completionHandler:^(NSError *error) {
    . . .
}];
```

When the `addAccessory:` method is called on `self.home`, the pairing process will be initiated by HomeKit. HomeKit will present another alert controller to request the pairing code from the user, as shown in Figure 8.8.

Figure 8.8   Sample app: HomeKit accessory pairing.

If the pairing code provided by the user matches the pairing code for the device, the accessory will be added to the home (see the section "Testing with HomeKit Accessory Simulator," later in the chapter, for more information on the pairing code). If not, or if the user cancels the pairing request, an instance of NSError will be returned in the completion handler for the addAccessory: method. If the accessory was successfully added to the home, it will be renamed using the name provided by the user for the accessory (from Figure 8.7) in the completion handler for adding the accessory.

```
if (!error) {
    [selectedAccessory updateName:newAccName completionHandler:^(NSError *error) {
        if (error) {
            NSLog(@"Error updating name for selected accessory");
        }
    }];
} else {
    NSLog(@"Error adding selected accessory");
}
```

After an accessory has been added to a home, it should also be added to a room in the home. By default, it is added to a room for the whole home; in the sample app, the user can tap the accessory that was just added in the accessory list to view the detail for it, as shown in Figure 8.9.

Figure 8.9   Sample app: accessory detail.

The user can then tap the room to select another room, as shown in Figure 8.10.

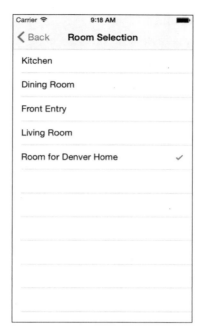

Figure 8.10   Sample app: select a room for the accessory.

When the user selects a room from the choices, the `tableView:didSelectRowAtIndexPath:` method will assign the accessory to the selected room on `self.home`. The selected room can be either a room in the `rooms` property for `self.home` or the `roomForEntireHome`.

```
HMRoom *selectedRoom = nil;
if (indexPath.row < [self.home.rooms count])
{
    selectedRoom = [self.home.rooms objectAtIndex:indexPath.row];
} else
{
    selectedRoom = [self.home roomForEntireHome];
}

[self.home assignAccessory:self.accessory
                    toRoom:selectedRoom
         completionHandler:^(NSError *error) {
    if (error)
    {
        NSLog(@"Error assigning accessory to room: %@", error.localizedDescription);
    }
}];
```

Services and Service Groups

Services are the functions that accessories perform. Services (instances of `HMService`) have a name, a service type, a reference to the containing accessory, and a list of characteristics that fulfill the service. Accessories typically have an information service that describes the accessory, and then at least one functional service that reports the status of the service and allows interaction with the service.

Characteristics are individual data points about a service. Characteristics (instances of `HMCharacteristic`) have a characteristic type, a reference to the containing service, an array of properties, and metadata.

The `characteristicType`, represented by a string constant, indicates the specific type of data for a characteristic and the meaning of that data. For example, a power state characteristic type (`HMCharacteristicTypePowerState`) means that the data for the characteristic is a `BOOL` value representing a power state of on or off. Alternatively, a characteristic type of `HMCharacteristicTypeCurrentTemperature` is a `float` value representing the current temperature reported by the accessory. There are characteristic types represented by several data types appropriate to the characteristic.

The properties array indicates whether the characteristic is readable, writable, or support event notification. A characteristic might support a combination of properties; for example, a brightness setting for a light bulb might be readable, be writable, and support event notification, whereas the model name of the light bulb might only be readable. A special case to be aware of is the Identify characteristic that is commonly available on accessories. Identify is typically a write-only characteristic; it can be used to instruct the accessory to identify itself using an appropriate method like flashing a light or making a noise. This is much better for users attempting to sort out similar accessories than having to read and compare serial numbers.

When the user selects an accessory that has already been added to a home in the sample app, the accessory detail view (`ICFAccessoryDetailTableViewController`) displays a section for the room that the accessory is assigned to, and then a section for each service that the accessory contains. The name of the service is displayed in the section header, and then information about the characteristics making up the service is displayed in the rows for the section, as shown in Figure 8.11.

To change the value of a characteristic, the user can tap on a supported table cell. As shown in Figure 8.12, the user has tapped on the Power State cell to turn off the light bulb.

Figure 8.11   Sample app: accessory services and characteristics.

Figure 8.12   Sample app: Operate Light.

To turn on the light bulb, the action block for the alert controller will use the `writeValue:completionHandler:` method on the characteristic:

```
[characteristic writeValue:[NSNumber numberWithBool:targetState]
        completionHandler:^(NSError *error) {
            if (error) {
                NSLog(@"Error changing state: %@",error.localizedDescription);
            } else {
                [self.tableView reloadRowsAtIndexPaths:@[indexPath]
                  ➡withRowAnimation:UITableViewRowAnimationAutomatic];
            }
}];
```

The `writeValue:completionHandler:` method can accept any `id` value, but will work only if the value passed is appropriate for the characteristic. The sample app approaches this simply by checking the characteristic type and using separate methods to handle different characteristic types; but any approach that ensures the correct value for a characteristic type will work.

A service group (instance of `HMServiceGroup`) provides a way to group services across accessories for easy management. A service group contains a name and an array of services (instances of `HMService`). Services can be added to or removed from a service group using the `addService:completionHandler:` and `removeService:completionHandler:` methods. Then a service group can be added to an `HMHome` instance and managed from there.

Actions and Action Sets

Actions and action sets currently provide a quick way to update characteristics on a group of accessories. This can be used to turn off all the light bulbs in the kitchen, or lock all the doors in the home.

`HMAction` is an abstract class with just one concrete implementation, `HMCharacteristicWriteAction`. Instances of `HMCharacteristicWriteAction` can be created using the `initWithCharacteristic:targetValue:` method, and then added to an instance of `HMActionSet`.

An instance of `HMActionSet` contains a name, an array of actions (instances of `HMAction`), and a property called `executing`. Actions can be added to or removed from an action set using the `addAction:completionHandler` and `removeAction:completionHandler:` methods. An action set is created by adding to an `HMHome`.

```
[self.home addActionSetWithName:@"Turn On Lights"
            completionHandler:^(HMActionSet *actionSet, NSError *error) {
    if (!error) {

        HMCharacteristicWriteAction *writeAction =
        ➡[[HMCharacteristicWriteAction alloc] initWithCharacteristic:characteristic
        ➡targetValue:[NSNumber numberWithBool:YES]];

        [actionSet addAction:writeAction completionHandler:^(NSError *error) {
            if (error) {
```

```
            NSLog(@"Error adding action to actionSet: %@",
            ➥error.localizedDescription);
        }
    }];
}
}];
```

An action set can then be added to a trigger to be executed on a schedule, or executed immediately with the `executeActionSet:` method on `HMHome`.

Testing with the HomeKit Accessory Simulator

At the time of writing, no HomeKit-compliant devices had been announced or were available. So a valid question is, how can a developer build and test a HomeKit app without any devices? Fortunately, Apple anticipated this issue and offers a solution: the HomeKit Accessory Simulator. The HomeKit Accessory Simulator is a Mac OS X app that enables a developer to set up any kind of HomeKit accessory virtually, and then interact with that accessory as if it were the real thing. The simulator advertises accessories over the network just as if they were the real thing, and enables HomeKit apps to connect to and communicate with the accessories.

To get the HomeKit Accessory Simulator, visit the Capabilities tab for the target in Xcode (as shown in Figure 8.2 earlier in the chapter). If the HomeKit capability has been enabled, there will be a button titled Download HomeKit Simulator in the HomeKit capability information. Tapping that button will navigate to the "Downloads for Apple Developers" section in the Apple developer Web site (registration required). Find and download the "Hardware IO Tools for Xcode" item, which includes the HomeKit Accessory Simulator. After it has downloaded, extract the simulator and install in `/Applications`.

When the HomeKit Accessory Simulator is first launched, there will be no data in it. To use the simulator, a new accessory (or bridge) must be added. To add an accessory, tap the plus (+) button in the lower-left corner of the app and select New Accessory. HomeKit will present an action sheet with information needed for a new accessory, as shown in Figure 8.13.

Figure 8.13   HomeKit Accessory Simulator: new accessory.

Provide an accessory name and a manufacturer name for the accessory, and click Finish (note that the simulator will provide a model and serial number). The simulator will add the accessory, which will then be visible in the list of accessories in the left section. Select the accessory and note the accessory information service visible with information about the accessory. Click Add Service to add a service to the accessory, and select a type of service to add when prompted. The simulator will add the service and standard characteristics to the accessory, as shown in Figure 8.14.

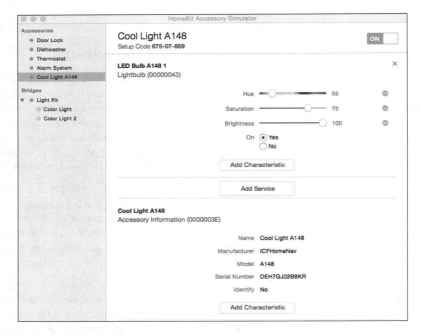

Figure 8.14   HomeKit Accessory Simulator: Accessory Information.

Characteristic information can be edited directly, and will be reflected in the HMCharacteristic information available to an app. The accessory can be turned on and off with the switch in the upper-right corner; when the accessory is on, it will be discoverable in the HMAccessoryBrowser. The Setup Code, shown just below the accessory name, is used to pair the accessory to the app when HomeKit requests a code for the accessory (refer to Figure 8.8).

When characteristic values are changed in an app that has paired with accessories from the HomeKit Accessory Simulator, those changes will be visible immediately in the simulator.

Scheduling Actions with Triggers

Triggers provide a way to kick off HomeKit-related actions when criteria are met. Currently, HomeKit supports a timer trigger (`HMTimerTrigger`), which can fire at a specified time and date, or with a recurrence interval from a time and date. This type of trigger is the only way to update HomeKit without an app being active in the foreground responding to user activity. HomeKit timer triggers are managed by iOS.

Triggers are based on action sets, as described previously in "Actions and Action Sets." To implement a trigger, first create actions and action sets as desired that should be executed by the trigger. Then initialize a trigger using the `initWithName:fireDate:timeZone:recurrence:recurrenceCalendar:` method. Add action sets to the trigger using the `addActionSet:completionHandler:` method. When the trigger is ready, call the `enable:completionHandler:` method to enable the trigger. When the trigger is enabled, it will fire on the specified fire date (and at each recurrence interval) and execute the attached action sets.

Scheduled triggers can be a great way to perform actions on a schedule, like turning holiday lights on in the evening and off in the morning, ensuring that home and garage doors are closed and locked after leaving for work, or even running a sprinkler system or fish feeding system while on vacation.

Because the triggers are maintained by iOS, the app does not need to be running in order for the triggered actions to occur.

Summary

This chapter looked at using HomeKit in an app. It covered the basic concepts of HomeKit and how to set up a project to use HomeKit. This chapter described all the components of HomeKit, how to set each of them up in an app, and how to maintain them. It explained how to set up and use the HomeKit Accessory Simulator to test a HomeKit-enabled app, and how to use triggers to schedule actions that run independently of a HomeKit app.

9

Working with and Parsing JSON

JSON is a great way to send data back and forth between servers, Web sites, and iOS apps. It is lighter and easier to handle than XML, and with iOS's built-in support for JSON, it is easy to integrate into an iOS project. Many popular Web sites, including Flickr, Twitter, and Google, offer APIs that provide results in JSON format, and many languages offer JSON support. This chapter demonstrates how to parse and present JSON from a sample message-board server in an app, and encode a new message entry in JSON to send to the server.

JSON

JavaScript Object Notation (JSON) is a lightweight format for sharing data. It is technically a part of the language JavaScript and provides a way to serialize JavaScript objects; however, practically, it is supported in a wide variety of programming languages, making it a great candidate for sharing data between different platforms. JSON also has the benefit of being human-readable.

JSON has a simple and intuitive syntax. At its most basic level, a JSON document can contain *objects,* which are essentially key-value dictionaries like what Objective-C programmers are familiar with, or arrays. JSON can contain arrays of objects and arrays of values, and can nest arrays and objects. Values stored in JSON, either in arrays or associated with a key, can be other JSON objects, strings, numbers, or arrays, or `true`, `false`, or `null`.

Benefits of Using JSON

There are many reasons to use JSON in an iOS app:

- **Server Support:** Communicating information to and from a remote server is a common use case for iOS apps. Since so many server languages have built-in support for JSON, it is a natural choice as a data format.

- **Lightweight:** JSON has little formatting overhead when compared to XML and can present a significant savings in the amount of bandwidth needed to transmit data between a server and a device.

- **iOS Support:** JSON is now fully supported as of iOS 5 with the addition of the `NSJSONSerialization` class. This class can conveniently provide an `NSDictionary` or `NSArray` (or even mutable varieties) from JSON data or can encode an `NSDictionary` or `NSArray` into JSON.

- **Presentation and Native Handling:** The simplest method to get data from a server to an iOS device is just to use a `UIWebView` and display a Web page; however, this approach has drawbacks in terms of performance and presentation. In many cases it is much better to just pull the data from the server, and present it on the device using native tools like `UITableView`. Performance can be much better, and presentation can be optimized to work on iOS screen sizes and take advantage of available retina displays.

JSON Resources

For more information on JSON, visit http://json.org. That site has a formal definition of JSON, with specific information on format and syntax.

The Sample App

The sample app for this chapter is Message Board, including a Ruby on Rails server and an iOS app.

The Ruby on Rails server consists of just one object: the message. It has been set up to support sending a list of messages in JSON, and to accept new messages in JSON format. The server also supports Web-based interactions.

The iOS app will pull messages from the server and display them in a standard table view and will be able to post new messages to the server in JSON format.

Accessing the Server

To view the Message Board Ruby on Rails server, visit http://freezing-cloud-6077.herokuapp. com/. The Messages home screen will be visible, as shown in Figure 9.1.

The messages server has been set up to handle creating and displaying messages on the Web and with JSON.

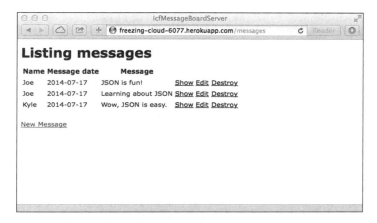

Figure 9.1   Messages home screen.

Getting JSON from the Server

To update the sample iOS app to handle JSON, the first thing to address is pulling the message list from the server and displaying it.

Building the Request

First, set up the URL so that the app can make calls to the right location:

```
NSString *const kMessageBoardURLString =
➥@"http://freezing-cloud-6077.herokuapp.com/messages.json";
```

In the `ICFViewController.m` implementation, look at the `viewWillAppear:` method. This code will initiate the request to the server:

```
NSURL *msgURL = [NSURL URLWithString:kMessageBoardURLString];
NSURLSession *session = [NSURLSession sharedSession];

NSURLSessionTask *messageTask = [session dataTaskWithURL:msgURL
  ➥completionHandler:^(NSData *data, NSURLResponse *response, NSError *error) {
  ...
}];
[messageTask resume];
```

This creates and initiates a network request to the `messages.json` resource at the server URL. The network request will run asynchronously, and when data comes back the completion handler block will be called. The important thing to note is that nothing special is required here for JSON; this is a standard network call. The only difference is that the `.json` extension used in the URL tells the server that the response should be in JSON format. Other servers might use a `Content-Type` and/or `Accept` HTTP header that specifies `application/json` as the mime-type to indicate that a JSON response is desired.

> **Note**
>
> Using the `.json` extension is not required for servers to return JSON format data; that is just how the sample server was set up. It is a common approach but is not required.

Inspecting the Response

When the network request has returned, the completion handler will be called. In the sample app, the data is converted into a UTF-8 string so that it can be logged to the console. This should not be done for every request in a production app; it is done here to demonstrate how to see the response for debugging when a problem parsing JSON is encountered.

```
NSString *retString =
➥ [NSString stringWithUTF8String:[data bytes]];

NSLog(@"json returned: %@", retString);
```

The log message will display on the console the data received:

```
json returned: [{"message":{"created_at":"2012-04-29T21:59:28Z",
"id":3, "message":"JSON is fun!", "message_date":"2012-04-29",
"name":"Joe","updated_at":"2012-04-29T21:59:28Z"}},
{"message":{"created_at":"2012-04-29T21:58:50Z","id":2,
"message":"Learning about JSON", "message_date":"2012-04-
29","name":"Joe", "updated_at":"2012-04-29T21:59:38Z"}},
{"message":{"created_at":"2012-04-29T22:00:00Z","id":4,
"message":"Wow, JSON is easy.", "message_date":"2012-04-
29","name":"Kyle", "updated_at":"2012-04-29T22:00:00Z"}},
{"message":{"created_at":"2012-04-29T22:46:18Z","id":5,
"message":"Trying a new message.", "message_date":"2012-04-
29","name":"Joe", "updated_at":"2012-04-29T22:46:18Z"}}]
```

Parsing JSON

Now that JSON has been received from the server, it is just a simple step to parse it. In the case of the sample app, an array of messages is expected, so parse the JSON into an `NSArray`:

```
NSError *parseError = nil;
NSArray *jsonArray =
➥ [NSJSONSerialization JSONObjectWithData:data
                         options:0
                           error:&parseError];
```

```
if (!parseError) {
    [self setMessageArray:jsonArray];
    NSLog(@"json array is %@", jsonArray);
} else {
    NSString *err = [parseError localizedDescription];
    NSLog(@"Encountered error parsing: %@", err);
}
```

NSJSONSerialization's method JSONObjectWithData:options:error: expects as parameters the data to be serialized, any desired options (for example, returning a mutable array instead of a regular array), and a reference to an NSError in case there are any parsing errors.

In this example, a local instance variable has been updated to the just-parsed array, the table view has been told to reload data now that there is data to display, and the activity view has been hidden. Note that the completion handler will most likely be called on a background queue, so if the user interface will be updated, it will be necessary to switch to the main queue.

```
dispatch_async(dispatch_get_main_queue(), ^{
    [self.messageTable reloadData];
    [self.activityView setHidden:YES];
    [self.activityIndicator stopAnimating];
});
```

Displaying the Data

Now that the JSON has been parsed into an NSArray, it can be displayed in a UITableView. The magic here is that there is no magic; the JSON received from the server is now just an array of NSDictionary instances. Each NSDictionary contains information for a message from the server, with attribute names and values. To display this in a table, just access the array and dictionaries as if they had been created locally.

```
- (UITableViewCell *)tableView:(UITableView *)tableView
        cellForRowAtIndexPath:(NSIndexPath *)indexPath
{
    UITableViewCell *cell =
    ➡ [tableView dequeueReusableCellWithIdentifier:@"MsgCell"];

    if (cell == nil) {
        cell = [[UITableViewCell alloc]
                ➡initWithStyle:UITableViewCellStyleSubtitle
                ➡reuseIdentifier:@"MsgCell"];

        cell.selectionStyle = UITableViewCellSelectionStyleNone;
    }
    NSDictionary *message =
    ➡ (NSDictionary *)[[self.messageArray
                    ➡objectAtIndex:indexPath.row]
                    ➡objectForKey:@"message"];
```

```
    NSString *byLabel =
➡  [NSString stringWithFormat:@"by %@ on %@",
➡  [message objectForKey:@"name"],
➡  [message objectForKey:@"message_date"]];

    cell.textLabel.text = [message objectForKey:@"message"];
    cell.detailTextLabel.text = byLabel;
    return cell;
}

- (NSInteger)tableView:(UITableView *)tableView
 numberOfRowsInSection:(NSInteger)section
{
    return [[self messageArray] count];
}
```

The parsed JSON data will be visible in a standard table view, as shown in Figure 9.2.

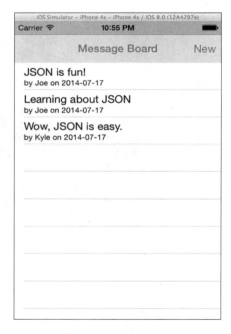

Figure 9.2   Sample app message table view.

Posting a Message

The sample app includes `ICFNewMessageViewController` to post new messages to the server. There are two fields on that controller: one for a name and one for a message (see Figure 9.3). After the user enters that information and hits Save, it will be encoded in JSON and sent to the server.

Figure 9.3   Sample app new message view.

Encoding JSON

An important detail for sending JSON to a Ruby on Rails server is to encode the data so that it mirrors what the Rails server provides. When a new message is sent to the server, it should have the same structure as an individual message received in the message list. To do this, a dictionary with the attribute names and values for the message is needed, and then a wrapper dictionary with the key "message" pointing to the attribute dictionary. This will exactly mirror what the server sends for a message. In the saveButtonTouched: method, set up this dictionary, like so:

```
NSMutableDictionary *messageDictionary =
➡ [NSMutableDictionary dictionaryWithCapacity:1];

[messageDictionary setObject:[nameTextField text]
                      forKey:@"name"];

[messageDictionary setObject:[messageTextView text]
                      forKey:@"message"];

NSDate *today = [NSDate date];

NSDateFormatter *dateFormatter =
➡ [[NSDateFormatter alloc] init];

NSString *dateFmt = @"yyyy'-'MM'-'dd'T'HH':'mm':'ss'Z'";
[dateFormatter setDateFormat:dateFmt];
[messageDictionary setObject:[dateFormatter stringFromDate:today]
                      forKey:@"message_date"];


NSDictionary *postDictionary = @{@"message" : messageDictionary};
```

Note that NSJSONSerialization accepts only instances of NSDictionary, NSArray, NSString, NSNumber, or NSNull. For dates or other data types not directly supported by NSJSONSerialization, they will need to be converted to a supported format. For example, in this example the date was converted to a string in a format expected by the server. Now that there is a dictionary, it is a simple step to encode it in JSON:

```
NSError *jsonSerializationError = nil;
NSData *jsonData = [NSJSONSerialization
                    ➡dataWithJSONObject:postDictionary
                    ➡options:NSJSONWritingPrettyPrinted
                    ➡error:&jsonSerializationError];

if (!jsonSerializationError)
{
    NSString *serJSON =
    [[NSString alloc] initWithData:jsonData
                          encoding:NSUTF8StringEncoding];

    NSLog(@"serialized json: %@", serJSON);
        ...
} else
{
```

```
      NSLog(@"JSON Encoding failed: %@",
            ➥ [jsonSerializationError localizedDescription]);
}
```

`NSJSONSerialization` expects three parameters:

1. An `NSDictionary` or `NSArray` with the data to be encoded.

2. Serialization options (in our case, we specified `NSJSONWritingPrettyPrinted` so that it's easy to read; otherwise, the JSON is produced with no whitespace for compactness).

3. A reference to an `NSError`.

If there are no errors encoding the JSON, it will look like this:

```
serialized json: {
  "message" : {
    "message" : "Six Test Messages",
    "name" : "Joe",
    "message_date" : "2012-04-01T14:31:11Z"
  }
}
```

Sending JSON to the Server

After the JSON is encoded, it is ready to be sent to the server. First, an instance of `NSMutableURLRequest` is needed. The request will be created with the URL for the server, and then will be customized with the HTTP method (`"POST"`) and HTTP headers to indicate that the uploaded content data is in JSON format.

```
NSURL *messageBoardURL =
➥ [NSURL URLWithString:kMessageBoardURLString];

NSMutableURLRequest *request = [NSMutableURLRequest
                               requestWithURL:messageBoardURL
                    cachePolicy:NSURLRequestUseProtocolCachePolicy
                  timeoutInterval:30.0];

[request setHTTPMethod:@"POST"];

[request setValue:@"application/json"
forHTTPHeaderField:@"Accept"];

[request setValue:@"application/json"
forHTTPHeaderField:@"Content-Type"];
```

When the request is completed, an `NSURLSessionUploadTask` can be created. The task requires the request, the JSON data, and a completion handler. The completion handler will be called on a background thread, so any user interface updates must be dispatched to the main queue.

```objc
NSURLSession *session = [NSURLSession sharedSession];

NSURLSessionUploadTask *uploadTask =
[session uploadTaskWithRequest:uploadRequest fromData:jsonData
➥ completionHandler:^(NSData *data, NSURLResponse *response, NSError *error) {

    NSHTTPURLResponse *httpResponse = (NSHTTPURLResponse *)response;
    BOOL displayError = (error || httpResponse.statusCode != 200);

    dispatch_async(dispatch_get_main_queue(), ^{
        [self.activityView setHidden:YES];
        [self.activityIndicator stopAnimating];
        if (displayError) {
            NSString *errorMessage = error.localizedDescription;
            if (!errorMessage) {
                errorMessage =
                ➥ [NSString stringWithFormat:@"Error uploading - http status: %i",
                ➥ httpResponse.statusCode];
            }

            UIAlertController *postErrorAlertController =
            ➥ [UIAlertController alertControllerWithTitle:@"Post Error"
                                          message:errorMessage
                                   preferredStyle:UIAlertControllerStyleAlert];

            [postErrorAlertController addAction:
            ➥ [UIAlertAction actionWithTitle:@"Cancel"
                              style:UIAlertActionStyleCancel
                            handler:nil]];

            [self presentViewController:postErrorAlertController
                               animated:YES
                             completion:nil];
        } else {
            [self.presentingViewController dismissViewControllerAnimated:YES
                                                     completion:nil];
        }
    });

}];
[uploadTask resume];
```

When `resume` is called on the `uploadTask`, the request will be made to the server, and the completion handler will be called when it is complete. Both the `error` returned in the completion handler and the `response` should be checked for errors; an `error` will be returned if there is a problem connecting (for example, the device is in airplane mode), or an HTTP status code might indicate a different problem if there is an issue on the server (for example, if the URL is not found, or if the server cannot process the data sent to it). If the request completes with no errors, the view controller will be dismissed and message board will be refreshed.

Summary

This chapter introduced JavaScript Object Notation (JSON). It explained how to request JSON data from a server in an iOS app, parse it, and display it in a table. The chapter also described how to encode an `NSDictionary` or `NSArray` into JSON, and send it over the network to a server.

10

Notifications

Notifications are Apple's method of keeping the user informed of important iOS app-related events when the user is not actively using an app. Because only one iOS app can be active and in the foreground at a time, notifications provide a mechanism to have inactive apps receive important and time-sensitive information and notify the user. This chapter guides you through how to set up your app to receive local and remote push notifications, and how to customize what happens when the user receives a notification with an app badge, a sound, and a message.

Differences Between Local and Push Notifications

Two types of notifications are supported by iOS: local notifications and remote, or push, notifications. Local notifications do not use or require any external infrastructure; they happen entirely on the device. That means that the device does not require any connectivity—besides being "on"—to present a local notification. Push notifications, however, require connectivity and a server infrastructure of some kind to send the notification through the Apple Push Notification service (APNs) to the intended device. It is important to note that push notification delivery is not guaranteed, so it is not appropriate to assume that every notification gets to its intended target. Do not make your application depend on push notifications.

To understand why push notification delivery is not guaranteed, you need to understand how push notifications get to a device. The APNs first will try to use the cellular network to communicate with an iOS device if it is available, and then will attempt over Wi-Fi. Some devices need to be in an active state (on fourth-generation iPod touches, for example, the screen actually has to be visible) in order to receive Wi-Fi communication. Other devices, like iPads, can be asleep and maintain a connection to a Wi-Fi network.

The process that each type of notification goes through is also different. For local notifications, these are the steps:

1. Create a local notification object, and specify options such as schedule time and date, message, sound, and badge update.

2. Schedule the local notification.

3. iOS presents the notification, plays a sound, and updates the badge.

4. Receive the local notification in the application delegate.

For push notifications, this is the process:

1. Register the application for push notifications and receive a token.

2. Notify your server that the device (identified by a token) would like to receive push notifications.

3. Create a push notification on your server and communicate to APNs.

4. APNs delivers the notification to the device.

5. iOS presents the notification, plays a sound, and updates the badge.

6. Receive the notification in the application's delegate.

With these differences, it is clear that there are different use cases in which local and push notifications make sense. If no information from outside the device is required, use a local notification. If information not available to the device is required, use a push notification.

The Sample App

The sample app for this chapter is called ShoutOut. It enables the user to prepare a test push message to the user's device and to add reminders to Shout Out. The sample app will illustrate setting up reminders as local notifications, as well as covering all the steps necessary to set up an app to receive push notifications, what information should be communicated to a push server, and how to have the server send push notifications via the APNs.

App Setup

There are several steps to prepare the app for remote push notifications. To begin, set up an App ID in the iOS Provisioning Portal. Visit the iOS Dev Center (https://developer.apple.com/devcenter/ios/index.action), log in, and choose Certificates, Identifiers & Profiles in the menu titled iOS Developer Program on the right side of the screen (you must be logged in to see this menu). Choose Identifiers from the menu on the left side of the screen. Then, click the button with a plus sign in the upper-right corner to create a new App ID, as shown in Figure 10.1.

Specify an App ID Description. The Description will be used to display the app throughout the iOS Provisioning Portal. Select an App ID Prefix (previously called the Bundle Seed ID). Scroll down to specify the App ID Suffix, as shown in Figure 10.2.

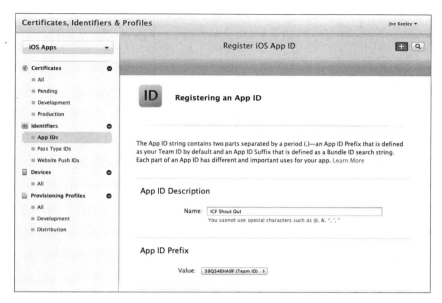

Figure 10.1   iOS Provisioning Portal: registering an App ID, App ID Description, and App ID Prefix.

App ID Suffix

◉ **Explicit App ID**

If you plan to incorporate app services such as Game Center, In-App Purchase, Data Protection, and iCloud, or want a provisioning profile unique to a single app, you must register an explicit App ID for your app.

To create an explicit App ID, enter a unique string in the Bundle ID field. This string should match the Bundle ID of your app.

Bundle ID: `com.explore-systems.icfshoutout`

We recommend using a reverse-domain name style string (i.e., com.domainname.appname). It cannot contain an asterisk (*).

○ **Wildcard App ID**

This allows you to use a single App ID to match multiple apps. To create a wildcard App ID, enter an asterisk (*) as the last digit in the Bundle ID field.

Bundle ID: _____

Example: com.domainname.*

Figure 10.2   iOS Provisioning Portal: registering an App ID, App ID Suffix.

Push notifications require an explicit App ID, so select that option and specify the same string as the Bundle ID for your app. Scroll down to select App Services, as shown in Figure 10.3.

Figure 10.3   iOS Provisioning Portal: registering an App ID, App Services.

Select the check box for Push Notifications in the list of App Services to indicate that push notifications should be enabled for the App ID. Click Continue to save the new App ID, and it will be visible in the list of App IDs. Click on the App ID to expand it and view the status of services for the App ID, as shown in Figure 10.4.

Now that the App ID is prepared, it needs to be configured for push notifications. Click Settings at the bottom of the App ID detail list, and scroll to the bottom to view the push notifications (see Figure 10.5).

Make sure that Enabled for Apple Push Notification service is checked. If so, the App ID is ready and push certificates can be created.

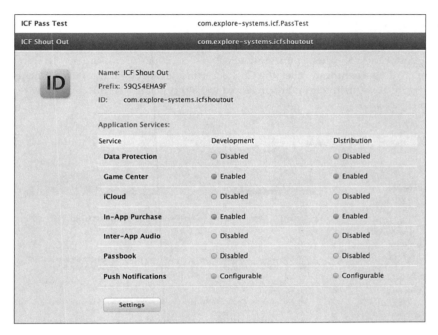

Figure 10.4   iOS Provisioning Portal: App ID in list.

Figure 10.5   iOS Provisioning Portal: App ID Push Notifications settings.

Creating Development Push SSL Certificate

A Development Push SSL Certificate is what the push server uses to identify and authorize a specific account to APNs when connecting to APNs to send push notifications. To start the process of creating a certificate, click the Create Certificate button on the Development line (refer to Figure 10.5). Instructions are presented to help generate a certificate signing request, as shown in Figure 10.6.

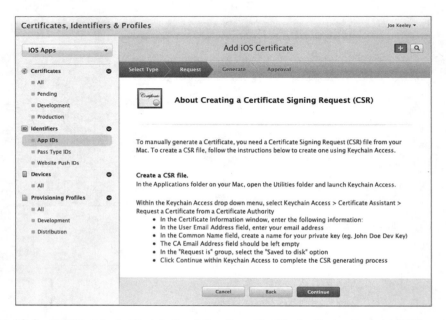

Figure 10.6   iOS Provisioning Portal: About Creating a Certificate Signing Request (CSR).

Leave the Add iOS Certificate page open in the browser, and open Keychain Access (in Applications, Utilities). Select Keychain Access, Certificate Assistant, Request a Certificate from a Certificate Authority from the application menu. A certificate request form will be presented, as shown in Figure 10.7.

Enter an email address and a common name (typically a company name or an entity name—it is safe to use your Apple Developer account name), and then select Saved to Disk. Click Continue, and specify where to save the request. When that step is complete, return to the iOS Provisioning Portal and click Continue. Select the saved request, as shown in Figure 10.8.

Figure 10.7   Keychain Access Certificate Assistant.

Figure 10.8   iOS Provisioning Portal: Add iOS Certificate: Generate Your Certificate.

After selecting it, click Generate. The development SSL Certificate will be generated, as shown in Figure 10.9.

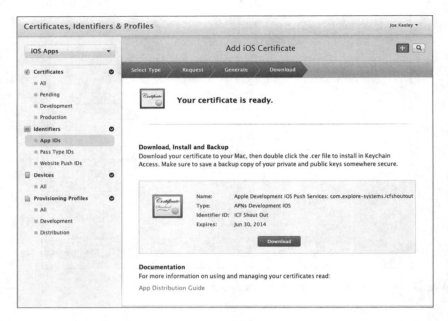

Figure 10.9   iOS Provisioning Portal: Add iOS Certificate: Your Certificate Is Ready.

After the certificate has been created, click the Download button to download the certificate so that the certificate can be installed on the notification server.

Double-click the downloaded certificate file, and it will automatically be installed in Keychain Access. It should be visible in the list of certificates, as shown in Figure 10.10. Click the triangle to confirm that the private key was matched with the certificate.

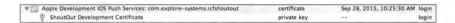

Figure 10.10   Keychain Access: Apple Development iOS Push Services SSL Certificate and private key.

Note that this procedure needs to be repeated to create Ad-Hoc and Production SSL Certificates when it is time to beta test and submit the application to the App Store.

The sample app includes a simple PHP file that can be executed from the command line to communicate with the APNs and send a test push notification. For that file to work, the certificate just generated needs to be converted into a format that can be included with an APNs request. This same conversion procedure will need to be performed for any server that communicates with APN. To convert the certificate, open Keychain Access and locate the certificate and key illustrated in Figure 10.10. Select them both, and choose File, Export Items. Save them as shoutout.p12 (any filename can be used with the p12 files). For communication with APNs, the certificate and key need to be in PEM format, so issue the following openssl command to convert them:

```
$ openssl pkcs12 -in shoutout.p12 –out shoutout.pem -nodes -clcerts
```

Copy the shoutout.pem file to the Xcode project Push Server group, and the sample app will be ready to send push notifications.

Development Provisioning Profile

For many apps, it is sufficient to use the team development provisioning profile automatically generated by Xcode to test on a device. To test push notifications, however, you need to create and use a development provisioning profile specific to the app to allow it to receive push notifications. To do this, click Provisioning Profiles in the left menu in the iOS Provisioning Portal.

> ### Note
>
> This presumes that a development certificate (under Certificates, Development) has already been created; if not, you should create one first. The procedure is well documented in the portal and similar to creating the SSL Certificate. This also presumes that you have set up at least one device for development in the portal; if not, you will need to do that as well (under Devices).

You are presented with a list of development provisioning profiles. To create a new one, click the button with the plus sign just above and to the right of the list. Select which type of provisioning profile to create (in this case, iOS App Development) and click Continue, as shown in Figure 10.11.

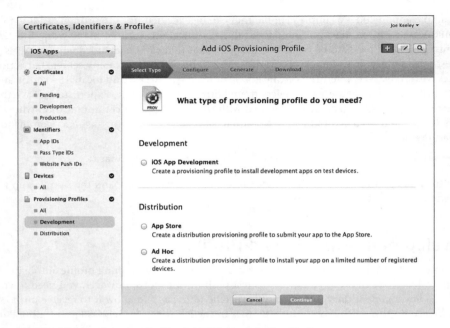

Figure 10.11   iOS Provisioning Profile: Add iOS Provisioning Profile.

Select the App ID just created, as shown in Figure 10.12, and click Continue.

Next, select the Development Certificate(s) to be used when signing the app with this provisioning profile, as shown in Figure 10.13, and click Continue.

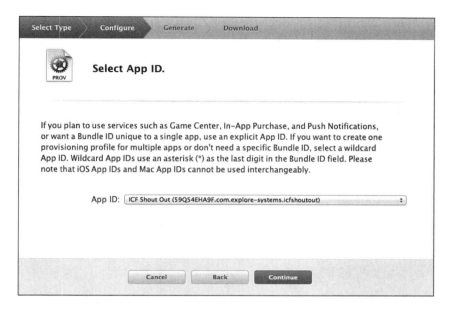

Figure 10.12   iOS Provisioning Profile: Add iOS Provisioning Profile: Select App ID.

Figure 10.13   iOS Provisioning Profile: Add iOS Provisioning Profile: Select Certificates.

Select the devices that can be used to run the app using this provisioning profile, as shown in Figure 10.14. It is generally a good practice to select all available devices to prevent having to regenerate the provisioning profile when it is discovered that a team member was not added the first time around.

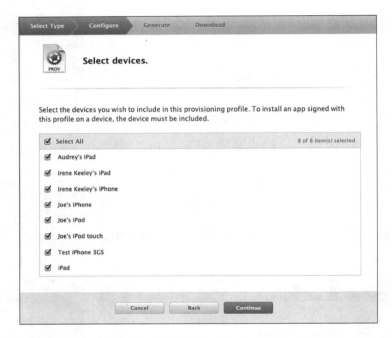

Figure 10.14   iOS Provisioning Profile: Add iOS Provisioning Profile: Select Devices.

Finally, provide a name for the provisioning profile, and review the summary presented for the provisioning profile, as shown in Figure 10.15. If the profile looks correct, click Generate to create it.

> **Note**
>
> Be descriptive with your provisioning profile name; these names tend to get confusing in Xcode when you have a lot of them. One approach is to use the app name and environment in the name, such as "ICF Shout Out Development."

Figure 10.15   iOS Provisioning Profile: Add iOS Provisioning Profile: Name This Profile and Generate.

When the provisioning profile has been created, a download page will be presented, as shown in Figure 10.16.

Click Download to get a copy of the provisioning profile. Double-click the profile after it is downloaded and it will be automatically installed and available in Xcode. One last step remains to make sure that the app is using the new provisioning profile. In Xcode, edit the Build Settings for your project (not the target). Find the section titled Code Signing, specifically Code Signing Identity. For Debug, choose iOS Developer under the Automatic section, as shown in Figure 10.17. To confirm that the provisioning profile is installed correctly on your system, check the Provisioning Profile section under the Code Signing Identity item and ensure that the provisioning profile is present in the list. Alternatively, select Preferences from the Xcode menu, and select Accounts. If your account information is not set up there, set it up. Select your account name and then View Details to see the provisioning profiles installed. Provisioning profiles can be refreshed directly from here rather than downloading directly from the portal; but provisioning profiles for individual apps must be created in the portal.

When that step is complete, you have completed all the configuration steps necessary on the app side to receive push notifications. Now you are ready to write some code.

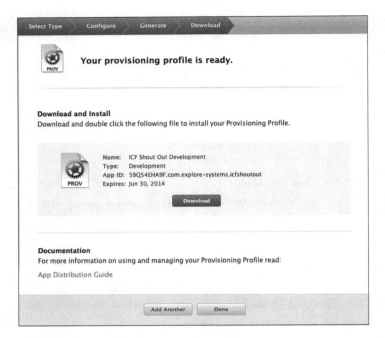

Figure 10.16   iOS Provisioning Profile: Your Provisioning Profile Is Ready.

Figure 10.17   Xcode Project Build Settings: Code Signing Identity.

Custom Sound Preparation

One detail that can really distinguish receipt of your push notification is a custom sound. iOS will play any specified sound less than 30 seconds in length if it is available in your app bundle. You can create a custom sound in GarageBand, for example (or any other audio app that can create sounds), and export the sound. It is worth exporting under each of the compression options to see what sounds good while meeting your size requirements (see Figure 10.18).

Figure 10.18   GarageBand: export song settings.

Now that you have a sound file, it will need to be converted to Core Audio format in order for your app to use it. Apple provides a command-line tool called afconvert that is up to the job. Open a Terminal session, navigate to the directory where the audio file is, and issue this command to convert your audio file to Core Audio format:

```
$ afconvert -f -caff -d ima4 shout_out.m4a shout_out.caf
```

This command will convert the `shout_out.m4a` file to ima4 format (which is a compressed format that works well on the device) and package it in a Core Audio–formatted sound file. When that process is complete, copy your new Core Audio format sound file into your Xcode project, and when it is specified in a notification, it will play.

Registering for Notifications

To enable the ShoutOut app to receive remote notifications, the app needs to register with the APNs to receive push notifications. In addition, the app needs to register settings for user notifications in order to update the badge, display a banner or an alert, or play a sound for both a local and remote notification. The app can be customized to register for push notifications at any point that makes sense, when the user has a good idea what value push notifications will provide from the app. For this example, however, the sample app will register with the APNs right away in the app delegate, in the `application:didFinishLaunchingWithOptions:` method:

```
- (BOOL)application:(UIApplication *)application
didFinishLaunchingWithOptions:(NSDictionary *)launchOptions
{
    [[UIApplication sharedApplication] registerForRemoteNotifications];

    UIUserNotificationSettings *notifSettings =
    ➡ [UIUserNotificationSettings settingsForTypes:UIUserNotificationTypeAlert |
    ➡ UIUserNotificationTypeBadge | UIUserNotificationTypeSound categories:nil];

    [[UIApplication sharedApplication]
    ➡ registerUserNotificationSettings:notifSettings];

    return YES;
}
```

UIUserNotificationSettings specify how the user can be alerted when a notification is received, including updating the application badge, presenting an alert, and playing a sound. The registerForRemoteNotifications: method will call the APNs and get a token to identify the device. Two delegate methods need to be implemented to handle receipt of that token, or an error in registering with APNs:

```
- (void)application:(UIApplication *)application
didRegisterForRemoteNotificationsWithDeviceToken:(NSData *)deviceToken {

    NSString *formattedTokenString = [deviceToken description];

    NSString *removedSpacesTokenString =
    ➡ [formattedTokenString stringByReplacingOccurrencesOfString:@" "
                                                      withString:@""];

    NSString *trimmedTokenString =
    ➡ [removedSpacesTokenString stringByTrimmingCharactersInSet:
    ➡ [NSCharacterSet characterSetWithCharactersInString:@"<>"]];

    [self setPushTokenString:trimmedTokenString];
}

- (void)application:(UIApplication *)application
➡didFailToRegisterForRemoteNotificationsWithError:(NSError *)error {
    NSLog(@"Error in push registration: %@", error.localizedDescription);
}
```

If the registration is successful, the token will be returned to the app in NSData format. For ShoutOut, the method will format a string by removing spaces and extra characters from the string representation provided by NSData, and store the string token so that it is available to create the command for sending test pushes. For typical apps, the device token might need to be sent to the push server for a user's account to facilitate sending pushes. Apple recommends that you perform this registration every time the app is launched, since the user might have switched devices or upgraded her version of iOS, which will require a new token. If there are specific failure actions that need to take place, they can be specified in the `didFailTo-RegiterForRemoteNotificationsWithError:` method. For the purposes of the sample app, just log the failure.

At this point, ShoutOut is ready to receive remote push notifications and display local notifications.

Scheduling Local Notifications

For local notifications, no additional setup is required for the app. In ShoutOut, a local notification will be used to schedule a reminder. In `ICFMainViewController`, there is a method that gets called when the user hits the Set Reminder button:

```
- (IBAction)setReminder:(id)sender
{
    NSDate *now = [NSDate date];
    UILocalNotification *reminderNotification = [[UILocalNotification alloc] init];
    [reminderNotification setFireDate:[now dateByAddingTimeInterval:15]];
    [reminderNotification setTimeZone:[NSTimeZone defaultTimeZone]];
    [reminderNotification setAlertBody:@"Don't forget to Shout Out!"];
    [reminderNotification setAlertAction:@"Shout Now"];
    [reminderNotification setSoundName:UILocalNotificationDefaultSoundName];
    [reminderNotification setApplicationIconBadgeNumber:1];

    [[UIApplication sharedApplication]
    ➥ scheduleLocalNotification:reminderNotification];


    UIAlertController *alert =
    ➥ [UIAlertController alertControllerWithTitle:@"Reminder"
                                    message:@"Your Reminder has been Scheduled"
                            preferredStyle:UIAlertControllerStyleAlert];

    UIAlertAction *dismissAction =
    ➥ [UIAlertAction actionWithTitle:@"OK Thanks!"
                            style:UIAlertActionStyleCancel
                          handler:^(UIAlertAction *action){
                              [self dismissViewControllerAnimated:YES
                                                       completion:nil];
                          }];

    [alert addAction:dismissAction];

    [self presentViewController:alert animated:YES completion:nil];
}
```

To create a local notification, create an instance of `UILocalNotification`. Specify the fire date for the notification. It also is generally a good idea to specify a time zone so that if the user is traveling, he will receive the reminder at the correct time. To make it easy to see, just set the fire date to 15 seconds from now. Then set how the user will receive the notification, including specifying alert text, setting whether a sound (or a specific sound) should be played, and updating the application badge. Finally, schedule the local notification. To see it in action, run the app, hit Set Reminder, and then close the app. In 15 seconds, an alert will appear with the custom text, sound, and alert badge.

In addition to scheduling local notifications by date and time, local notifications can be scheduled for a region. When the device enters the region, the notification will fire. Refer to the "Geofencing" section in Chapter 2, "Core Location, MapKit, and Geofencing," for more information on how to set up a `CLRegion` to assign to the `region` property on a local notification.

> **Note**
> Local notifications can be tested in the simulator, but remote push notifications cannot.

Receiving Notifications

When a device receives a notification, either local or remote, the device will check whether the app associated with the notification is currently active and in the foreground. If not, the parameters included guide the device to play a sound, display an alert, or update the badge on the app icon. If an alert is displayed, the user will have the opportunity to dismiss the alert or to follow the alert into the app.

If the user chooses to go into the app, then either the app delegate's `appDidFinish-LaunchingWithOptions:` method is called if the app is in a terminated state and is launching, or a delegate method will be called when the app is brought to the foreground. The same delegate method will be called if the app happens to be in the foreground when the notification is received.

If the app was launched as a result of tapping on a notification, the notification payload will be present in the launch options passed to the `appDidFinishLaunchingWithOptions:` method, and can be used to drive any desired custom functionality, like navigating to a view specific to the notification or displaying a message.

```
NSDictionary *notif = [launchOptions
objectForKey:UIApplicationLaunchOptionsRemoteNotificationKey];

if (notif) {
    //custom logic here using notification info dictionary
}
```

If the notification is received while the app is active or in the background, there are two delegate methods for receiving notifications, one for local and one for remote:

```
- (void)application:(UIApplication *)application
didReceiveRemoteNotification:(NSDictionary *)userInfo {
    NSString *message =
    [[[userInfo objectForKey:@"aps"] objectForKey:@"alert"] objectForKey:@"body"];

    NSString *appState = ([application applicationState] ==
    ➡UIApplicationStateActive) ? @"app Active" : @"app in Background";

    [self presentAlertWithMessage:
     [NSString stringWithFormat:@"Received remote push for app state %@: %@",
      ➡ appState, message]];
}

- (void)application:(UIApplication *)application
➡ didReceiveLocalNotification:(UILocalNotification *)notification {
    NSString *message = [notification alertBody];

    NSString *appState = ([application applicationState] ==
    ➡ UIApplicationStateActive) ? @"app Active" : @"app in Background";

    [self presentAlertWithMessage:
     ➡ [NSString stringWithFormat:@"Received local notification for app state %@: %@",
      ➡ appState, message]];
}
```

The local notification delegate method receives the local notification, and the remote notification delegate receives a dictionary with the notification information. That information can be
inspected and acted upon. In this example an alert is displayed to the user, but other apps can
use the information to navigate to a view in the app that is directly relevant to the notification.
In both cases the `application` parameter can be inspected to determine the state of the app
when the notification was received. Then the response to the notification can be customized
depending on whether the app is currently active or whether the app was awakened from the
background.

Push Notification Server

After the app is prepared to receive notifications, a server needs to be set up to send push notifications. Push notifications can be sent via the APNs from any type of server that can communicate over a secure TCP socket connection (an SSL stack is required). Apple requires that the
server maintain a persistent connection while sending push notification requests to APNs to
avoid the overhead of establishing connections. Many open source libraries support APNs for
several different platforms, and third-party providers provide API access for push notifications.
For the sample app, a simple PHP command-line utility is included to send test push messages
through the sandbox APNs.

At a minimum, the server will need to know the device token in order to send a push to a device. For "data available" type notifications, this might be all that is required to inform the app to download new data. For other requirements, the server might need to specify a message, a sound to play, a number to set the badge on the app, or a custom hash of data to assist the app in navigating to relevant information.

The push server will create a message payload that contains the information to be sent to the device. This payload is in JSON format, and must contain a hash for the key aps:

```
{"aps":{"alert":"Hello Joe","sound":"shout_out.caf"}}
```

If the destination app has been localized, the server can include a hash for the alert item instead of just providing an alert string:

```
{"aps":{"alert": {"loc-key": "push-msg-key",
➥"action-loc-key": "see-push-key"}, "sound":"shout_out.caf"}}
```

Alternatively, the device can pass up locale information to the server when registering the device token, and the server can localize the message before sending through APNs. The action-loc-key item can be specified to customize the title of the button presented with the notification.

> **Note**
>
> For more detail on communication with APNs, look at Apple's documentation at https://developer.apple.com/library/ios/documentation/NetworkingInternet/Conceptual/RemoteNotificationsPG/Chapters/ApplePushService.html#//apple_ref/doc/uid/TP40008194-CH100-SW9.

Sending the Push Notifications

To send a test push using the sample app, run the app on a device. Enter some text in the text field presented, and tap the Shout button. The sample app will use that text to create a command that can be copied and then executed from a terminal session via the installed version of PHP. It requires a message parameter and device parameter to function correctly.

```
php shout.php "testing1..2..3"
➥"f1313af4d5af93d53ba595fdd9a9dc8799bcf10c3e7b3e2cb53662816d5bcc89"
```

To execute the command, right-click on the shout.php file in the Push Server group in the sample app in Xcode, and select Show in Finder. Open a Terminal session, and navigate to the same directory where the shout.php file is. Ensure that the certificate has been created (as shown in Figure 10.10), has been exported to pem format, and is present in the same directory as shout.php. The code currently assumes that no passphrase was set for the certificate; however, if you set a passphrase you can uncomment the passphrase line in shout.php and add your passphrase there. Copy and paste the command from the Xcode console to the

Terminal window and execute it. The script will create a push message in JSON using the provided message and device ID, and will send it to the APNs. Note that this version will send only one push per connection and is suitable only for very light testing in the sandbox; any volume testing should use a more robust version that will maintain a persistent connection with the APNs.

After the script has been executed, the notification will appear quickly on your device (see Figure 10.19). Visit Settings.app (under Notifications, ShoutOut) to change whether the notification is displayed alert style or banner style, and see how each looks on your device.

Figure 10.19   ShoutOut notification received and displayed on the home screen.

Handling APNs Feedback

APNs can provide feedback to each server that connects to it and sends notifications. If any of the device tokens specified in the messages have errors (for example, if the user has deleted the app from her device), the server should prevent sending future notifications to the disabled devices. Many APNs libraries have facilities built in to communicate with the feedback endpoint, which can be scheduled to run periodically. After the feedback has been obtained, stored device tokens on the server should be updated or removed to prevent sending additional notifications to them.

Summary

This chapter introduced you to Apple's method of communicating with apps that are not active and in the foreground: notifications. It explained the differences between local and remote push notifications. It showed how to set up an app to receive remote push notifications, and how to schedule local notifications. This chapter guided you through how to use the utility push script to send test push notifications to your app via the Apple Push Notification service.

Cloud Persistence with CloudKit

iCloud is a set of cloud-based services provided by Apple. It was introduced with iOS 5 as a replacement for MobileMe, and generally provides cloud storage and automatic syncing among iOS devices, OS X devices, and the Web. iCloud includes email, address book, notes, reminders, and calendar syncing; automated iOS device backup and restore; a Find My iPhone feature to locate and/or disable a lost device; a Find My Friends feature to share locations with family or friends; Photo Stream, which automatically syncs photos to other devices; Back to My Mac, which allows for configurationless access to a user's Mac over the Internet; iTunes Match, which provides access to a user's music library without uploading and syncing; iCloud Keychain, which syncs passwords; and iCloud Drive, which allows for storing files and documents in the cloud. In addition, iCloud provides the ability for apps to store app-specific data in the cloud and automatically sync between devices. At the time of this writing, iCloud provides 5GB of storage free, and offers paid plans for additional storage.

For app-specific storage and syncing, iCloud supports four different approaches: document-based storage and syncing (based on `NSDocument` or `UIDocument`), key-value storage and syncing (similar to `NSUserDefaults`), remote structured data storage with CloudKit, and Core Data syncing. This chapter explains how to set up an app to use remote structured data storage with CloudKit.

CloudKit Basics

CloudKit was introduced with iOS 8. CloudKit offers remote data storage, data syncing between the local device and remote storage, and push notification-based subscriptions for data changes for users with iCloud accounts. Apple provides CloudKit free of charge up to certain storage and data transfer limits, based on the number of users in the app. If the limits are exceeded, Apple charges for CloudKit, but pricing has not been disclosed at the time of writing.

CloudKit includes a Web interface for setting up and managing the database schema and public data, and CloudKit includes an API for accessing, retrieving, and maintaining data from an iOS (or OS X) client. Note that CloudKit does not offer any mechanism for local data storage, so it is up to the app developer to select and implement a local storage approach, and integrate that local storage with CloudKit. See Chapter 15, "Getting Up and Running with Core Data," for more discussion on selecting a local storage mechanism. In addition, CloudKit does not offer a way to implement any logic on the server, so any application logic related to the data must be performed on the client.

The Sample App

The sample app for this chapter is called CloudTracker, which is a basic data-tracking app for races and practice runs that stores data using CloudKit. CloudTracker takes advantage of the public database to store race results and the private database to store practice run results. CloudTracker illustrates iCloud user discovery to get and display information about the current user. In addition, CloudTracker uses a CloudKit subscription to be notified when new race data is available.

Setting Up a CloudKit Project

To set up an app to use iCloud, several steps used to be required. Entitlements for the app needed to be set up, and the app needed to be configured in the iOS Provisioning Portal for iCloud support. Some iCloud functions can be tested only on the device, so the provisioning profile work needed to be completed in order for an iCloud app to work. Since Xcode 5, this process has been significantly streamlined and can be done entirely within Xcode.

Account Setup

Xcode needs iOS developer account information in order to connect to the Member Center and perform all the setup necessary for iCloud on the developer's behalf. Select Xcode, Preferences from the Xcode menu, and then select the Accounts tab, as shown in Figure 11.1.

To add a new account, click the plus sign in the lower left of the Accounts tab, and select Apple ID. Enter the account credentials and click the Add button. Xcode validates the credentials and gathers account information if valid. Click the View Details button to see what certificates and provisioning profiles are currently configured for an account, as shown in Figure 11.2.

Figure 11.1   Xcode Accounts tab.

Figure 11.2   Xcode Accounts detail view.

Enabling iCloud Capabilities

After Xcode has account credentials, it can configure apps with capabilities on behalf of the account. It can set up App IDs, entitlements, and provisioning profiles as needed. To set up the iCloud capability, view the CloudTracker Target in Xcode, click the Capabilities tab, and find the iCloud section. Change the iCloud switch to On, and Xcode will automatically create an entitlements file for the project. Check the CloudKit checkbox to enable CloudKit for the app. Xcode will automatically populate an entry with the project's bundle ID in the Ubiquity Containers table. For the sample app, this is all that is needed; for a more complex app that shares with a Mac OS X application and that would need to support more than one ubiquity container name, additional ubiquity container names can be added here. Xcode will check with the developer portal to see whether the App ID is configured correctly for iCloud. If not, Xcode will display the issue, as shown in Figure 11.3. Tap the Fix Issues button, and Xcode will communicate with the developer portal and fix any issues with the app setup.

Figure 11.3   Xcode Target Capabilities—iCloud.

After the iCloud capability is enabled, and there are check marks by CloudKit and all the listed steps, the app is ready to use CloudKit.

CloudKit Concepts

CloudKit introduces several concepts to consider when developing a CloudKit app.

Containers

The container object, CKContainer, represents the iCloud container where all the CloudKit information is stored. iCloud uses a special directory in the iOS file system called the ubiquity container to manage data syncing between the app and iCloud. A container is identified with a container identifier, which can be either the default container identifier (which is the same as the bundle ID), or a custom container identifier. The CKContainer object has class methods to get references to the default container or a custom container by ID (defaultContainer and containerWithIdentifier:). A reference to the container is needed in order to access the CloudKit databases.

Databases

CloudKit supports both a publicly accessible database and a private database. Each database can store data defined by record types. The public database can be read by any user (even a user without an iCloud account), but can be written to only by an iCloud user. The public database is theoretically accessible by any user, but access to it is limited by the design of the app in practice. Records stored in the public database count against the app's CloudKit storage quota. To access the public database, use the `publicCloudDatabase` method on the container:

```
CKDatabase *publicDatabase = [[CKContainer defaultContainer] publicCloudDatabase];
```

The private database is specific to an iCloud user for the app. Data in the private database can be read and updated only by the user; even the app administrator cannot see or update data in the private database. Records stored in the private database count against the iCloud user's storage quota. To access the private database, use the `privateCloudDatabase` method on the container:

```
CKDatabase *privateDatabase = [[CKContainer defaultContainer] privateCloudDatabase];
```

Records

CloudKit stores structured data in records, or instances of `CKRecord`. Records are defined by record types (similar to an "entity" or "table" in relational database terminology), which can be set up either in the CloudKit dashboard or just by saving a new record while operating in the development environment. The server will return an error when attempting to save unknown record types or unknown attributes for record types in the production environment.

`CKRecord` instances can function much like instances of `NSMutableDictionary`, in that the attribute or object values can be set for keys, or attribute names. Records support several attribute types, as shown in Table 11.1. CloudKit has special support for querying by `CLLocation`, and supports relationships with other records using a `CKReference`. In addition, records can use a `CKAsset` to store data (see the "Assets" section).

Table 11.1 **CloudKit-Supported Data Types**

Data Types	Objective-C Storage
String	NSString
Date/Time	NSDate
Int(64)	NSNumber
Double	NSNumber
Bytes	NSData
Location	CLLocation
Reference to another CKRecord	CKReference
Asset	CKAsset

Users represent a special type of CKRecord. User records cannot be queried; rather, a user record has to be fetched directly using the record ID, or the user record needs to be accessed through the user discovery process, which will find users that exist in the iCloud user's list of contacts (by email address). See the section "User Discovery and Management" for more details.

Record Zones

Record zones (CKRecordZone) are a way to organize related record types together. A record zone functions as a container for related record types. In the public database for an app, there is only one record zone, which is called the default zone. Customized record zones can be created for the private database. Note that changes to records in the same record zone can be committed or rolled back together. References between records can exist only within a record zone.

Record Identifiers

Each instance of CKRecord by default is given a unique identifier by CloudKit when it is initialized, which is an instance of CKRecordID. This record identifier will be based on a UUID and is guaranteed to be unique, is safe to store locally, and can be used to fetch instances of CKRecord when they are needed.

CloudKit can also support custom record identifiers. Record identifiers can be supplied when a record is created, and must be unique to the database the record will be saved to. Custom record identifiers must be used when saving records outside the default zone for a database.

Assets

A CKAsset can be used to store attribute data in a file, rather than directly in an attribute for a record. This approach is appropriate for images, sounds, or any other relatively large pieces of data. Remember that a CKRecord can have a maximum of 1MB of data, and an asset can store up to 250MB.

When the related CKRecord is fetched, the CKAsset will also be downloaded. The data for the CKAsset can be loaded from the fileURL of the CKAsset.

If the data for the asset should be available locally while offline, it should be copied from the CKAsset to a locally accessible file URL.

CloudKit Basic Operations

CloudKit offers two different approaches to working with data: robust NSOperation-based tools and block-based convenience methods from the CKDatabase object. This chapter illustrates working with CloudKit using the block-based approaches in order to be easier to follow; but be advised that the NSOperation-based approaches provide some additional power that the convenience methods do not, such as the ability to save multiple records simultaneously or get progress updates on larger operations.

Fetching Records

To fetch records from a CloudKit database, a query is needed. In the sample app, both the races view and the practice runs view use a query to pull records from CloudKit, and then display those records in a table view. Because the races view pulls race information from the public database, a reference to the public database is needed:

```
CKDatabase *publicDatabase = [[CKContainer defaultContainer] publicCloudDatabase];
```

Queries in CloudKit leverage the power of NSPredicate. To query records from CloudKit, build an NSPredicate that expresses the conditions to be satisfied, using the attribute names for the record in the selection criteria (see the "Using Predicates" section in Chapter 15, "Getting Up and Running with Core Data," for more information on building predicates). If all records are desired, a predicate is still needed for the query. In this case, there is a special way to declare a predicate for everything:

```
NSPredicate *predicate = [NSPredicate predicateWithFormat:@"TRUEPREDICATE"];
```

After a predicate has been created, a CKQuery instance can be created, specifying the record type and the predicate.

```
CKQuery *query = [[CKQuery alloc] initWithRecordType:@"Race" predicate:predicate];
```

Then a convenience method on the database can be used to execute the query. The convenience method either will return matching records in an instance of NSArray, or will return an error in an instance of NSError. Note that passing a zone ID of nil, as shown in the example, will execute the query in the default zone.

```
__weak ICFRaceListTableViewController *weakSelf = self;

[publicDatabase performQuery:query
            inZoneWithID:nil
       completionHandler:^(NSArray *results, NSError *error) {
           dispatch_async(dispatch_get_main_queue(), ^{
               weakSelf.raceList =
               ➥ [[NSMutableArray alloc] initWithArray:results];
               [weakSelf.tableView reloadData];
           });
       }];
```

The completion handler will be executed on an arbitrary queue. It is not likely to be executed on the main queue, so it is absolutely necessary to dispatch to the main queue to handle the results if there will be any user interface updates as a result. Dispatching asynchronously reduces the likelihood of a deadlock.

In this example, the view controller stores the results array in a property, and then informs the table view that it should reload to display the data from the stored results, so dispatching to the main queue is a requirement. The races in the public database will be displayed, as shown in Figure 11.4.

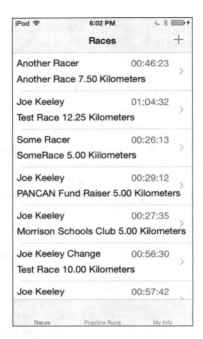

Figure 11.4   CloudTracker Sample App—race list.

Create and Save a Record

To create a new record in the sample app, tap the plus sign in the upper-right corner of the race view (as shown in Figure 11.4). The app will present a form that will accept data for a new race record. When the user has filled out the form and tapped the Save button, the view controller will present an activity indicator since the save operation will likely take a noticeable amount of time. A reference to the public database will be established, and then an instance of `CKRecord` will be initialized for the record type "Race."

```
if (!self.raceData)
{
    self.raceData = [[CKRecord alloc] initWithRecordType:@"Race"];
}
```

The race record will be updated with data from the user interface. First, the racer, or user who is entering the record, will be pulled from the app delegate and set up as a reference to the user record using a `CKReference`. See the "User Discovery and Management" section later in this chapter for more information on how the user record was populated. The racer's name will be pulled from the user record and stored for convenience on the race record.

```
if (![self.raceData objectForKey:@"racer"])
```

```
{

    AppDelegate *appDelegate =
    ➥(AppDelegate *)[[UIApplication sharedApplication] delegate];

    CKRecord *userRecord = appDelegate.myUserRecord;

    if (userRecord)
    {
        CKReference *racerReference =
        ➥[[CKReference alloc] initWithRecord:userRecord
                                      action:CKReferenceActionNone];

        self.raceData[@"racer"] = racerReference;
        self.raceData[@"racerName"] = userRecord[@"name"];
    }
}
```

Next each attribute will be given a value from the associated form object.

```
self.raceData[@"raceName"] = self.raceName.text;
self.raceData[@"location"] = self.location.text;
self.raceData[@"distance"] =
➥[NSNumber numberWithFloat:[self.distance.text floatValue]];
self.raceData[@"distanceUnits"] = [self selectedDistanceUnits];
self.raceData[@"hours"] =
➥[NSNumber numberWithInteger:[self.hours.text integerValue]];
self.raceData[@"minutes"] =
➥[NSNumber numberWithInteger:[self.minutes.text integerValue]];
self.raceData[@"seconds"] =
➥[NSNumber numberWithInteger:[self.seconds.text integerValue]];
self.raceData[@"raceDate"] = [self.datePicker date];
```

Finally, the race record will be saved, using a convenience method on the database. The save method requires a `CKRecord` parameter and completion handler.

```
__weak ICFRaceDetailViewController *weakSelf = self;
[publicDatabase saveRecord:self.raceData
        completionHandler:^(CKRecord *record, NSError *error) {
            dispatch_async(dispatch_get_main_queue(), ^{
                [weakSelf.saveRaceActivityIndicator setHidden:YES];
                if (weakSelf.indexPathForRace) {
                    [weakSelf.raceDataDelegate raceUpdated:record
                      ➥forIndexPath:weakSelf.indexPathForRace];
                } else {
                    [weakSelf.raceDataDelegate raceAdded:record];
                }
```

```
            [weakSelf.navigationController popViewControllerAnimated:YES];
        });
    }];
```

Again, note that the completion handler will be called on an arbitrary queue, so if the user interface will be updated, it is necessary to dispatch to the main queue. The completion handler will hide the activity indicator, tell the race list view controller to either update the saved record or handle adding a new race record, and then dismiss the detail view controller.

Update and Save a Record

To update a race record, tap on a race row in the race list in the sample app. The CKRecord for the race associated with the view will be passed to the detail view controller in the prepareForSegue:sender: method. The index path will also be passed to the detail view controller so that when the update is complete, only the affected row will need to be refreshed.

```
if ([segue.identifier isEqualToString:@"updateRaceDetail"])
{
    NSIndexPath *tappedRowIndexPath = [self.tableView indexPathForSelectedRow];
    CKRecord *raceData = [self.raceList objectAtIndex:tappedRowIndexPath.row];
    [detail setIndexPathForRace:tappedRowIndexPath];
    [detail setRaceData:raceData];
    [detail setConnectedToiCloud:self.connectedToiCloud];
}
```

The user interface for the detail view will be populated from the passed-in race record.

```
if (!race)
{
    return;
}
[self.raceName setText:race[@"raceName"]];
[self.location setText:race[@"location"]];
[self.distance setText:[race[@"distance"] stringValue]];

[self.distanceUnit setSelectedSegmentIndex:
 [self segmentForDistanceUnitString:race[@"distanceUnits"]]];

[self.hours setText:[race[@"hours"] stringValue]];
[self.minutes setText:[race[@"minutes"] stringValue]];
[self.seconds setText:[race[@"seconds"] stringValue]];
[self.datePicker setDate:race[@"raceDate"]];
```

After the information has been updated and the user has tapped the Save button, the race record will be saved using the same logic as a new record (as illustrated in the preceding section).

Subscriptions and Push

CloudKit offers the capability to subscribe to, or listen for, data changes, and then receive notifications when relevant data has changed. This enables an application to be very responsive to data changes without expensive polling, and even enables an application to keep up-to-date when it is not actively being used. CloudKit leverages push notifications (refer to Chapter 10, "Notifications," for more details, and recall that push notification delivery is not guaranteed) and predicates to enable this powerful feature.

Push Setup

For the app to receive push notifications related to subscriptions, some setup is required. First, the app needs to register for remote notifications and receive a device token in order for CloudKit to be able to send pushes to the device. Note that a push certificate does not need to be set up for CloudKit notifications; CloudKit manages the notifications internally.

The sample app registers for push notifications in the `application:didFinishLaunchingWithOptions:` method in the app delegate. It will frequently be better to place the push registration logic in a different context in the app so that the user understands what benefits push notifications will provide and will be more likely to accept them. First, the sample app registers for remote notifications:

```
[application registerForRemoteNotifications];
```

Then the sample app registers the desired user notification settings, which can be customized.

```
UIUserNotificationSettings *notifSettings =
[UIUserNotificationSettings settingsForTypes:UIUserNotificationTypeAlert |
 UIUserNotificationTypeBadge | UIUserNotificationTypeSound categories:nil];

[application registerUserNotificationSettings:notifSettings];
```

After the two registrations are complete, the app is ready to receive push notifications from CloudKit.

Subscribing to Data Changes

The sample app sets up a subscription for race data after the registration for remote notifications is complete (in the `application:didRegisterForRemoteNotificationsWithDeviceToken:` method in the app delegate). In a real app it is more likely that a subscription would be set up in a different context in the app. The sample app subscription will receive notifications for any new or updated race records. The subscription (an instance of `CKSubscription`) requires a record type, a predicate, a unique identifier, and some options. One good option for a unique identifier is to use the vendor identifier, since it will be unique to the device and app combination. It can be augmented with additional information to make it specific to a record type or predicate just by appending data to it. The unique identifier is necessary to remove the subscription, so it needs to either be stored when created, or be reproducible in some other way. The subscription options indicate under what circumstances the notification should fire (creates, updates, deletes), and can be specified in any combination desired. Multiple subscriptions can be registered to handle different situations.

```
CKDatabase *publicDatabase = [[CKContainer defaultContainer] publicCloudDatabase];
NSPredicate *allRacesPredicate = [NSPredicate predicateWithFormat:@"TRUEPREDICATE"];
NSString *subscriptionIdentifier =
➡[[[UIDevice currentDevice] identifierForVendor] UUIDString];


CKSubscription *raceSubscription =
[[CKSubscription alloc] initWithRecordType:@"Race"
➡predicate:allRacesPredicate
➡subscriptionID:subscriptionIdentifier
➡options:CKSubscriptionOptionsFiresOnRecordCreation |
➡CKSubscriptionOptionsFiresOnRecordUpdate];
```

After the subscription is instantiated, notification preferences need to be set for it. The sample app will just use an alert, but badging and sounds can also be used. Note that the alert message can be customized to use replacement variables as well.

```
CKNotificationInfo *notificationInfo = [[CKNotificationInfo alloc] init];
[notificationInfo setAlertBody:@"New race info available!"];
[raceSubscription setNotificationInfo:notificationInfo];
```

The subscription then needs to be saved to the database to become active.

```
[publicDatabase saveSubscription:raceSubscription
              completionHandler:^(CKSubscription *subscription, NSError *error) {
    if (error)
    {
        NSLog(@"Could not subscribe for notifications: %@",
        ➡error.localizedDescription);
    } else
    {
        NSLog(@"Subscribed for notifications");
    }
}];
```

The completion handler will be called on an arbitrary queue, and will contain the subscription if it was saved successfully, or an error if not. After the subscription is saved, the app will receive notifications any time the criteria for the subscription are met, as shown in Figure 11.5.

Figure 11.5   CloudTracker sample app—new data notification.

User Discovery and Management

To fully use CloudKit in an app, the user must have an iCloud account. For non-iCloud users, CloudKit will allow read-only access to the public database; in order to write to the public database or have any access to a private database, an iCloud account is required. At the same time, Apple requires that apps using CloudKit not require an iCloud account, so a CloudKit app must know whether an iCloud account is present, and adjust the user interface accordingly.

> **Tip**
>
> Although the simulator can be used to test with an iCloud account (just sign into iCloud in the simulator just as on the device), testing without an iCloud account on the simulator does not work in all cases. For non-iCloud account testing, use a device to be certain everything works.

In the sample app, the race list is the only view that can function correctly without an iCloud account. A non-iCloud user should be able to view the race list but not add or update races. The race list view controller will use the `accountStatusWithCompletionHandler:` method on the CloudKit container to determine the current iCloud account status of the device:

```
[[CKContainer defaultContainer] accountStatusWithCompletionHandler:
➥^(CKAccountStatus accountStatus, NSError *error) {
    dispatch_async(dispatch_get_main_queue(), ^{
        self.connectedToiCloud = (accountStatus == CKAccountStatusAvailable);
        [self.addRaceButton setEnabled:self.connectedToiCloud];
    });
}];
```

The completion handler will store the information as to whether there is a current iCloud account so that the detail screen can be updated accordingly when a row is tapped, and will update the Add Race button to be enabled only when an iCloud account is available.

In CloudKit, the user record is a special case of CKRecord. The user record always exists in the public database with no custom attributes, and custom attributes can be added to it. Information about the current user cannot be queried directly; rather, the app has to go through the user discovery process to see what users are visible to the iCloud account, using email addresses in the user's address book. After that process is complete, the current user's information will be accessible to the app. That user information can be used to update the user record.

The My Info view will perform the user discovery task, beginning with the permissions check.

```
[[CKContainer defaultContainer] requestApplicationPermission:
➥CKApplicationPermissionUserDiscoverability
➥completionHandler:^(CKApplicationPermissionStatus applicationPermissionStatus,
➥NSError *error) {
    if (error)
    {
        NSLog(@"Uh oh - error requesting discoverability permission:
        ➥%@",error.localizedDescription);
    } else
    {
        if (applicationPermissionStatus == CKApplicationPermissionStatusGranted)
        {
            [self lookUpUserInfo];
        }
    }
}];
```

The app will present an alert to request the user's permission to perform the user discovery process. The dialog will be presented only once. Assuming that the user grants permission, the next step is to fetch the recordID of the current user, which will be used to determine which user information belongs to the current user:

```
[[CKContainer defaultContainer] fetchUserRecordIDWithCompletionHandler:
➥^(CKRecordID *recordID, NSError *error) {
    if (error)
    {
        NSLog(@"Error fetching user record ID: %@",error.localizedDescription);
```

```
    } else
    {
        [self discoverUserInfoForRecordID:recordID];
    }
}];
```

After the `recordID` is available, the user discovery process will be performed with a call to the `discoverAllContactUserInfosWithCompletionHandler:` method on the container:

```
[[CKContainer defaultContainer] discoverAllContactUserInfosWithCompletionHandler:
➥^(NSArray *userInfos, NSError *error) {
    if (error)
    {
        NSLog(@"Error discovering contacts: %@",error.localizedDescription);
    } else
    {
        NSLog(@"Got info: %@", userInfos);

        for (CKDiscoveredUserInfo *info in userInfos) {
            if ([info.userRecordID.recordName
            ➥isEqualToString:recordID.recordName]) {
                //this is the current user's record
                dispatch_async(dispatch_get_main_queue(), ^{
                    NSString *myName = [NSString stringWithFormat:
                                        @"%@ %@",info.firstName, info.lastName];

                    [self.name setText:myName];
                    self.myUserRecordName = info.userRecordID.recordName;

                    self.currentUserInfo = @{@"name":myName,
                                             @"location":self.location.text,
                                             @"recordName":
                                             ➥info.userRecordID.recordName};

                    NSUserDefaults *defaults =
                    ➥[NSUserDefaults standardUserDefaults];

                    [defaults setObject:self.currentUserInfo
                                 forKey:@"currentUserInfo"];

                    [defaults synchronize];

                    [self fetchMyUserRecord];
                });
            }
        }
    }
}];
```

If the user discovery process is successful, it will return an array of CKDiscoveredUserInfo instances. The logic will iterate over that array, and compare the CKDiscoveredUserInfo's userRecordID to the recordID of the current user. If they are the same, the first and last name will be pulled from the CKDiscoveredUserInfo and put into the name text field. A dictionary of information about the current user, including the name, provided location, and record name, will be created and stored in NSUserDefaults so that it will persist across launches without the need to refetch.

With the record name of the current user saved, the current user record can be fetched.

```
CKRecordID *myUserRecordID =
➥[[CKRecordID alloc] initWithRecordName:self.myUserRecordName];

CKDatabase *publicDatabase = [[CKContainer defaultContainer] publicCloudDatabase];
➥[publicDatabase fetchRecordWithID:myUserRecordID
                completionHandler:^(CKRecord *record, NSError *error) {
    if (error)
    {
        NSLog(@"Error fetching user record: %@", error.localizedDescription);
        [self setMyUserRecord:nil];
    } else
    {
        AppDelegate *appDelegate =
        ➥(AppDelegate *)[[UIApplication sharedApplication] delegate];

        [appDelegate setMyUserRecord:record];
        [self setMyUserRecord:record];
    }
}];
```

If the fetch is successful, the CKRecord representing the current user will be stored on the app delegate so that it will be easily accessible to the race detail view controller that will use it when saving new races.

If the user updates the name and location and taps the Save button, the changes will be saved to the user record.

```
if (self.myUserRecord) {
    self.myUserRecord[@"location"] = self.location.text;
    self.myUserRecord[@"name"] = self.name.text;
    CKDatabase *publicDatabase =
    ➥[[CKContainer defaultContainer] publicCloudDatabase];
    [publicDatabase saveRecord:self.myUserRecord
            completionHandler:^(CKRecord *record, NSError *error) {
        if (error) {
            NSLog(@"Error saving my user record: %@", error.localizedDescription);
        }
    }];
}
```

> **Note**
>
> Any CloudKit app that stores data locally specific to an iCloud account should also listen for the `NSUbiquityIdentityDidChangeNotification`, which will identify when the iCloud account status has changed, and then be able to handle the use case in which the user has logged out, or in which a different iCloud user has logged in.

Managing Data in the Dashboard

In addition to the iOS SDK, CloudKit provides a Web-based dashboard to manage the server portion of CloudKit. To access the dashboard, click the CloudKit Dashboard button from the iCloud Capabilities tab, as shown in Figure 11.6.

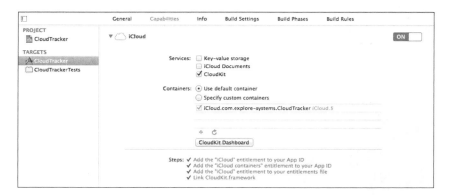

Figure 11.6   Xcode Target Capabilities—iCloud.

The CloudKit dashboard will open in the default Web browser, and will request authentication. Provide developer account credentials to access the dashboard. The dashboard will display several categories of information about the server in the left panel. Selecting a category will display more detailed information or additional choices in the middle panel. Selecting a choice in the middle panel will present detailed information or editing capabilities in the right panel.

Record types can be edited by selecting the Record Types item under the Schema header, as shown in Figure 11.7. A record type can be added or deleted by the icons at the top of the right panel, and attributes and index settings for a selected record type can be managed in the lower part of the right panel.

Figure 11.7   CloudKit Dashboard—Record Types.

Data in the public database can also be viewed and managed through the dashboard. Users can be viewed by selecting the User Records item under the Public Data header. Data can be viewed by selecting the Default Zone header under the Public Data header. After the Default Zone is selected, data for record types can be viewed and edited by selecting a record type in the upper part of the middle panel, as shown in Figure 11.8. Sorting can be adjusted, and records can be searched. Individual records can be viewed, added, edited, or deleted.

Figure 11.8   CloudKit Dashboard—Public Data, Default Zone.

Private data is visible only to the individual iCloud user. Selecting Default Zone under the Private Data heading will display data only for the currently logged-in iCloud user in the dashboard.

In the Deployment section under the Admin heading (as shown in Figure 11.9), there are options to reset the development environment or to deploy to production. Resetting the development environment is the "nuclear option"—it will change all the record types back to match the production environment, and will delete all the data in the development environment.

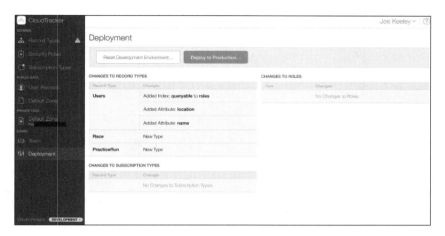

Figure 11.9   CloudKit Dashboard: Deployment.

Summary

This chapter discussed using CloudKit in an app. It covered setting up the app to use CloudKit, some of the basic CloudKit concepts, and how to perform basic CloudKit operations, such as querying records, displaying data from records, and creating, updating, and saving records. The chapter then explained how to set up a subscription to receive data update notifications via push. It showed how to customize user records and how to perform user discovery. Finally, this chapter explained managing CloudKit using the CloudKit dashboard.

Extensions

Since the dawn of the iOS platform, apps have been sandboxed. Third-party apps could not influence any other app with the exception of some simple URL scheming. With the introduction of iOS 8, Apple has given developers the ability to run code from their apps outside of the sandbox for the first time. Although extensions are limited in functionality, they add a great amount of flexibility to the developer's tool belt. Six types of extensions are available on the iOS platform (Finder Sync is uniquely OS X), each with its own specific function. This doesn't include Apple's choice to use extensions to power WatchKit, which is discussed in the "Apple Watch Extension" section of this chapter.

This chapter covers two of the most popular extensions. The first is a Today widget, which enables the app to post quick at-a-glance information in the Notification Center. The second extension is an Apple Watch Extension, which enables an iOS app to post information and receive feedback to the Apple Watch.

Types of Extensions

Apple has broken out extensions into seven unique types (six of which are available on iOS). Each extension is limited and restricted to protect the user from malicious activity and provides a unique type of functionality. It is possible for a single app to provide more than one type of extension. The types of extensions are detailed in this section.

Today

Today Extensions, often simply referred to as widgets, appear in the Notification Center of an iOS device. They are called Today Extensions because the section of the Notification Center they appear in is the Today area. These widgets are designed to provide quick at-a-glance information or accept a quick action like a button press.

Some developers are already pushing the limits of what Apple intended with Today Extensions. When the popular calculator app PCCalc added a full calculator to the Notification Center through a Today Extension, Apple initially rejected the app, only later reversing their decision due to public outcry.

Share

The Share Extension gives the user an easy and convenient method to share content with other services or Web sites. The extension will add functionality to the built-in share dialog on iOS. For example, if developers were to create a new service that competed with Twitter, they could write an extension into their native iOS app. That extension would allow other apps to share content through the extension directly with their service by appearing directly in the sharing sheet.

Action

An Action Extension helps users view or transform content from the originating app. For example, if you have an app that enables the user to edit a selection of text, a new Action Extension can be created to bring in text from other apps. For example, a developer could write an extension that translated Spanish text into English. An Action Extension must specify the type of data that it is designed to work with such as text, video, or PDFs.

Photo Editing

The Photo Editing Extension enables the user to edit a photo or video within Photos.app. In a sense, this creates a custom modification plug-in that the user can then access from the standard Photo app. For example, a developer could create a Photo Editing Extension that applies a set of custom filters that would become available to the user on his photo library. As with any other changes to images in Photos.app, the original is always saved so that the user can easily revert any changes.

Document Provider

The Document Provider Extension enables a developer to share a custom type of file across multiple apps. The Document Provider Extension stores all these associated files in a shared location. For example, Adobe could release a Photoshop Document Extension, which would enable apps to work with and share PSD documents.

Custom Keyboard

One of the most requested features from iOS users before iOS 8 was to be able to install custom keyboards. The Custom Keyboard Extension does exactly this, and enables users to install third-party keyboards with varying purposes into the system keyboard selector. The Keyboard Extension is limited to inputting data into the user's selected text field or other text input area.

Understanding Extensions

There are many types of extensions; however, they all share something in common: They allow the execution of functionality inside an app that might not be created by the same developer who made the extension. This is a radical shift from the first six years of iOS development.

Previously, to get functionality like extensions, the user was required to be running a jailbroken device. Apple has made tremendous efforts to ensure that extensions do not cross the line into malware, and in doing so has placed various limitations on developing extensions. To work effectively with extensions, you need to first understand how they function.

Extensions are not standalone apps; they are attached to another app, called the host app, through which the user installs and activates the extension. If the user uninstalls the host app, the extension is removed along with it. Because the extension isn't a standalone app, it isn't constantly running in the background; the extension remains unlaunched until the user chooses it from an app's interface or from a presented activity view controller. The host app defines the parameters of the extension and waits for the user to activate it. After the extension is activated, it performs its duty and then terminates. Extensions are not designed to continue running in the background and performing long processes.

While an extension is running, there is no direct communication between the extension and the containing app. The containing app will pass any information required for the extension to perform its duties upon launch and then wait for the extension to terminate.

Note

An app extension can be run only at the request of a user; there is no way to auto-launch or auto-execute an extension based on the state of the app.

API Limitations

App extensions have limitations that are unique when dealing with iOS development. Many APIs cannot be accessed from within an extension due to security or other concerns:

- Extensions cannot access `sharedApplication` or any of the associated methods such as `openURL`, `delegate`, `applicationState`, or accessing push or local notification settings.

- Apple has also marked certain APIs with the `NS_EXTENSION_UNAVAILABLE` macro, which will restrict use within an extension. Examples of these APIs include calendar events and HealthKit interaction.

- An extension might not activate or work directly with the camera or microphone.

- Extensions might not perform long-running background tasks and are subject to app store rejection or runtime termination for processes that take too long to run in the background.

- AirDrop is not accessible from within the extension; however, the extension can access data sending through AirDrop via the `UIActivityViewController`.

Extensions are brand-new technology from both a code standpoint and a user-interaction standpoint. Apple has been known to adapt the rules for their developer technologies on the fly to ensure the best possible user experience.

Creating Extensions

Because extensions are a separate target that belongs to a host app, that new host app must first be created. Extensions can be added to any normal iOS project. To create a new extension in Xcode 6, select File, New, Target. This opens a new window (see Figure 12.1); select Application Extension from the list on the left. The six types of iOS extensions will be presented, so select the type of extension that will be added to your project.

Figure 12.1   Adding a new extension to a project.

Upon creation of the extension, a new group will be created in the project with the extension's name. This group will contain a class file and an associated storyboard. If a Today Extension was chosen, running the project now will display a Hello World widget to the Notification Center (see Figure 12.2). Each extension has default properties and will show up differently when testing.

Figure 12.2   A Hello World Today Extension running on the iOS Simulator.

When an extension is being run, it is important that the simulator already be running and that your host app has been installed. Failing to do so might result in an error, as shown in Figure 12.3. If an extension fails to load or compiles new source, try cleaning the project and rebuilding the host app and then the extension again.

Figure 12.3   An unable-to-launch-extension error due to the iOS Simulator not being launched.

Today Extension

The first of two sample apps for this chapter will create a Today Extension. ICFToday will be the host app but has no specific functionality itself other than hosting the extension. As for the extension, it will use Yahoo's Finance API to pull down the most recent ask price for Apple's Stock and display it to the Notification Center. A refresh button is also provided to demonstrate user action from the Today Extension.

Following the directions from the preceding section, a new project is created and a new Today Extension is added to it. The extension storyboard is set up with a single label to reflect the price of the stock and a single button to force a refresh of the price.

A new method is created by default, `widgetPerformUpdateWithCompletionHandler`. This method will be called when the Today Extension or Widget is ready to be updated. This usually occurs when the Notification Center is presented for display. Setting a breakpoint on this method will cause it to fire every time Notification Center refreshes or is reloaded. The first thing that needs to be done is to set the dimensions that will be used for the extension; since this is a very small extension it needs a height of only 20 points. The second line of this method performs a call to refresh the stock price.

```
- (void)widgetPerformUpdateWithCompletionHandler:
➥(void (^)(NCUpdateResult))completionHandler
{
        self.preferredContentSize = CGSizeMake(0, 20);
        [self refreshAction: nil];

        completionHandler(NCUpdateResultNewData);
}
```

Yahoo provides a simple API to fetch the stock price of any listed company. The URL provided in the following method simply requests the current ask price of the AAPL stock. The results are delivered in a CSV file; however, with only one line item in that file, it can be treated as plain text.

```
-(NSString *)getStockPrice
{
        NSURL *url = [NSURL URLWithString:
        ➥@"http://finance.yahoo.com/d/quotes.csv?s=AAPL&f=a"];

        NSError *error = nil;

        NSString *quote = [NSString stringWithContentsOfURL:url
        ➥encoding:NSASCIIStringEncoding error:&error];

        return quote;
}
```

Running the extension target will now launch into the Notification Center and display the current asking price for AAPL, as shown in Figure 12.4.

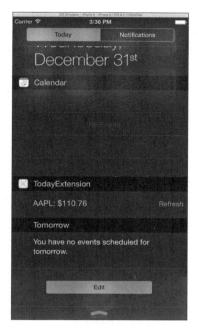

Figure 12.4   Viewing a Today Extension that shows the current stock price for AAPL.

Sharing Code and Information between Host App and Extension

An extension cannot directly communicate with its host app, nor can it share code in the typical sense. In the real world, both of these requirements are often necessary. To share code between the extension and the host app, an embedded framework can be created. The embedded framework can then be referenced from both targets and code can effectively be shared between the host app and the extension.

To create a new framework, select the project in the Project Navigator and add a new target by selecting Editor, Add Target. Select iOS, Framework & Library, and then Cocoa Touch Framework from the prompt window. The Framework can now be added to both targets, and class files can be shared between the extension and the host app.

Often, an extension needs to be able to share data between itself and the host app. Because both targets do not share the same sandbox, they cannot directly interact with each other. However, with the leveraging of another iOS 8 technology, simple data sharing becomes possible.

Apple allows for App Groups that allow a set of apps from the same developer to share limited data. The same technology can be used to share data between an extension and an app. App Groups can be turned on through the capabilities section of the project editor. Sharing `NSUserDefaults` through App Groups after it's enabled is as easy as working with `NSUserDefaults` on older versions of iOS. A new instance of `NSUserDefaults` is created and stored using the group identifier that was created in the App Groups project settings.

```
[[NSUserDefaults alloc] initWithSuiteName:@"<group identifier>"];
```

> **Note**
>
> When you are using App Groups and `NSUserDefaults`, it is important to remember that `NSUserDefaults` for both targets still exist and this is different than referencing the shared groups `NSUserDefaults`. Items saved into each target's defaults do not automatically become available in the shared defaults.

Apple Watch Extension

The Apple Watch was announced at a special Apple event on September 9, 2014. There had been rumors of an Apple-branded watch for several years before the release. Those rumors were put to bed when Tim Cook showed the first device onstage. Apple has had a history of revolutionizing industries, from the personal computer to MP3 player, smartphones, and tablet computing. Whether the Apple Watch will be the next great technology revolution ushered in by Apple remains to be seen.

Apple has promised two software development rollouts for the Apple Watch. The first WatchKit is available in Xcode 6.2 or newer; the second, a true native SDK, is expected sometime in 2015. This first phase of Apple rolling out Apple Watch app development centers on extensions. The current WatchKit development package works much like a Today Extension, covered earlier in this chapter.

> **Note**
>
> Apple WatchKit Development requires Xcode 6.2 Beta 3 or newer.

To create a new WatchKit project, a host app needs to be first created. Apple has not allowed for standalone apps on the Apple Watch yet. Every third-party app currently allowed on the Apple Watch must be hosted on another external iOS device. The process for adding a WatchKit component to an existing app is the same as for the Today Extension, with the difference of selecting Apple Watch from the template target menu (see Figure 12.5).

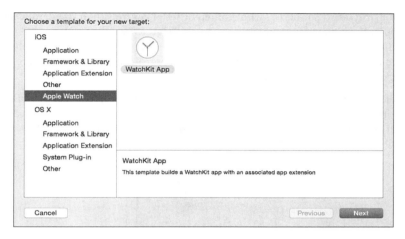

Figure 12.5   Creating a new WatchKit app.

Creating the new WatchKit app target will also generate several new files, an `InterfaceController` and `NotificationController`, as well as supporting files such as `info.plist` and asset catalogs. Unlike with a Today Extension, no WatchKit storyboard is created. Running the WatchKit app will produce a blank AppleWatch interface (see Figure 12.6). The interface contains just a clock and power indicator. Create a new storyboard from the Add File menu, and select a WatchKit storyboard from the available options.

Figure 12.6   A WatchKit Extension running on the iOS Simulator.

The WatchKit storyboard contains a whole different set of controls than standard iOS develop-ment. Although there are many familiar items to a veteran iOS developer, there is a significant amount of difference in their appearance and behavior. Familiar controls such as labels, tables, and standard controls are available. Some customized controls such as steppers, date display, and date pickers are made available as well.

When you are working with the storyboard file, it will quickly become apparent not only that items snap into position unlike iOS but also that there are no standard autolayout controls. However, this might certainly change as Xcode 6.2 progresses through betas and WatchKit is refined. Instead, WatchKit uses several positioning controls (see Figure 12.7).

Figure 12.7   Positioning controls on WatchKit differ from the standard autolayout approach found on iOS.

Hooking up controls like outlets and actions is identical to standard iOS development practices. In the sample app, a new label and button are created. The only difference is that `UILabel` is called `WKInterfaceLabel` on the Apple Watch. The WatchKit simulator has significant lag between interactions and responses. Whether this will carry over to physical devices or is a symptom of the simulator is currently unknown. However, since WatchKit is functioning as an extension that runs on another device, some lag would be expected.

This simple WatchKit app should provide the groundwork required to expand on the inter-face and functionality with existing iOS development knowledge. The platform, though in its infancy, already provides a lot of functionality and options.

> **Note**
>
> Apple WatchKit Development has been rapidly changing since introduction. The materials in this chapter were written while WatchKit was in early stages of beta. A number of bugs are being worked out in each release, and the material in this section was kept as simple as possible in the hopes that it will remain functional through future releases.

Summary

Extensions are a new and exciting shift in thinking on iOS. Extensions are expected to continue to be refined and adapted in the future. The basic initial functionality of extensions allows for a great amount of flexibility and features that were not previously available in iOS development. The use of extension-like behavior for the Apple Watch shows that Apple is behind this technology and that they are taking the slow and proper approach to allowing cross-app interaction. Security, stability, and user safety have always been of the utmost importance for Apple, and extensions enable them to maintain that focus while giving developers functionality that has been requested since the initial iOS release.

Although extensions are a fairly large topic covering various types of interactions, the material provided in this chapter should provide a comfort level enabling a developer to dig into and begin working with and exploring the power of app extensions. There have been only a handful of times in the evolution of the iOS developer platform when a new technology allows for a radical change in the flexibility of the developer. Extensions are one of these few giant leaps forward. No one, including Apple, has any idea what developers will do with this technology, and that always makes for a very interesting development platform.

13

Handoff

Handoff is one of several features introduced with iOS 8 and OS X Yosemite to support Continuity. Given the proliferation of devices including desktop computers, laptop computers, iPhones, iPads, and iPod touches, Continuity is intended to help those devices work together seamlessly. Continuity includes features that leverage proximity of devices and special features that devices support, such as placing a call or sending a text message from a laptop or an iPad using a nearby iPhone, or having an Internet hotspot connection instantly available for another device that does not have a cellular Internet capability. Handoff provides the capability for an app or application to advertise what user activity it is currently performing so that the activity can be picked up and continued on another device.

The Sample App

The sample app for this chapter is called HandoffNotes, which is a basic note app built to demonstrate the basics of Handoff. The app enables a user to keep a list of notes using two different storage approaches: iCloud key-value storage and iCloud document storage. Each note includes a title, note text, and a date when the note was created. The Handoff capability will be advertised when a user is editing a note in either approach. Note that the sample app requires the device to be logged in to a valid iCloud account to work correctly.

Handoff Basics

Handoff requires two devices running either iOS 8 or higher or OS X Yosemite or higher. Each device must be logged in to the same iCloud account, and each device must support Bluetooth version 4.0 (also known as BTLE or Bluetooth Low Energy). This setup will allow iOS and OS X to perform automatic device pairing and enable Handoff.

When a user is engaging in a Handoff-capable activity on a device, the Handoff activity will be advertised to other nearby devices. For example, if a user is viewing a Web page in Safari on an iOS device and then opens her laptop nearby, OS X will show that an activity is available for Handoff in the Dock, as shown in Figure 13.1.

Figure 13.1   Handoff advertisement shown in OS X Dock.

Similarly, if a user is editing a note in HandoffNotes and opens another iOS device nearby, the lock screen will show that HandoffNotes has an activity available for Handoff in the lower-left portion of the screen, by displaying the HandoffNotes app icon next to the Slide to Unlock view, as shown in Figure 13.2.

Figure 13.2   Handoff advertisement shown on the iOS lock screen.

In either case, if the user taps the advertisement in the Dock in OS X, or slides up the icon on the lock screen in iOS, the target app will be displayed. In the Safari example the Web page that the user was browsing will be displayed, and in the HandoffNotes example the app will navigate to the note the user was editing, and include any in-progress updates to the note.

Handoff utilizes a simple mechanism to facilitate advertisement and continuation: NSUserActivity. In iOS, many UIKit classes (including UIResponder) have an NSUserActivity property so that a user activity can be set and propagate through the responder chain. This enables the developer to determine the best representation of a user activity, whether that is viewing some content, editing some text, or performing some other activity, and tie a Handoff activity to that directly in the user interface. In addition, UIDocument has support for NSUserActivity that makes supporting Handoff in document-based apps simple.

An instance of NSUserActivity contains two critical pieces of information: an activityType that identifies what the user is doing, and a userInfo dictionary that contains specific information about the user activity. An activityType should be a reverse DNS string identifier that uniquely identifies an activity. When a user activity is set, iOS will be able to advertise it, as shown in Figures 13.1 and 13.2. When the user continues the activity on another device, the activity will be passed to the destination app, and then the activityType and userInfo can be used by the destination device to navigate to the right place in the app and pick up the activity where it left off. Note that the userInfo dictionary is not intended to be a data transport mechanism. Apple recommends that the userInfo dictionary contain the minimum of information required to restart the user activity on another device, and that other transport mechanisms such as iCloud be used to move the actual data. NSUserActivity does provide a capability to establish a data stream between devices to move data between them if other transport mechanisms are not sufficient.

Tip

Before attempting Handoff in an app, be sure that Handoff works with test devices using Apple's apps that support Handoff (like Safari, Keynote, or Pages, for example). This will ensure that the test devices are properly configured to meet all the Handoff requirements, like having Bluetooth 4.0–enabled and matching iCloud accounts. Without this step, it is easy to spend a lot of time investigating Handoff issues in the wrong place.

Implementing Handoff

For apps that are not document based, Handoff can be implemented directly. The developer must determine what activity or activities the app should advertise, and how the Handoff should occur. A Handoff will frequently require navigation to the right place in an app, and potentially some data transfer of in-progress updates.

To get started, the app needs to declare what activity types are supported. In the Info.plist for the target, there needs to be an entry called NSUserActivityTypes. That entry should contain an array of activity type strings, each of which represents a reverse DNS identifier for an activity type that the app supports, as shown in Figure 13.3.

Figure 13.3 `NSUserActivityTypes` entry for manual `NSUserActivity`.

After the app info is configured, it can be customized to advertise a user activity and continue a user activity.

Creating the User Activity

The sample app uses the iCloud key-value store as a trivial storage and transport mechanism to illustrate the manual approach to Handoff; production apps will likely have a more complex and robust approach to storage and data transport. The sample app maintains a list of notes in an array in the key-value store, and ensures that the key-value store is consistent across devices. To communicate which note is being edited, the sample app just needs to know the index of the note in the note array. In addition, the sample app will capture in-progress updates to the note to communicate as well.

When the user is editing a note in `ICFManualNoteViewController`, an instance of `NSUserActivity` will be created and configured with an activity type. The activity type string must match the string declared in the `Info.plist` file. The sample app configures the user activity in the `viewWillAppear:` method, but other apps should take a close look at what the user is doing to determine the right timing for setting up the user activity.

```
NSUserActivity *noteActivity = [[NSUserActivity alloc]
➥initWithActivityType:@"com.explore-systems.handoffnotes.manual.editing"];

noteActivity.userInfo = @{@"noteIndex":@(self.noteIndex),
                          @"noteTitle":self.note[@"title"],
                          @"noteText":self.note[@"note"]};

[noteActivity setDelegate:self];
 self.userActivity = noteActivity;
```

The user activity is configured with a `userInfo` dictionary containing information about the current activity, is assigned the current view controller as the delegate, and then is assigned to the current view controller's `userActivity` property. After that is done, the app will automatically start advertising the user activity to other devices.

As the user is performing an activity, the `userActivity` should be kept up-to-date to correctly reflect the state of the activity. In the sample app, as the user updates the text and title of the note, the `userActivity` will be updated. To efficiently update the `userActivity`, the sample app indicates that something has happened that requires the `userActivity` to be updated. In this case when the user changes the text in either the note text view or the title text label, the `setNeedsSave:` method will be called.

```
- (BOOL)textField:(UITextField *)textField
  shouldChangeCharactersInRange:(NSRange)range
  replacementString:(NSString *)string {

    [self.userActivity setNeedsSave:YES];
    return YES;
}
- (void)textViewDidChange:(UITextView *)textView {
    [self.userActivity setNeedsSave:YES];
}
```

Then, the delegate method called `updateUserActivityState:` can be implemented to the update the user activity.

```
- (void)updateUserActivityState:(NSUserActivity *)activity {
    activity.userInfo = @{@"noteIndex":@(self.noteIndex),
                          @"noteTitle":self.noteTitle.text,
                          @"noteText":self.noteDetail.text};
    NSLog(@"user info is: %@",activity.userInfo);
}
```

The delegate method will be called periodically and will keep the user activity up-to-date. As the user activity is advertised, it will be visible on other devices, as shown in Figure 13.2. When the user leaves the editing view, the user activity will be automatically invalided and the advertisement will stop. If a user activity should be ended independently of a view controller, the `invalidate` method can be called.

Continuing an Activity

When a user swipes up the icon as shown in Figure 13.2 to continue an activity, the app delegate will be notified that the user would like to continue an activity. First, the `application:willContinueUserActivityWithType:` method will be called to determine whether the app can continue the activity. This method should return a YES or NO to indicate whether the activity will be continued, and any custom logic required to determine whether an activity will be continued can be implemented there. In addition, this is a good opportunity to update the user interface to notify the user that an activity will be continued, in case the continuation is not instantaneous.

Next, the `application:continueUserActivity:restorationHandler:` method will be called to perform the continuation. This method should check the `activityType` of the passed-in `userActivity`, and do any necessary setup or navigation to get the app to the right place to continue the activity. After the setup is complete, the `restorationHandler` can be called with an array of view controllers that should perform additional configuration to restore the activity. In the sample app, the method will synchronize the iCloud key-value store to ensure that state is the same across devices. Then, it will navigate to the manual note list, and call the restoration handler passing the manual note list view controller to perform the rest of the navigation and setup.

```
UIStoryboard *storyboard = [UIStoryboard storyboardWithName:@"Main"
                                              bundle:[NSBundle mainBundle]];

ICFManualNoteTableViewController *manualListVC =
➥[storyboard instantiateViewControllerWithIdentifier:
➥@"ICFManualNoteTableViewController"];

[navController pushViewController:manualListVC animated:NO];

restorationHandler(@[manualListVC]);
```

When the `restorationHandler` block is called, it will call the `restoreUserActivity-State:` method on each view controller included in the array parameter. In the sample app, the method will navigate to the right note for the index included in the `userInfo` of the user activity.

```
if ([activity.userInfo objectForKey:@"noteIndex"]) {
    NSNumber *resumeNoteIndex = [[activity userInfo] objectForKey:@"noteIndex"];

    NSIndexPath *resumeIndexPath =
    ➥[NSIndexPath indexPathForRow:[resumeNoteIndex integerValue]
                        inSection:0];
    [self.tableView selectRowAtIndexPath:resumeIndexPath
                         animated:NO
                   scrollPosition:UITableViewScrollPositionNone];

    [self performSegueWithIdentifier:@"showNoteDetail" sender:activity];
}
```

The method passes the user activity as a parameter when performing the segue to the detail screen; this enables the segue to customize the note with in-progress information.

```
if ([segue.identifier isEqualToString:@"showNoteDetail"]) {

    ICFManualNoteViewController *noteVC =
    ➥(ICFManualNoteViewController *)segue.destinationViewController;
```

```
    NSUInteger selectedIndex = [[self.tableView indexPathForSelectedRow] row];
    NSDictionary *note = [self.noteList objectAtIndex:selectedIndex];

    if ([sender isKindOfClass:[NSUserActivity class]]) {
        NSUserActivity *activity = (NSUserActivity *)sender;
        note = @{@"title":activity.userInfo[@"noteTitle"],
                 @"note":activity.userInfo[@"noteText"],
                 @"date":note[@"date"]};
    }
    [noteVC setNote:note];
    [noteVC setNoteIndex:selectedIndex];
}
```

After the segue is complete, the note detail screen reflects the state of the note on the originating device. Because the originating user activity has been successfully continued, it should stop advertising to other devices. To do that, the note detail view controller implements the `user-ActivityWasContinued:` method, which calls the `invalidate` method on the `userActivity` so that it stops advertising from the originating device.

```
- (void)userActivityWasContinued:(NSUserActivity *)userActivity {
    [self.userActivity invalidate];
}
```

Now that the app has communicated the state of a user activity from one device to another, the user can pick up on the new device where he left off the originating device with minimal effort.

Implementing Handoff in Document-Based Apps

Instances of `UIDocument` have an `NSUserActivity` property that is automatically set up, called `userActivity`. If the document is saved in iCloud, the file URL of the document will be included in the `userInfo` of the `userActivity` so that the receiving device can access the document. In the sample app, the document notes demonstrate this approach. To see it in action, tap UIDocument from the top menu, and tap an existing note. When the document has been opened in the `viewDidLoad` method of `ICFDocumentNoteViewController`, an `NSUserActivity` is created and assigned to the document automatically, with no custom code required.

```
self.noteDocument =
[[ICFNoteDocument alloc] initWithFileURL:[self noteURL]];

[self.noteDocument openWithCompletionHandler:^(BOOL success) {

    [self.noteTitle setText:[self.noteDocument noteTitle]];
    [self.noteDetail setText:[self.noteDocument noteText]];

    UIDocumentState state = self.noteDocument.documentState;
```

```
    if (state == UIDocumentStateNormal) {
        [self.noteTitle becomeFirstResponder];
        NSLog(@"opened and first responder.");
    }
}];
```

In order for the NSUserActivity instance to be created automatically for the UIDocument instance, some additional set up in the project is required. For each document type supported by an app, an NSUbiquitousDocumentUserActivityType entry needs to be included in the CFBundleDocumentTypes entry in the Info.plist file as shown in Figure 13.4.

▼ Document types		Array	(1 item)
▼ Item 0 (ICFHandoffNote)		Dictionary	(6 items)
▼ CFBundleTypeExtensions		Array	(1 item)
Item 0		String	icfnote
▶ CFBundleTypeIconFiles		Array	(0 items)
Document Type Name		String	ICFHandoffNote
Handler rank		String	Owner
▶ Document Content Type UTIs		Array	(1 item)
NSUbiquitousDocumentUserActivityType		String	com.explore-systems.handoffnotes.document.editing

Figure 13.4   NSUbiquitousDocumentUserActivityType entry for automatic NSUserActivity on UIDocument.

In addition, a Uniform Type Indicator (UTI) needs to be declared for the document in the Info.plist file as shown in Figure 13.5.

▼ Exported Type UTIs		Array	(1 item)
▼ Item 0 (com.explore-systems.handoffnotes.icfnote)		Dictionary	(4 items)
Conforms to UTIs		String	public.data
Description		String	ICFMyNoteDocument
Identifier		String	com.explore-systems.handoffnotes.icfnote
▼ Equivalent Types		Dictionary	(1 item)
▼ public.filename-extension		Array	(1 item)
Item 0		String	icfnote

Figure 13.5   Uniform Type Indicator (UTI) entry for UIDocument file type.

When the activity is continued on another device, the application:continueUserActivity: restorationHandler: method in the app on the receiving device will check the activity type, and then will navigate to the document note list screen and call the restorationHandler.

```
UINavigationController *navController =
➥(UINavigationController *)self.window.rootViewController;

[navController popToRootViewControllerAnimated:NO];

UIStoryboard *storyboard =
➥[UIStoryboard storyboardWithName:@"Main" bundle:[NSBundle mainBundle]];
```

```
ICFDocumentNoteTableViewController *documentListVC =
➥[storyboard instantiateViewControllerWithIdentifier:
➥@"ICFDocumentNoteTableViewController"];

[navController pushViewController:documentListVC animated:NO];
restorationHandler(@[documentListVC]);
```

The `restorationHandler` will call the `restoreUserActivityState:` method in the document note table view controller, which will get the file URL for the document in the `userInfo` of the `userActivity` passed in, using the key `NSUserActivityDocumentURLKey`.

```
if ([activity.userInfo objectForKey:NSUserActivityDocumentURLKey]) {

    self.navigateToURL =
    ➥[activity.userInfo objectForKey:NSUserActivityDocumentURLKey];

    [self performSegueWithIdentifier:@"showDocNoteDetail"
                              sender:activity];
}
```

The document note detail screen will be displayed, the document for the file URL in the activity will be loaded, and the user can pick up on the new device where she left off the originating device.

Summary

This chapter looked at using Handoff to continue a user's activity between devices in an app. It covered the basic requirements of Handoff, such as having Bluetooth 4.0–enabled devices running either OS X Yosemite or iOS 8.0 or higher on the same iCloud account. It explained how to set up a user activity so that it will be advertised to other devices, and how to continue a user activity from another device. This chapter also explained how to support automatic user activity creation and handling with `UIDocument`.

AirPrint

Without a doubt, printing is going the way of the dodo bird and the Tasmanian tiger, but it will not happen overnight. Plenty of solid autumn years remain for physical printing. Print will most likely cling to life for a long time, along with the fax. Apple has provided an SDK feature, aptly named AirPrint, since iOS 4, which allows for physical printing to compatible wireless printers.

With the expansion and trust of mobile software into more established traditional fields over the past few years, AirPrint is becoming more popular. Point-of-sales apps and medical-processing apps both have a strong need for being able to print physical documents.

AirPrint Printers

There is a limited selection of AirPrint-enabled printers, even more than four years after the release of AirPrint. Most major printer manufacturers now have at least a few models that support AirPrint. Apple also maintains a list of compatible printers through a tech note (http://support.apple.com/kb/HT4356). In addition, some third-party Mac applications enable AirPrint for any existing printer, such as Printopia ($19.95 at www.ecamm.com/mac/printopia).

Since the release of AirPrint, there have been numerous blogs, articles, and how-tos written on testing AirPrint. Apple seems to have taken notice of the need and has started to bundle an app with the developer tools called Printer Simulator (`Developer/Platforms/iPhoneOS.platform/Developer/Applications`), as shown in Figure 14.1. Printer Simulator enables your Mac to host several printer configurations for the iOS Simulator to print to; using this tool, you can test a wide range of compatibility.

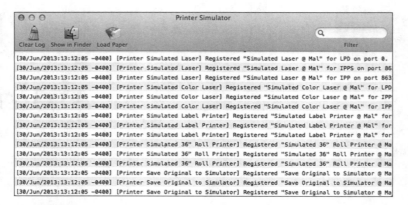

Figure 14.1   The Printer Simulator tool.

The sample app for this chapter is a simple iPhone app that provides the user with two views, as shown in Figure 14.2. The first view is a simple text editor, which will demo how to position pages and text. The second view is a Web browser, which will demo how to print rendered HTML as well as PDF screen grabs.

Figure 14.2   Print, the sample app for AirPrint.

The Print app is simple and does not contain a significant amount of overhead code. It is based on the Apple TabBarController default project, containing two tabs. The text editor contains a `UITextView` as well as two buttons: one to hide the keyboard, the other to begin the print process. The Web browser view contains a Print button but also needs a URL entry text field.

Testing for AirPrint

It is important to test for AirPrint support in your software before enabling the functionality to users, because some of your users might be running an iOS version that does not support AirPrint. In the sample app, this is performed as part of the `application:didFinish-LaunchingWithOptions:` method using the following code snippet:

```
if (![UIPrintInteractionController isPrintingAvailable])
{
    UIAlertView *alert = [[UIAlertView alloc]
    initWithTitle:@"Error"
    message:@"This device does not support printing!"
    delegate:nil
    cancelButtonTitle:@"Dismiss"
    otherButtonTitles:nil];

    [alert show];
}
```

Note
AirPrint is defined as part of `UIKit` so there are no additional headers or frameworks that need to be imported.

Printing Text

Printing text is probably the most common use case for not just AirPrint but any kind of print job. Using AirPrint to print text can be complex if you aren't familiar with printing terminology. The following code is from the `ICFFirstViewController.m` class of the sample app. Look at it as a whole first; later in this section, it will be broken down by each line and discussed.

```
- (IBAction)print:(id)sender
{
    UIPrintInteractionController *print =
    [UIPrintInteractionController sharedPrintController];

    print.delegate = self;
```

```
UIPrintInfo *printInfo = [UIPrintInfo printInfo];
printInfo.outputType = UIPrintInfoOutputGeneral;
printInfo.jobName = @"Print for iOS";
printInfo.duplex = UIPrintInfoDuplexLongEdge;
print.printInfo = printInfo;

print.showsPageRange = YES;

UISimpleTextPrintFormatter *textFormatter =
➥[[UISimpleTextPrintFormatter alloc] initWithText:[theTextView
➥text]];

textFormatter.startPage = 0;

textFormatter.contentInsets = UIEdgeInsetsMake(36.0, 36.0,36.0,
➥36.0);

textFormatter.maximumContentWidth = 540;

print.printFormatter = textFormatter
}
```

The preceding code takes the contents of a text view and prints it formatted for 8 1/2- by 11-inch paper with 1/2-inch margins on all sides. The first thing you need to do whenever you want to prepare for a print operation is create a reference to the sharedPrintController using the following code snippet:

```
UIPrintInteractionController *print = [UIPrintInteractionController
➥sharedPrintController];
```

In the next line of the sample app, a delegate is set. The delegate methods for printing are defined in the upcoming section "UIPrintInteractionControllerDelegate."

Print Info

The next step is to configure the print info. This specifies a number of controls and modifiers for how the print job is set up. You can obtain a new default UIPrintInfo object using the provided UIPrintInfo singleton.

The first property that is set on the print info in the sample app is outputType. In the example, the output is set as UIPrintInfoOutputGeneral. This specifies that the print job can be a mix of text, graphics, and images, as well as setting the default paper size to letter. Other options for outputType include UIPrintInfoOutputPhoto and UIPrintInfoOutputGrayscale.

The next property that is set is the jobName. This is an optional field that is used to identify the print job in the print center app. If you do not set a jobName, it is defaulted to the app's name.

Duplexing in the printer world refers to how the printer handles double-sided printing. If the printer does not support double-sided printing, these properties are ignored. You can supply UIPrintInfoDuplexNone if you would like to prevent double-sided printing. To use double-sided printing, you have two options: UIPrintInfoDuplexLongEdge, which will flip the back page along the long edge of the paper, and UIPrintInfoDuplexShortEdge, which, as the name implies, flips the back page along the short side of the paper.

In addition to the printInfo properties that are used in the sample code, there are two additional properties. The first, orientation, enables you to specify printing in either landscape or portrait. The second is printerID, which enables you to specify a hint on which printer to use. PrinterID is often used to automatically select the last used printer, which can be obtained using the UIPrintInteractionControllerDelegate.

After you configure the printInfo for the print job, you need to set the associated property on the UIPrintInteractionController. An example is shown in the next code snippet:

```
print.printInfo = printInfo;
```

Setting Page Range

In many cases, a print job will consist of multiple pages, and occasionally you will want to provide the user with the option of selecting which of those pages is printed. You can do this through the showsPageRange property. When set to YES, it will allow the user to select pages during the printer selection stage.

```
print.showsPageRange = YES;
```

UISimpleTextPrintFormatter

After configuring the printInfo, the UIPrintInteractionController has a good idea of what type of print job is coming but doesn't yet have any information on what to print. This data is set using a print formatter; this section discusses the print formatter for text. In following sections, additional print formatters are discussed in depth.

```
UISimpleTextPrintFormatter *textFormatter =
➥[[UISimpleTextPrintFormatter alloc] initWithText:[theTextView
➥text]];

textFormatter.startPage = 0;

textFormatter.contentInsets = UIEdgeInsetsMake(36.0, 36.0, 36.0, 36.0);

textFormatter.maximumContentWidth = 540;

print.printFormatter = textFormatter;
```

When you create a new instance of the `UISimpleTextPrintFormatter`, it is allocated and initialized with the text you will be printing. The sample app will print any text that appears in the `UITextView`.

The first property that is set in the sample app is for the `startPage`. This is a zero-based index of the first page to be printed. The sample app will begin printing from page one (index 0).

On the following line `contentInserts` are set. A value of `72.0` equals one inch on printed paper. The sample app will be providing half-inch values on all sides; this will print the text with half-inch margins on the top, bottom, left, and right. Additionally, the maximum width is set to 504, which specifies a 7 1/2-inch printing width (72.0×7.0).

There are two additional properties that were not used in the sample app. The `font` property enables you to specify a `UIFont` that the text is to be printed in. `font` is an optional property; if you do not specify a font, the system font at 12-point is used. You can also specify a text color using the `color` property. If you do not provide a color, `[UIColor blackColor]` is used.

When you finish configuring the `textFormatter`, you will need to set it to the `printFormatter` property of the `UIPrintInteractionController` object.

Error Handling

It is always important to gracefully handle errors, even more so while printing. With printing, there are any number of things that can go wrong outside of the developer's control, from out-of-paper issues to the printer not even being on.

The sample app defines a new block called `completionHandler`. This is used to handle any errors that are returned from the print job. In the next section, you will begin a new print job with the `completionHandler` block as one of the arguments.

```
void (^completionHandler)(UIPrintInteractionController *,BOOL, NSError
*) = ^(UIPrintInteractionController *print,BOOL completed, NSError
*error)
{
    if (!completed && error)
    {
        NSLog(@"Error!");
    }
};
```

Starting the Print Job

After you have created a new `UIPrintInteractionController`, specified the `printInfo` and the `printFormatter`, and created a block to handle any errors that are returned, you can finally print something. Call the method `presentAnimated:completionHandler:` on the `UIPrintInteractionController` object using the completion block that was created in the preceding section. This will present the user with the Printer Options view, as shown in Figure 14.3.

```
[print presentAnimated:YES completionHandler:completionHandler];
```

Figure 14.3   Print options for printing text with multiple pages on a printer that supports double-sided printing.

Depending on the selected printer and the amount of text being printed, the options will vary. For example, if the print job is only one page, the user will not be presented with a range option; likewise, if the printer does not support double-sided printing, this option will be disabled.

Printer Simulator Feedback

If you printed to the Printer Simulator app as discussed in the "AirPrint Printers" section, after the print job is finished, a new page will be opened in preview (or your default PDF viewing application) showing how the final page will look. An example using the print info and print formatter information from this section is shown in Figure 14.4.

Figure 14.4   A print preview shown when the Printer Simulator is used; notice the highlighted margins.

Print Center

Just as on desktop computers, iOS provides users a way to interact with the current print queue. Although any print job is active on an iOS device, a new app appears in the active app area. The Print Center app itself is shown in Figure 14.5. The Print Center was removed in iOS 7 and printing feedback is now handled during the print process.

Figure 14.5   Print Center app provides information about the current print job.

UIPrintInteractionControllerDelegate

As shown earlier in the "Printing Text" section, you can optionally provide a delegate for a `UIPrintInteractionController` object. The possible delegate callbacks are used in both views of the sample app. Table 14.1 describes these delegate methods.

Table 14.1   Available **UIPrintInteractionControllerDelegate** Methods

Method Name	Description
printInteractionControllerWillPresent-PrinterOptions:	The API will present the options for the user to configure the print job.
printInteractionControllerDidPresent-PrinterOptions:	The API did present the options for the user to configure the print job.
printInteractionControllerWill-DismissPrinterOptions:	The API will dismiss the print options view.
printInteractionControllerDid-DismissPrinterOptions:	The API did dismiss the print options view.

Method Name	Description
printInteractionControllerWillStartJob:	The method is called right before the print job is started.
printInteractionControllerDidFinishJob:	This method is called when the print job has been completed or has failed.

Printing Rendered HTML

Printing rendered HTML is handled automatically through a print formatter in an almost identical manner as printing plain text. The following method handles printing an HTML string, which is retrieved from the UIWebView in the sample app. You might notice that this is similar to how text was printed in the previous example. Take a look at the method as a whole; it is discussed in detail later in this section.

```
- (IBAction)print:(id)sender
{
    UIPrintInteractionController *print =
    ➥[UIPrintInteractionController sharedPrintController];

    print.delegate = self;

    UIPrintInfo *printInfo = [UIPrintInfo printInfo];
    printInfo.outputType = UIPrintInfoOutputGeneral;
    printInfo.jobName = @"Print for iOS";
    printInfo.duplex = UIPrintInfoDuplexLongEdge;
    print.printInfo = printInfo;

    print.showsPageRange = YES;

    NSURL *requestURL = [[theWebView request] URL];
    NSError *error;

    NSString *contentHTML = [NSString
    stringWithContentsOfURL:requestURL
    encoding:NSASCIIStringEncoding
    error:&error];

    UIMarkupTextPrintFormatter *textFormatter =
    ➥[[UIMarkupTextPrintFormatter alloc]
    ➥initWithMarkupText:contentHTML];

    textFormatter.startPage = 0;
```

```
textFormatter.contentInsets = UIEdgeInsetsMake(36.0, 36.0, 36.0,
➦36.0);

textFormatter.maximumContentWidth = 540;
print.printFormatter = textFormatter;


void (^completionHandler)(UIPrintInteractionController *,BOOL,
➦NSError *) = ^(UIPrintInteractionController *print,BOOL
➦ completed, NSError *error)
{
    if (!completed && error)
    {
        NSLog(@"Error!");
    }
};

[print presentAnimated:YES completionHandler:completionHandler];
}
```

The first thing that needs to be done as it was in the text printing is to create a new reference to a UIPrintInteractionController. The next step is to set the printInfo for the upcoming print job. Nothing in this code block dealing with printing differs from the printing text example; refer to that section for details on these properties.

Printing PDFs

AirPrint has built-in support for printing PDF files. PDF is arguably the easiest type of file to print when you have the PDF data. Before a PDF file can be printed, first the UIPrintInteractionController and associated UIPrintInfo need to be set up. This setup is done exactly the same as in the preceding example in the section "Printing Rendered HTML." In the sample app, the PDF is generated from the UIWebView from the preceding section; however, you can specify any source for the PDF data. After the data has been created using the renderInContext method, you can assign that image value to printingItem. This method can also be used to print any UIImage data.

> Note
>
> The sample app does not currently have an action hooked up to the print PDF method. You will have to assign a button to that method in order to use it.

```
- (IBAction)printPDF:(id)sender
{
    UIPrintInteractionController *print =
    [UIPrintInteractionController sharedPrintController];
```

```objc
    print.delegate = self;
    UIPrintInfo *printInfo = [UIPrintInfo printInfo];
    printInfo.outputType = UIPrintInfoOutputGeneral;
    printInfo.jobName = @"Print for iOS";
    printInfo.duplex = UIPrintInfoDuplexLongEdge;
    print.printInfo = printInfo;

    print.showsPageRange = YES;

    UIGraphicsBeginImageContext(theWebView.bounds.size);

    [theWebView.layer
    renderInContext:UIGraphicsGetCurrentContext()];

    UIImage *image = UIGraphicsGetImageFromCurrentImageContext();
    UIGraphicsEndImageContext();

    print.printingItem = image;

    void (^completionHandler)(UIPrintInteractionController *,BOOL,
    ➥NSError *) = ^(UIPrintInteractionController *print,BOOL
    ➥completed,NSError *error)
    {
        if (!completed && error)
        {
            NSLog(@"Error!");
        }
    };

    [print presentAnimated:YES completionHandler:completionHandler];
}
```

Summary

In this chapter, you learned how to print documents, images, and HTML from an iOS device using AirPrint. You should have a firm grasp of the knowledge required to create new print jobs, provide the materials to be printed, format the output, handle errors, and interact with various printers. The sample app provided for this chapter walked you through the process of printing plain text, HTML, and PDF data. You should feel confident adding AirPrint support into any of your existing or future iOS projects.

15

Getting Up and Running with Core Data

For many apps, being able to locally store and retrieve data that persists beyond a single session is a requirement. Since iOS 3.0, Core Data has been available to address this need. Core Data is a powerful object database; it provides robust data storage and management capabilities.

Core Data has its roots in NeXT's Enterprise Object Framework (EOF), which was capable of mapping objects to relational databases. There are great advantages to writing business logic to objects, and to not having to build database or persistence-specific logic. Mainly, there is a lot less code to write, and that code tends to be focused on the needs of the app rather than the needs of the database. EOF could support several brands of relational databases. Since Core Data was built to support single-user applications in Mac OS X, Core Data supports storing data in an embedded relational database called SQLite, which provides the benefits of an SQL database without the hassle and overhead of maintaining a database server.

Some features of Core Data include the following:

- Modeling data objects with a visual model editor
- Automatic and manual migration tools to handle when object schema changes
- Establishing relationships between objects (one-to-one, one-to-many, many-to-many)
- Storing data in separate files and different file formats
- Validation of object attributes
- Querying and sorting data
- Lazy-loading data
- Interacting closely with iOS table views and collection views
- Managing related object changes with commit and undo capabilities

At first glance, Core Data can look difficult and overwhelming. Several books are devoted solely to Core Data, and the official Apple documentation is lengthy and challenging to get through since it covers the entire breadth and depth of the topic. However, most apps do not require all the features that Core Data has to offer. The goal of this chapter is to get you up and running with the most common Core Data features that apps need.

This chapter describes how to set up a project to use Core Data, and illustrates how to implement several common use cases with the sample app. It covers how to set up your data model, how to populate some starting data, and how to display data in a table using a fetched results controller. This chapter also demonstrates how to add, edit, and delete data, how to fetch data, and how to use predicates to fetch specific data. With this knowledge, you will have a good foundation for implementing Core Data quickly in your apps.

Deciding on Core Data

Before we dive into Core Data, it is generally worthwhile to take a look at the persistence requirements of an app and compare those to the available persistence options. If the app's requirements can be met without implementing Core Data, that can save some development effort and reduce the overall complexity of the app, making it easier to maintain in the long run. A few options are available to iOS developers who want to use persistent data:

- **NSUserDefaults:** This method is typically used to save app preferences. NSUserDefaults functions very much like an NSDictionary with key-value storage, and supports storing values that can be expressed as NSNumber, NSString, NSDate, NSData, NSDictionary, NSArray, or any object that conforms to the NSCoding protocol. If an app's persistence needs can be satisfied using key-value pairs, dictionaries, and arrays, then NSUserDefaults is a viable option.

- **iCloud Key-Value Storage:** This method works just like NSUserDefaults, except that it is supported by iCloud and can sync data across devices. There are fairly strict limits on how much data can be stored and synced. If an app's persistence needs can be satisfied using key-value pairs, dictionaries, and arrays, and syncing between devices is desired, then iCloud key-value storage is a viable option.

- **Property List (plist):** NSDictionary and NSArray each support reading from and saving to a user-specified property list file, which is an XML file format supporting NSNumber, NSString, NSDate, NSData, NSDictionary, and NSArray. If an app's persistence needs can be satisfied using a dictionary or an array, a property list file is a viable option.

- **Coders and Keyed Archives:** NSCoder and NSKeyedArchiver support saving an arbitrary object graph into a binary file. These options require implementing NSCoder methods in each custom object to be saved, and require the developer to manage saving and loading. If an app's persistence needs can be satisfied with a handful of custom objects, the coder/ archiver approach is a viable option.

- **Structured Text Files (JSON, CSV, etc.):** Structured text files such as CSV or JSON can be used to store data. JSON in particular can take advantage of built-in serialization and deserialization support (see Chapter 9, "Working with and Parsing JSON," for more details); but any structured text method will require building additional support for custom model objects and any searching and filtering requirements. If an app's persistence needs can be satisfied with a handful of custom objects, or a dictionary or an array, then using structured text files can be a viable option.

- **Direct SQLite:** Using the C library `libsqlite`, apps can interact with SQLite databases directly. SQLite is an embedded relational database that does not need a server; it supports most of the standard SQL language as described by SQL92. Any data persistence logic that can be built using SQL can likely be built into an iOS app utilizing SQLite, including defining database tables and relationships, inserting data, querying data, and updating and deleting data. The drawback of this approach is that the app needs to map data between application objects and SQL files, requires writing SQL queries to retrieve and save data, and requires code to track which objects need to be saved.

- **Core Data:** This provides most of the flexibility of working with SQLite directly, while insulating the app from the mechanics of working with the database. If the app requires more than a handful of data, needs to maintain relationships between different objects, or needs to be able to access specific objects or groups of objects quickly and easily, Core Data might be a good candidate.

One feature that really makes Core Data stand out as an exceptional persistence approach is called the `NSFetchedResultsController`. With an `NSFetchedResultsController`, a table view or a collection view can be easily tied to data, and can be informed when the underlying data changes. Both table views and collection views have methods built in to allow for animation of cell insertions, deletions, and moves, which are provided when the `NSFetchedResultsController` detects changes to the relevant data. This feature can be used to great effect when an app needs to pull data from a server and store it locally, and then update a table or collection on the screen with the new data. This chapter explains how to implement an `NSFetchedResultsController` in an app.

Sample App

The sample app for this chapter is called MyMovies. It is a Core Data–based app that will keep track of all your physical media movies and, if you have loaned a movie to someone, who you loaned it to and when (as shown in Figure 15.1).

The sample app has three tabs: Movies, Friends, and Shared Movies. The Movies tab shows the whole list of movies that the user has added and tracked in a table view. There are two sections in the table view demonstrating how data can be segregated with a fetched results controller. Users can add new movies from this tab, and can edit existing movies. The Friends tab lists the friends set up to share movies with, shows which friends have borrowed movies, and enables the user to add and edit friends. The Shared Movies tab displays which movies have currently been shared with friends.

Figure 15.1   Sample App: Movies tab.

Starting a Core Data Project

To start a new Core Data project, open Xcode and select File from the menu, New, and then Project. Xcode will present some project template options to get you started (see Figure 15.2).

The quickest method to start a Core Data project is to select the Master-Detail template. Click Next to specify options for your new project, and then make sure that Use Core Data is selected (see Figure 15.3). This ensures that your project has the Core Data plumbing built in.

When Next is clicked, Xcode creates the project template. The project template includes a "master" view controller, which includes a table view populated by an `NSFetchedResultsController`, a specialized controller that makes pairing Core Data with a table view a snap. The project template includes a "detail" view to display a single data record. In the sample app, the master and detail views have been renamed to fit the project.

> ### Note
>
> To add Core Data to an existing project quickly, create an empty template project with Core Data support as described, and then copy the elements described in the following section, "Core Data Environment," into the existing project. Add a new managed object model file to the project, and be sure to add the Core Data framework to the existing project as well.

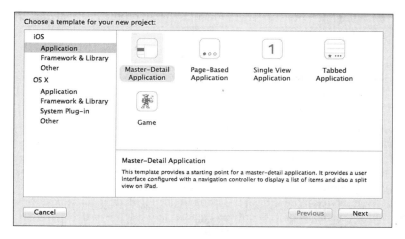

Figure 15.2   Xcode new project template choices.

Figure 15.3   Xcode new project options.

Core Data Environment

The project template sets up the Core Data environment for the project in the class that implements the UIApplicationDelegate protocol; in the sample app this is ICFAppDelegate. The project template uses a lazy-loading pattern for each of the properties needed in the Core Data environment, so each is loaded when needed.

The process of loading the Core Data environment is kicked off the first time the managed object context is referenced in the app. The managed object context (NSManagedObjectContext) is a working area for managed objects. To create a new object, delete an object, or query existing objects, the app interacts with the managed object context. In addition, the managed object context can manage related changes. For example, the app could insert a few objects, update some objects, delete an object, and then save all those changes together or even roll them back if they are not needed.

More than one managed object context can be used at the same time to separate or confine work. Imagine that an app needs to display a set of data while it is importing some new data from a Web service. In that case, one managed object context would be used in the main thread to query and display existing data. Another managed object context could be created as a child of the main context, which would then be used in a background thread to import the data from the Web service. When the app is done importing data, it can quickly and automatically merge the two managed object contexts together and dispose of the background context. Core Data is powerful enough to handle cases in which the same object is updated in both contexts, and can merge the changes.

Note that one change to the template setup is needed as of this writing: Instead of a normal alloc / init for the managed object context, the initWithConcurrencyType: method should be used. As of iOS 8, the thread confinement approach for Core Data (in which the developer is responsible for managing which thread Core Data operations run on) has been deprecated. Instead, for basic apps with relatively small data requirements, use the main queue concurrency type, which requires performing Core Data operations in a block. This approach ensures that all the Core Data access takes place on the correct thread, and avoids potentially challenging threading and debugging issues. For more complex apps in which data updates need to take place on background threads, more advanced Core Data stacks can be established with parent/child relationships to handle background operations and efficient merging with the main queue managed object context.

The managed object context accessor method will check to see whether the managed object context instance variable has a reference. If not, it will get the persistent store coordinator and instantiate a new managed object context with it, assign the new instance to the instance variable, and return the instance variable.

```
- (NSManagedObjectContext *)managedObjectContext
{
  if (__managedObjectContext != nil)
  {
    return __managedObjectContext;
  }

  NSPersistentStoreCoordinator *coordinator =
➥[self persistentStoreCoordinator];

  if (coordinator != nil)
  {
    __managedObjectContext = [[NSManagedObjectContext alloc]
    ➥initWithConcurrencyType:NSMainQueueConcurrencyType];
```

```
    [__managedObjectContext
    ➥setPersistentStoreCoordinator:coordinator];
  }
  return __managedObjectContext;
}
```

The persistent store coordinator is the class that Core Data uses to manage the persistent stores (or files) where the data for the app is stored. To instantiate it, an instance of NSManagedObjectModel is needed so that the persistent store coordinator knows what object model the persistent stores are implementing. The persistent store coordinator also needs a URL for each persistent store to be added; if the file does not exist, Core Data will create it. If the persistent store doesn't match the managed object model (Core Data uses a hash of the managed object model to uniquely identify it, which is kept for comparison in the persistent store), then the template logic will log an error and abort. In a shipping application, logic would be added to properly handle errors with a migration from the old data model to the new one; in development having the app abort can be a useful reminder when the model changes to retest with a clean installation of the app.

```
- (NSPersistentStoreCoordinator *)persistentStoreCoordinator
{
  if (__persistentStoreCoordinator != nil)
  {
    return __persistentStoreCoordinator;
  }

  NSURL *storeURL =
  ➥[[self applicationDocumentsDirectory]
  ➥URLByAppendingPathComponent:@"MyMovies.sqlite"];

  NSError *error = nil;
  __persistentStoreCoordinator =
  ➥[[NSPersistentStoreCoordinator alloc]
  ➥initWithManagedObjectModel:[self managedObjectModel]];

  if (![__persistentStoreCoordinator
    ➥addPersistentStoreWithType:NSSQLiteStoreType
    ➥configuration:nil URL:storeURL options:nil
    ➥error:&error])
  {
    NSLog(@"Unresolved error %@, %@", error,
      [error userInfo]);

    abort();
  }

  return __persistentStoreCoordinator;
}
```

The managed object model is loaded from the app's main bundle. Xcode will give the managed object model the same name as your project.

```
- (NSManagedObjectModel *)managedObjectModel
{
  if (__managedObjectModel != nil)
  {
    return __managedObjectModel;
  }

  NSURL *modelURL =
  ➥[[NSBundle mainBundle] URLForResource:@"MyMovies"
                          withExtension:@"momd"];

  __managedObjectModel =
  ➥[[NSManagedObjectModel alloc]
    initWithContentsOfURL:modelURL];

  return __managedObjectModel;
}
```

Building Your Managed Object Model

With the project template, Xcode will create a data model file with the same name as your project. In the sample project this file is called MyMovies.xdatamodeld. To edit your data model, click the data model file, and Xcode will present the data model editor (see Figure 15.4).

Xcode has two styles for the data model editor: Table and Graph. The Table style presents the entities in your data model in a list on the left. Selecting an entity will display and enable you to edit the attributes, relationships, and fetched properties for that entity.

To change to Graph style, click the Editor Style Graph button in the lower-right corner of the data model editor (see Figure 15.5). There will still be a list of entities on the left of the data model editor, but the main portion of the editor will present an entity relationship diagram of your data model. Each box presented in the diagram represents an entity, with the name of the entity at the top, the attributes listed in the middle, and any relationships listed in the bottom. The graph will have arrows connecting entities that have relationships established, with arrows indicating the cardinality of the relationship.

When you are working with your data model, it is often convenient to have more working space available and to have access to additional detail for selected items. Use Xcode's View options in the upper-right corner of the window to hide the Navigator panel and display the Utilities panel (see Figure 15.5).

Figure 15.4   Xcode data model editor, Table style.

Figure 15.5   Xcode data model editor, Graph style.

Creating an Entity

To create an entity, click the Add Entity button. A new entity will be added to the list of entities, and if the editor is in Graph style, a new entity box will be added to the view. Xcode will
highlight the name of the entity and enable you to type in the desired name for the entity. The
name of the entity can be changed at any time by just clicking twice on the entity name in
the list of entities, or by selecting the desired entity and editing the entity name in the Utilities
panel.

Core Data supports entity inheritance. For any entity, you can specify a parent entity from
which your entity will inherit attributes, relationships, validations, and custom methods. To
do that, ensure that the entity to be inherited from has been created, and then select the child
entity and choose the desired parent entity in the Utilities panel.

> ### Note
>
> If you are using SQLite as your persistent store, Core Data implements entity inheritance by
> creating one table for the parent entity and all child entities, with a superset of all their attri-
> butes. This can obviously have unintended performance consequences if you have a lot of data
> in the entities, so use this feature wisely.

Adding Attributes

To add attributes to an entity, first select the entity in either the graph or the list of entities.
Then click the Add Attribute button in the lower part of the editor, just to the left of the Editor
Style buttons. Xcode will add an attribute called `attribute` to the entity. Select a Type for the
attribute. (See Table 15.1 for supported data types.) Note that Core Data treats all attributes as
Objective-C objects, so if Integer 32 is the selected data type, for example, Core Data will treat
the attribute as an `NSNumber`.

One thing to note is that Core Data will automatically give each instance a unique object ID,
called `objectID`, which it uses internally to manage storage and relationships. You can also
add a unique ID or another candidate key to the entity and add an index to it for quick access,
but note that Core Data will manage relationships with the generated object ID.

`NSManagedObject` instances also have a method called `description`; if you want to have a
`description` attribute, modify the name slightly to avoid conflicts. In the sample app, for
example, the `Movie` entity has a `movieDescription` attribute.

Table 15.1   Core Data Supported Data Types

Data Types	Objective-C Storage
Integer 16	`NSNumber`
Integer 32	`NSNumber`
Integer 64	`NSNumber`

Data Types	Objective-C Storage
Decimal	NSNumber
Double	NSNumber
Float	NSNumber
String	NSString
Boolean	NSNumber
Date	NSDate
Binary Data	NSData
Transformable	Uses value transformer

Establishing Relationships

Having relationships between objects can be a powerful technique to model the real world in an app. Core Data supports one-to-one and one-to-many relationships. In the sample app, a one-to-many relationship between friends and movies is established. Since a friend might borrow more than one movie at a time, that side of the relationship is "many," but a movie can be lent to only one friend at a time, so that side of the relationship is "one."

To add a relationship between entities, select one of the entities, and then Ctrl-click and drag to the destination entity. Alternatively, click and hold the Add Attribute button, and select Add Relationship from the menu that appears. Xcode will create a relationship to the destination entity and will call it "relationship." In the Utilities panel, select the Data Model inspector, and change the name of the relationship. In the Data Model inspector, you can do the following:

- Indicate whether the relationship is transient.
- Specify whether the relationship is optional or required with the Optional check box.
- Specify whether the relationship is ordered.
- Establish an inverse relationship. To do this, create and name the inverse relationship first, and then select it from the drop-down. The inverse relationship allows the "to" object to have a reference to the "from" object, in addition to the original relationship.
- Specify the cardinality of the relationship by checking or unchecking the Plural check box. If checked, it indicates a to-many relationship.
- Specify minimum and maximum counts for a relationship.
- Set up the rule for Core Data to follow for the relationship when the object is deleted. Choices are No Action (no additional action taken on delete), Nullify (relationship set to nil), Cascade (objects on the other side of the relationship are deleted too), and Deny (error issued if relationships exist).

Custom Managed Object Subclasses

A custom `NSManagedObject` subclass can be useful if you have custom logic for your model object, or if you would like to be able to use dot syntax for your model object properties and have the compiler validate them.

Xcode has a menu option to automatically create a subclass for you. To use it, ensure that you have completed setup of your entity in the data model editor. Select your entity (or multiple entities) in the data model editor, select Editor from the Xcode menu, and then select Create NSManagedObject Subclass. Xcode will ask where you want to save the generated class files. Specify a location and click Create, and Xcode will generate the header and implementation files for each entity you specified. Xcode will name each class with the class prefix specified for your project concatenated with the name of the entity.

In the generated header file, Xcode will create a property for each attribute in the entity. Note that Xcode will also create a property for each relationship specified for the entity. If the relationship is to-one, Xcode will create an `NSManagedObject` property (or `NSManagedObject` subclass if the destination entity is a custom subclass). If the relationship is to-many, Xcode will create an `NSSet` property.

In the generated implementation file, Xcode will create `@dynamic` instructions for each entity, rather than `@synthesize`. This is because Core Data dynamically handles accessors for Core Data managed attributes, and does not need the compiler to build the accessor methods.

> **Note**
>
> A project called mogenerator will generate two classes per entity: one for the attribute accessors and one for custom logic. That way, you can regenerate classes easily when making model changes without overwriting your custom logic. Mogenerator is available at http://rentzsch. github.com/mogenerator/.

Setting Up Default Data

When a Core Data project is first set up, there is no data in it. Although this might work for some use cases, frequently it is a requirement to have some data prepopulated in the app for the first run. In the sample app there is a custom data setup class called `ICFDataStarter`, which illustrates one method to populate Core Data with some initial data. A `#define` variable is set up in `MyMovies-Prefix.pch` called `FIRSTRUN`, which can be uncommented to have the app run the logic in `ICFDataStarter`.

Inserting New Managed Objects

To create a new instance of a managed object for data that does not yet exist in your model, a reference to the managed object context is needed. The sample app passes the managed object context property from the `ICFAppDelegate` to the `setupStarterDataWithMOC:` method in `ICFDataStarter`:

```
[ICFDataStarter setupStarterDataWithMOC:[self managedObjectContext]];
```

To prevent threading errors, all activities against Core Data objects should take place in a block performed by the managed object context. There are two options: `performBlock:` and `performBlockAndWait:`. The first option will submit the block to the managed object context's queue asynchronously, and then will continue executing code in the current scope. The second approach will submit the block to the managed object context's queue asynchronously, and then wait until all the operations are completed before continuing to execute code in the current scope. When there are no dependencies in the current scope, use `performBlock:` to avoid deadlocks and waiting; if there are dependencies, use `performBlockAndWait:`. In this case, because the managed object context is on the main queue and the code is executing on the main queue, using `performBlockAndWait:` ensures that everything executes in the sequence shown in the code and prevents any confusion from items potentially executing out of sequence.

```
[moc performBlockAndWait:^{
```

To insert data, Core Data needs to know what entity the new data is for. Core Data has a class called `NSEntityDescription` that provides information about entities. Create a new instance using `NSEntityDescription`'s class method:

```
NSManagedObject *newMovie1 =
➡ [NSEntityDescription insertNewObjectForEntityForName:@"Movie"
                               inManagedObjectContext:moc];
```

After an instance is available, populate the attributes with data:

```
[newMovie1 setValue:@"The Matrix" forKey:@"title"];
[newMovie1 setValue:@"1999" forKey:@"year"];

[newMovie1 setValue:@"Take the blue pill."
            forKey:@"movieDescription"];

[newMovie1 setValue:@NO forKey:@"lent"];
[newMovie1 setValue:nil forKey:@"lentOn"];
[newMovie1 setValue:@20 forKey:@"timesWatched"];
```

Core Data uses key-value coding to handle setting attributes. If an attribute name is incorrect, it will fail at runtime. To get compile-time checking of attribute assignments, create a custom `NSManagedObject` subclass and use the property accessors for each attribute directly.

The managed object context acts as a working area for changes, so the sample app sets up more initial data:

```
NSManagedObject *newFriend1 =
➡ [NSEntityDescription insertNewObjectForEntityForName:@"Friend"
                               inManagedObjectContext:moc];

[newFriend1 setValue:@"Joe" forKey:@"friendName"];
[newFriend1 setValue:@"joe@dragonforged.com" forKey:@"email"];
```

The last step after setting up all the initial data is to save the managed object context, and close the block.

```
NSError *mocSaveError = nil;

if ([moc save:&mocSaveError])
{
    NSLog(@"Save completed successfully.");
} else
{
    NSLog(@"Save did not complete successfully. Error: %@",
    ➥[mocSaveError localizedDescription]);
}
}];
```

After the managed object context is saved, Core Data will persist the data in the data store. For this instance of the app, the data will continue to be available through shutdowns and restarts. If the app is removed from the simulator or device, the data will no longer be available. One technique to populate data for first run is to copy the data store from the app's storage directory back into the app bundle. This will ensure that the default set of data is copied into the app's directory on first launch and is available to the app.

Other Default Data Setup Techniques

Two other default data setup techniques are commonly used: data model version migrations and loading data from a Web service or an API.

Core Data managed object models are versioned. Core Data understands the relationship between the managed object model and the current data store. If the managed object model changes and is no longer compatible with the data store (for example, if an attribute is added to an entity), Core Data will not be able to initiate the persistent store object using the existing data store and new managed object model. In that case, a migration is required to update the existing data store to match the updated managed object model. In many cases Core Data can perform the migration automatically by passing a dictionary of options when instantiating the persistent store; in some cases, additional steps need to be taken to perform the migration. Migrations are beyond the scope of this chapter, but be aware that migrations can be used and are recommended by Apple to do data setup.

The other approach is to pull data from a Web service or an API. This approach is most applicable when an app needs to maintain a local copy of a subset of data on a Web server, and Web calls need to be written for the app to pull data from the API in the course of normal operation. To set up the app's initial data, the Web calls can be run in a special state to pull all needed initial data and save it in Core Data.

Displaying Your Managed Objects

To display or use existing entity data in an app, managed objects need to be fetched from the managed object context. Fetching is analogous to running a query in a relational database, in that you can specify what entity you want to fetch, what criteria you want your results to match, and how you want your results sorted.

Creating Your Fetch Request

The object used to fetch managed objects in Core Data is called `NSFetchRequest`. Refer to `ICFFriendChooserViewController` in the sample app. This view controller displays the friends set up in Core Data and enables the user to select a friend to lend a movie to (see Figure 15.6).

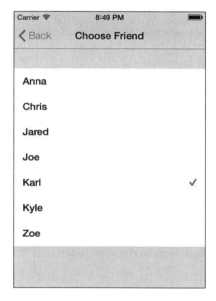

Figure 15.6   Sample App: friend chooser.

To get the list of friends to display, the view controller performs a standard fetch request when the view controller has loaded. The first step is to create an instance of `NSFetchRequest` and associate the entity to be fetched with the fetch request:

```
NSManagedObjectContext *moc = kAppDelegate.managedObjectContext;

[moc performBlockAndWait:^{
    NSFetchRequest *fetchReq = [[NSFetchRequest alloc] init];
```

```
    NSEntityDescription *entity =
  ➥[NSEntityDescription entityForName:@"Friend"
                 inManagedObjectContext:moc];

    [fetchReq setEntity:entity];
```

The next step is to tell the fetch request how to sort the resulting managed objects. To do this, we associate a sort descriptor with the fetch request, specifying the attribute name to sort by:

```
NSSortDescriptor *sortDescriptor =
➥[[NSSortDescriptor alloc] initWithKey:@"friendName"
                           ascending:YES];

NSArray *sortDescriptors = @[sortDescriptor];

[fetchReq setSortDescriptors:sortDescriptors];
```

Because the friend chooser should show all the available friends to choose from, it is not necessary to specify any matching criteria. All that remains is to execute the fetch:

```
NSError *error = nil;

self.friendList = [moc executeFetchRequest:fetchReq
                               error:&error];

 if (error)
{
  NSString *errorDesc =
  ➥[error localizedDescription];

    UIAlertController *alertController =
    ➥[UIAlertController alertControllerWithTitle:@"Error fetching friends"
                                     message:errorDesc
                              preferredStyle:UIAlertControllerStyleAlert];

    [alertController addAction:
    ➥[UIAlertAction actionWithTitle:@"OK"
                          style:UIAlertActionStyleCancel
                        handler:nil]];

    [self presentViewController:alertController
                    animated:YES
                  completion:nil];
}
```

To execute a fetch, create an instance of NSError and set it to nil. Then have the managed object context execute the fetch request that has just been constructed. If an error is encountered, the managed object context will return the error to the instance you just created. The sample app will display the error in an instance of `UIAlertController`. If no error is encountered, the results will be returned as an `NSArray` of `NSManagedObjects`. The view controller will store those results in an instance variable to be displayed in a table view.

Fetching by Object ID

When only one specific managed object needs to be fetched, Core Data provides a way to quickly retrieve that managed object without constructing a fetch request. To use this method, you must have the `NSManagedObjectID` for the managed object.

To get the `NSManagedObjectID` for a managed object, you must already have fetched or created the managed object. Refer to `ICFMovieListViewController` in the sample app, in the `prepareForSegue:sender:` method. In this case, the user has selected a movie from the list, and the view controller is about to segue from the list to the detail view for the selected movie. To inform the detail view controller which movie to display, the `objectID` for the selected movie is set as a property on the `ICFMovieDisplayViewController`:

```
if ([[segue identifier] isEqualToString:@"showDetail"])
{

  NSIndexPath *indexPath =
➥[self.tableView indexPathForSelectedRow];

  ICFMovie *movie =
➥[[self fetchedResultsController]
➥objectAtIndexPath:indexPath];

  ICFMovieDisplayViewController *movieDispVC =
➥(ICFMovieDisplayViewController *)
➥[segue destinationViewController];

  [movieDispVC setMovieDetailID:[movie objectID]];
}
```

When the `ICFMovieDisplayViewController` is loaded, it uses a method on the managed object context to load a managed object using the `objectID`:

```
[kAppDelegate.managedObjectContext performBlockAndWait:^{
    ICFMovie *movie = (ICFMovie *)[kAppDelegate.managedObjectContext
➥objectWithID:self.movieDetailID];

    [self configureViewForMovie:movie];
}];
```

When this is loaded, the movie is available to the view controller to configure the view using the movie data (see Figure 15.7).

It is certainly possible to just pass the managed object from one view controller to the next with no problems, instead of passing the objectID and loading the managed object in the destination view controller. However, there are cases when using the objectID is highly preferable to using the managed object:

- If the managed object has been fetched or created on a different thread than the destination view controller will use to process and display the managed object—this approach must be used since managed objects are not thread safe!

- If a background thread might update the managed object in another managed object context between fetching and displaying—this will avoid possible issues with displaying the most up-to-date changes.

Figure 15.7   Sample App: movie display view.

Displaying Your Object Data

After managed objects have been fetched, accessing and displaying data from them is straightforward. For any managed object, using the key-value approach will work to retrieve attribute values. As an example, refer to the configureCell:atIndexPath method in ICFFriendsViewController in the sample app. This code will populate the table cell's text label and detail text label.

```
NSManagedObject *object =
➥[self.fetchedResultsController objectAtIndexPath:indexPath];

cell.textLabel.text = [object valueForKey:@"friendName"];

NSInteger numShares = [[object valueForKey:@"lentMovies"] count];

NSString *subtitle = @"";

switch (numShares)
{
  case 0:
    subtitle = @"Not borrowing any movies.";
    break;

  case 1:
    subtitle = @"Borrowing 1 movie.";
    break;

  default:
    subtitle =
    ➥[NSString stringWithFormat:@"Borrowing %d movies.",
    ➥numShares];

    break;
}

cell.detailTextLabel.text = subtitle;
```

To get the attribute values from the managed object, call `valueForKey:` and specify the attribute name. If the attribute name is specified incorrectly, the app will fail at runtime.

For managed object subclasses, the attribute values are also accessible by calling the property on the managed object subclass with the attribute name. Refer to the `configureViewForMovie:` method in `ICFMovieDisplayViewController` in the sample app.

```
- (void)configureViewForMovie:(ICFMovie *)movie

{
  NSString *movieTitleYear = [movie yearAndTitle];

  [self.movieTitleAndYearLabel
  ➥setText:movieTitleYear];

  [self.movieDescription setText:[movie movieDescription]];

  BOOL movieLent = [[movie lent] boolValue];
```

```
NSString *movieShared = @"Not Shared";
if (movieLent)
{
  NSManagedObject *friend =
➥[movie valueForKey:@"lentToFriend"];

  NSDateFormatter *dateFormatter =
➥[[NSDateFormatter alloc] init];

  [dateFormatter setDateStyle:NSDateFormatterMediumStyle];

  NSString *sharedDateTxt =
➥[dateFormatter stringFromDate:[movie lentOn]];

  movieShared =
➥[NSString stringWithFormat:@"Shared with %@ on %@",
➥[friend valueForKey:@"friendName"],sharedDateTxt];
}

  [self.movieSharedInfoLabel setText:movieShared];
}
```

If the property-based approach to get attribute values from managed object subclasses is used, errors will be caught at compile time.

Using Predicates

Predicates can be used to narrow down your fetch results to data that match your specific criteria. They are analogous to a where clause in an SQL statement, but they can be used to filter elements from a collection (like an NSArray) as well as a fetch request from Core Data. To see how a predicate is applied to a fetch request, refer to method fetchedResults-Controller in ICFSharedMoviesViewController. This method lazy-loads and sets up an NSFetchedResultsController, which helps a table view interact with the results of a fetch request (this is described in detail in the next section). Setting up a predicate is simple; for example:

```
NSPredicate *predicate =
➥[NSPredicate predicateWithFormat:@"lent == %@",@YES];
```

In the format string, predicates can be constructed with attribute names, comparison operators, Boolean operators, aggregate operators, and substitution expressions. A comma-separated list of expressions will be substituted in the order of the substitution expressions in the format string. Dot notation can be used to specify relationships in the predicate format string. Predicates support a large variety of operators and arguments, as shown in Table 15.2.

Table 15.2   **Core Data Predicate-Supported Operators and Arguments**

Type	Operators and Arguments
Basic Comparisons	`=, ==, >=, =>, <=, =<, >, <, !=, <>, BETWEEN {low,high}.`
Boolean	`AND, && OR, || NOT, !.`
String	`BEGINSWITH, CONTAINS, ENDSWITH, LIKE, MATCHES.`
Aggregate	`ANY, SOME, ALL, NONE, IN.`
Literals	`FALSE, NO, TRUE, YES, NULL, NIL, SELF.` Core Data also supports string and numeric literals.

Tell the fetch request to use the predicate:

```
[fetchRequest setPredicate:predicate];
```

Now the fetch request will narrow the returned result set of managed objects to match the criteria specified in the predicate (see Figure 15.8).

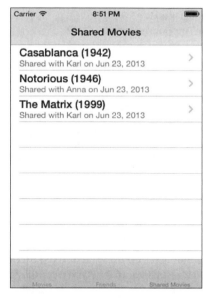

Figure 15.8   Sample App: Shared Movies tab.

Introducing the Fetched Results Controller

A fetched results controller (`NSFetchedResultsController`) is a very effective liaison between Core Data and a `UITableView` or `UICollectionView`. The fetched results controller provides a way to set up a fetch request so that the results are returned in sections and rows, accessible by index paths. In addition, the fetched results controller can listen to changes in Core Data and update the table accordingly using delegate methods.

In the sample app, refer to `ICFMovieListViewController` for a detailed example of a fetched results controller in action (see Figure 15.9).

Figure 15.9   Sample App: movie list view controller.

Preparing the Fetched Results Controller

When the "master" view controller is set up using Xcode's Master Detail template, Xcode creates a property for the fetched results controller, and overrides the accessor method (`fetchedResultsController`) to lazy-load or initialize the fetched results controller the first time it is requested. First the method checks to see whether the fetched results controller has already been initialized:

```
if (__fetchedResultsController != nil)
{
  return __fetchedResultsController;
}
```

If the fetched results controller is already set up, it is returned. Otherwise, a new fetched results controller is set up, starting with a fetch request:

```
NSFetchRequest *fetchRequest = [[NSFetchRequest alloc] init];
```

The fetch request needs to be associated with an entity from the managed object model, and a managed object context:

```
NSManagedObjectContext *moc = kAppDelegate.managedObjectContext;

NSEntityDescription *entity =
➡[NSEntityDescription entityForName:@"Movie"
               inManagedObjectContext:moc];

[fetchRequest setEntity:entity];
```

A batch size can be set up to prevent the fetch request from fetching too many records at once:

```
[fetchRequest setFetchBatchSize:20];
```

Next, the sort order is established for the fetch request using NSSortDescriptor instances. An important point to note is that the attribute used for sections needs to be the first in the sort order so that the records can be correctly divided into sections. The sort order is determined by the order of the sort descriptors in the array of sort descriptors attached to the fetch request.

```
NSSortDescriptor *sortDescriptor =
➡[[NSSortDescriptor alloc] initWithKey:@"title" ascending:YES];

NSSortDescriptor *sharedSortDescriptor =
➡[[NSSortDescriptor alloc] initWithKey:@"lent" ascending:NO];

NSArray *sortDescriptors = @[sharedSortDescriptor,sortDescriptor];

[fetchRequest setSortDescriptors:sortDescriptors];
```

After the fetch request is ready, the fetched results controller can be initialized. It requires a fetch request, a managed object context, a key path or an attribute name to be used for the table view sections, and a name for a cache (if nil is passed, no caching is done). The fetched results controller can specify a delegate that will respond to any Core Data changes. When this is complete, the fetched results controller is assigned to the view controller's property:

```
NSFetchedResultsController *aFetchedResultsController =
➡[[NSFetchedResultsController alloc]
➡initWithFetchRequest:fetchRequest
➡managedObjectContext:moc
➡sectionNameKeyPath:@"lent"
➡cacheName:nil];

aFetchedResultsController.delegate = self;
self.fetchedResultsController = aFetchedResultsController;
```

Now that the fetched results controller has been prepared, the fetch can be executed to obtain a result set the table view can display, and the fetched results controller can be returned to the caller:

```
NSError *error = nil;
if (![self.fetchedResultsController performFetch:&error])
{
  NSLog(@"Unresolved error %@, %@", error, [error userInfo]);
  abort();
}

return __fetchedResultsController;
```

Integrating Table View and Fetched Results Controller

Integrating the table view and fetched results controller is just a matter of updating the table view's datasource and delegate methods to use information from the fetched results controller. In ICFMovieListViewController, the fetched results controller tells the table view how many sections it has:

```
- (NSInteger)numberOfSectionsInTableView:(UITableView *)tableView
{
  return [[self.fetchedResultsController sections] count];
}
```

The fetched results controller tells the table view how many rows are in each section, using the NSFetchedResultsSectionInfo protocol:

```
- (NSInteger)tableView:(UITableView *)tableView
➥numberOfRowsInSection:(NSInteger)section
{
  id <NSFetchedResultsSectionInfo> sectionInfo =
  ➥[[self.fetchedResultsController sections]
  ➥objectAtIndex:section];

  return [sectionInfo numberOfObjects];
}
```

The fetched results controller provides section titles, which are the values of the attribute specified as the section name. Since the sample app is using a Boolean attribute for the sections, the values that the fetched results controller returns for section titles are not user-friendly titles: 0 and 1. The sample app looks at the titles from the fetched results controller and returns more helpful titles: Shared instead of 1 and Not Shared instead of 0.

```
- (NSString *)tableView:(UITableView *)tableView
➥titleForHeaderInSection:(NSInteger)section
{
  id <NSFetchedResultsSectionInfo> sectionInfo =
```

```
➥[[self.fetchedResultsController sections]
➥objectAtIndex:section];

   if ([[sectionInfo indexTitle] isEqualToString:@"1"])
   {
      return @"Shared";
   }
   else
   {
      return @"Not Shared";
   }
}
```

To populate the table cells, the sample app dequeues a reusable cell, and then calls the configureView: method, passing the indexPath for the cell:

```
- (UITableViewCell *)tableView:(UITableView *)tableView
➥cellForRowAtIndexPath:(NSIndexPath *)indexPath
{
   UITableViewCell *cell =
   ➥[tableView dequeueReusableCellWithIdentifier:@"Cell"];

   [self configureCell:cell atIndexPath:indexPath];

   return cell;
}
```

The fetched results controller knows which movie should be displayed at each index path, so the sample app can get the correct movie to display by calling the objectAtIndexPath: method on the fetched results controller. Then, it is simple to update the cell with data from the movie instance.

```
- (void)configureCell:(UITableViewCell *)cell
➥atIndexPath:(NSIndexPath *)indexPath
{
   ICFMovie *movie =
   ➥[self.fetchedResultsController objectAtIndexPath:indexPath];

   cell.textLabel.text = [movie cellTitle];

   cell.detailTextLabel.text = [movie movieDescription];
}
```

The last table-view integration detail would typically be handling table cell selection in the tableView:didSelectRowAtIndexPath: method. In this case, no integration in that method is needed since selection is handled by storyboard segue. In the prepareForSegue:sender: method, selection of a table cell is handled with an identifier called showDetail:

```
if ([[segue identifier] isEqualToString:@"showDetail"])
{
NSIndexPath *indexPath =
➥[self.tableView indexPathForSelectedRow];

    ICFMovie *movie =
    ➥[[self fetchedResultsController]
    ➥objectAtIndexPath:indexPath];

    ICFMovieDisplayViewController *movieDisplayVC =
    ➥(ICFMovieDisplayViewController *)
    ➥[segue destinationViewController];

    [movieDisplayVC setMovieDetailID:[movie objectID]];
}
```

This method gets the index path of the selected row from the table view, and then gets the movie instance from the fetched results controller using the index path. The method then sets the `movieDetailID` of the `ICFMovieDisplayViewController` instance with the movie instance's `objectID`.

Responding to Core Data Changes

For the fetched results controller to respond to Core Data changes and update the table view, methods from the `NSFetchedResultsControllerDelegate` protocol need to be implemented. First the view controller needs to declare that it will implement the delegate methods:

```
@interface ICFMovieListViewController : UITableViewController
➥<NSFetchedResultsControllerDelegate>
```

The fetched results controller delegate will be notified when content will be changed, giving the delegate the opportunity to animate the changes in the table view. Calling the `begin-Updates` method on the table view tells it that all updates until `endUpdates` is called should be animated simultaneously.

```
- (void)controllerWillChangeContent:
➥(NSFetchedResultsController *)controller
{
   [self.tableView beginUpdates];
}
```

There are two delegate methods that might be called based on data changes. One method will tell the delegate that changes occurred that affect the table-view sections; the other will tell the delegate that the changes affect objects at specified index paths, so the table view will need to update the associated rows. Because the data changes are expressed by type, the delegate will be notified if the change is an insert, a delete, a move, or an update, so a typical pattern is to build a `switch` statement to perform the correct action by change type. For sections, the sample app will only make changes that can insert or delete a section (if a section name is changed, that might trigger a case in which a section might move and be updated as well).

```
- (void)controller:(NSFetchedResultsController *)controller
➡didChangeSection:(id <NSFetchedResultsSectionInfo>)sectionInfo
➡atIndex:(NSUInteger)sectionIndex
➡forChangeType:(NSFetchedResultsChangeType)type
{
  switch(type)
  {
    case NSFetchedResultsChangeInsert:
      ...
      break;

    case NSFetchedResultsChangeDelete:
      ...
      break;
  }
}
```

Table views have a convenient method to insert new sections, and the delegate method receives all the necessary information to insert new sections:

```
[self.tableView
➡insertSections:[NSIndexSet indexSetWithIndex:sectionIndex]
➡withRowAnimation:UITableViewRowAnimationFade];
```

Removing sections is just as convenient:

```
[self.tableView
➡deleteSections:[NSIndexSet indexSetWithIndex:sectionIndex]
➡withRowAnimation:UITableViewRowAnimationFade];
```

For object changes, the delegate will be informed of the change type, the object that changed, the current index path for the object, and a "new" index path if the object is being inserted or moved. Using switch logic to respond by change type works for this method as well.

```
- (void)controller:(NSFetchedResultsController *)controller
➡didChangeObject:(id)anObject
➡atIndexPath:(NSIndexPath *)indexPath
➡forChangeType:(NSFetchedResultsChangeType)type
➡newIndexPath:(NSIndexPath *)newIndexPath
{
  UITableView *tableView = self.tableView;

  switch(type)
  {
    case NSFetchedResultsChangeInsert:
      ...
      break;
```

```
    case NSFetchedResultsChangeDelete:
      ...
      break;

    case NSFetchedResultsChangeUpdate:
      ...
      break;

    case NSFetchedResultsChangeMove:
      ...
      break;
  }
}
```

Table views have convenience methods to insert rows by index path. Note that the `newIndex-Path` is the correct index path to use when inserting a row for an inserted object.

```
[tableView
➡insertRowsAtIndexPaths:[NSArray arrayWithObject:newIndexPath]
➡withRowAnimation:UITableViewRowAnimationFade];
```

To delete a row, use the `indexPath` passed to the delegate method.

```
[tableView
➡deleteRowsAtIndexPaths:[NSArray arrayWithObject:indexPath]
➡withRowAnimation:UITableViewRowAnimationFade];
```

To update a row, call the `configureCell:atIndexPath:` method for the current `indexPath`. This is the same configure method called from the table view delegate's `tableView:cellForRowAtIndexPath:` method.

```
[self configureCell:[tableView cellForRowAtIndexPath:indexPath]
➡atIndexPath:indexPath];
```

To move a row, delete the row for the current `indexPath` and insert a row for the `newIndexPath`.

```
[tableView
➡deleteRowsAtIndexPaths:[NSArray arrayWithObject:indexPath]
➡withRowAnimation:UITableViewRowAnimationFade];
```

```
[tableView
➡insertRowsAtIndexPaths:[NSArray arrayWithObject:newIndexPath]
➡withRowAnimation:UITableViewRowAnimationFade];
```

The fetched results controller delegate will be notified when the content changes are complete, so the delegate can tell the table view there will be no more animated changes by calling the `endUpdates` method. After that method is called, the table view will animate the accumulated changes in the user interface.

```
- (void)controllerDidChangeContent:
➥ (NSFetchedResultsController *)controller
{
    [self.tableView endUpdates];
}
```

Adding, Editing, and Removing Managed Objects

Although it is useful to be able to fetch and display data, apps often need to add new data, edit existing data, and remove unneeded data at the user's request.

Inserting a New Managed Object

In the sample app, view the Movies tab. To insert a new movie, the user can tap the Add button in the navigation bar. The Add button is wired to perform a segue to the ICFMovieEditViewController. In the segue logic, a new movie managed object is inserted into Core Data, and the new movie's object ID is passed to the edit movie view controller. This approach is used in the sample app to prevent having logic in the edit view controller to handle both creating new managed objects and editing existing managed objects; however, it would be perfectly acceptable to create the new movie managed object in the edit view controller if that makes more sense in a different app.

To create a new instance of a movie managed object, a reference to the managed object context is needed.

```
NSManagedObjectContext *moc =
➥[kAppDelegate managedObjectContext];
```

Set up a variable to capture the managed object ID of the new movie in block storage so that it can be used to pass along in the segue.

```
__block NSManagedObjectID *newMovieID = nil;
```

Again, use the performBlockAndWait: technique to isolate core data changes to the managed object context's thread:

```
[moc performBlockAndWait:^{
```

To insert data, Core Data needs to know what entity the new data is for. Core Data has a class called NSEntityDescription that provides information about entities. Create a new instance using NSEntityDescription's class method:

```
ICFMovie *newMovie = [NSEntityDescription
➥insertNewObjectForEntityForName:@"Movie"
➥inManagedObjectContext:moc];
```

Populate the new movie managed object's attributes with data:

```
[newMovie setTitle:@"New Movie"];
[newMovie setYear:@"2014"];
[newMovie setMovieDescription:@"New movie description."];
[newMovie setLent:@NO];
[newMovie setLentOn:nil];
[newMovie setTimesWatched:@0];
```

Prepare an NSError variable to capture any potential errors, save the managed object context, and close the perform block.

```
NSError *mocSaveError = nil;

if (![moc save:&mocSaveError])
{
  NSLog(@"Save did not complete successfully. Error: %@",
  ➡[mocSaveError localizedDescription]);
}
```

After the managed object context has been successfully saved, the fetched results controller will be notified if the save affects the results of the controller's fetch, and the delegate methods described earlier in this chapter will be called.

Removing a Managed Object

On the Movies tab in the sample app, the user can swipe on the right side of a table cell, or can tap the Edit button to reveal the delete controls for each table cell. When Delete is tapped on a cell, the table view delegate method tableView:commitEditingStyle: forRowAtIndexPath: is called. That method checks whether the editingStyle is equal to UITableViewCellEditingStyleDelete. If so, that indicates the user has tapped the Delete button for the table cell, so the method prepares to delete the corresponding movie by getting a reference to the managed object context from the fetched results controller. The fetched results controller keeps a reference to the managed object context it was initialized with, which is needed to delete the object.

```
NSManagedObjectContext *context =
➡[self.fetchedResultsController managedObjectContext];
```

The method determines which managed object should be deleted, by asking the fetched results controller for the managed object at the specified index path.

```
[context performBlockAndWait:^{
➡NSManagedObject *objectToBeDeleted =
➡[self.fetchedResultsController objectAtIndexPath:indexPath];
```

To delete the managed object, the method tells the managed object context to delete it.

```
[context deleteObject:objectToBeDeleted];
```

The deletion is not permanent until the managed object context is saved. After it is saved, the delegate methods described earlier in the chapter will be called and the table will be updated.

```
NSError *error = nil;
if (![context save:&error])
{
  NSLog(@"Error deleting movie, %@", [error userInfo]);
}
```

Editing an Existing Managed Object

On the Movies tab in the sample app, the user can tap a movie to see more detail about it. To change any of the information about the movie, tap the Edit button in the navigation bar, which will present an instance of `ICFMovieEditViewController`. When the view is loaded, it will load an instance of `ICFMovie` using the `objectID` passed in from the display view or list view, will save that instance into the property `editMovie`, and will configure the view using information from the movie managed object.

If the user decides to edit the year of the movie, for example, another view controller will be presented with a `UIPickerView` for the user to select a new year. The `ICFMovieEditViewController` is set up as a delegate for the year chooser, so when the user has selected a new year and taps Save, the delegate method `chooserSelectedYear:` is called. In that method, the `editMovie` is updated with the new date and the display is updated.

```
- (void)chooserSelectedYear:(NSString *)year
{
    [self.editMovie setYear:year];
    [self.movieYearLabel setText:year];
}
```

Note that the managed object context was not saved after `editMovie` was updated. The managed object `editMovie` can keep updates temporarily until the user makes a decision about whether to make the changes permanent, indicated by tapping the Save or Cancel button.

Saving and Rolling Back Your Changes

If the user taps the Save button, he has indicated his intention to keep the changes made to the `editMovie`. In the `saveButtonTouched:` method, the fields not updated with delegate methods are saved to the `editMovie` property:

```
[kAppDelegate.managedObjectContext performBlockAndWait:^{
    NSString *movieTitle = [self.movieTitle text];
    [self.editMovie setTitle:movieTitle];

    NSString *movieDesc = [self.movieDescription text];
    [self.editMovie setMovieDescription:movieDesc];
```

```
   BOOL sharedBool = [self.sharedSwitch isOn];
   NSNumber *shared = [NSNumber numberWithBool:sharedBool];
   [self.editMovie setLent:shared];
```

Then the managed object context is saved, making the changes permanent.

```
NSError *saveError = nil;
[kAppDelegate.managedObjectContext save:&saveError];
if (saveError)
{
    UIAlertController *alertController =
    ➥[UIAlertController alertControllerWithTitle:@"Error saving movie"
    ➥message:[saveError localizedDescription]
    ➥preferredStyle:UIAlertControllerStyleAlert];

    [alertController addAction:
    ➥[UIAlertAction actionWithTitle:@"OK"
                                style:UIAlertActionStyleCancel
                              handler:nil]];

    [self presentViewController:alertController
                       animated:YES
                     completion:nil];
}
else
{
    NSLog(@"Changes to movie saved.");
}
```

If the user decides that the changes should be thrown away and not be made permanent, the user will tap the Cancel button, which calls the cancelButtonTouched: method. That method will first check whether the managed object context has any unsaved changes. If so, the method will instruct the managed object context to roll back or throw away the unsaved changes. After that is completed, the managed object context will be back to the state it was in before any of the changes were made. Rather than the user interface being updated to reflect throwing away the changes, the view is dismissed.

```
if ([kAppDelegate.managedObjectContext hasChanges])
{
  [kAppDelegate.managedObjectContext rollback];
  NSLog(@"Rolled back changes.");
}

[self.navigationController.presentingViewController
➥dismissModalViewControllerAnimated:YES];
```

The managed object context can be saved at any time while making updates; be advised that saving large numbers of changes with a main queue managed object context tied to the persistent store can result in a noticeable delay and potentially affect the user interface. It is generally advisable to keep saves relatively small and related; if saves must be large (for example, when pulling a lot of information from a Web API), then it is worth considering a more complex Core Data stack with multiple contexts in a parent/child relationship to prevent writing to the persistent store on the main queue.

Summary

This chapter described how to set up a new project to use Core Data and how to set up all the Core Data environment pieces. The chapter detailed how to create a managed object model, including how to add a new entity, add attributes to an entity, and set up relationships between entities. It also described why an `NSManagedObject` subclass is useful and how to create one.

This chapter explained how to set up some initial data for the project, and demonstrated how to insert new managed objects. Alternative techniques for initial data setup were discussed.

This chapter then detailed how to create a fetch request to get saved managed objects, and how to fetch individual managed objects using an `objectID`. It described how to display data from managed objects in the user interface of an app. It explained how to use predicates to fetch managed objects that match specific criteria.

This chapter introduced the fetched results controller, a powerful tool for integrating Core Data with the `UITableView`; described how to set up a `UITableView` with a fetched results controller; and explained how to set up a fetched results controller delegate to automatically update a table view from Core Data changes.

Finally, this chapter explained how to add, edit, and delete managed objects, and how to save changes or roll back unwanted changes.

With all these tools, you should now have a good foundation for using Core Data effectively in your apps.

16

Integrating Twitter and Facebook Using Social Framework

Social networking is here to stay, and users want to be able to access their social media accounts on everything from the newest iOS game to their refrigerators (Samsung Model RF4289HARS). Before iOS 5, adding Twitter and Facebook to an app was a frustrating and challenging endeavor; third-party libraries written by people who didn't understand the platform were rampant, often not even compiling. Starting with iOS 5, Apple introduced Social Framework, which enabled developers to directly integrate Twitter services into their apps with little effort. With iOS 6, Apple expanded the Social Framework functionality to include Facebook and Sina Weibo (China's leading social network).

Not only are users craving social integration in just about everything with a screen, but social integration can be highly beneficial to the app developer as well. When a user tweets a high score from a game or shares a Facebook message about an app, it will reach a market that a developer would not be able to penetrate. Not only is the app reaching new customers, but it also is getting a personalized endorsement from a potential new customer's friends. There are few apps that could not benefit from the inclusion of social media, and with iOS 8 it has become easier than ever to add this functionality.

The Sample App

The sample app for this chapter is called SocialNetworking (see Figure 16.1). The app features a single text view with a character-count label and a button to attach an image. There are two buttons on the title bar as well that enable the user to access Twitter and Facebook functionality. The sample app enforces a 140-character count on Facebook posts and Twitter; in reality, Facebook supports much longer text posts.

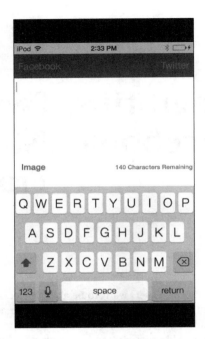

Figure 16.1   A first look at the sample app, SocialNetworking, for this chapter.

Tapping the buttons for each of the services brings up three options: composer, auto-post, and timeline. The composer option will take you to the built-in SLComposeViewController and is the easiest and fastest way to post a message to a social service. The auto-post option will post the text and optional image from the main screen without the user needing to take any additional steps; this step can also be considered programmatic posting. The timeline option will bring up the user's Twitter timeline or Facebook feed. The sample app does not include functionality for Sina Weibo, although this service can be adapted with relative ease.

Logging In

The Social Framework uses a centralized login system for Facebook and Twitter, which can be found under the Settings.app, as shown in Figure 16.2.

In the event that a user is not currently logged in to Twitter or Facebook and attempts to access Twitter and Facebook functionality, the user will be prompted to set up a new account, as shown in Figure 16.3. This system works only when the `SLComposeViewController` is being used; otherwise, a simple access-denied message is presented if no accounts are configured. In addition to the no-accounts message, you might occasionally see an "Error 6" returned if the accounts in Settings.app are not properly configured. This is typically caused by an account set with incorrect credentials.

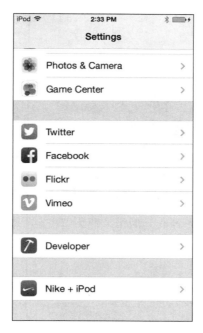

Figure 16.2   Logging in to a social service on iOS requires the user to leave the app and visit the Settings app.

Figure 16.3   The user being prompted to configure a Twitter account for the device.

> **Note**
> There is currently no Apple-approved method of loading the user directly into the configure
> screen for Twitter and Facebook outside of the SLComposeViewController built-in message.

Using `SLComposeViewController`

The easiest way to post a new message to Twitter or Facebook is to use the
SLComposeViewController. It requires no fiddling with permissions and, if the
user has not set up an account, it prompts him to configure one. The downside of
SLComposeViewController is that there is no way to customize the appearance of the view
that the user is presented with, as shown in Figure 16.4.

Figure 16.4   Posting a new tweet with an image using the SLComposeViewController.

Before your app can interact with SLComposeViewController, the Social.framework must first be imported into the project. In addition, the header file "Social" will need to be imported; note the capitalization of the header files.

The following code is the most effortless method of presenting an SLComposeViewController for Twitter. The first step is a call to isAvailableForServiceType; in the event that the device is not capable of posting to Twitter, it will gracefully exit. A new SLComposeViewController is created and a new block is made to handle the results of the action. The completion handler for the SLComposeViewController is set to the newly created block and it is presented with presentViewController. These are the bare minimum steps that need to be completed in order to post from an iOS app to Twitter. This option is demonstrated in the sample app as the Composer option under the Twitter menu.

```
if([SLComposeViewController
➥isAvailableForServiceType:SLServiceTypeTwitter])
{

        SLComposeViewController *controller =
        ➥[SLComposeViewController
        ➥composeViewControllerForServiceType: SLServiceTypeTwitter];
```

```
        SLComposeViewControllerCompletionHandler myBlock =
      ^(SLComposeViewControllerResult result){
            if (result == SLComposeViewControllerResultCancelled)
            {
                  NSLog(@"Cancelled");
            }

            else
            {
                  NSLog(@"Done");
            }

            [controller dismissViewControllerAnimated:YES
            ➥completion:nil];
        };

        controller.completionHandler = myBlock;

        [self presentViewController:controller animated:YES
        ➥completion:nil];
}

else
{
      NSLog(@"Twitter Composer is not available.");
}
```

You can also customize an SLComposeViewController by setting the initial text, images, and URLs.

```
[controller setInitialText:@"Check out my app:"];
[controller addImage:[UIImage imageNamed:@"Kitten.jpg"]];
[controller addURL:[NSURL URLWithString:@"http://amzn.to/Um85L0"]];
```

Multiple attachments can also be added by stacking addImage or addURL calls.

```
[controller addImage:[UIImage imageNamed:@"Kitten1.jpg"]];
[controller addImage:[UIImage imageNamed:@"Kitten2.jpg"]];
```

In the event that it is necessary to remove URLs or images from the SLComposeViewController after they have been added, it can be done with a single method call.

```
[controller removeAllImages];
[controller removeAllURLs];
```

The approach for SLComposeViewController with Facebook is identical to that for Twitter with one exception: Both uses of SLServiceTypeTwitter should be replaced with SLServiceTypeFacebook.

Posting with a Custom Interface

It might become necessary to move beyond the capabilities of the `SLComposeViewController` and implement a ground-up solution. Luckily, Social Framework fully supports this kind of customization. When `SLComposeViewController` was used in the preceding example, the differences between posting to Facebook and posting to Twitter were minor, but this will no longer be the case when you're dealing with customized interfaces. Twitter and Facebook implementations when working at a lower level are almost entirely different. This section is broken into two subsections: one for Twitter and one for Facebook. Twitter support is the simpler of the two, so that is covered first.

Posting to Twitter

In addition to importing the `Social.framework` and importing the `"Social/Social.h"` header from the `SLComposeViewController`, the `"Accounts/Accounts.h"` header will also need to be imported. To begin working with more direct access to Twitter's APIs, two new objects first need to be created.

```
ACAccountStore *account = [[ACAccountStore alloc] init];
ACAccountType *accountType = [account
➥accountTypeWithAccountTypeIdentifier: ACAccountTypeIdentifierTwitter];
```

The `ACAccountStore` will allow the code base to access the Twitter account that has been configured in the Settings.app, and the `ACAccountType` contains the information needed for a particular type of account. The `accountType` object can be queried to see whether access has already been granted to the user.

```
if (accountType.accessGranted)
{
    NSLog(@"User has already granted access to this service");
}
```

To prompt the user to grant access to the Twitter account information, a call on the `ACAccountStore` for `requestAccessToAccountsWithType:options:completion:` is required. If the account has already been authorized, the completion block will return YES for `granted` without prompting the user again.

```
[account requestAccessToAccountsWithType:accountType options:nil
➥completion:^(BOOL granted, NSError *error)
```

If the user grants access or if access has already been granted, a list of the user's Twitter accounts will need to be retrieved. A user can add multiple Twitter accounts to his device and you cannot determine which one he will want to post from. In the event that multiple accounts are found, the user should be prompted to specify which account he would like to use.

```
if (granted == YES)
{
    NSArray *arrayOfAccounts = [account accountsWithAccountType:
    ➥accountType];
}
```

In the sample app, for the sake of simplicity, if multiple accounts are found, the last one is automatically selected. In an App Store app, it will be important to present the user with an option to select which account she would like to use if more than one is found.

```
if ([arrayOfAccounts count] > 0)
{
    ACAccount *twitterAccount = [arrayOfAccounts lastObject];
}
```

After a reference to the account is created and stored in an ACAccount object, the post data can be configured. Depending on whether the post will include an image or other media, a different post URL needs to be used.

```
NSURL *requestURL = nil;

if(hasAttachmentedImage)
{
    requestURL = [NSURL URLWithString:
    ➥@"https://upload.twitter.com/1.1/statuses/
    ➥update_with_media.json"];
}

else
{
    requestURL = [NSURL URLWithString:
    ➥@"http://api.twitter.com/1.1/statuses/update.json"];
}
```

Warning

Posting a tweet to the improper URL will result in its failing to be processed. You cannot post an image tweet to the update.json endpoint, and you cannot post a non-image tweet to the update_with_media.json endpoint.

After the endpoint URL has been determined, a new SLRequest object is created. The SLRequest is the object that will contain all the information needed to post the full tweet details to Twitter's API.

```
SLRequest *postRequest = [SLRequest
➥requestForServiceType:SLServiceTypeTwitter
➥requestMethod:SLRequestMethodPOST
➥URL:requestURL parameters:nil];
```

After the `SLRequest` has been created, an account must be defined for it. Using the account that was previously determined, the account property is then set.

```
postRequest.account = twitterAccount;
```

To add text to this tweet, a call on the `postRequest` to `addMultipartData:withName: type:filename:` is used. The text is a simple string with `NSUTF8StringEncoding`. The name used here correlates to the Twitter API documentation; for text it is `status`. For `type`, `multipart/form-data` is used in accordance with the Twitter API. No filename is required for text.

```
[postRequest addMultipartData:[socialTextView.text dataUsingEncoding:
➥NSUTF8StringEncoding] withName:@"status"
➥type:@"multipart/form-data"filename:nil];
```

Note

For more information on Twitter's API and where these constants are pulled from, visit https://dev.twitter.com/docs.

If the tweet has an image associated with it, add it next. A `UIImage` first needs to be converted to `NSData` using `UIImageJPEGRepresentation`. This example is similar to the preceding text-based example except that a filename is specified.

```
NSData *imageData = UIImageJPEGRepresentation(self.attachmentImage, 1.0);

[postRequest addMultipartData:imageData withName:@"media"
type:@"image/jpeg" filename:@"Image.jpg"];
```

Note

Multiple images can be added with repetitive calls to `addMultipartData:withName:type: filename:`.

After the `postRequest` has been fully populated with all the information that should appear in the tweet, it is time to post it to Twitter's servers. This is done with a call to `performRequest-WithHandler:`. A URLResponse code of `200` indicates a success; every other response code indicates a type of failure. A successful post from the sample is shown in Figure 16.5.

Figure 16.5   A successful tweet to Twitter using a custom interface as shown in the sample app.

> **Note**
>
> It is important to remember that `UIAlertViews` cannot be shown from within a completion
> block, because the completion block will not necessarily be executed on the main thread. In the
> sample app, error messages are passed to a main thread method to display alerts.

```
[postRequest performRequestWithHandler:^(NSData *responseData,
➥NSHTTPURLResponse *urlResponse, NSError *error)
{
    if(error != nil)
    {
        [self performSelectorOnMainThread:
        ➥@selector(reportSuccessOrError:) withObject:[error
        ➥localizedDescription] waitUntilDone:NO];
    }

    if([urlResponse statusCode] == 200)
    {
```

```
        [self performSelectorOnMainThread:
        ➥@selector(reportSuccessOrError:) withObject:@"Your
        ➥message has been posted to Twitter" waitUntilDone:NO];
    }
}];
```

This concludes all the required steps to post a string and an image to Twitter using a custom interface. In the following subsection, Facebook posting will be fully explored.

 Tip

Inside of the sample app, the process of posting to Twitter is fully laid out in the method `twitterPost`.

Posting to Facebook

The same basic principles apply when you are working with a Facebook post as with Twitter; however, multiple additional are steps required to deal with a number of authentication and permission requirements. Unlike Twitter, Facebook has various levels of permissions. If users authorize an app to access their feed, they might not want the app to be able to publish to their feeds. To make matters more complex, permissions have to be requested in certain orders, and requests for read and write permission cannot be made at the same time.

Creating a Facebook App

To post or interact with Facebook from a mobile app, a Facebook App that corresponds to the mobile app must first be created.

Log in to https://developers.facebook.com/apps using a Facebook account that you want to have ownership of the app.

Click the button + Create New App, as shown in Figure 16.6. Enter values for App Name and App Namespace. Clicking the question mark icon next to any field will provide additional details.

After a new Facebook App has been created (see Figure 16.7), copy down the App ID number. Browse through all the pages for the new app and ensure that it is configured to suit the needs of the iOS app. By default, there are no options you need to change to continue working through this section.

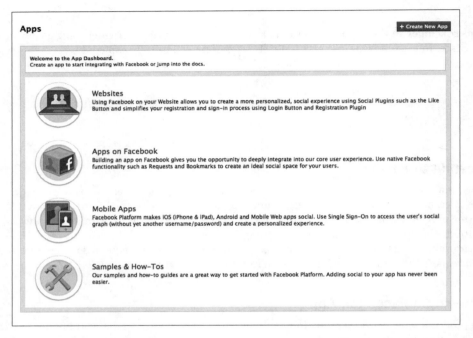

Figure 16.6   Creating a new Facebook App ID from the Developers Portal on Facebook's Web site.

Figure 16.7   A newly created Facebook App. The App ID will be needed to make any Facebook calls from within an iOS app.

Basic Facebook Permissions

The first group of permissions that every Facebook-enabled app needs to request (except if you are using only the SLComposeViewController) is basic profile access. You do this by requesting any of the following attributes: id, name, first_name, last_name, link, username, gender, or locale. Requesting any of these items grants access to all the remaining basic profile items.

If the app has not yet been set up according to the instructions from the preceding section for Twitter, the proper headers and frameworks need to be first imported. Basic permission is requested upon app launch or entering into the section of the app that requires Facebook inter-action. It is not recommended to access basic permissions after the user has already attempted to make a post; this will create a chain of pop-up alerts that a user will have trouble under-standing. The following code is part of the viewDidLoad: method of ICFViewController.m in the sample app:

```objectivec
ACAccountStore *accountStore = [[ACAccountStore alloc] init];
ACAccountType *facebookAccountType = [accountStore
➥accountTypeWithAccountTypeIdentifier: ACAccountTypeIdentifierFacebook];

NSDictionary *options = @{
ACFacebookAudienceKey : ACFacebookAudienceEveryone,
ACFacebookAppIdKey : @"363120920441086",
ACFacebookPermissionsKey : @[@"email"] };

[accountStore requestAccessToAccountsWithType:facebookAccountType
➥options:options completion:^(BOOL granted, NSError *error)
{
    if (granted)
    {
        NSLog(@"Basic access granted");
    }

    else
    {
        NSLog(@"Basic access denied");
    }
}];
```

The ACAccountStore and ACAccountType are configured in the same fashion as for
Twitter, as described in the preceding section. A new dictionary called options is created;
this will be used to supply the API parameters for whatever call is to be made. For basic
permissions ACFacebookAudienceEveryone is passed for ACFacebookAudienceKey. The
ACFacebookAppIdKey is the App ID that was created in the section "Creating a Facebook
App." Since any of the basic permissions can be used to request access to all basic permissions,
the email attribute is used for the ACFacebookPermissionsKey. A call of requestAccess-
ToAccountWithType:options:completion: is made on the accountStore. The user will be
presented with a dialog similar to the one shown in Figure 16.8. The result of the user granting
or denying permissions is logged.

Figure 16.8   A user being prompted to allow the sample app SocialNetworking to access basic profile information.

Publishing to Stream Permissions

Before an app can post to a user's stream, it first needs to request write permissions. This step must be done after basic permissions have been authorized. Requesting publish permissions is nearly identical to requesting permissions to the basic profile information. Instead of requesting access to email for ACFacebookPermissionsKey, permission is requested for publish_ stream. The user will be prompted to grant access to publish a new post on behalf of the user. After a user has granted permission, he will not be prompted again unless he removes the app's permissions from within Facebook.

```
ACAccountStore *accountStore = [[ACAccountStore alloc] init];
ACAccountType *facebookAccountType = [accountStore
➥accountTypeWithAccountTypeIdentifier:ACAccountTypeIdentifierFacebook];

NSDictionary *options = @{
ACFacebookAudienceKey : ACFacebookAudienceEveryone,
ACFacebookAppIdKey : @"363120920441086",
ACFacebookPermissionsKey : @[@"publish_stream"]};
```

```
[accountStore requestAccessToAccountsWithType:facebookAccountType
➥options:options completion:^(BOOL granted, NSError *error)
{
     if (granted)
     {
          NSLog(@"Publish permission granted");
     }

     else
     {
          NSLog(@"Publish permission denied");
     }
}];
```

> **Note**
>
> *Important:* Do not forget to change the `ACFacebookAppIdKey` to match the ID of the Facebook
> App that you will be publishing under.

Posting to the Facebook Stream

After the user has granted permission to publish to her timeline on her behalf, the app is
ready to create a new post. The first step to creating a new Facebook post is to create an
NSDictionary that will store a single object under the key @"message". This key/value pair
will hold the text that will appear in the post.

```
NSDictionary *parameters = [NSDictionary
➥dictionaryWithObject:socialTextView.text forKey:@"message"];
```

If the post does not contain any media such as images, the message is posted to https://graph.
facebook.com/me/feed; however, if the new post will contain photos or media, it will need to
be posted to https://graph.facebook.com/me/photos. These URLs cannot be mixed; for example,
posting a feed item with no image to https://graph.facebook.com/me/photos will result in a
failure. The sample app performs a simple check to determine which endpoint to use.

```
if(self.attachmentImage)
{
    feedURL = [NSURL URLWithString:
    ➥@"https://graph.facebook.com/me/photos"];
}

else
{
    feedURL = [NSURL URLWithString:
    ➥@"https://graph.facebook.com/me/feed"];
}
```

After the proper URL for posting has been determined, a new `SLRequest` object is created specifying the URL and the parameters.

```
SLRequest *feedRequest = [SLRequest

requestForServiceType:SLServiceTypeFacebook
                        requestMethod:SLRequestMethodPOST
                        URL:feedURL
                        parameters:parameters];
```

In the event that the post contains an image, that data needs to be added to the `feedRequest`. This is done using the `addMultipartData:withName:type:filename:` method.

```
if(self.attachmentImage)
{
    NSData *imageData =
    ➥UIImagePNGRepresentation(self.attachmentImage);
    ➥[feedRequest addMultipartData:imageData withName:@"source"
    ➥type:@"multipart/form-data" filename:@"Image"];
}
```

After the optional image data is added, a `performRequestWithHandler:` is called in the same fashion as Twitter. Facebook will return a `urlResponse` code of `200` if the post was successful.

```
[feedRequest performRequestWithHandler:^(NSData *responseData,
➥NSHTTPURLResponse *urlResponse, NSError *error)
{
    NSLog(@"Facebook post statusCode: %d", [urlResponse
    ➥statusCode]);

    if([urlResponse statusCode] == 200)
    {
        [self performSelectorOnMainThread:@selector
        ➥(reportSuccessOrError:) withObject:@"Your message has
        ➥been posted to Facebook" waitUntilDone:NO];
    }

    else if(error != nil)
    {
        [self performSelectorOnMainThread:
        ➥@selector(faceBookError:) withObject:error
        ➥waitUntilDone:NO];
    }
}];
```

Additional information about formatting posts and embedding media for Facebook can be found through the documentation at http://developers.facebook.com.

Accessing User Timelines

There might be times when posting a status update is not enough to satisfy an app's social interaction requirements. Accessing a timeline on Twitter or Facebook is complex, and there is an abundance of tricky edge cases and data types to support, from Twitter's retweets to Facebook embedded data. This section takes a cursory look at accessing the raw data from a timeline and displaying it to a `tableView`. It has been left simple because the subject of timelines is a rabbit hole that can very well occupy a book in and of itself.

Twitter

As shown in previous sections, Twitter has been easier to interact with than the more complex Facebook APIs, due mainly to the multiple permission hierarchy implemented with Facebook. Accessing a user's Twitter timeline begins in the same fashion as posting new a tweet; references to `ACAccountStore` and `ACAccountType` are created.

```
ACAccountStore *account = [[ACAccountStore alloc] init];

ACAccountType *accountType = [account
➥accountTypeWithAccountTypeIdentifier: ACAccountTypeIdentifierTwitter];
```

Continuing in the same fashion as posting a new tweet, a call to `requestAccessTo-AccountWithType:` is performed on the account object. Basic error handling is also set up here.

```
[account requestAccessToAccountsWithType:accountType options:nil
➥completion:^(BOOL granted, NSError *error)
{
     if(error != nil)
     {
          [self
performSelectorOnMainThread:@selector(reportSuccessOrError:)
➥withObject:[error localizedDescription]
➥waitUntilDone:NO];
     }

}];
```

If no errors are returned and access is granted, a copy of the `ACAccount` object for the user is obtained. The sample app, once again, just uses the last object in the account array; however, it is important to keep in mind that some users might be logged in to several Twitter accounts at once and should be given the option of selecting which account they want to use. The request URL used to retrieve a copy of the user's timeline is http://api.twitter.com/1.1/statuses/home_timeline.json. A number of options will also need to be specified. The first option, `count`, specifies the number of tweets that will be retrieved per call. The second option is a Boolean value used to specify whether tweet entities should be included. A tweet entity will include additional details such as users mentioned, hashtags, URLs, and media.

After it has been created, the SLRequest is submitted in the same fashion used when posting to a new status update. The performRequestWithHandler success block will contain the responseData that can then be displayed. The following code is part of the twitterTimeline method of ICFViewController.m:

```
if (granted == YES)
{
    NSArray *arrayOfAccounts = [account
    accountsWithAccountType:accountType];

    if ([arrayOfAccounts count] > 0)
    {
        ACAccount *twitterAccount = [arrayOfAccounts
        lastObject];

        NSURL *requestURL = [NSURL URLWithString:
        @"http://api.twitter.com/1.1/statuses/home_timeline.json"];

        NSDictionary *options = @{
        @"count" : @"20",
        @"include_entities" : @"1"};

        SLRequest *postRequest = [SLRequest
        requestForServiceType:SLServiceTypeTwitter
        requestMethod:SLRequestMethodGET
        URL:requestURL parameters:options];

        postRequest.account = twitterAccount;

        [postRequest performRequestWithHandler:^(NSData
        *responseData, NSHTTPURLResponse *urlResponse, NSError
        *error)
        {
            if(error != nil)
            {
                [self performSelectorOnMainThread:@selector
                (reportSuccessOrError:) withObject:[error
                localizedDescription] waitUntilDone:NO];
            }

            [self performSelectorOnMainThread:
            @selector(presentTimeline:) withObject:
            [NSJSONSerialization JSONObjectWithData:responseData
            options:NSJSONReadingMutableLeaves error:&error]
            waitUntilDone:NO];
        }];
    }
}
```

Provided is a sample of the `responseData` with tweet entities enabled from a typical Twitter timeline fetch; in addition, a sample of how this tweet shows up on the Twitter Web site is shown in Figure 16.9. As shown in the following console output, Twitter provides a considerable amount of information to which the developer has access. For more information on working with JSON data, refer to Chapter 9, "Working with and Parsing JSON."

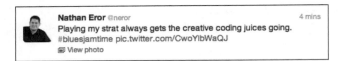

Figure 16.9   A fully rendered tweet as seen on the Twitter Web site. The data that makes up this tweet can be seen in the log statements earlier in this section.

```
2013-02-27 21:50:54.562 SocialNetworking[28672:4207] (
        {
        contributors = "<null>";
        coordinates = "<null>";
        "created_at" = "Thu Feb 28 02:50:41 +0000 2013";
        entities =          {
            hashtags =          (
                            {
                    indices =                   (
                        63,
                        76
                    );
                    text = bluesjamtime;
                }
            );
            media =             (
                            {
                    "display_url" = "pic.twitter.com/CwoYlbWaQJ";
                    "expanded_url" =
➥"http://twitter.com/neror/status/306959580582248448/photo/1";
                    id = 306959580586442753;
                    "id_str" = 306959580586442753;
                    indices =                   (
                        77,
                        99
                    );
                    "media_url" =
➥"http://pbs.twimg.com/media/BEKKHLlCAAEUQ6x.jpg";
                    "media_url_https" =
➥"https://pbs.twimg.com/media/BEKKHLlCAAEUQ6x.jpg";
                    sizes =                 {
                        large =                 {
```

```
                    h = 768;
                    resize = fit;
                    w = 1024;
                };
                medium =                     {
                    h = 450;
                    resize = fit;
                    w = 600;
                };
                small =                       {
                    h = 255;
                    resize = fit;
                    w = 340;
                };
                thumb =                       {
                    h = 150;
                    resize = crop;
                    w = 150;
                };
            };
            type = photo;
            url = "http://t.co/CwoYlbWaQJ";
        }
    );
    urls =              (
    );
    "user_mentions" =              (
    );
};
favorited = 0;
geo = "<null>";
id = 306959580582248448;
"id_str" = 306959580582248448;
"in_reply_to_screen_name" = "<null>";
"in_reply_to_status_id" = "<null>";
"in_reply_to_status_id_str" = "<null>";
"in_reply_to_user_id" = "<null>";
"in_reply_to_user_id_str" = "<null>";
place =           {
    attributes =            {
    };
    "bounding_box" =               {
        coordinates =                 (
                                (
                                    (
                    "-95.90998500000001",
                    "29.537034"
```

```
                            ),
                                                (
                            "-95.01449599999999",
                            "29.537034"
                            ),
                                                (
                            "-95.01449599999999",
                            "30.110792"
                            ),
                                                (
                            "-95.90998500000001",
                            "30.110732"
                            )
                        )
                    );
                    type = Polygon;
                };
                country = "United States";
                "country_code" = US;
                "full_name" = "Houston, TX";
                id = 1c69a67ad480e1b1;
                name = Houston;
                "place_type" = city;
                url =
➥"http://api.twitter.com/1/geo/id/1c69a67ad480e1b1.json";
            };
            "possibly_sensitive" = 0;
            "retweet_count" = 0;
            retweeted = 0;
            source = "<a href=\"http://tapbots.com/software/tweetbot/mac\
➥rel=\"nofollow\">Tweetbot for Mac</a>";
            text = "Playing my strat always gets the creative coding juices
➥going. #bluesjamtime http://t.co/CwoYlbWaQJ";
            truncated = 0;
            user =            {
                "contributors_enabled" = 0;
                "created_at" = "Mon Sep 04 02:05:35 +0000 2006";
                "default_profile" = 0;
                "default_profile_image" = 0;
                description = "Dad, iOS & Mac game and app developer,
➥Founder of Free Time Studios, Texan";
                "favourites_count" = 391;
                "follow_request_sent" = "<null>";
                "followers_count" = 2254;
                following = 1;
                "friends_count" = 865;
                "geo_enabled" = 1;
```

```
            id = 5250;
            "id_str" = 5250;
            "is_translator" = 0;
            lang = en;
            "listed_count" = 182;
            location = "Houston, Texas";
            name = "Nathan Eror";
            notifications = "<null>";
            "profile_background_color" = 1A1B1F;
            "profile_background_image_url" =
➥"http://a0.twimg.com/images/themes/theme9/bg.gif";
            "profile_background_image_url_https" =
➥"https://si0.twimg.com/images/themes/theme9/bg.gif";
            "profile_background_tile" = 0;
            "profile_image_url" =
➥"http://a0.twimg.com/profile_images/1902659692/36A2FDF8-72F4-
➥485E-B574-892C1FF16534_normal";
            "profile_image_url_https" =
➥"https://si0.twimg.com/profile_images/1902659692/36A2FDF8-72F4-
➥485E-B574-892C1FF16534_normal";
            "profile_link_color" = 2FC2EF;
            "profile_sidebar_border_color" = 181A1E;
            "profile_sidebar_fill_color" = 252429;
            "profile_text_color" = 666666;
            "profile_use_background_image" = 1;
            protected = 0;
            "screen_name" = neror;
            "statuses_count" = 5091;
            "time_zone" = "Central Time (US & Canada)";
            url = "http://www.freetimestudios.com";
            "utc_offset" = "-21600";
            verified = 0;
        };
    }
)
```

Facebook

Retrieving a Facebook timeline is done through the endpoint https://graph.facebook.com/me/
feed. To begin, a new NSURL is created and then used to generate a new SLRequest. The following example assumes that the app has previously authenticated the user's permissions and that
request was granted. See the earlier section "Basic Facebook Permissions" for more details.

```
NSURL *feedURL = [NSURL URLWithString:
➥@"https://graph.facebook.com/me/feed"];

SLRequest *feedRequest = [SLRequest
```

```
requestForServiceType:SLServiceTypeFacebook
                           requestMethod:SLRequestMethodGET
                           URL:feedURL
                           parameters:nil];
```

```
feedRequest.account = self.facebookAccount;
```

After the SLRequest has been set up, a call to performRequestWithHandler: is invoked on
the feedRequest object. In the event of a success, Facebook will return a urlResponse status
code of 200; any other status code indicates a failure.

```
[feedRequest performRequestWithHandler:^(NSData *responseData,
➡NSHTTPURLResponse *urlResponse, NSError *error)
{
      NSLog(@"Facebook post statusCode: %d", [urlResponse
      ➡statusCode]);

      if([urlResponse statusCode] == 200)
      {
          NSLog(@"%@", [[NSJSONSerialization
          ➡JSONObjectWithData:responseData
          ➡options:NSJSONReadingMutableLeaves error:&error]
          ➡objectForKey:@"data"]);

          [self performSelectorOnMainThread:
          ➡@selector(presentTimeline:) withObject:
          ➡[[NSJSONSerialization JSONObjectWithData:responseData
          ➡options:NSJSONReadingMutableLeaves error:&error]
          ➡objectForKey:@"data"] waitUntilDone:NO];
      }

      else if(error != nil)
      {
          [self performSelectorOnMainThread:
          ➡@selector(faceBookError:) withObject:error
          ➡waitUntilDone:NO];
      }
}];
```

Facebook supports many types of post updates, from likes, comments, and new friends to wall
updates. Many of these dictionaries use different key sets for the information that is typically
displayed. The sample app will handle the most common types of Facebook posts. Following
are three standard post types with all the accompanying data. The first is a message indicating
that a new Facebook friend has been connected. The second item in the array represents a post
in which the user likes a link. The final example shows the user adding a comment to a post
by another user. It is important to thoroughly test any use of Facebook timeline parsing on a
wide selection of Facebook events to ensure proper compatibility. More information on the

formatting and behavior of Facebook posts can be found at http://developers.facebook.com. For more information on working with JSON data, refer to Chapter 9.

```
(
        {
        actions =            (
                        {
                link =
➥"http://www.facebook.com/1674990377/posts/4011976152528";
                name = Comment;
            },
                        {
                link =
➥"http://www.facebook.com/1674990377/posts/4011976152528";
                name = Like;
            }
        );
        comments =            {
            count = 0;
        };
        "created_time" = "2013-02-10T18:26:44+0000";
        from =            {
            id = 1674990377;
            name = "Kyle Richter";
        };
        id = "1674990377_4011976152528";
        privacy =              {
            value = "";
        };
        "status_type" = "approved_friend";
        story = "Kyle Richter and Kirby Turner are now friends.";
        "story_tags" =              {
            0 =               (
                            {
                    id = 1674990377;
                    length = 12;
                    name = "Kyle Richter";
                    offset = 0;
                    type = user;
                }
            );
            17 =                (
                            {
                    id = 827919293;
                    length = 12;
                    name = "Kirby Turner";
                    offset = 17;
                    type = user;
```

```
            }
        );
    };
    type = status;
    "updated_time" = "2013-02-10T18:26:44+0000";
},
    {
    comments =            {
        count = 0;
    };
    "created_time" = "2013-01-03T00:58:41+0000";
    from =            {
        id = 1674990377;
        name = "Kyle Richter";
    };
    id = "1674990377_3785554092118";
    privacy =             {
        value = "";
    };
    story = "Kyle Richter likes a link.";
    "story_tags" =            {
        0 =                (
                            {
                id = 1674990377;
                length = 12;
                name = "Kyle Richter";
                offset = 0;
                type = user;
            }
        );
    };
    type = status;
    "updated_time" = "2013-01-03T00:58:41+0000";
},
    {
    application =            {
        id = 6628568379;
        name = "Facebook for iPhone";
        namespace = fbiphone;
    };
    comments =             {
        count = 0;
    };
    "created_time" = "2013-01-02T19:20:59+0000";
    from =            {
        id = 1674990377;
        name = "Kyle Richter";
```

```
        };
        id = "1674990377_3784462784836";
        privacy =           {
            value = "";
        };
        story = "\"Congrats!\" on Dan Burcaw's link.";
        "story_tags" =          {
            15 =                (
                                    {
                    id = 10220084;
                    length = 10;
                    name = "Dan Burcaw";
                    offset = 15;
                    type = user;
                }
            );
        };
        type = status;
        "updated_time" = "2013-01-02T19:20:59+0000";
    })
```

Summary

This chapter covered the basics of integrating both Twitter and Facebook into an iOS app. Topics ranged from working with the built-in composer to writing highly customized posting engines. In addition, readers learned how to pull down the timeline and feed data and display it for consumption.

Social media integration has never been an easy topic, but with the enhancements made to Social Framework as well as Apple's commitment to bring social intergeneration to more third-party apps, it continues to get easier. The skills required to build a rich social app that includes Twitter and Facebook interaction should now be much clearer.

17

Working with Background Tasks

When iOS was first introduced in 2008, only one third-party app at a time could be active—the foreground app. This meant that any tasks that the app needed to complete had to finish while the app was in the foreground being actively used, or those tasks had to be paused and resumed the next time the app was started. With the introduction of iOS 4, background capabilities were added for third-party apps. Since iOS devices have limited system resources and battery preservation is a priority, background processing has some limitations to prevent interference with the foreground app and to prevent using too much power. An app can accomplish a lot with correct usage of backgrounding capabilities. This chapter explains what options are available and how to use them.

Two approaches to background-task processing are supported by iOS:

- The first approach is finishing a long-running task in the background. This method is appropriate for completing things like large downloads or data updates that stretch beyond the time the user spends interacting with the app.

- The second approach is supporting specific types of background activities allowed by iOS, such as playing music, interacting with Bluetooth devices, fetching newly available app content, monitoring the GPS for large changes, or maintaining a persistent network connection to allow VoIP-type apps to work.

> **Note**
>
> The term "background task" is frequently used interchangeably for two different meanings: a task executed when the app is not in the foreground (described in this chapter), and a task executed asynchronously off the main thread (described in Chapter 18, "Grand Central Dispatch for Performance"). In addition, NSURLSession provides the capability to upload and download files while the app is terminated, and can restart the app when an upload or download is complete.

The Sample App

The sample app for this chapter is called BackgroundTasks. This app demonstrates the two backgrounding approaches: completing a long-running task while the app is in the background, and playing audio continuously while the app is in the background. The user interface is simple—it presents a button to start and stop background music and a button to start the background task (see Figure 17.1).

Figure 17.1   BackgroundTasks sample app.

Checking for Background Availability

All devices capable of running iOS 5 or higher support performing activities in the background, referred to as multitasking in Apple's documentation. If the target app needs to support iOS 4 (or potentially a new device released in the future), note that a few devices do not support multitasking. Any code written to take advantage of multitasking should check to ensure that multitasking is supported by the device. When the user taps the Start Background Task button in the sample app, the `startBackgroundTaskTouched:` method in `ICFViewController` will be called to check for multitasking support.

```
- (IBAction)startBackgroundTaskTouched:(id)sender
{
    UIDevice* device = [UIDevice currentDevice];

    if (! [device isMultitaskingSupported])
    {
        NSLog(@"Multitasking not supported on this device.");
        return;
    }

    [self.backgroundButton setEnabled:NO];
    NSString *buttonTitle =@"Background Task Running";

    [self.backgroundButton setTitle:buttonTitle
                           forState:UIControlStateNormal];

    dispatch_queue_t background =
➥dispatch_get_global_queue(DISPATCH_QUEUE_PRIORITY_DEFAULT, 0);

    dispatch_async(background, ^{
        [self performBackgroundTask];
    });

}
```

To check for multitasking availability, use the class method `currentDevice` on `UIDevice` to get information about the current device. Then, call the `isMultitaskingSupported` method to determine whether multitasking is supported. If multitasking is supported, the user interface is updated and the `performBackgroundTask` method is called asynchronously to start the background task (see Chapter 18 for more info on executing tasks asynchronously).

Finishing a Task in the Background

To execute a long-running task in the background, the application needs to be informed that the task should be capable of running in the background. Consideration should also be given to the amount of memory needed for the task, and the total amount of time needed to complete the task. If the task will be longer than 10 to 15 minutes, it is likely that the app will be terminated before the task can complete. The task logic should be able to handle a quick termination, and be capable of being restarted when the app is relaunched. Apps are given a set amount of time to complete their background tasks, and can be terminated earlier than the given amount of time if the operating system detects that resources are needed.

To see the background task in action, start the sample app, as shown in Figure 17.1, from Xcode. Tap the Start Background Task button, and then tap the Home button to exit the app. Observe the console in Xcode to see log statements generated by the app; this will confirm that the app is running in the background.

```
Background task starting, task ID is 1.
Background Processed 0. Still in foreground.
Background Processed 1. Still in foreground.
Background Processed 2. Still in foreground.
Background Processed 3. Still in foreground.
Background Processed 4. Still in foreground.
Background Processed 5. Still in foreground.
Background Processed 6. Time remaining is: 599.579052
Background Processed 7. Time remaining is: 598.423525
Background Processed 8. Time remaining is: 597.374849
Background Processed 9. Time remaining is: 596.326780
Background Processed 10. Time remaining is: 595.308253
```

The general process to execute a background task is as follows:

1. Request a background task identifier from the application, specifying a block as an expiration handler. The expiration handler will get called only if the app runs out of background time or if the system determines that resource usage is too high and the app should be terminated.

2. Perform the background task logic. Any code between the request for background task identifier and the background task end will be included.

3. Tell the application to end the background task, and invalidate the background task identifier.

Background Task Identifier

To start a task that can complete running in the background, a background task identifier needs to be obtained from the application. The background task identifier helps the application keep track of which tasks are running and which are complete. The background task identifier is needed to tell the application that a task is complete and background processing is no longer required. The performBackgroundTask method in ICFViewController obtains the background task identifier before beginning the work to be done in the background.

```
__block UIBackgroundTaskIdentifier bTask =
➥[[UIApplication sharedApplication]
➥beginBackgroundTaskWithExpirationHandler:
➥^{
    ...
}];
```

When a background task is being obtained, an expiration handler block should be specified. The reason the __block modifier is used when the background task identifier is declared is that the background task identifier is needed in the expiration handler block, and needs to be modified in the expiration handler block.

Expiration Handler

The expiration handler for a background task will get called if the operating system decides the app has run out of time and/or resources and needs to be shut down. The expiration handler will get called on the main thread before the app is about to be shut down. Not much time is provided (at most it is a few seconds), so the handler should do a minimal amount of work.

```
__block UIBackgroundTaskIdentifier bTask =
➡[[UIApplication sharedApplication]
➡beginBackgroundTaskWithExpirationHandler:
➡^{
    NSLog(@"Background Expiration Handler called.");
    NSLog(@"Counter is: %d, task ID is %u.",counter,bTask);

    [[UIApplication sharedApplication]
    ➡endBackgroundTask:bTask];

    bTask = UIBackgroundTaskInvalid;
}];
```

The minimum that the expiration handler should do is to tell the application that the background task has ended by calling the endBackgroundTask: method on the shared application instance, and invalidate the background task ID by setting the bTask variable to UIBackgroundTaskInvalid so that it will not inadvertently be used again.

```
Background Processed 570. Time remaining is: 11.482063
Background Processed 571. Time remaining is: 10.436456
Background Processed 572. Time remaining is: 9.394706
Background Processed 573. Time remaining is: 8.346616
Background Processed 574. Time remaining is: 7.308527
Background Processed 575. Time remaining is: 6.260324
Background Processed 576. Time remaining is: 5.212251
Background Expiration Handler called.
Counter is: 577, task ID is 1.
```

Completing the Background Task

After a background task ID has been obtained, the actual work to be done in the background can commence. In the performBackgroundTask method some variables are set up to know where to start counting, to keep count of iterations, and to know when to stop. A reference to NSUserDefaults standardUserDefaults is established to retrieve the last counter used, and store the last counter with each iteration.

```
NSInteger counter = 0;

NSUserDefaults *userDefaults =
➡[NSUserDefaults standardUserDefaults];
```

```
NSInteger startCounter =
➥[userDefaults integerForKey:kLastCounterKey];


NSInteger twentyMins = 20 * 60;
```

The background task for the sample app is trivial—it puts the thread to sleep for a second in a loop to simulate lots of long-running iterations. It stores the current counter for the iteration in `NSUserDefaults` so that it will be easy to keep track of where it left off if the background task expires. This logic could be modified to handle keeping track of any repetitive background task.

```
NSLog(@"Background task starting, task ID is %u.",bTask);
for (counter = startCounter; counter<=twentyMins; counter++)
{
    [NSThread sleepForTimeInterval:1];
    [userDefaults setInteger:counter
                    forKey:kLastCounterKey];

    [userDefaults synchronize];

    NSTimeInterval remainingTime =
    ➥[[UIApplication sharedApplication] backgroundTimeRemaining];

    NSLog(@"Background Processed %d. Time remaining is: %f",
    ➥counter,remainingTime);
}
```

When each iteration is complete, the time remaining for the background task is obtained from the application. This can be used to determine whether additional iterations of a background task should be started.

Note

The background task is typically expired when there are a few seconds remaining, to give it time to wrap up, so any decision to start a new iteration should take that into consideration.

After the background task work is done, the last counter is updated in `NSUserDefaults` so that it can start over correctly, and the UI is updated to enable the user to start the background task again.

```
NSLog(@"Background Completed tasks");

[userDefaults setInteger:0
                forKey:kLastCounterKey];

[userDefaults synchronize];
```

```
dispatch_sync(dispatch_get_main_queue(), ^{
    [self.backgroundButton setEnabled:YES];
    [self.backgroundButton setTitle:@"Start Background Task"
                            forState:UIControlStateNormal];
});
```

Finally, two key items need to take place to finish the background task: tell the application to end the background task, and invalidate the background task identifier. Every line of code between obtaining the background task ID and ending it will execute in the background.

```
[[UIApplication sharedApplication] endBackgroundTask:self.backgroundTask];

self.backgroundTask = UIBackgroundTaskInvalid;
```

Implementing Background Activities

iOS supports a specific set of background activities that can continue processing without the limitations of the background task identifier approach. These activities can continue running or being available without a time limit, and need to avoid using too many system resources to keep the app from getting terminated.

Types of Background Activities

These are the background activities:

- Playing background audio
- Tracking device location
- Supporting a Voice over IP app
- Downloading new Newsstand app content
- Communicating with an external or Bluetooth accessory
- Fetching content in the background
- Initiating a background download with a push notification

To support any of these background activities, the app needs to declare which background activities it supports in the `Info.plist` file. To do this, select the app target in Xcode, and select the Capabilities tab. Turn Background Modes to On, and then check the desired modes to support. Xcode will add the entries to the `Info.plist` file for you. Or edit the `Info.plist` file directly by selecting the app target in Xcode, and then select the Info tab. Look for the Required Background Modes entry in the list; if it is not present, hover over an existing entry and click the plus sign to add a new entry, and then select Required Background Modes. An array entry will be added with one empty `NSString` item. Select the desired background mode, as shown in Figure 17.2.

Figure 17.2   Xcode's Info editor showing required background modes.

After the Required Background Modes entry is established, activity-specific logic can be built into the app and it will function when the app is in the background.

Playing Music in the Background

To play music in the background, the first step is to adjust the audio session settings for the app. By default, an app uses the AVAudioSessionCategorySoloAmbient audio session category. This ensures that other audio is turned off when the app is started, and that the app audio is silenced when the screen is locked or the ring/silent switch on the device is set to silent. This session will not work, since audio will be silenced when the screen is locked or when another app is brought to the foreground. The viewDidLoad method in ICFViewController adjusts the audio session category to AVAudioSessionCategoryPlayback, which will ensure that the audio will continue playing when the app is in the background or the ring/silent switch is set to silent.

```
AVAudioSession *session = [AVAudioSession sharedInstance];

NSError *activeError = nil;
if (![session setActive:YES error:&activeError])
{
    NSLog(@"Failed to set active audio session!");
}

NSError *categoryError = nil;
if (![session setCategory:AVAudioSessionCategoryPlayback
                error:&categoryError])
{
    NSLog(@"Failed to set audio category!");
}
```

The next step in playing audio is to initialize an audio player. This is also done in the `view-DidLoad` method so that the audio player is ready whenever the user indicates that audio should be played.

```
NSError *playerInitError = nil;

NSString *audioPath =
➡[[NSBundle mainBundle] pathForResource:@"background_audio"
                                  ofType:@"mp3"];

NSURL *audioURL = [NSURL fileURLWithPath:audioPath];

self.audioPlayer = [[AVAudioPlayer alloc]
➡initWithContentsOfURL:audioURL error:&playerInitError];
```

The Play Background Music button is wired to the `playBackgroundMusicTouched:` method. When the user taps that button, the logic checks to see whether audio is currently playing. If audio is currently playing, the method stops the audio and updates the title of the button.

```
if ([self.audioPlayer isPlaying])
{
    [self.audioPlayer stop];

    [self.audioButton setTitle:@"Play Background Music"
                      forState:UIControlStateNormal];

}
else
{ ...
}
```

If music is not currently playing, the method starts the audio and changes the title of the button.

```
[self.audioPlayer play];

[self.audioButton setTitle:@"Stop Background Music"
                  forState:UIControlStateNormal];
```

While the audio is playing, the user can press the lock button on the device or the home button to send the app to the background, and the audio will continue playing. A really nice feature when audio is playing and the screen is locked is to display the currently playing information on the lock screen. To do this, first set up a dictionary with information about the playing media.

```
UIImage *lockImage = [UIImage imageNamed:@"book_cover"];

MPMediaItemArtwork *artwork =
➡[[MPMediaItemArtwork alloc] initWithImage:lockImage];
```

```
NSDictionary *mediaDict =
➡@{
    MPMediaItemPropertyTitle: @"BackgroundTask Audio",
    MPMediaItemPropertyMediaType: @(MPMediaTypeAnyAudio),
    MPMediaItemPropertyPlaybackDuration:
    @(self.audioPlayer.duration),
    MPNowPlayingInfoPropertyPlaybackRate: @1.0,
    MPNowPlayingInfoPropertyElapsedPlaybackTime:
    @(self.audioPlayer.currentTime),
    MPMediaItemPropertyAlbumArtist: @"Some User",
    MPMediaItemPropertyArtist: @"Some User",
    MPMediaItemPropertyArtwork: artwork };
```

Various options can be set. Note that a title and an image are specified; these will be displayed on the lock screen. The duration and current time are provided and can be displayed at the media player's discretion, depending on the state of the device and the context in which it will be displayed. After the media information is established, the method starts the audio player, and then informs the media player's MPNowPlayingInfoCenter about the playing media item info. It sets self to be the first responder, since the media player's info center requires the view or view controller playing audio to be the first responder in order to work correctly. It tells the app to start responding to "remote control" events, which will allow the lock screen controls to control the audio in the app with delegate methods implemented.

```
[[MPNowPlayingInfoCenter defaultCenter]
➡setNowPlayingInfo:mediaDict];

[self becomeFirstResponder];

[[UIApplication sharedApplication]
➡beginReceivingRemoteControlEvents];
```

Now when the audio is playing in the background, the lock screen will display information about it, as shown in Figure 17.3.

In addition, the Control Center will display information about the audio, as shown in Figure 17.4.

Figure 17.3   Lock screen showing sample app playing background audio.

Figure 17.4   Lock screen Control Center showing sample app playing background audio.

Summary

This chapter illuminated two approaches to executing tasks while the app is in the background, or while it is not the current app that the user is interacting with.

The first approach to background task processing described was finishing a long-running task in the background. The sample app demonstrated how to check whether the device is capable of running a background task, showed how to set up and execute a background task, and explained how to handle the case when iOS terminates the app and notifies the background task that it will be ended (or expired).

The second approach to background tasks described was supporting very specific types of background activities allowed by iOS, such as playing music, interacting with Bluetooth devices, monitoring the GPS for large changes, and maintaining a persistent network connection to enable VoIP-type apps to work. The chapter explained how to configure an Xcode project to enable a background activity to take place, and then the sample app demonstrated how to play audio in the background while displaying information about the audio on the lock screen.

Grand Central Dispatch for Performance

Many apps have challenging performance requirements, involving multiple processor-intensive and high-latency tasks that need to take place simultaneously. This chapter demonstrates the negative effects of blocking the main queue, which makes the user interface slow or completely unusable—not at all desirable for a good user experience. It then examines tools supported by iOS that enable the programmer to perform tasks "in the background," meaning that a processing task will take place and not directly delay updating the user interface. Apple provides several tools with varying degrees of control over how background tasks are accomplished.

Concurrent programming is frequently done using threads. It can be challenging to get the desired performance improvements from a multicore device by managing threads directly in an app, because effective thread management requires real-time monitoring and management of system resources and usage. To address this problem, Apple introduced Grand Central Dispatch (GCD). GCD manages queues, which are an abstracted level above threads. Queues can operate concurrently or serially, and can automatically handle thread management and optimization at a system level.

This chapter introduces several approaches to background processing of long-running tasks and highlights the benefits and drawbacks of each.

The Sample App

The sample app is called LongRunningTasks. It will demonstrate a trivial long-running task on the main thread, and then several techniques for handling the same long-running task off the main thread. The trivial long-running tasks are five loops to add ten items each with a time delay to an array, which can then be displayed in a table view. The sample app has a table view, which will present a list of the available approaches. Selecting an approach will present a table view for the approach. The table view has five starting items, so it is clear when attempting to scroll whether the main thread is being interrupted by the long-running task. The long-running tasks will then create 50 more items in batches of ten to display in the table view. The table view will be notified upon completion to update the UI on the main thread, and the new items will appear.

The sample app (as shown in Figure 18.1) illustrates the following techniques:

- **performSelectorInBackground:withObject:** This is the simplest approach to running code off the main thread, and it works well when the task has simple and straightforward requirements. The system does not undertake any additional management of tasks performed this way, so this is best suited to nonrepetitive tasks.

- **NSOperationQueue:** This is a slightly more complex method for running code off the main thread, and it provides some additional control capabilities, such as running serially, concurrently, or with dependencies between tasks. Operation queues are implemented with and are a higher level of abstraction of GCD queues. Operation queues are best suited to repetitive, well-defined asynchronous tasks, for example, network calls or parsing.

- **GCD Queues:** This is the most "low-level" approach to running code off the main thread, and it provides the most flexibility. The sample app will demonstrate running tasks serially and concurrently using GCD queues. GCD can be used for anything from just communicating between the background and the main queue to quickly performing a block of code for each item in a list, to processing large, repetitive asynchronous tasks.

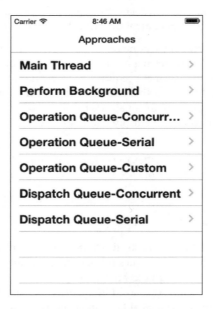

Figure 18.1   Sample app, long-running task approach list.

Introduction to Queues

Some of the terminology related to concurrent processing can be a bit confusing. *Thread* is a commonly used term; in the context of an iOS app, a thread is a standard POSIX thread. Technically, a thread is just a set of instructions that can be handled independently within a process (an app is a process), and multiple threads can exist within a process, sharing memory and resources. Since threads function independently, work can be split across threads to get it done more quickly. It is also possible to run into problems when multiple threads need access to the same resource or data. All iOS apps have a main thread that handles the run loop and updating the UI. For an app to remain responsive to user interaction, the main thread must be given only tasks that can be completed in less than 1/60 of a second.

Queue is a term that Apple uses to describe the contexts provided by Grand Central Dispatch. A queue is managed by GCD as a group of tasks to be executed. Depending on the current system utilization, GCD will dynamically determine the right number of threads to use to process the tasks in a queue. The main queue is a special queue managed by GCD that is associated with the main thread. So when you run a task on the main queue, GCD executes that task on the main thread.

People frequently toss around the terms *thread* and *queue* interchangeably; just remember that a queue is really just a managed set of threads, and *main* is just referring to the thread that handles the main run loop and UI.

Running on the Main Thread

Run the sample app and select the row called Main Thread. Notice that the five initial items in the table view are initially visible, but they cannot be scrolled and the UI is completely unresponsive while the additional items are being added. There is logging to demonstrate that the additional items are being added while the UI is frozen—view the debugging console while running the app to see the logging. The frozen UI is obviously not a desirable user experience, and it is unfortunately easy to get a situation like this to happen in an app. To see why this is happening, take a look at the ICFMainThreadLongRunningTaskViewController class. First, the array to store display data is set up and given an initial set of data:

```
- (void)viewDidLoad
{
    [super viewDidLoad];

    self.displayItems =
    ➥[[NSMutableArray alloc] initWithCapacity:45];

    [self.displayItems addObject:@[@"Item Initial-1",
    ➥@"Item Initial-2",@"Item Initial-3",
    ➥@"Item Initial-4",@"Item Initial-5"]];
}
```

After the initial data is set up and the view is visible, the long-running task is started:

```
- (void)viewDidAppear:(BOOL)animated
{
    [super viewDidAppear:animated];

    for (int i=1; i<=5; i++)
    {
        NSNumber *iteration = [NSNumber numberWithInt:i];
        [self performLongRunningTaskForIteration:iteration];
    }
}
```

The app is calling the `performLongRunningTaskForIteration:` method five times to set up additional table data. This does not appear to be doing anything that would slow down the main thread. Examine the `performLongRunningTaskForIteration:` method to see what is hanging the main thread. The intention is for the long-running task to add ten items to an array, which will then be added to the `displayItems` array, which is the data source for the table view.

```
- (void)performLongRunningTaskForIteration:(NSNumber *)iterationNumber
{
    NSMutableArray *newArray =
    ➥[[NSMutableArray alloc] initWithCapacity:10];

    for (int i=1; i<=10; i++)
    {

        [newArray addObject:
        [NSString stringWithFormat:@"Item %@-%d",
        ➥iterationNumber,i]];

        [NSThread sleepForTimeInterval:.1];

        NSLog(@"Main Added %@-%d",iterationNumber,i);
    }

    [self.displayItems addObject:newArray];
    [self.tableView reloadData];
}
```

Because the main thread is responsible for keeping the user interface updated, any activity that takes longer than 1/60 of a second can result in noticeable delays. In this case, notice that the method is calling `sleepForTimeInterval:` on `NSThread` for every iteration. Obviously, this is not something that would make sense to do in a typical app, but it clearly illustrates the point that a single method call that takes a little bit of time and blocks the main thread can cause severe performance issues.

Note

Finding the method calls that take up an appreciable amount of time is rarely as clear as in this example. See Chapter 26, "Debugging and Instruments," for techniques to discover where performance issues are taking place.

In this case, the `sleepForTimeInterval:` method call is quickly and frequently blocking the main thread, so even after the `for` loop is complete, the main thread does not have enough time to update the UI until all the calls to `performLongRunningTaskForIteration:` are complete.

Running in the Background

Run the sample app, and select the row called Perform Background. Notice that the five initial items in the table view are initially visible, and they are scrollable while the long-running tasks are being processed (view the debugging console to confirm that they are being processed while scrolling the table view). After the tasks are completed, the additional rows become visible.

This approach sets up the initial data in exactly the same way as the Main Thread approach. View `ICFPerformBackgroundViewController` in the sample app source code to see how it is set up. After the initial data is set up and the view is visible, the long-running task is started; this is where performing the task in the background is specified.

```
- (void)viewDidAppear:(BOOL)animated
{
    [super viewDidAppear:animated];

    SEL taskSelector =
    ➥@selector(performLongRunningTaskForIteration:);

    for (int i=1; i<=5; i++)
    {

        NSNumber *iteration = @(i);

        [self performSelectorInBackground:taskSelector
                               withObject:iteration];
    }
}
```

A selector is set up; this is just the name of the method to perform in the background. `NSObject` defines the method `performSelectorInBackground:withObject:`, which requires an Objective-C object to be passed as the parameter `withObject:`. This method will spawn a new thread, execute the method with the passed parameter in that new thread, and return to the calling thread immediately. This new thread is the developer's responsibility to manage, so it is entirely possible to create too many new threads by calling this method frequently and overwhelm the system. If testing indicates that this is a problem, an operation queue or dispatch queue (both described later in the chapter) can be used to provide more precise control over the execution of the tasks and better management of system resources.

The method `performLongRunningTaskForIteration:` performs exactly the same task as in the Main Thread approach; however, instead of adding the `newArray` to the `displayItems` array directly, the method calls the `updateTableData:` method using `NSObject`'s method `performSelectorOnMainThread:withObject:waitUntilDone:`. Using that approach is necessary for two reasons. First, UIKit objects, including our table view, will update the UI only if they are updated on the main thread. Second, the property `displayItems` is declared as `nonatomic`, meaning that the getter and setter methods generated are not thread-safe. To "fix" this, the `displayItems` property could be declared `atomic`, but that would add some performance overhead to lock the array before updating it. If the property is updated on the main thread, locking is not required.

```
- (void)performLongRunningTaskForIteration:(NSNumber *)iterationNumber
{
    NSMutableArray *newArray =
    [[NSMutableArray alloc] initWithCapacity:10];

    for (int i=1; i<=10; i++)
    {

        [newArray addObject:
        ➥[NSString stringWithFormat:@"Item %@-%d",
        ➥iterationNumber,i]];

        [NSThread sleepForTimeInterval:.1];

        NSLog(@"Background Added %@-%d",iterationNumber,i);
    }

    [self performSelectorOnMainThread:@selector(updateTableData:)
                           withObject:newArray
                        waitUntilDone:NO];
}
```

The `updateTableData:` method simply adds the newly created items to the `displayItems` array and informs the table view to reload and update the UI.

An interesting side effect is that the order in which the additional rows are added is not deterministic—it will potentially be different every time the app is run.

```
10:51:09.324 LongRunningTasks[29382:15903] Background Added 3-1
10:51:09.324 LongRunningTasks[29382:16303] Background Added 5-1
10:51:09.324 LongRunningTasks[29382:15207] Background Added 1-1
10:51:09.324 LongRunningTasks[29382:15e03] Background Added 4-1
10:51:09.324 LongRunningTasks[29382:15107] Background Added 2-1
```

```
10:51:09.430 LongRunningTasks[29382:15207] Background Added 1-2
10:51:09.430 LongRunningTasks[29382:16303] Background Added 5-2
10:51:09.430 LongRunningTasks[29382:15e03] Background Added 4-2
10:51:09.430 LongRunningTasks[29382:15107] Background Added 2-2
10:51:09.430 LongRunningTasks[29382:15903] Background Added 3-2
...
```

This is a symptom of the fact that using this technique makes no promises about when a task will be completed or in what order it will be processed, since the tasks are all performed on different threads. If the order of operation is not important, this technique can be just fine; if order matters, an operation queue or dispatch queue is needed to process the tasks serially (both described later, in the sections "Serial Operations" and "Serial Dispatch Queues").

Running in an Operation Queue

Operation queues (NSOperationQueue) are available to manage a set of tasks or operations (NSOperation). An operation queue can specify how many operations can run concurrently, can be suspended and restarted, and can cancel all pending operations. Operations can be a simple method invocation, a block, or a custom operation class. Operations can have dependencies established to make them run serially. Operations and operation queues are actually managed by Grand Central Dispatch, and are implemented with dispatch queues.

The sample app illustrates three approaches using an operation queue: concurrent operations, serial operations with dependencies, and custom operations to support cancellation.

Concurrent Operations

Run the sample app, and select the row called Operation Queue-Concurrent. The five initial items in the table view are visible, and they are scrollable while the long-running tasks are being processed (view the debugging console to confirm that they are being processed while scrolling the table view). After the tasks are completed, the additional rows become visible.

Examine the ICFOperationQueueConcurrentViewController in the sample app source code to see how this approach is set up. Before operations are added, the operation queue needs to be set up in the viewDidLoad: method:

```
self.processingQueue = [[NSOperationQueue alloc] init];
```

This approach sets up the initial data in exactly the same way as the Main Thread approach. After the initial data is set up and the view is visible, the long-running tasks are added to the operation queue as instances of NSInvocationOperation:

```
- (void)viewDidAppear:(BOOL)animated
{
    [super viewDidAppear:animated];
```

```
SEL taskSelector =
➥@selector(performLongRunningTaskForIteration:);

for (int i=1; i<=5; i++)
{

    NSNumber *iteration = @(i);

    NSInvocationOperation *operation =
    ➥[[NSInvocationOperation alloc] initWithTarget:self
    ➥selector:taskSelector object:iteration];

    [operation setCompletionBlock:^{
        NSLog(@"Operation #%d completed.",i);
    }];

    [self.processingQueue addOperation:operation];
}
}
```

Each operation is assigned a completion block that will run when the operation is finished processing. The method `performLongRunningTaskForIteration:` performs exactly the same task as in the Perform Background approach; in fact, the method is not changed in this approach. The `updateTableData:` method is also not changed. The results will be similar to the Perform Background approach in that the items will not be added in a deterministic order.

```
21:00:16.165 LongRunningTasks[31009] OpQ Concurrent Added 1-1
21:00:16.165 LongRunningTasks[31009] OpQ Concurrent Added 3-1
21:00:16.165 LongRunningTasks[31009] OpQ Concurrent Added 4-1
21:00:16.165 LongRunningTasks[31009] OpQ Concurrent Added 2-1
21:00:16.165 LongRunningTasks[31009] OpQ Concurrent Added 5-1
...
21:00:17.107 LongRunningTasks[31009] Operation #4 completed.
21:00:17.108 LongRunningTasks[31009] Operation #2 completed.
21:00:17.107 LongRunningTasks[31009] Operation #5 completed.
21:00:17.108 LongRunningTasks[31009] Operation #3 completed.
21:00:17.109 LongRunningTasks[31009] Operation #1 completed.
```

The main difference here is that the NSOperationQueue is managing the threads, and will process only up to the default maximum concurrent operations for the queue. This can be very important when your app has many different competing tasks that need to happen concurrently and need to be managed to avoid overloading the system.

Note

The default maximum concurrent operations for an operation queue is a dynamic number determined in real time by the system. It can vary based on the current system load. The maximum number of operations can also be specified for an operation queue, in which case the queue will process only up to the specified number of operations simultaneously.

Serial Operations

Visit the sample app and select the row called Operation Queue-Serial. The five initial items in the table view are visible, and they are scrollable while the long-running tasks are being processed (view the debugging console to confirm that they are being processed while scrolling the table view). After the tasks are completed, the additional rows become visible.

The setups of the initial data and operation queue are identical to the Operation Queue-Concurrent approach. To have the operations process serially in the correct order, they need to be set up with dependencies. To accomplish this task, the `viewDidAppear:` method adds an array to store the operations as they are created, and an `NSInvocationOperation` (prev-Operation) to track the previous operation created.

```
NSMutableArray *operationsToAdd = [[NSMutableArray alloc] init];

NSInvocationOperation *prevOperation = nil;
```

While the operations are being created, the method keeps track of the previously created operation. The newly created operation adds a dependency to the previous operation so that it cannot run until the previous operation completes. The new operation is added to the array of operations to add to the queue.

```
for (int i=1; i<=5; i++)
{

    NSNumber *iteration = @(i);

    NSInvocationOperation *operation =
    ➥[[NSInvocationOperation alloc] initWithTarget:self
    ➥selector:taskSelector object:iteration];

    if (prevOperation)
    {
        [operation addDependency:prevOperation];
    }

    [operationsToAdd addObject:operation];

    prevOperation = operation;
}
```

After all the operations are created and added to the array, they are added to the queue. Because an operation will start executing as soon as it is added to an operation queue, the operations need to be added all at once to ensure that the queue can respect the dependencies.

```
for (NSInvocationOperation *operation in operationsToAdd)
{
    [self.processingQueue addOperation:operation];
}
```

The operation queue will analyze the added operations and dependencies, and determine the optimum order in which to execute them. Observe the debugging console to see that the operations execute in the correct order serially.

```
16:51:45.216 LongRunningTasks[29554:15507] OpQ Serial Added 1-1
16:51:45.318 LongRunningTasks[29554:15507] OpQ Serial Added 1-2
16:51:45.420 LongRunningTasks[29554:15507] OpQ Serial Added 1-3
16:51:45.522 LongRunningTasks[29554:15507] OpQ Serial Added 1-4
16:51:45.625 LongRunningTasks[29554:15507] OpQ Serial Added 1-5
16:51:45.728 LongRunningTasks[29554:15507] OpQ Serial Added 1-6
16:51:45.830 LongRunningTasks[29554:15507] OpQ Serial Added 1-7
16:51:45.931 LongRunningTasks[29554:15507] OpQ Serial Added 1-8
16:51:46.034 LongRunningTasks[29554:15507] OpQ Serial Added 1-9
16:51:46.137 LongRunningTasks[29554:15507] OpQ Serial Added 1-10
16:51:46.246 LongRunningTasks[29554:14e0b] OpQ Serial Added 2-1
16:51:46.349 LongRunningTasks[29554:14e0b] OpQ Serial Added 2-2
16:51:46.452 LongRunningTasks[29554:14e0b] OpQ Serial Added 2-3
16:51:46.554 LongRunningTasks[29554:14e0b] OpQ Serial Added 2-4
16:51:46.657 LongRunningTasks[29554:14e0b] OpQ Serial Added 2-5
16:51:46.765 LongRunningTasks[29554:14e0b] OpQ Serial Added 2-6
. . .
```

The serial approach increases the total amount of time needed to complete all the tasks, but successfully ensures that the tasks execute in the correct order.

Canceling Operations

Back in the sample app, select the row called Operation Queue-Concurrent. Quickly tap the Cancel button at the top of the table while the operations are running. Notice that nothing appears to happen after the Cancel button has been tapped, and the operations will finish. When the Cancel button is touched, the operation queue is instructed to cancel all outstanding operations:

```
- (IBAction)cancelButtonTouched:(id)sender
{
    [self.processingQueue cancelAllOperations];
}
```

This does not work as expected because `Cancelled` is just a flag on an operation object—the logic of the operation must dictate how the operation behaves when it is canceled. The call to `cancelAllOperations:` dutifully sets the flag on all the outstanding operations, and since they are not checking their own cancellation status while running, they proceed until they complete their tasks.

To properly handle cancellation, a subclass of `NSOperation` must be created, or a weak reference to an instance of `NSBlockOperation` must be checked like so:

```
NSBlockOperation *blockOperation =
➡[[NSBlockOperation alloc] init];

__weak NSBlockOperation *blockOperationRef = blockOperation;
[blockOperation addExecutionBlock:^{
    if (![blockOperationRef isCancelled])
    {
        NSLog(@"...not canceled, execute logic here");
    }
}];
```

In the next section, creating a custom NSOperation subclass with cancellation handling is
discussed.

Custom Operations

Return to the sample app, and select the row called Operation Queue-Custom. The five initial
items in the table view are visible, and they are scrollable while the long-running tasks are
being processed (view the debugging console to confirm that they are being processed while
scrolling the table view). Quickly hit the Cancel button at the top of the table before the operations complete. Notice that this time the tasks stop immediately.

The setups of the initial data and operation queue are nearly identical to the Operation Queue-
Serial approach. The only difference is the use of a custom NSOperation subclass called
ICFCustomOperation:

```
- (void)viewDidAppear:(BOOL)animated
{
    [super viewDidAppear:animated];

    NSMutableArray *operationsToAdd =
    ➡[[NSMutableArray alloc] init];

    ICFCustomOperation *prevOperation = nil;
    for (int i=1; i<=5; i++)
    {

        NSNumber *iteration = [NSNumber numberWithInt:i];

        ICFCustomOperation *operation =
        ➡[[ICFCustomOperation alloc] initWithIteration:iteration
                                         andDelegate:self];

        if (prevOperation)
        {
            [operation addDependency:prevOperation];
        }
```

```
        [operationsToAdd addObject:operation];

        prevOperation = operation;
    }

    for (ICFCustomOperation *operation in operationsToAdd)
    {
        [self.processingQueue addOperation:operation];
    }
}
```

ICFCustomOperation is declared as a subclass of NSOperation, and declares a protocol so that it can inform a delegate that processing is complete and pass back the results:

```
@protocol ICFCustomOperationDelegate <NSObject>

- (void)updateTableWithData:(NSArray *)moreData;

@end
```

An NSOperation subclass needs to implement the main method. This is where the processing logic for the operation should go:

```
- (void)main
{
    NSMutableArray *newArray =
    ➥[[NSMutableArray alloc] initWithCapacity:10];

    for (int i=1; i<=10; i++)
    {

        if ([self isCancelled])
        {
            break;
        }

        [newArray addObject:
        ➥[NSString stringWithFormat:@"Item %@-%d",
        ➥self.iteration,i]];

        [NSThread sleepForTimeInterval:.1];
        NSLog(@"OpQ Custom Added %@-%d",self.iteration,i);
    }

    [self.delegate updateTableWithData:newArray];
}
```

At the beginning of the `for` loop, the cancellation status is checked:

```
if ([self isCancelled])
{
    break;
}
```

This check enables the operation to respond immediately to a cancellation request. When designing a custom operation, give careful consideration to how cancellations should be processed, and whether any rollback logic is required.

Properly handling cancellations is not the only benefit to creating a custom operation subclass; it is a very effective way to encapsulate complex logic in a way that can be run in an operation queue.

Running in a Dispatch Queue

Dispatch queues are provided by Grand Central Dispatch to execute blocks of code in a managed environment. GCD is designed to maximize concurrency and take full advantage of multicore processing power by managing the number of threads allocated to a queue dynamically based on the status of the system.

GCD offers three types of queues: the main queue, concurrent queues, and serial queues. The main queue is a special queue created by the system, which is tied to the application's main thread. In iOS, several global concurrent queues are available: the high-, normal-, low-, and background-priority queues. Private concurrent and serial queues can be created by the application and must be managed like any other application resource. The sample app demonstrates using concurrent and serial GCD queues, and how to interact with the main queue from those queues.

> **Note**
>
> As of iOS 6, created dispatch queues are managed by ARC, and they do not need to be retained or released.

Concurrent Dispatch Queues

Open the sample app, and select the row called Dispatch Queue-Concurrent. The five initial items in the table view are visible, and they are scrollable while the long-running tasks are being processed (view the debugging console to confirm that they are being processed while scrolling the table view). After the tasks are completed, the additional rows become visible. Notice that this approach completes significantly faster than any of the previous approaches.

To start the long-running tasks in the `viewDidAppear:` method, the app gets a reference to the high-priority concurrent dispatch queue:

```
dispatch_queue_t workQueue =
➥dispatch_get_global_queue(DISPATCH_QUEUE_PRIORITY_HIGH, 0);
```

Using `dispatch_get_global_queue` provides access to the three global, system-maintained concurrent dispatch queues. References to these queues do not need to be retained or released. After a reference to the queue is available, logic can be submitted to it for execution inside a block:

```
for (int i=1; i<=5; i++)
{

    NSNumber *iteration = @(i);

    dispatch_async(workQueue, ^{
        [self performLongRunningTaskForIteration:iteration];
    });
}
```

The use of `dispatch_async` indicates that the logic should be performed asynchronously. In that case, the work in the block will be submitted to the queue, and the call to do that will return immediately without blocking the main thread. Blocks can also be submitted to the queue synchronously using `dispatch_sync`, which will cause the calling thread to wait until the block has completed processing.

In the `performLongRunningTaskForIteration:` method, there are a few differences from previous approaches that need to be highlighted. The `newArray` used to keep track of created items needs a `__block` modifier so that the block can update it.

```
__block NSMutableArray *newArray =
➥[[NSMutableArray alloc] initWithCapacity:10];
```

The method then gets a reference to the low-priority concurrent dispatch queue.

```
dispatch_queue_t detailQueue =
➥dispatch_get_global_queue(DISPATCH_QUEUE_PRIORITY_LOW, 0);
```

The low-priority dispatch queue is then used for a powerful GCD technique: processing an entire enumeration simultaneously.

```
dispatch_apply(10, detailQueue, ^(size_t i)
{
    [NSThread sleepForTimeInterval:.1];

    [newArray addObject:[NSString stringWithFormat:
    ➥@"Item %@-%zu",iterationNumber,i+1]];

    NSLog(@"Dispatch Q Added %@-%zu",iterationNumber,i+1);
});
```

With `dispatch_apply`, all that is needed is a number of iterations, a reference to a dispatch queue, a variable to express which iteration is being processed (it must be `size_t`), and a block to be processed for each iteration. GCD will fill the queue with all the possible iterations, and they will be processed as close to simultaneously as possible, within the constraints of the system. This technique enables this approach to process so much more quickly than the other approaches, and it can be effective if the task order is not important.

> **Note**
>
> Methods on collection classes can achieve a similar effect at a higher level of abstraction. For example, `NSArray` has a method called `enumerateObjectsWithOptions:usingBlock:`. This method can enumerate the objects in an array serially, serially in reverse, or concurrently.

After the iterations are complete and the array of new items has been created, the method needs to inform the UI to update the table view.

```
dispatch_async(dispatch_get_main_queue(), ^{
    [self updateTableData:newArray];
});
```

This `dispatch_async` call uses the function `dispatch_get_main_queue` to access the main queue. Note that this technique can be used from anywhere to get to the main queue, and can be a very handy way to update the UI to report status on long-running tasks.

Serial Dispatch Queues

Run the sample app, and select the row called Dispatch Queue-Serial. The five initial items in the table view are visible, and they are scrollable while the long-running tasks are being processed (view the debugging console to confirm that they are being processed while scrolling the table view). After the tasks are completed, the additional rows become visible. This approach is not as fast as the concurrent dispatch queue approach, but it will process the items in the order in which they are added to the queue.

To start the long-running tasks in the `viewDidAppear:` method, the app creates a serial dispatch queue:

```
dispatch_queue_t workQueue =
➥dispatch_queue_create("com.icf.serialqueue", NULL);
```

Blocks of work can be added to the serial queue asynchronously:

```
for (int i=1; i<=5; i++)
{

    NSNumber *iteration = @(i);

    dispatch_async(workQueue, ^{
        [self performLongRunningTaskForIteration:iteration];
    });
}
```

The method `performLongRunningTaskForIteration:` performs exactly the same task as in the main thread, perform background, and concurrent operation queue approaches; however, the method calls the `updateTableData:` method using `dispatch_async` to the main queue.

```
- (void)performLongRunningTaskForIteration:(id)iteration
{
    NSNumber *iterationNumber = (NSNumber *)iteration;

    NSMutableArray *newArray =
    ➥[[NSMutableArray alloc] initWithCapacity:10];

    for (int i=1; i<=10; i++)
    {

        [newArray addObject:[NSString stringWithFormat:
        ➥@"Item %@-%d",iterationNumber,i]];

        [NSThread sleepForTimeInterval:.1];
        NSLog(@"DispQ Serial Added %@-%d",iterationNumber,i);
    }

    dispatch_async(dispatch_get_main_queue(), ^{
        [self updateTableData:newArray];
    });
}
```

The serial dispatch queue will execute the long-running tasks in the order in which they are added to the queue, first in, first out. The debugging console will show that the operations execute in the correct order.

```
20:41:00.340 LongRunningTasks[30650:] DispQ Serial Added 1-1
20:41:00.444 LongRunningTasks[30650:] DispQ Serial Added 1-2
20:41:00.546 LongRunningTasks[30650:] DispQ Serial Added 1-3
20:41:00.648 LongRunningTasks[30650:] DispQ Serial Added 1-4
20:41:00.751 LongRunningTasks[30650:] DispQ Serial Added 1-5
20:41:00.852 LongRunningTasks[30650:] DispQ Serial Added 1-6
20:41:00.955 LongRunningTasks[30650:] DispQ Serial Added 1-7
20:41:01.056 LongRunningTasks[30650:] DispQ Serial Added 1-8
20:41:01.158 LongRunningTasks[30650:] DispQ Serial Added 1-9
20:41:01.261 LongRunningTasks[30650:] DispQ Serial Added 1-10
20:41:01.363 LongRunningTasks[30650:] DispQ Serial Added 2-1
20:41:01.465 LongRunningTasks[30650:] DispQ Serial Added 2-2
20:41:01.568 LongRunningTasks[30650:] DispQ Serial Added 2-3
20:41:01.671 LongRunningTasks[30650:] DispQ Serial Added 2-4
20:41:01.772 LongRunningTasks[30650:] DispQ Serial Added 2-5
...
```

Again, the serial approach increases the total amount of time needed to complete all the tasks, but successfully ensures that the tasks execute in the correct order. Using a dispatch queue to process tasks serially is simpler than managing dependencies in an operation queue, but does not offer the same high-level management options.

Summary

This chapter introduced several techniques to process long-running tasks without interfering with the UI, including `performSelectorInBackground:withObject:`, operation queues, and GCD queues.

Using the `performSelectorInBackground:withObject:` method on `NSObject` to execute a task in the background is the simplest approach, but provides the least support and management.

Operation queues can process tasks concurrently or serially, using a method call, a block, or a custom operation class. Operation queues can be managed by specifying a maximum number of concurrent operations, they can be suspended and resumed, and all the outstanding operations can be canceled. Operation queues can handle custom operation classes. Operation queues are implemented by GCD.

Dispatch queues can also process tasks concurrently or serially. There are three global concurrent queues, and applications can create their own serial queues. Dispatch queues accept blocks to be executed, and can execute blocks synchronously or asynchronously.

No technique is described as "the best," because each technique has pros and cons relative to the requirements of an application, and testing should be done to understand which technique is most appropriate.

Using Keychain and Touch ID to Secure and Access Data

Securing sensitive user data is a critical and often-overlooked step of mobile development. The technology press is constantly plagued by stories of large companies storing password or credit-card information in plain text. Users put their trust in developers to treat sensitive information with the care and respect it deserves. This includes encrypting remote and local copies of that information to prevent unauthorized access. It is the duty of every developer to treat users' data as they would like their own confidential information to be handled.

Apple has long provided a security framework called Keychain to store encrypted information on an iOS device. The Keychain also has several additional benefits beyond standard application and data security. Information stored in the Keychain persists even after an app has been deleted from the device, and Keychain information can even be shared among multiple apps by the same developer.

This chapter demonstrates the use of Apple's `KeychainItemWrapper` class (version 1.2) to secure and retrieve sensitive information. Although it is completely acceptable and occasionally required to write a Keychain wrapper from the ground up, leveraging Apple's libraries can be a tremendous time-saver and will often provide all the functionality required. This chapter does not cover creating a custom Keychain wrapper class but leverages Apple's provided code to quickly add Keychains to an iOS app. Keychain interaction can be complex, and small mistakes might cause the data to not truly be secure, but using Apple's class minimizes these risk.

> **Tip**
>
> The most up-to-date version of Apple's `KeychainItemWrapper` class can be found at http://developer.apple.com/library/ios/#samplecode/GenericKeychain/Listings/Classes_KeychainItemWrapper_m.html.

It is important to remember that while securing information on disk, it is only a small part of complete app security; other factors, such as transmitting data over a network, remote storage, and password enforcement, are just as critical in providing a well-rounded secure app.

The Sample App

The Keychain sample app is a single-view app that will secure a credit card number along with relevant user information, such as name and expiration date. To access the information, the user sets a PIN on first launch. Both the PIN and the credit card information are secured using the Keychain.

> **Note**
>
> The Keychain does not work on the iOS simulator as of iOS 8. The wrapper class provided by Apple and used in this chapter does make considerable efforts to properly simulate the Keychain behaviors. In addition, since code being executed on the simulator is not code signed, it is important to keep in mind that there are no restrictions on which apps can access Keychain items. It is highly recommended that Keychain development be thoroughly debugged on the device after it's working correctly on the simulator.

The sample app itself is simple. It consists of four text fields and a button. The majority of the sample code not directly relating to the Keychain handles laying out information.

> **Note**
>
> Deleting the app from a device does not remove the Keychain for that app, which can make debugging considerably more difficult. The simulator does have a Reset Contents and Settings option, which will wipe the Keychain. It is highly recommended that a Keychain app not be debugged on a device until it is functional on the simulator due to the hassle of returning to a clean state.

Setting Up and Using Keychain

Keychain is part of the Security.framework and has been available for iOS starting with the initial SDK release. Keychain has its roots in Mac OS X development, where it was first introduced with OS X 10.2. However, Keychain's history predates even OS X with roots back into OS 8.6. Keychain was initially developed for Apple's email system called PowerTalk. This makes Keychain one of the oldest available frameworks on iOS.

Keychain can be used to secure small amounts of data such as passwords, keys, certificates, and notes. However, if an app is securing large amounts of information such as encoded images or videos, implementing a third-party encryption library is usually a better fit than Keychain. Core data also provides encryption capabilities, and is worth exploring if the app will be Core Data–based.

Before work can be done with Keychain, the Security.framework must be added to the project and `<Security/Security.h>` needs to be imported to any classes directly accessing Keychain methods and functions.

Setting Up a New `KeychainItemWrapper`

iOS Keychains are unlocked based on the code signing of the app that is requesting it. Since there is no systemwide password as seen on OS X, there needs to be an additional step to secure data. Since the app controls which Keychain data can be accessed to truly secure information, the app itself should be password protected. This is done through the sample app using a PIN entry system.

When the app is launched for the first time, it will prompt the user to enter a new PIN and repeat it. To securely store the PIN, a new `KeychainItemWrapper` is created.

```
pinWrapper = [[KeychainItemWrapper
➥alloc]initWithIdentifier:@"com.ICF.Keychain.pin" accessGroup:nil];
```

Creating a new `KeychainItemWrapper` is done using two attributes. The first attribute is an identifier for that Keychain item. It is recommended that a reverse DNS approach be used here, such as com.company.app.id. `accessGroup` is set to `nil` in this example, and the `accessGroup` parameter is used for sharing Keychains across multiple apps. Refer to the section "Sharing a Keychain Between Apps" for more information on `accessGroups`.

The next attribute that needs be set on the new `KeychainItemWrapper` is the `kSecAttr-Accessible`. This controls when the data will be unlocked. In the sample app the data becomes available when the device is unlocked, securing the data for a locked device. There are several possible options for this parameter, as detailed in Table 19.1.

```
[pinWrapper setObject:kSecAttrAccessibleWhenUnlocked forKey:
➥(id)kSecAttrAccessible];
```

Table 19.1 **All Possible Constants and Associated Descriptions to Be Supplied to**
`kSecAttrAccessible`

Constant	Description
kSecAttrAccessibleAfterFirstUnlock	This Keychain will unlock data on the first device unlock after a restart; items will remain locked until the device is restarted. This setting is recommended for items that might be required by background tasks. These items will move to a new device when the user upgrades.
kSecAttrAccessibleAfterFirst UnlockThisDeviceOnly	This setting will duplicate the functionality described in `kSecAttrAccessibleAfter-FirstUnlock` but will not transfer to a new device if the user upgrades or restores from a backup.
kSecAttrAccessibleAlways	This item is always unlocked whether or not the device is unlocked. This setting is not recommended for secure information. These items will migrate when a user upgrades his device.

Constant	Description
`kSecAttrAccessibleAlwaysThis DeviceOnly`	This setting will duplicate the functionality described in `kSecAttrAccessibleAlways` but will not transfer to a new device if the user upgrades or restores from a backup.
`kSecAttrAccessibleWhenUnlocked`	This item is unlocked only when the user has unlocked the device. This parameter is recommended when an app needs access to secure information when it is in the foreground. This is also the most common setting for `kSecAttr-Accessible`. This item will also migrate when a user upgrades his device.
`kSecAttrAccessibleWhenUnlocked ThisDeviceOnly`	This setting will duplicate the functionality described in `kSecAttrAccessibleWhen-Unlocked` but will not transfer to a new device if the user upgrades or restores from a backup.

The app now knows the identifier for the Keychain as well the security level that is required. However, an additional parameter needs to be set before data can begin to be stored. The `kSecAttrService` is used to store a username for the password pair that will be used for the PIN. A PIN does not have an associated password; for the purposes of the sample app, `pinIdentifer` is used here. Although Keychains will often work while the `kSecAttr-Service` is omitted, having a value set here corrects many hard-to-reproduce failures, and is recommended.

```
[pinWrapper setObject:@"pinIdentifer" forKey: (id)kSecAttrAccount];
```

Storing and Retrieving the PIN

After a new `KeychainItemWrapper` has been configured in the manner described in the preceding section, data can be stored into it. Storing information in a Keychain is similar to storing data in a dictionary. The sample app first checks to make sure that both of the PIN text fields match; then it calls `setObject:` on the `pinWrapper` that was created in the preceding section. For the key identifier `kSecValueData` is used. This item is covered more in depth in the section "Keychain Attribute Keys"; for now, however, it is important to use this constant.

```
if([pinField.text isEqualToString: pinFieldRepeat.text])
{
    [pinWrapper setObject:[pinField text] forKey:kSecValueData];
}
```

After a new value has been stored into the Keychain, it can be retrieved in the same fashion. To test whether the user has entered the correct PIN in the sample app, the following code is used:

```
if([pinField.text isEqualToString: [pinWrapper
➥objectForKey:kSecValueData]])
```

After the PIN number being entered has been confirmed as the PIN number stored in the Keychain, the user is allowed to access the next section of the app, described in the section "Securing a Dictionary."

Keychain Attribute Keys

Keychain items are stored similar to NSDictionaries; however, they have very specific keys that can be associated with them. Unlike an NSDictionary, a Keychain cannot use any random string for a key value. Each Keychain is associated with a Keychain class; if using Apple's KeychainItemWrapper, it defaults to using CFTypeRef kSecClassGenericPassword. However, other options exist for kSecClassInternetPassword, kSecClassCertificate, kSecClassKey, and kSecClassIdentity. Each class has different associated values attached to it. For the purposes of this chapter as well as for the KeychainItemWrapper, the focus will be on kSecClassGenericPassword.

kSecClassGenericPassword contains 14 possible keys for storing and accessing data, as described in Table 19.2. It is important to keep in mind that these keys are optional and are not required to be populated in order to function correctly.

Table 19.2 **Keychain Attribute Keys Available When Working with kSecClassGenericPassword**

Attribute	Description
kSecAttrAccessible	The locking behavior key, discussed in Table 19.1.
kSecAttrAccessGroup	The string for the access group as seen during a new Keychain initialized and discussed in depth in the section "Sharing a Keychain Between Apps."
kSecAttrCreationDate	A CFDateRef representing the date the Keychain item was created.
kSecAttrModificationDate	A CFDateRef representing the date the Keychain item was last modified.
kSecAttrDescription	A string that represents a user-visible description for the Keychain, such as Twitter Password.
kSecAttrComment	A string that corresponds to a user-editable comment for the Keychain item.
kSecAttrCreator	A four-digit CFNumberRef representation of character code that reflects the creator code for the Keychain, such as aCrt. This will identify the creator of the Keychain if needed for custom implementations.

Attribute	Description
kSecAttrType	A four-digit `CFNumberRef` representation of character code that reflects the item type for the Keychain, such as `aTyp`. This will identify the type for a Keychain if needed for custom implementations.
kSecAttrLabel	A string that represents a user-visible label for the Keychain item.
kSecAttrIsInvisible	A `CFBooleanRef` representation of whether the item is invisible. `kCFBooleanTrue` represents invisible.
kSecAttrIsNegative	A `CFBooleanRef` indicating whether a valid password is associated with this item. This is useful if you do not want to store a password and force a user to enter it each time.
kSecAttrAccount	The account name attribute as discussed in the section "Setting up a New `KeychainItemWrapper`."
kSecAttrService	A `CFStringRef` that represents the service associated with this item.
kSecAttrGeneric	A generic attribute key that can be used to store a user-defined attribute.

Securing a Dictionary

Securing a more complex data type such as a dictionary follows the same approach taken to secure the PIN in earlier sections. The Keychain wrapper allows for the storage only of strings; to secure a dictionary, it is first turned into a string. The approach chosen for the sample code is to first save the dictionary to a JSON string using the `NSJSONSerialization` class. (See Chapter 9, "Working with and Parsing JSON," for more info.)

```
NSMutableDictionary *secureDataDict = [[[NSMutableDictionary alloc]
➥init] autorelease];

NSError *error = nil;

if(numberTextField.text)
    [secureDataDict setObject:numberTextField.text
    ➥forKey:@"numberTextField"];

if(expDateTextField.text)
    [secureDataDict setObject:expDateTextField.text
    ➥forKey:@"expDateTextField"];

if(CV2CodeTextField.text)
    [secureDataDict setObject:CV2CodeTextField.text
    ➥forKey:@"CV2CodeTextField"];
```

```
if(nameTextField.text)
    [secureDataDict setObject:nameTextField.text
    ➡forKey:@"nameTextField"];


NSData *rawData = [NSJSONSerialization
➡dataWithJSONObject:secureDataDict
           options:0
              error:&error];


if(error != nil)
{
    NSLog(@"An error occurred: %@", [error localizedDescription]);
}


NSString *dataString = [[NSString alloc] initWithData:rawData
➡encoding:NSUTF8StringEncoding];
```

After the value of the dictionary has been converted into a string representation of the dictionary data, it can be added to the Keychain in the same fashion as previously discussed.

```
KeychainItemWrapper *secureDataKeychain = [[KeychainItemWrapper alloc]
➡initWithIdentifier:@"com.ICF.keychain.securedData" accessGroup:nil];


[secureDataKeychain setObject:@"secureDataIdentifer" forKey:
➡(id)kSecAttrAccount];


[secureDataKeychain setObject:kSecAttrAccessibleWhenUnlocked forKey:
➡(id)kSecAttrAccessible];


[secureDataKeychain setObject:dataString forKey:kSecValueData];
```

To retrieve the data in the form of a dictionary, the steps must be followed in reverse. Starting with an NSString from the Keychain, it is turned into an NSData value. The NSData is used with NSJSONSerialization to retrieve the original dictionary value. After the dictionary is re-created, the text fields that display the user's credit card information are populated.

```
KeychainItemWrapper *secureDataKeychain = [[KeychainItemWrapper alloc]
➡initWithIdentifier:@"com.ICF.keychain.securedData" accessGroup:nil];


NSString *secureDataString = [secureDataKeychain
➡objectForKey:kSecValueData];


if([secureDataString length] != 0)
{
    NSData* data = [secureDataString
    ➡dataUsingEncoding:NSUTF8StringEncoding];

    NSError *error = nil;
```

```objc
NSDictionary *secureDataDictionary = [NSJSONSerialization
➥JSONObjectWithData:data
➥options:NSJSONReadingMutableContainers
➥error:&error];

if(error != nil)
{
    NSLog(@"An error occurred: %@", [error localizedDescription]);
}

numberTextField.text = [secureDataDictionary
➥objectForKey:@"numberTextField"];

expDateTextField.text = [secureDataDictionary
➥objectForKey:@"expDateTextField"];

CV2CodeTextField.text = [secureDataDictionary
➥objectForKey:@"CV2CodeTextField"];

nameTextField.text = [secureDataDictionary
➥objectForKey:@"nameTextField"];
}

else
{
    NSLog(@"No Keychain data stored yet");
}
```

Resetting a Keychain Item

At times, it might be necessary to wipe out the data in a Keychain while not replacing it with another set of user data. This can be done using Apple's library by invoking the `reset-KeyChainItem` method on the Keychain wrapper that needs to be reset.

```objc
[pinWrapper resetKeychainItem];
```

Sharing a Keychain Between Apps

A Keychain can be shared across multiple iOS apps if they are published by the same developer and under specific conditions. The most important requirement for sharing Keychain data between two apps is that both apps must have the same bundle seed. For example, consider two apps with the bundle identifiers 659823F3DC53.com.ICF.firstapp and 659823F3DC53.com. ICF.secondapp. These apps would be able to access and modify each other's Keychain data. Keychain sharing with a wildcard ID does not seem to work, although the official documentation remains quiet on this situation. Bundle seeds can be configured from the developer portal when new apps are created.

When you have two apps that share the same bundle seed, each app will need to have its entitlements configured to allow for a Keychain access group. Keychain groups are configured from the summary tab of the target, as shown in Figure 19.1.

Figure 19.1   Setting up a new Keychain group using Xcode 6.

For the shared Keychain to be accessed, the Keychain group first needs to be set. With a modification of the PIN example from earlier in the chapter, it would look like the following code snippet:

```
[pinWrapper setObject:@"659823F3DC53.com.ICF.appgroup"
forKey:(id)kSecAttrAccessGroup];
```

> **Note**
>
> Remember that when setting the access group in Xcode, you do not need to specify the bundle seed. However, when you are setting the `kSecAttrAccessGroup` property, the bundle seed needs to be specified and the bundle seeds of both apps must match.

After an access group has been set on a `KeychainItemWrapper`, it can be created, modified, and deleted in the typical fashion discussed throughout this chapter.

Keychain Error Codes

The Keychain can return several specialized error codes depending on any issues encountered at runtime. These errors are described in Table 19.3.

Table 19.3   **Keychain Error Codes**

Code	Value	Description
errSecSuccess	0	No error encountered.
errSecUnimplemented	-4	Function or operation not implemented.
errSecParam	-50	One or more parameters passed to the function were not valid.
errSecAllocate	-108	Failed to allocate memory.
errSecNotAvailable	-25291	No trust results are available.
errSecAuthFailed	-25293	Authorization/authentication failed.
errSecDuplicateItem	-25299	The item already exists.
errSecItemNotFound	-25300	The item cannot be found.
errSecInteractionNotAllowed	-25308	Interaction with the Security Server is not allowed.
errSecDecode	-26275	Unable to decode the provided data.

Implementing Touch ID

The iPhone 5s was the first iOS device to feature hardware-level fingerprint recognition. This technology, collectively referred to as Touch ID, enables the user to authenticate and make purchases using only their fingerprint. Third-party developers can implement Touch ID to authenticate a user. It is important to know that the fingerprint data itself is stored on the A7 chip and cannot be accessed outside of Touch ID. Whenever you are working with Touch ID, it is important to realize that not all users will have a device capable of using fingerprint authentication, nor will everyone who is capable opt into using the technology.

Touch ID enables the user to authenticate with a fingerprint, enter her password, or cancel the authentication action. If a user chooses not to authenticate with her fingerprint, the app must supply a fallback method to conform to Apple's Review Guidelines. To begin using Touch ID in your app, first add the Local Authentication Framework. The <LocalAuthentication/LocalAuthentication.h> header must also be imported.

A new local Authentication Context is created.

```
LAContext *myContext = [[LAContext alloc] init];
```

The app then needs to check to make sure that Touch ID exists and is enabled for the device. This is done using the `canEvaluatePolicy:` method. If the app allows for Touch ID authentication, `evaluatePolicy:` can be called; otherwise, the app should fall back to alternative authentication methods.

```
NSError *authError = nil;
NSString *myReasonString = @"Human readable string for reason
➥access is being requested";

if ([myContext canEvaluatePolicy:LAPolicyDeviceOwnerAuthenticationWithBiometrics
➥error:&authError])
{
    [myContext evaluatePolicy:LAPolicyDeviceOwnerAuthenticationWithBiometrics
➥localizedReason:myReasonString reply:^(BOOL succes, NSError *error)
{
        if (success)
        {
                // Authenticated successfully
        }
        else
        {
                // Authenticate failed
        }
    }];
}
else
{
    // Could not evaluate policy; check authError
}
```

The `LAContext` can return several possible errors on failure; they are detailed in Table 19.4.

Table 19.4 **Touch ID Error Codes**

Code	Description
LAErrorAuthenticationFailed	Authentication was not successful because the user failed to provide valid credentials.
LAErrorUserCancel	Authentication was canceled by the user (e.g., tapped Cancel button).
LAErrorUserFallback	Authentication was canceled because the user tapped the fallback button (Enter Password).
LAErrorSystemCancel	Authentication was canceled by the system (e.g., another application went to the foreground).

Code	Description
LAErrorPasscodeNotSet	Authentication could not start because the passcode is not set on the device.
LAErrorTouchIDNotAvailable	Authentication could not start because the Touch ID is not available on the device.
LAErrorTouchIDNotEnrolled	Authentication could not start because the Touch ID has no enrolled fingerprints.

Summary

This chapter covered using Keychain to secure small amounts of app data. The sample app covered setting and checking a PIN number for access to an app on launch. It also covered the storage and retrieval of multiple fields of credit card data. The chapter also introduced Touch ID, which is supported on the iPhone 5s and newer to enable the user to use his fingerprint to authenticate.

Keychain and data security is a large topic, and this chapter merely touches the tip of the iceberg. The development community is also seeking security professionals, especially in the mobile marketplace. Keychain is an exciting and vast topic that should now be much less intimidating. Hopefully, this introduction to securing data with Keychain will set you as a developer down a path of conscious computer security and prevent yet another story in the news about the loss of confidential information by a careless developer.

Working with Images and Filters

Images and image handling are central to many iOS apps. At a basic level, images are a necessary part of customizing the user interface, from custom view backgrounds to custom buttons and view elements. Beyond that, iOS 6 added sophisticated support for customizing user-provided images with the Core Image library. Previous to iOS 6, doing image manipulations required custom image-handling code using Quartz or custom C libraries. With the addition of Core Image, many complex image-editing functions demonstrated by successful apps, like Instagram, can now be handled by iOS with minimal effort.

This chapter describes basic image handling: how to load and display an image, how to handle images on devices with different capabilities, and some basic image display techniques. It also describes how to acquire an image from the device's image library or camera. In addition, this chapter demonstrates and describes how to use the Core Image library to apply effects to user-provided images.

The Sample App

The sample app for this chapter is called ImagePlayground. It demonstrates selecting an image from the device's photo library or acquiring an image from the camera to be used as a source image, which the app then resizes to a smaller size. The user can select and chain filters to apply to the source image to alter how it looks, with the effect of each filter displayed in a table alongside the name of each selected filter. The filter selection process demonstrates how Core Image filters are organized into categories, and enables the user to customize a selected filter and preview its effect.

Basic Image Data and Display

Some basic image-handling techniques are required to support the images displayed in the sample app. This section describes different techniques for displaying images in a view and for handling stretchable images that can be used in buttons of different sizes, and it explains the basic approach needed to acquire an image from the user's photo library or camera.

Instantiating an Image

To use an image in an app, iOS provides a class called `UIImage`. This class supports many image formats:

- Portable Network Graphics (PNG): `.png`
- Tagged Image File Format (TIFF): `.tiff`, `.tif`
- Joint Photographic Experts Group (JPEG): `.jpeg`, `.jpg`
- Graphics Interchange Format (GIF): `.gif`
- Windows Bitmap Format (DIB): `.bmp`, `.BMPf`
- Windows Icon Format: `.ico`
- Windows Cursor: `.cur`
- X BitMap: `.xbm`

When images are used for backgrounds, buttons, or other elements in the user interface, Apple recommends using the PNG format. `UIImage` has a class method called `imageNamed:` that can be used to instantiate an image. This method provides a number of advantages:

- Looks for and loads the image from the app's main bundle without needing to specify the path to the main bundle.
- Automatically loads a PNG image with no file extension. So specifying `myImage` will load `myImage.png` if that exists in the app's main bundle.
- Takes into consideration the scale of the screen when loading the image, and `@2x` or `@3x` is automatically appended to the image name if the scale of the screen is greater than 1.0. In addition, it will check for `~ipad` and `~iphone` versions of the images and use those if available.
- Supports in-memory caching. If the same image has already been loaded and is requested again, it will return the already-loaded image and not reload it. This is useful when the same image is used multiple times in the user interface.

For images that are not present in the app's main bundle, when the `imageNamed:` method is not appropriate, there are several other approaches to instantiate images. A `UIImage` can be instantiated from a file, as in this code example, which will load `myImage.png` from the app's `Documents` directory:

```
NSArray *pathForDocuments =
➥NSSearchPathForDirectoriesInDomains(NSDocumentDirectory,
                                    NSUserDomainMask, YES);

NSString *imagePath =
➥[[pathForDocuments lastObject]
➥stringByAppendingPathComponent:@"myImage.png"];

UIImage *myImage =
➥[UIImage imageWithContentsOfFile:imagePath];
```

A UIImage can be instantiated from NSData, as in the next code example. NSData can be from any source; typically, it is from a file or from data pulled from a network connection.

```
NSData *imageData = [NSData dataWithContentsOfFile:imagePath];

UIImage *myImage2 = [UIImage imageWithData:imageData];
```

A UIImage can be created from Core Graphics images, as in this code example, which uses Core Graphics to take a sample rectangle from an existing image. A Core Graphics image (CGImage or CGImageRef) represents the Core Graphics image data.

```
CGImageRef myImage2CGImage = [myImage2 CGImage];
CGRect subRect = CGRectMake(20, 20, 120, 120);

CGImageRef cgCrop =
➥CGImageCreateWithImageInRect(myImage2CGImage, subRect);

UIImage *imageCrop = [UIImage imageWithCGImage:cgCrop];
```

A UIImage can be created from Core Image images, as described in detail later in "Core Image Filters," in the subsection "Rendering a Filtered Image."

Displaying an Image

After an instance of UIImage is available, there are a few ways to display it in the user interface. The first is UIImageView. When an instance of UIImageView is available, it has a property called image that can be set:

```
[self.sourceImageView setImage:scaleImage];
```

UIImageView can also be instantiated with an image, which will set the bounds to the size of the image:

```
UIImageView *newImageView =
➥[[UIImageView alloc] initWithImage:myImage];
```

For images displayed in a UIImageView, setting the contentMode can have interesting and useful effects on how the image is displayed, as shown in Figure 20.1.

The content mode setting tells the view how to display its contents. Aspect fit and fill modes will preserve the aspect ratio of the image, whereas scale to fill mode will skew the image to fit the view. Modes such as center, top, bottom, left, and right will preserve the dimensions of the image while positioning it in the view.

Figure 20.1　Sample app: content mode effects.

Several other UIKit items support or use images, for example, UIButton. A useful technique for buttons or especially other resizable user interface elements is to utilize the resizable image capability provided by the UIImage class. This can be used to provide the same style for buttons of different sizes without warping or distorting the edges of the button image, as shown in Figure 20.2. Resizing images this way is optimized in UIKit and is quick and efficient; it can greatly reduce the number and size of assets needed in an app.

Figure 20.2　Sample app: custom button using resizable background image.

The source image for the button is only 28 pixels by 28 pixels. The resizable image used in the background is created from the original image; edge insets are specified to indicate which parts of the image should be kept static, and which parts can be stretched or tiled to fill in the additional space.

```
UIImage *startImage =
➥[UIImage imageNamed:@"ch_20_stretch_button"];

CGFloat topInset = 10.0f;
CGFloat bottomInset = 10.0f;
CGFloat leftInset = 10.0f;
CGFloat rightInset = 10.0f;

UIEdgeInsets edgeInsets =
➥UIEdgeInsetsMake(topInset, leftInset, bottomInset, rightInset);

UIImage *stretchImage =
➥[startImage resizableImageWithCapInsets:edgeInsets];

[self.selectImageButton setBackgroundImage:stretchImage
                               forState:UIControlStateNormal];

[self.selectImageButton setBackgroundImage:stretchImage
                               forState:UIControlStateSelected];

[self.selectImageButton setBackgroundImage:stretchImage
                               forState:UIControlStateHighlighted];

[self.selectImageButton setBackgroundImage:stretchImage
                               forState:UIControlStateDisabled];
```

Tip

Update old projects in Xcode 5 and later to use the Asset Catalog, which can automatically support resizable images with no code. The Asset Catalog includes a visual editor to establish the image slicing, and calling `imageNamed:` for a sliced asset name will return a resizable image.

Using the Image Picker

It is common for apps to make use of images provided by the user. To allow an app access to the user's photos in the camera roll and photo albums, iOS provides two approaches: the `UIImagePickerController` and the asset library. The `UIImagePickerController` provides a modal user interface to navigate through the user's albums and photos, so it is appropriate to use when Apple's provided styling works for the app and there are no special requirements for photo browsing and selection. The photo library provides full access to the photos and albums, so it is appropriate to use when there are specific user-interface and styling requirements for navigating and selecting images. The photo library is fully described in Chapter 24, "Accessing the Photo Library."

To see how to use a `UIImagePickerController`, refer to the `selectImageTouched:` method in `ICFViewController` in the sample app. The method starts by allocating and initializing an instance of `UIImagePickerController`.

```
UIImagePickerController *imagePicker =
➡[[UIImagePickerController alloc] init];
```

The method then customizes the picker. The `UIImagePickerController` can be customized to acquire images or videos from the camera, from the photo library, or from the saved photos album. In this case, the photo library is specified.

```
[imagePicker setSourceType:
➡UIImagePickerControllerSourceTypePhotoLibrary];
```

A `UIImagePickerController` can be customized to select images, videos, or both, by specifying an array of media types. Note that the media types which can be specified are constants that are defined in the MobileCoreServices framework, so it is necessary to add that framework to the project and import it in the view controller. For the sample app, only photos are desired, so the `kUTTypeImage` constant is used.

```
[imagePicker setMediaTypes:@[(NSString*)kUTTypeImage]];
```

The picker can be customized to allow or prevent editing of the selected image. If editing is allowed, the user will be able to pinch and pan the image to crop it within a square provided in the user interface.

```
[imagePicker setAllowsEditing:YES];
```

Lastly, the picker receives a delegate. The delegate is informed when the user has selected an image or has cancelled image selection according to the `UIImagePickerControllerDelegate` protocol. The delegate is responsible for dismissing the image picker view controller.

```
[imagePicker setDelegate:self];
```

In the sample app, the image picker is presented in a popover view controller using the source image container view as its anchor view.

```
self.imagePopoverController = [[UIPopoverController alloc]
➡initWithContentViewController:imagePicker];
```

```
[self.imagePopoverController
➡presentPopoverFromRect:self.sourceImageContainer.frame
➡inView:self.view
➡permittedArrowDirections:UIPopoverArrowDirectionAny
➡animated:YES];
```

When the user has selected an image and cropped it, the delegate method is called.

```
- (void)imagePickerController:(UIImagePickerController *)picker
➡didFinishPickingMediaWithInfo:(NSDictionary *)info
{
...
}
```

The delegate is provided with a dictionary of information about the selected media. If editing occurred during the selection process, information about the editing that the user performed is included in the dictionary. The keys and information contained in the info dictionary are described in Table 20.1.

Table 20.1 **UIImagePickerControllerDelegate Media Info Dictionary**

Key	Value
UIImagePickerControllerMediaType	An NSString constant indicating whether the user selected an image (kUTTypeImage) or a video (kUTTypeMovie).
UIImagePickerControllerOriginalImage	A UIImage containing the image selected by the user with no cropping or editing applied.
UIImagePickerControllerEditedImage	A UIImage containing the image selected by the user, with cropping or editing applied. If the image was not edited, this will not be available in the dictionary.
UIImagePickerControllerCropRect	An NSValue containing a CGRect of the cropping rectangle applied to the original image. If the image was not edited, this will not be available in the dictionary.
UIImagePickerControllerMediaURL	An NSURL pointing to the location of the data for a movie in the device's file system. This URL is accessible to the app and can be used to upload the movie data or use in a movie player. This will not be available if the media type is image.
UIImagePickerControllerReferenceURL	An NSURL representing the corresponding ALAsset. This can be used to interact with the asset directly using the asset library as described in Chapter 24.
UIImagePickerControllerMediaMetadata	An NSDictionary containing metadata for a photo taken from the camera. This is not available for images or movies from the photo library.

In the sample app, the selected image is resized to 200px by 200px so that it will be easy to work with and will fit nicely in the display. First, a reference to the editing image is acquired.

```
UIImage *selectedImage =
➡[info objectForKey:UIImagePickerControllerEditedImage];
```

Then a `CGSize` is created to indicate the desired size, and a scale method in a category set up for `UIImage` is called to resize the image. The resized image is then set as the image to display in the user interface.

```
CGSize scaleSize = CGSizeMake(200.0f, 200.0f);

UIImage *scaleImage =
➡[selectedImage scaleImageToSize:scaleSize];

[self.sourceImageView setImage:scaleImage];
```

After the image is set, the popover with the image picker is dismissed.

Resizing an Image

When images are being displayed, it is advisable to work with the smallest image possible while still maintaining a beautiful user interface. Although the sample app certainly could use the full-size selected image, performance will be affected if a larger image is used and there will be increased memory requirements to handle a larger image. Therefore, the sample app will resize a selected image to work with the image at the exact size needed for the user interface and no larger. To scale an image in iOS, the method will need to use Core Graphics. The sample app includes a category called `Scaling` on `UIImage` (in `UIImage+Scaling`), with a method called `scaleImageToSize:`. The method accepts a `CGSize` parameter, which is a width and a height.

The first step in resizing an image is to create a Core Graphics context, which is a working area for images.

```
UIGraphicsBeginImageContextWithOptions(newSize, NO, 0.0f);
```

UIKit provides the convenience function `UIGraphicsBeginImageContextWithOption`, which will create a Core Graphics context with the options provided. The first parameter passed in is a `CGSize`, which specifies the size of the context; in this case, the method uses the size passed in from the caller. The second parameter is a `BOOL`, which tells Core Graphics whether the context and resulting image should be treated as opaque (`YES`) or should include an alpha channel for transparency (`NO`). The final parameter is the scale of the image, where `1.0f` is nonretina and `2.0f` is retina. Passing in `0.0f` will tell the function to use the scale of the current device's screen. After a context is available, the method draws the image into the context using the `drawInRect:` method.

```
CGFloat originX = 0.0f;
CGFloat originY = 0.0f;

CGRect destinationRect =
➡CGRectMake(originX, originY, newSize.width, newSize.height);

[self drawInRect:destinationRect];
```

The `drawInRect:` method will draw the content of the image into the Core Graphics context, using the position and dimensions specified in the destination rectangle. If the width and height of the source image are different from the new dimensions, the `drawInRect:` method will resize the image to fit in the new dimensions.

Note that it is important to take the aspect ratios of the source image and destination into consideration when doing this. The aspect ratio is the ratio of the width to the height of the image. If the aspect ratios are different, the `drawInRect:` method will stretch or compress the image as needed to fit into the destination context, and the resulting image will appear distorted.

Next, the method creates a new `UIImage` from the context, ends the context since it is no longer required, and returns the newly resized image.

```
UIImage *newImage = UIGraphicsGetImageFromCurrentImageContext();
UIGraphicsEndImageContext();
return newImage;
```

Core Image Filters

The sample app enables the user to select a starting image, and select a sequence of filters to apply to that image to arrive at a final image. As a general rule, Core Image filters require an input image (except in cases in which the filter generates an image) and some parameters to customize the behavior of the filter. When requested, Core Image will process the filter against the input image to provide an output image. Core Image is efficient in the application of filters. A list of filters will be applied only when the final output image is requested, not when each filter is specified. In addition, Core Image will combine the filters mathematically wherever possible so that a minimum of calculations are performed to process the filters.

> Note
>
> To use Core Image in a project, add the Core Image framework to the project and `@import CoreImage;` in each class that requires it.

Filter Categories and Filters

Core Image filters are organized into categories internally. A filter can belong to more than one category; for example, a color effect filter like Sepia Tone belongs to six categories, including `CICategoryColorEffect`, `CICategoryVideo`, `CICategoryInterlaced`, `CICategoryNonSquarePixels`, `CICategoryStillImage`, and `CICategoryBuiltIn`. These categories are useful to the developer to determine what Core Image filters are available for a desired task, and can be used as in the sample app to enable the user to browse and select available filters.

In the sample app, when a user taps the Add Filter button, a popover segue is initiated. This segue will initialize a `UIPopoverController`, a `UINavigationController`, and an instance of `ICFFilterCategoriesViewController` as the top root view controller in the navigation controller. The instance of `ICFViewController` implements `ICFFilterProcessingDelegate` and is set as the delegate so that it will be notified when a filter is selected or when the selection process is cancelled. The instance of `ICFFilterCategoriesViewController` sets up a dictionary of user-readable category names in the `viewDidLoad` method to correspond with some of Core Image's category keys for presentation in a table.

```
self.categoryList = @{
    @"Blur" : kCICategoryBlur,
    @"Color Adjustment" : kCICategoryColorAdjustment,
    @"Color Effect" : kCICategoryColorEffect,
    @"Composite" : kCICategoryCompositeOperation,
    @"Distortion" : kCICategoryDistortionEffect,
    @"Generator" : kCICategoryGenerator,
    @"Geometry Adjustment" : kCICategoryGeometryAdjustment,
    @"Gradient" : kCICategoryGradient,
    @"Halftone Effect" : kCICategoryHalftoneEffect,
    @"Sharpen" : kCICategorySharpen,
    @"Stylize" : kCICategoryStylize,
    @"Tile" : kCICategoryTileEffect,
    @"Transition" : kCICategoryTransition
};
self.categoryKeys = [self.categoryList allKeys];
```

The table looks as shown in Figure 20.3.

Figure 20.3   Sample app: Add Filter, Category selection.

When the user selects a category, a segue is initiated. In the `prepareForSegue:sender:` method the destination instance of `ICFFiltersViewController` is updated with the Core Image constant for the selected category, and is assigned the `ICFFilterProcessingDelegate` delegate. In the `viewDidLoad` method, the `ICFFiltersViewController` will get a list of available filters for the filter category.

```
self.filterNameArray =
➥[CIFilter filterNamesInCategory:self.selectedCategory];
```

The filters are displayed in a table as shown in Figure 20.4.

Figure 20.4   Sample app: Add Filter, Filter selection.

Core Image filters can be instantiated by name, so the `tableView:cellForRowAtIndexPath:` method instantiates a `CIFilter`, and examines the filter's attributes to get the display name of the filter.

```
NSString *filterName =
➥[self.filterNameArray objectAtIndex:indexPath.row];

CIFilter *filter = [CIFilter filterWithName:filterName];
NSDictionary *filterAttributes = [filter attributes];

NSString *categoryName =
➥[filterAttributes valueForKey:kCIAttributeFilterDisplayName];

[cell.textLabel setText:categoryName];
```

When the user selects a filter, a segue is initiated. In the `prepareForSegue:sender:` method the destination instance of `ICFFilterViewController` is updated with an instance of `CIFilter` for the selected filter, and is assigned the `ICFFilterProcessingDelegate` delegate. When the `ICFFilterViewController` instance appears, it will display the customizable attributes for the selected filter.

Filter Attributes

Core Image filters have a flexible approach to customization. All instances of `CIFilter` have a dictionary property called `attributes` that contains information about the filter and all the customizations to the filter. Instances of `CIFilter` have a property called `inputKeys`, which lists the keys of each customizable input item, and a property called `outputKeys`, which lists the output items from the filter.

The sample app has specialized table cells to enable the user to see what attributes are available for a selected filter, adjust those attributes, and preview the image based on the current attribute parameters, as shown in Figure 20.5.

Figure 20.5   Sample app: Add Color Monochrome Filter, Filter Attributes.

Each attribute has information that can be used to determine how to display and edit the attribute in the user interface. In `ICFFilterViewController` the `tableView:cellForRowAt-IndexPath:` method determines which attribute to look at based on the index path.

```
NSString *attributeName =
➥[[self.selectedFilter inputKeys] objectAtIndex:indexPath.row];
```

Using the attribute name from the filter's `inputKeys` property, the method can then get an `NSDictionary` of info about the attribute.

```
NSDictionary *attributeInfo =
➥[[self.selectedFilter attributes] valueForKey:attributeName];
```

With the attribute info available, the method can inspect what type the attribute is and what class the filter expects the attribute information to be expressed in. With that info the method can dequeue the correct type of custom cell to use to edit the attribute. `ICFInputInfoCell` is a superclass with several subclasses to handle images, colors, numbers, vectors, and transforms.

```
NSString *cellIdentifier =
➥[self getCellIdentifierForAttributeType:attributeInfo];

ICFInputInfoCell *cell = (ICFInputInfoCell *)
➥[tableView dequeueReusableCellWithIdentifier:cellIdentifier
                                  forIndexPath:indexPath];
```

The custom `getCellIdentifierForAttributeType:` method uses the attribute type and class to determine what type of cell to return. Note that the filters are not completely consistent with attribute types and classes; one filter might specify an attribute type of `kCIAttribute-TypeColor`, whereas another might specify an attribute class of `CIColor`. The method corrects for this by allowing either approach.

```
NSString *attributeType = @"";
if ([attributeInfo objectForKey:kCIAttributeType])
{
    attributeType =
    ➥[attributeInfo objectForKey:kCIAttributeType];
}

NSString *attributeClass =
➥[attributeInfo objectForKey:kCIAttributeClass];

NSString *cellIdentifier = @"";

if ([attributeType isEqualToString:kCIAttributeTypeColor] ||
    ➥[attributeClass isEqualToString:@"CIColor"])
{
    cellIdentifier = kICSInputColorCellIdentifier;
}

if ([attributeType isEqualToString:kCIAttributeTypeImage] ||
    ➥[attributeClass isEqualToString:@"CIImage"])
{
    cellIdentifier = kICSInputImageCellIdentifier;
}
```

```
if ([attributeType isEqualToString:kCIAttributeTypeScalar] ||
    ➥[attributeType isEqualToString:kCIAttributeTypeDistance] ||
    ➥[attributeType isEqualToString:kCIAttributeTypeAngle] ||
    ➥[attributeType isEqualToString:kCIAttributeTypeTime])
{
    cellIdentifier = kICSInputNumberCellIdentifier;
}

if ([attributeType isEqualToString:kCIAttributeTypePosition] ||
    ➥[attributeType isEqualToString:kCIAttributeTypeOffset] ||
    ➥[attributeType isEqualToString:kCIAttributeTypeRectangle])
{
    cellIdentifier = kICSInputVectorCellIdentifier;
}

if ([attributeClass isEqualToString:@"NSValue"])
{
    cellIdentifier = kICSInputTransformCellIdentifier;
}

return cellIdentifier;
```

Each of the cell subclasses can accept the attribute dictionary, configure the cell display with provided or default values, manage editing of the parameter values, and then return an instance of the expected class when requested.

Initializing an Image

To apply a filter to an image, Core Image requires an image to be an instance of `CIImage`. To get an instance of `CIImage` from a `UIImage`, a conversion to `CGImage` and then to `CIImage` is needed. If the `UIImage` has image data already in memory, these conversions are quick; otherwise, the image data must be loaded into memory before they can occur.

In `ICFFilterViewController`, the `tableView:cellForRowAtIndexPath:` method handles the `inputImage` by checking with the filter delegate to get either the starting image or the image from the previous filter. The filter delegate keeps an array of `UIImages`, which it will use to return the last image from the `imageWithLastFilterApplied` method.

If the starting image is provided, it is converted to `CGImage` and then used to create a `CIImage`. If the input image is from another filter, it is safe to assume that `UIImage` has an associated `CIImage` (asking a `UIImage` for a `CIImage` works only when the `UIImage` has been created from a `CIImage`; otherwise, it returns `nil`).

```
if ([attributeName isEqualToString:@"inputImage"])
{
    UIImage *sourceImage =
    ➥[self.filterDelegate imageWithLastFilterApplied];
```

```
[[(ICFInputImageTableCell *)cell inputImageView]
➥setImage:sourceImage];

CIImage *inputImage = nil;
if ([sourceImage CIImage])
{
    inputImage = [sourceImage CIImage];
}
else
{
    CGImageRef inputImageRef = [sourceImage CGImage];
    inputImage = [CIImage imageWithCGImage:inputImageRef];
}

[self.selectedFilter setValue:inputImage
                       forKey:attributeName];
}
```

Rendering a Filtered Image

To render a filtered image, all that is required is to request the `outputImage` from the filter's attributes, and to call one of the available methods to render it to a context, an image, a bitmap, or a pixel buffer. At that point the filter operations will be applied to the `inputImage` and the `outputImage` will be produced. In the sample app, this occurs in two instances: if the user taps Preview in the filter view controller (as shown in Figure 20.5), or if the user taps Add Filter. When the user taps the Preview button in `ICFFilterViewController`, the `previewButtonTouched:` method is called. This method begins by initializing a Core Image context (note that the context can be initialized once as a property, but is done here to illustrate it all in one place).

```
CIContext *context = [CIContext contextWithOptions:nil];
```

The method then gets a reference to the `outputImage` from the filter, and sets up a rectangle that will be used to tell the context what part of the image to render. In this case the rectangle is the same size as the image and might seem superfluous; however, note that there are some filters that generate infinitely sized output images (see the Generator category of filters), so it is prudent to specify desired dimensions.

```
CIFilter *filter = self.selectedFilter;
CIImage *resultImage = [filter valueForKey:kCIOutputImageKey];
CGRect imageRect = CGRectMake(0.0f, 0.0f, 200.0f, 200.0f);
```

The method then asks the context to create a Core Graphics image using the `outputImage` and the rectangle.

```
CGImageRef resultCGImage =
➥[context createCGImage:resultImage fromRect:imageRect];
```

The Core Graphics result image can then be used to create a UIImage to display on the screen.

```
UIImage *resultUIImage =
[UIImage imageWithCGImage:resultCGImage];

[self.previewImageView setImage:resultUIImage];
```

The preview image is displayed in the lower-right corner of the filter view, as shown in Figure 20.5.

Chaining Filters

Chaining filters is the process of applying more than one filter to a source image. With the combination of filters applied to a source image, interesting effects can be produced, as shown in Figure 20.6.

Figure 20.6   Sample app: filter list.

When a user taps Add Filter (refer to Figure 20.5), the addFilter: method of the ICFFilterProcessing protocol gets called in ICFViewController. The method checks to see whether the filter to be added is the first filter, in which case it leaves the source image as the inputImage for the filter. If it is not the first filter, the method uses the outputImage of the last filter as the inputImage for the filter to be added.

```
CIFilter *lastFilter = [self.filterArray lastObject];

if (lastFilter)
{
    if ([[filter inputKeys] containsObject:@"inputImage"] )
    {
        [filter setValue:[lastFilter outputImage]
                forKey:@"inputImage"];
    }
}

[self.filterArray addObject:filter];
```

Using this technique, any number of filters can be chained together. With the last filter, the method renders the final image.

```
CIContext *context = [CIContext contextWithOptions:nil];
CIImage *resultImage = [filter valueForKey:kCIOutputImageKey];

CGImageRef resultCGImage =
➡[context createCGImage:resultImage
            fromRect:CGRectMake(0.0f, 0.0f, 200.0f, 200.0f)];

UIImage *resultUIImage =
➡[UIImage imageWithCGImage:resultCGImage];
```

The final image is added to the list of images, and the filter list table is reloaded to display the images for each filter step.

```
[self.resultImageView setImage:resultUIImage];

[self.filteredImageArray addObject:self.resultImageView.image];
[self.filterList reloadData];

[self.filterPopoverController dismissPopoverAnimated:YES];
```

Core Image will automatically optimize the filter chain to minimize the number of calculations necessary; in other words, Core Image will not process each step in the filter individually; rather, it will combine the math operations indicated by the filters and perform the filter operation in one step.

Feature Detection

Core Image provides the capability to detect features, including faces, and facial features as of iOS 7, and QR codes and rectangles as of iOS 8, in an image or a video. Feature detection can be used for a number of useful things; for example, the standard Camera app can highlight faces in the viewfinder. Face locations and dimensions can be used in filters to make faces anonymous or highlight faces in a number of engaging ways. Rectangle dimensions can be used similarly to apply filters to specific portions of an image, opening a wide potential for creative application of filters to images. The sample app contains functionality to detect and highlight faces and face features in the source image; the same techniques can be used for QR codes and rectangles.

Setting Up a Face Detector

To use a face detector, Core Image needs an instance of `CIImage` as a source image to analyze. In the `detectFacesTouched:` method in `ICFViewController`, an instance of `CIImage` is created from the source image displayed.

```
UIImage *detectUIImage = [self.sourceImageView image];
CGImageRef detectCGImageRef = [detectUIImage CGImage];

CIImage *detectImage =
➥[CIImage imageWithCGImage:detectCGImageRef];
```

Face detection in Core Image is provided by the `CIDetector` class. The class method to create a detector accepts a dictionary of options; in this case, a face detector can use either a high- or low-accuracy setting. The high-accuracy setting is more accurate but takes more time to complete, so it is appropriate for cases in which performance is not the primary consideration. The low-accuracy setting is appropriate for cases like a real-time video feed in which performance is more important than precision. A Core Image context can be provided but is not required.

```
NSDictionary *options =
➥@{CIDetectorAccuracy : CIDetectorAccuracyHigh};

CIDetector *faceDetector =
➥[CIDetector detectorOfType:CIDetectorTypeFace
                    context:nil
                    options:options];
```

After the detector is created, calling the `featuresInImage:` method will provide an array of features detected in the source image.

```
NSArray *features = [faceDetector featuresInImage:detectImage];
```

Features discovered will be returned as instances of `CIFaceFeature`, which is a subclass of `CIFeature`. Instances of `CIFeature` have a `bounds` property, which is a rectangle outlining the feature's relative position inside the source image.

Processing Face Features

The `detectFacesTouched:` method in `ICFViewController` will iterate over the found faces, and will visually highlight them in the source image, as shown in Figure 20.7. The method will also log detailed information about each face feature to a text view in the display.

For each face, the method first gets a rectangle to position the red square around the face.

```
CGRect faceRect =
➥[self adjustCoordinateSpaceForMarker:face.bounds
                           andHeight:detectImage.extent.size.height];
```

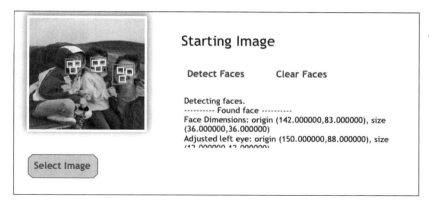

Figure 20.7   Sample app: detect faces.

To determine where to draw the rectangle for a face, the method needs to adjust the positions provided by Core Image, which uses a different coordinate system than UIKit. Core Image's coordinate system is flipped in the Y or vertical direction so that position zero is at the bottom of an image instead of the top. The adjustCoordinateSpaceForMarker:andHeight: method will adjust a marker rectangle by shifting the marker by the height of the image and flipping it, so the new coordinates are expressed the same way as in UIKit's coordinate system.

```
CGAffineTransform scale = CGAffineTransformMakeScale(1, -1);

CGAffineTransform flip =
➥CGAffineTransformTranslate(scale, 0, -height);

CGRect flippedRect = CGRectApplyAffineTransform(marker, flip);
return flippedRect;
```

With the correct coordinates, the method will add a basic view with a red border to the source image view to highlight the face.

```
UIView *faceMarker = [[UIView alloc] initWithFrame:faceRect];
faceMarker.layer.borderWidth = 2;
faceMarker.layer.borderColor = [[UIColor redColor] CGColor];
[self.sourceImageView addSubview:faceMarker];
```

The CIFaceFeature class has methods to indicate whether a face has detected a left eye, a right eye, and a mouth. As of iOS 7, it has methods to indicate whether a detected face is smiling (hasSmile), or whether either of the eyes is blinking (leftEyeClosed and rightEyeClosed).

```
if (face.hasLeftEyePosition)
{
...
}
```

If an eye or a mouth has been detected, a position will be available for that face feature expressed as a `CGPoint`. Since only a position is provided for each face feature (and not dimensions), the method uses a default width and height for the rectangles to indicate the location of a face feature.

```
CGFloat leftEyeXPos = face.leftEyePosition.x - eyeMarkerWidth/2;
CGFloat leftEyeYPos = face.leftEyePosition.y - eyeMarkerWidth/2;

CGRect leftEyeRect =
➥CGRectMake(leftEyeXPos, leftEyeYPos, eyeMarkerWidth, eyeMarkerWidth);

CGRect flippedLeftEyeRect =
➥[self adjustCoordinateSpaceForMarker:leftEyeRect
➥andHeight:self.sourceImageView.bounds.size.height];
```

With the calculated and adjusted rectangle, the method adds a yellow square to the source image view to highlight the left eye.

```
UIView *leftEyeMarker =
➥[[UIView alloc] initWithFrame:flippedLeftEyeRect];

leftEyeMarker.layer.borderWidth = 2;

leftEyeMarker.layer.borderColor =
➥[[UIColor yellowColor] CGColor];

[self.sourceImageView addSubview:leftEyeMarker];
```

The same approach is repeated for the right eye and the mouth.

Summary

This chapter described basic image handling, including how to load and display an image, how to specify a content mode to adjust how an image is displayed, and how to create a stretchable image to reuse a source image for elements of different sizes. It demonstrated how to get an image from the user's photo library or from the camera, and how to customize the image picker with options, such as which albums to use and whether to allow cropping of the selected image. It also explained how to resize an image.

Then, this chapter explained how to make use of Core Image filters, including how to get information about the available filters and filter categories, how to apply a filter to an image, and how to chain filters together to achieve interesting effects. Finally, this chapter described how to utilize Core Image's face detection.

21

Collection Views

Collection views were added in iOS 6 to provide a convenient new way to display scrollable cell-based information in a view with arbitrary layouts. Consider the iOS 6+ versions of Photos. app, which present thumbnails of images in a scrollable grid. Before iOS 6, implementing a grid view would require setting up a table view with logic to calculate which thumbnail (or cell) should go in each position in each table row, or would require custom logic to place thumbnails in a scroll view and manage them all as scrolling occurs. Both approaches are challenging, time-consuming, and error prone to implement. Collection views address this situation by providing a cell-management architecture that is similar to row management in a table view, while abstracting the layout of cells.

There is a default collection view layout called flow layout, which can be used to quickly and easily implement many common grid-style layouts for both horizontal and vertical scrolling. Custom layouts can be created to implement specialized grids or any nongrid layout that can be visualized and calculated at runtime.

Collection views can be organized into sections, with section header and section footer views that depend on section data. In addition, decoration views not related to content data can be specified to enhance the look of the collection view.

Last but not least, collection views support lots of types of animation, including custom states while cells are scrolling, animations for inserting or removing cells, and transitioning between layouts.

The Sample App

The sample app for this chapter is called PhotoGallery. The app demonstrates presenting the user's photo library in a few different implementations of a collection view:

- The first implementation is a basic collection view of thumbnails, organized by album, which can be scrolled vertically. It has section headers displaying album names, and can be created with a minimum of custom code.

- The second implementation uses a custom subclass of the flow layout so that it can display decoration views.

- The third implementation uses a custom layout to present items in a nongrid layout, and includes the capability to change to another layout with a pinch gesture.

Introducing Collection Views

A collection view needs a few different classes in order to work. The base class is called UICollectionView and is a subclass of UIScrollView. It will manage the presentation of cells provided by the datasource (which can be any class implementing the UICollectionViewDataSource protocol), according to the layout referenced by the collection view, which will be an instance of UICollectionViewLayout. A delegate conforming to the UICollectionViewDelegate protocol can be specified to manage selection and highlighting of cells.

The class that conforms to the UICollectionViewDataSource protocol will return configured cells to the collection view, which will be instances of UICollectionViewCell. If the collection view is configured to use section headers and/or section footers, the data source will return configured instances of UICollectionReusableView.

In the sample app, refer to the Basic Flow Layout to see these classes all working together, as shown in Figure 21.1.

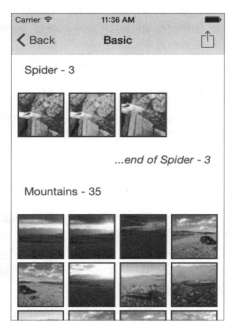

Figure 21.1   Sample app: Basic Flow Layout.

Setting Up a Collection View

The Basic Flow Layout example in the sample app demonstrates setting up a collection view with a minimum of customization, to show how quickly and easily a collection view can be created. Instead of using a basic `UIViewController` subclass, the basic flow used a `UICollectionViewController` subclass called `PHGBasicFlowViewController`, which conforms to the `UICollectionViewDataSource` and `UICollectionViewDelegate` protocols. This approach is not required; it is convenient when the collection view is all that is being displayed for a view controller. A collection view can be used with a standard view controller with no issues:

1. In the MainStoryboard, examine the Basic Flow View Controller–Basic Scene.

2. Expand the scene to see the collection view controller, as shown in Figure 21.2.

3. With the collection view controller selected, note the custom class specified in the identity inspector.

This ensures that the collection view controller will use the custom subclass `PHGBasicFlowViewController`.

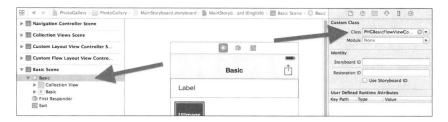

Figure 21.2   Xcode storyboard: specify custom class for collection view controller.

`UICollectionViewController` instances have a property called `collectionView`, which is represented in Interface Builder as the collection view object. With the collection view object selected, note that several settings can be configured: the type of layout, the scrolling direction, and whether a section header and/or section footer should be used, as shown in Figure 21.3.

Figure 21.3   Xcode storyboard: custom collection view settings.

Interface Builder will present objects for the section header, collection view cell, and section footer that can be customized as well. For each of these, a custom subclass has been set up to simplify managing the subviews that need to be configured at runtime. This is not required; the `UICollectionViewCell` and `UICollectionReusableView` classes can be used directly if preferred.

The collection view cell subclass is called `PHGThumbCell`, and has one property called `thumb-ImageView`, which will be used to display the thumbnail image. The collection view object in Interface Builder is configured to use the custom subclass in the identity inspector, and references a `UIImageView` object for the `thumbImageView` property. The key item to set up for the collection view cell is the identifier, as shown in Figure 21.4; this is how the data source method will identify the type of cell to be configured and displayed.

Figure 21.4   Xcode storyboard: collection view cell identifier.

The collection view section header subclass is called `PHGSectionHeader`, and the section footer subclass is called `PHGSectionFooter`. Each subclass has a property for a label that will be used to display the header or footer title for the section. Both objects in Interface Builder are configured to use their respective custom subclasses in the identity inspector, and reference `UILabel` objects for their title properties. Just as the collection view cell "identifier" was specified for the collection view cell, separate identifiers are specified for the section header and section footer.

Implementing the Collection View Data Source Methods

After all the objects are configured in Interface Builder, the data source methods need to be implemented for the collection view to work. Confirm that the collection view object in the storyboard has the data source set to the basic flow view controller, as shown in Figure 21.5.

The sample app is a gallery app that displays photos from the user's photo library organized by photo album, so there is logic implemented in the `viewDidLoad` method that builds an array of image asset fetch results by album and a fetch request of photo albums. See Chapter 24, "Accessing the Photo Library," for more details on that process.

Figure 21.5   Xcode storyboard: collection view data source setting.

The collection view needs to know how many sections to present, which is returned in the numberOfSectionsInCollectionView: method. The method is set up to return the count of albums (or groups) from the array of asset groups built in viewDidLoad.

```
- (NSInteger)numberOfSectionsInCollectionView:(UICollectionView *)collectionView
{
    return [self.albumsResult count];
}
```

Next the collection view needs to know how many cells to present in each section. This method is called collectionView:numberOfItemsInSection:. The method has been built to find the correct asset array for the section index, and then return the count of assets in that array.

```
- (NSInteger)collectionView:(UICollectionView *)view
     numberOfItemsInSection:(NSInteger)section;
{
    PHFetchResult *albumAssets = self.albumAssetsResults[section];
    return [albumAssets count];
}
```

After the collection view has the counts of sections and items, it can determine how to lay out the view. Depending on where in the scrollable bounds the current view is, the collection view will request section headers, footers, and cells for the visible area of the view. Section headers and footers are requested from the collectionView:viewForSupplementary-ElementOfKind:atIndexPath: method. Section headers and footers both need to be instances (or subclasses) of UICollectionReusableView. The method declares a nil instance of UICollectionReusableView, which will be populated with either a configured section header or a section footer. In addition, the method gets information about the photo album and assets in the album to display in the header or footer.

```
UICollectionReusableView *supplementaryView = nil;
PHAssetCollection *album = [self.albumsResult objectAtIndex:indexPath.section];
PHFetchResult *albumAssets =
➥ [self.albumAssetsResults objectAtIndex:indexPath.section];
```

The logic in the method must check the value of the `kind` parameter (which will be either `UICollectionElementKindSectionHeader` or `UICollectionElementKindSectionFooter`) to determine whether to return a section header or section footer.

```
if ([kind isEqualToString:UICollectionElementKindSectionHeader]) {

    PHGSectionHeader *sectionHeader =
    ➥[collectionView dequeueReusableSupplementaryViewOfKind:kind
    ➥withReuseIdentifier:kSectionHeader forIndexPath:indexPath];

    [sectionHeader.headerLabel
    ➥setText:[NSString stringWithFormat:@"%@ - %lu",album.localizedTitle,
    ➥ (unsigned long)albumAssets.count]];

    supplementaryView = sectionHeader;
}
```

To get an instance of the custom `PHGSectionHeader`, the collection view is asked to provide a supplementary view for the specified index path, using the dequeue with reuse identifier method. Note that the reuse identifier must be the same as specified in Interface Builder previously for the section header. This method will either instantiate a new view or reuse an existing view that is no longer being displayed. Then the title of the section is looked up in the group array, and put in the header's title label.

For cells, the `collectionView:cellForItematIndexPath:` method is called. In this method, a cell is dequeued for the reuse identifier specified (this must match the reuse identifier specified for the cell in Interface Builder).

```
PHGThumbCell *cell =
[cv dequeueReusableCellWithReuseIdentifier:kThumbCell
                             forIndexPath:indexPath];
```

The cell is then configured to display the thumbnail image for the asset at the `indexPath` and returned for display.

```
PHFetchResult *albumAssets = self.albumAssetsResults[indexPath.section];
PHAsset *asset = albumAssets[indexPath.row];

PHImageManager *imageManager = [PHImageManager defaultManager];
[imageManager requestImageForAsset:asset
                        targetSize:CGSizeMake(50, 50)
                       contentMode:PHImageContentModeAspectFill
                           options:nil
                     resultHandler:^(UIImage *result, NSDictionary *info){
                         [cell.thumbImageView setImage:result];
                         [cell setNeedsLayout];
                     }];

return cell;
```

Customizing Collection View and Flow Layout

Various customizations are possible for a flow layout collection view. The size of each cell can be customized individually, as well as the size of each section header and section footer. Guidelines can be provided to ensure that a minimum amount of spacing is respected between cells, as well as between cells, section headers and footers, and section boundaries. In addition, decoration views, which are views that enhance the collection view aesthetically but are not directly related to the collection view's data, can be placed anywhere in the collection view.

Basic Customizations

The flow layout provided in the SDK can be customized to provide a wide variety of grid-based layouts. The flow layout has logic built in to calculate, based on scrolling direction and all the parameters set for cell size, spacing and sections, how many cells should be presented per row, and then how big the scroll view should be. When these parameters are manipulated, collection views can be created that display one cell per row (or even per screen), multiple cells packed tightly together in a row (as in iOS7's Photos.app), or anything in between. These parameters are illustrated in Figure 21.7.

Figure 21.7   Collection view customizable parameters.

There are a few approaches to performing basic customizations on a flow layout collection view. The simplest approach is to set the defaults for the collection view in Interface Builder, by selecting the collection view object (or collection view flow layout object) and using the Size Inspector, as shown in Figure 21.8. Note that adjustments to these values affect the flow layout object associated with the collection view.

Figure 21.8   Xcode Interface Builder: Size Inspector for the collection view object.

Another approach is to update the items in code, in an instance or a subclass of
`UICollectionViewFlowLayout`. In `PHGCustomFlowLayout`, the attributes for the custom flow
layout are set in the `init` method.

```
self.scrollDirection = UICollectionViewScrollDirectionVertical;

self.itemSize = CGSizeMake(60, 60);
self.sectionInset = UIEdgeInsetsMake(10, 26, 10, 26);
self.headerReferenceSize = CGSizeMake(300, 50);
self.minimumLineSpacing = 20;
self.minimumInteritemSpacing = 40;
```

Finally, the collection view's delegate can implement methods from the
`UICollectionViewDelegateFlowLayout` protocol. These methods can be used to customize
dimensions for individual cells based on data, or individual section headers or footers based on
data. For example, photos with a higher user rating could be made bigger, or a section header
or footer could be expanded as needed to accommodate an extra row of text for a long title.

> **Note**
>
> As of iOS 8, collection views using flow layout can automatically resize their cells based on the
> intrinsic content size of the UI elements in the cell. To get this behavior, set up the cells using
> Auto Layout constraints that will allow one or more UI elements to expand in the scroll direction
> of the layout (vertical or horizontal). Then, in code set the estimated item size on the flow lay-
> out for the collection view. After that is set, the collection view will use the estimated item size
> to initially lay out the collection view, and will then ask each cell for an actual size based on the
> Auto Layout constraints and content.

Decoration Views

Decoration views can be used to enhance the visual look of the collection view, independently of cells and section headers and footers. They are intended to be independent of collection view data, and as such are not handled by the collection view's data source or delegate. Since decoration views can be placed anywhere in a collection view, logic must be provided to tell the collection view where the decoration views should go. This necessitates creating a subclass of `UICollectionViewFlowLayout` to calculate locations for decoration views and to place them in the collection view when they should be visible in the currently displayed area.

In the sample app, tap the Custom Flow Layout option from the top menu to view an example that uses decoration views. The tilted shelf with a shadow below each row of photos is a decoration view, as shown in Figure 21.9.

Figure 21.9   Sample app: Custom Flow Layout example.

The first step in using a decoration view is to register a class or nib that can be used for decoration view. In `PHGCCustomFlowLayout`, a subclass of `UICollectionReusableView` called `PHGRowDecorationView` is registered in the `init` method.

```
[self registerClass:[PHGRowDecorationView class]
➥forDecorationViewOfKind:[PHGRowDecorationView kind]];
```

The `PHGCCustomFlowLayout` class has custom drawing logic to draw the shelf and shadow. Note that multiple types of decoration views can be registered for a collection view if desired; they can be distinguished using the `kind` parameter. After a decoration view class or nib is registered, the layout needs to calculate where the decoration views should be placed. To do this, the custom layout overrides the `prepareLayout` method, which gets called every time the layout needs to be updated. The method will calculate frame `rects` for each needed decoration view and store them in a property so that they can be pulled as needed.

In the `prepareLayout` method, `[super prepareLayout]` is called first to get the base layout. Then some calculations are performed to determine how many cells can fit in each row, presuming that they are uniform in size.

```
[super prepareLayout];

NSInteger sections = [self.collectionView numberOfSections];

CGFloat availableWidth = self.collectionViewContentSize.width -
➥(self.sectionInset.left + self.sectionInset.right);

NSInteger cellsPerRow =
➥floorf((availableWidth + self.minimumInteritemSpacing) /
➥(self.itemSize.width + self.minimumInteritemSpacing));
```

A mutable dictionary to store the calculated frames for each decoration is created, and a float to track the current y position in the layout while performing calculations is created.

```
NSMutableDictionary *rowDecorationWork =
➥[[NSMutableDictionary alloc] init];

CGFloat yPosition = 0;
```

With that established, the method will iterate over the sections to find rows needing decoration views.

```
for (NSInteger sectionIndex = 0; sectionIndex < sections; sectionIndex++)
{
...
}
```

Within each section, the method will calculate how much space the section header takes up, and how much space is needed between the section and the top of the cells in the first row. Then the method will calculate how many rows there will be in the section based on the number of cells.

```
yPosition += self.headerReferenceSize.height;
yPosition += self.sectionInset.top;

NSInteger cellCount =
➥[self.collectionView numberOfItemsInSection:sectionIndex];

NSInteger rows = ceilf(cellCount/(CGFloat)cellsPerRow);
```

Then the method will iterate over each row, calculate the frame for the decoration view for that row, create an index path for the row and section, store the frame rectangle in the work dictionary using the index path as the key, and adjust the current y position to account for minimum line spacing unless it is the final row of the section.

```
for (int row = 0; row < rows; row++)
{
    yPosition += self.itemSize.height;

    CGRect decorationFrame = CGRectMake(0,
    ➥yPosition-kDecorationYAdjustment,
    ➥self.collectionViewContentSize.width,
    ➥kDecorationHeight);

    NSIndexPath *decIndexPath = [NSIndexPath
    ➥indexPathForRow:row inSection:sectionIndex];

    rowDecorationWork[decIndexPath] =
    ➥ [NSValue valueWithCGRect:decorationFrame];

    if (row < rows - 1)
        yPosition += self.minimumLineSpacing;
}
```

> **Note**
>
> The index path for the decoration item does not need to be strictly correct because the layout uses it only for a unique identifier for the decoration view. The developer can use any scheme that makes sense for the decoration view's index path, and is unique for the decoration views of the same type in the collection view. Non-unique index paths will generate an assertion failure.

The method will then adjust for any space required at the end of the section, including the section inset and footer.

```
yPosition += self.sectionInset.bottom;
yPosition += self.footerReferenceSize.height;
```

After all the sections have been iterated, the dictionary of decoration view frames will be stored in the layout's property for use during layout.

```
self.rowDecorationRects =
➥ [NSDictionary dictionaryWithDictionary:rowDecorationWork];
```

Now that the decoration view frames have been calculated, the layout can use them when the collection view asks for layout attributes for the visible bounds in the overridden `layout-AttributesForElementsInRect:` method. First the method gets the attributes for the cells and section headers from the superclass, and then it will update those attributes to ensure that the cells are presented in front of the decoration views.

```
NSArray *layoutAttributes =
➡[super layoutAttributesForElementsInRect:rect];

for (UICollectionViewLayoutAttributes *attributes
     ➡in layoutAttributes)
{
    attributes.zIndex = 1;
}
```

The method will set up a mutable copy of the attributes so that it can add the attributes needed for the decoration views. It will then iterate over the dictionary of the calculated decoration view frames, and check to see which frames are in the collection view's visible bounds. Layout attributes will be created for those decoration views, and adjusted to ensure that they are presented behind the cell views. The updated array of attributes will be returned.

```
NSMutableArray *newLayoutAttributes =
➡[layoutAttributes mutableCopy];

[self.rowDecorationRects enumerateKeysAndObjectsUsingBlock:
 ^(NSIndexPath *indexPath, NSValue *rowRectValue, BOOL *stop) {

    if (CGRectIntersectsRect([rowRectValue CGRectValue], rect))
    {
        UICollectionViewLayoutAttributes *attributes =
        ➡[UICollectionViewLayoutAttributes
        ➡layoutAttributesForDecorationViewOfKind:
        ➡[PHGRowDecorationView kind] withIndexPath:indexPath];

        attributes.frame = [rowRectValue CGRectValue];
        attributes.zIndex = 0;
        [newLayoutAttributes addObject:attributes];
    }
}];

layoutAttributes = [NSArray arrayWithArray:newLayoutAttributes];

return layoutAttributes;
```

With the attributes for the decoration views being included in the whole set of layout attributes, the collection view will display the decoration views, as shown in Figure 21.9.

Creating Custom Layouts

Custom layouts can be created for collection views that do not fit well into a grid format. In the sample app tap Custom Layout from the main menu to see an example of a layout that is more complex than a grid format. This layout presents images from the photo library in a continuous sine curve, even between section breaks, as shown in Figure 21.10.

Figure 21.10   Sample app: custom layout example with sine curve layout.

To create a subclass of `UICollectionViewLayout`, several methods need to be implemented:

- The `collectionViewContentSize` method tells the collection view how to size the scroll view.

- The `layoutAttributesForElementsInRect:` method tells the collection view all the layout attributes necessary for cells, section headers and footers, and decoration views in the rectangle specified.

- The `layoutAttributesForItemAtIndexPath:` method returns the layout attributes for a cell at an index path.

- The `layoutAttributesForSupplementaryViewOfKind:atIndexPath:` method returns the layout attributes for a section header or footer at the index path. Does not need to be implemented if section headers or footers are not used in the collection view.

- The `layoutAttributesForDecorationViewOfKind:atIndexPath:` method returns the layout attributes for a decoration view at the index path. Does not need to be implemented if decoration views are not used in the collection view.

- The `shouldInvalidateLayoutForBoundsChange:` method is used for animation of items in the layout. If this method returns `yes`, the collection view will recalculate all the layout attributes for the visible bounds. This will allow layout attributes to change based on their position on the screen.

- The `prepareLayout` method, though optional, is a good place to calculate the layout since it gets called every time the layout needs to be updated.

In `PHGCustomLayout`, the `prepareLayout` method begins by determining the number of sections to be displayed, creates a float variable to track the current y position during the calculations, creates a dictionary to store the center points of the cells, and creates an array to store the frames of the section headers.

```
NSInteger numSections = [self.collectionView numberOfSections];

CGFloat currentYPosition = 0.0;
self.centerPointsForCells = [[NSMutableDictionary alloc] init];
self.rectsForSectionHeaders = [[NSMutableArray alloc] init];
```

The method then iterates over the sections. For each section it will calculate and store the frame for the section header, and then update the current y position from the top of the calculated section header to the vertical center of the first cell to be displayed. It will then determine the number of cells to be presented for the section.

```
for (NSInteger sectionIndex = 0; sectionIndex < numSections;
     sectionIndex++)
{
    CGRect rectForNextSection = CGRectMake(0, currentYPosition,
    ➥self.collectionView.bounds.size.width, kSectionHeight);

    self.rectsForSectionHeaders[sectionIndex] =
    ➥[NSValue valueWithCGRect:rectForNextSection];

    currentYPosition +=
    ➥kSectionHeight + kVerticalSpace + kCellSize / 2;

    NSInteger numCellsForSection =
    ➥[self.collectionView numberOfItemsInSection:sectionIndex];
    ...
}
```

Next the method will iterate over the cells. It will calculate the horizontal center of the cell using the sine function, and store the center point in the dictionary with the index path for the cell as the key. The method will update the current vertical position and continue.

```
for (NSInteger cellIndex = 0; cellIndex < numCellsForSection;
     cellIndex++)
{
    CGFloat xPosition =
    ➥[self calculateSineXPositionForY:currentYPosition];

    CGPoint cellCenterPoint =
    ➥CGPointMake(xPosition, currentYPosition);
```

```
    NSIndexPath *cellIndexPath = [NSIndexPath
    ➥indexPathForItem:cellIndex inSection:sectionIndex];

    self.centerPointsForCells[cellIndexPath] =
    ➥[NSValue valueWithCGPoint:cellCenterPoint];

    currentYPosition += kCellSize + kVerticalSpace;
}
```

After all the section header frames and cell center points have been calculated and stored, the method will calculate and store the content size of the collection view in a property so that it can be returned from the collectionViewContentSize method.

```
self.contentSize =
➥CGSizeMake(self.collectionView.bounds.size.width,
➥currentYPosition + kVerticalSpace);
```

When the collection view is displayed, the layoutAttributesForElementsInRect: method will be called for the visible bounds of the collection view. That method will create a mutable array to store the attributes to be returned, and will iterate over the section frame array to determine which section headers should be displayed. It will call the layoutAttributesFor-SupplementaryViewOfKind:atIndexPath: method for each section header to be displayed to get the attributes for the section headers, and store the attributes in the work array.

```
NSMutableArray *attributes = [NSMutableArray array];
for (NSValue *sectionRect in self.rectsForSectionHeaders)
{
    if (CGRectIntersectsRect(rect, sectionRect.CGRectValue))
    {
        NSInteger sectionIndex =
        ➥[self.rectsForSectionHeaders indexOfObject:sectionRect];

        NSIndexPath *secIndexPath =
        ➥[NSIndexPath indexPathForItem:0 inSection:sectionIndex];

        [attributes addObject:
        ➥[self layoutAttributesForSupplementaryViewOfKind:
        ➥UICollectionElementKindSectionHeader
        ➥atIndexPath:secIndexPath]];
    }
}
```

The method will then iterate over the dictionary containing index paths and cell center points to determine which cells should be displayed, will fetch the necessary cell attributes from the layoutAttributesForItemAtIndexPath: method, and will store the attributes in the work array.

```
[self.centerPointsForCells enumerateKeysAndObjectsUsingBlock:
  ➥^(NSIndexPath *indexPath, NSValue *centerPoint, BOOL *stop) {
```

```
    CGPoint center = [centerPoint CGPointValue];

    CGRect cellRect = CGRectMake(center.x - kCellSize/2,
    ➥center.y - kCellSize/2, kCellSize, kCellSize);

    if (CGRectIntersectsRect(rect, cellRect)) {
        [attributes addObject:
        ➥[self layoutAttributesForItemAtIndexPath:indexPath]];
    }
}];
```

To determine the layout attributes for each section header, the `layoutAttributesFor-SupplementaryViewOfKind:atIndexPath:` method will begin by getting a default set of attributes for the section header by calling the `UICollectionViewLayoutAttributes` class method `layoutAttributesForSupplementaryViewOfKind:withIndexPath:`. Then the method will update the size and center point of the section header using the frame calculated in the `prepareLayout` method earlier, and return the attributes.

```
UICollectionViewLayoutAttributes *attributes =
➥[UICollectionViewLayoutAttributes
➥layoutAttributesForSupplementaryViewOfKind:
➥UICollectionElementKindSectionHeader withIndexPath:indexPath];

CGRect sectionRect =
➥[self.rectsForSectionHeaders[indexPath.section] CGRectValue];

attributes.size =
➥CGSizeMake(sectionRect.size.width, sectionRect.size.height);

attributes.center =
➥CGPointMake(CGRectGetMidX(sectionRect),
➥CGRectGetMidY(sectionRect));

return attributes;
```

To determine the layout attributes for each cell, the `layoutAttributesForItem-WithIndexPath:` method will get a default set of attributes for the cell by calling the `UICollectionViewLayoutAttributes` class method `layoutAttributesForCellWithIndex-Path:`. Then the method will update the size and center point of the cell using the point calculated in the `prepareLayout` method earlier, and return the attributes.

```
UICollectionViewLayoutAttributes *attributes =
➥[UICollectionViewLayoutAttributes
➥layoutAttributesForCellWithIndexPath:path];

attributes.size = CGSizeMake(kCellSize, kCellSize);
```

```
NSValue *centerPointValue = self.centerPointsForCells[path];

attributes.center = [centerPointValue CGPointValue];
return attributes;
```

With all those methods implemented, the collection view is able to calculate the positions for all the items in the view, and properly retrieve the positioning information as needed to display the custom layout shown in Figure 21.10.

Collection View Animations

Collection views have extensive built-in support for animations. A collection view can change layouts, and animate all the cells from the positions in the first layout to the positions in the new layout. Within a layout, collection views can animate each cell individually by adjusting the layout attributes as scrolling occurs. Changes to the cells in the layout, including insertions and deletions, can all be animated.

Collection View Layout Changes

In the sample app, tap the Custom Flow item in the menu. Perform a pinch-out gesture on any image in the view, and observe the layout changing to a new layout with animations. The cells will all move from their original positions to the new positions, and the collection view will be scrolled to display the pinched cell in the center of the view. The logic to do this is set up in the PHGCustomLayoutViewController. When the view controller is loaded, two pinch gesture recognizers are created and stored in properties. The gesture recognizer for a pinch out is added to the collection view. For more information on gesture recognizers, see Chapter 23, "Gesture Recognizers."

```
self.pinchIn = [[UIPinchGestureRecognizer alloc]
               initWithTarget:self
               action:@selector(pinchInReceived:)];

self.pinchOut = [[UIPinchGestureRecognizer alloc]
                initWithTarget:self
                action:@selector(pinchOutReceived:)];

[self.collectionView addGestureRecognizer:self.pinchOut];
```

When a pinch out is received, the pinchOutReceived: method is called. That method will check the state of the gesture to determine the correct course of action. If the state is UIGestureRecognizerStateBegan, the method will determine which cell the user has pinched over and will store that in order to navigate to it after the transition has occurred.

```
if (pinchRecognizer.state == UIGestureRecognizerStateBegan)
{
    CGPoint pinchPoint =
    ➥[pinchRecognizer locationInView:self.collectionView];
```

```
        self.pinchedIndexPath =
        ➥[self.collectionView indexPathForItemAtPoint:pinchPoint];
}
```

When the pinch gesture is completed, the method will be called again, and the method will
check whether the state is ended. If so, the method will remove the pinch recognizer from the
view to prevent any additional pinches from accidentally occurring during the transition, and
will then create the new layout and initiate the animated transition. The method defines a
completion block to execute when the transition to the new layout is complete. This completion block will add the pinch-in gesture recognizer so that the user can pinch and return to the
previous view, and will perform the animated navigation to the cell that the user pinched over.

```
[self.collectionView removeGestureRecognizer:self.pinchOut];

UICollectionViewFlowLayout *individualLayout =
➥[[PHGAnimatingFlowLayout alloc] init];

__weak UICollectionView *weakCollectionView = self.collectionView;
__weak UIPinchGestureRecognizer *weakPinchIn = self.pinchIn;
__weak NSIndexPath *weakPinchedIndexPath = self.pinchedIndexPath;
void (^finishedBlock)(BOOL) = ^(BOOL finished) {

    [weakCollectionView scrollToItemAtIndexPath:weakPinchedIndexPath
    ➥atScrollPosition:UICollectionViewScrollPositionCenteredVertically
    ➥animated:YES];

    [weakCollectionView addGestureRecognizer:weakPinchIn];
};
[self.collectionView setCollectionViewLayout:individualLayout
                                    animated:YES
                                  completion:finishedBlock];
```

> **Note**
>
> All the animations are handled by the collection view. No custom logic was required to perform
> any calculations for the animations.

Collection View Layout Animations

After a pinch out has occurred on the custom layout, the newly presented layout has a unique
feature. The cells in each row are larger the closer they are to the center of the view along the y
axis, as shown in Figure 21.11.

Figure 21.11   Sample app: custom layout example with animations.

As the user scrolls, the size of the cells will change dynamically depending on their proximity to the center of the view. To achieve this effect, some custom logic is implemented in the PHGAnimatingFlowLayout class. The first piece is required to tell the layout that it should recalculate the layout attributes of each cell when scrolling occurs. This is done by returning YES from the shouldInvalidateLayoutForBoundsChange: method.

```
- (BOOL)shouldInvalidateLayoutForBoundsChange:(CGRect)oldBounds
{
    return YES;
}
```

When the flow layout has invalidated the layout during a scroll, it will call the layout-AttributesForElementsInRect: method to get new layout attributes for each visible cell. This method will determine which layout attributes are for cells in the visible rect so that they can be modified.

```
NSArray *layoutAttributes =
➥[super layoutAttributesForElementsInRect:rect];

CGRect visibleRect;
visibleRect.origin = self.collectionView.contentOffset;
visibleRect.size = self.collectionView.bounds.size;
```

```
for (UICollectionViewLayoutAttributes *attributes
    ➥in layoutAttributes)
{
    if (attributes.representedElementCategory ==
        ➥UICollectionElementCategoryCell &&
        ➥CGRectIntersectsRect(attributes.frame, rect))
    {
        ...
    }
}
```

For each cell, the method will calculate how far away from the center of the view the cell is along the y axis. The method will then calculate how much to scale up the cell based on how far away from the center it is. The layout attributes are updated with the 3D transform and returned.

```
CGFloat distanceFromCenter =
➥CGRectGetMidY(visibleRect) - attributes.center.y;

CGFloat distancePercentFromCenter =
➥distanceFromCenter / kZoomDistance;

if (ABS(distanceFromCenter) < kZoomDistance) {
    CGFloat zoom =
    ➥1 + kZoomAmount * (1 - ABS(distancePercentFromCenter));

    attributes.transform3D =
    ➥CATransform3DMakeScale(zoom, zoom, 1.0);
}
else
{
    attributes.transform3D = CATransform3DIdentity;
}
```

Collection View Change Animations

Collection views offer support for animations when items are being inserted or deleted. This animation is not demonstrated in the sample app, but can be covered with some discussion. To build support for animating insertions and deletions, there are a few methods in the collection view layout subclass to implement. First is the prepareForCollectionViewUpdates: method, which can be used for any preparation needed before animations occur. That method receives an array of updates that can be inspected so that the method can be customized to perform preparations by individual items and by type of update.

For insertions, the initialLayoutAttributesForAppearingItemAtIndexPath: method can be implemented. This method can be used to tell the layout where to display the item before putting it in the calculated position in the layout with animation. In addition, any other initial attributes assigned to the item will animate to the final layout attributes, meaning that an item can be scaled, can be rotated, or can make any other change as it flies in.

For deletions, the `finalLayoutAttributesForDisappearingItemAtIndexPath:` method can be implemented. This method can be used to tell the layout where the final position for an item should be as it is pulled out of the layout with animation. Again, any other final attributes can be assigned to the item for additional animation.

Finally, the `finalizeCollectionViewUpdates` method can be implemented. This method will be executed when all the inserts and deletes have completed, so it can be used to clean up any state saved during the preparations.

Summary

This chapter covered collection views. It described how to implement a basic collection view with minimal custom code, and then explored some more advanced customizations to collection views, including customizations to the flow layout, decoration views, and completely custom layouts. This chapter discussed what animation options are supported by collection views, and how to implement animations while changing layouts, while scrolling through a collection view, and while inserting or deleting items.

22

Introduction to TextKit

Both the iPhone and, later, the iPad have supported numerous text presentation elements from their inception. Text fields, labels, text views, and Web views have been with the OS since its release. Over time these classes have been expanded and improved with the goal of giving developers more flexibility and power with regard to text rendering.

In the early days of iOS (then called iPhone OS), the only practical way to display attributed text was to use a UIWebView and use HTML to render custom attributes; however, this was difficult to implement and carried with it terrible performance. iOS 3.2 introduced Core Text, which brought the full power of NSAttributedString to the mobile platform from the Mac. Core Text, however, was complex and unwieldy and was largely shunned by developers who were not coming from the Mac or did not have an abundance of time to invest in text rendering for their apps.

Enter TextKit. First announced as part of iOS 7, TextKit is not a framework in the traditional sense. Instead, TextKit is the nomenclature for a set of enhancements to existing text-displaying objects to easily render and work with attributed strings. Although TextKit adds several new features and functionalities beyond what Core Text offered, a lot of that functionality is re-created in TextKit, albeit in a much simpler-to-work-with fashion. Existing Core Text code likewise is easily portable to TextKit, often needing no changes or only very minor changes through the use of toll-free bridges.

An introduction to TextKit is laid out over the following pages. It will demonstrate some of the basic principles of text handling on iOS 7; however, working with text on modern devices is a vast topic, worthy of its own publication. Apple has put considerable time and effort into making advanced text layout and rendering easier than it has ever been in the past. The techniques and tools described will provide a stepping-stone into a world of virtually limitless text presentation.

The Sample App

The sample app (shown in Figure 22.1) is a simple table view–based app that will enable the user to explore four popular features of TextKit. There is little overhead for the sample app not directly related to working with the new TextKit functionality. It consists of a main view built on a `UINavigationController` and a table view that offers the selection of one of four items. The sample app provides demos for Dynamic Link Detection, which will automatically detect and highlight various data types; Hit Detection, which enables the user to select a word from a `UITextView`; and Content Specific Highlighting, which demos TextKit's capability to work with attributed strings. Lastly, the sample app exhibits Exclusion Paths, which offers the capability to wrap text around objects or Bézier paths.

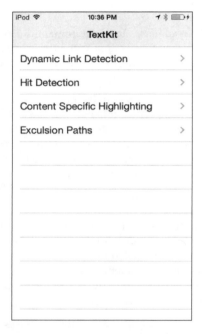

Figure 22.1   A look at the sample app showing a table view with options for different TextKit functionalities.

Introducing `NSLayoutManager`

`NSLayoutManager` was first introduced as part of the TextKit additions in iOS 7. It can be used to coordinate the layout and display of characters held in an `NSTextStore`, which is covered in the following section. `NSLayoutManager` can be used to render multiple `NSTextViews` together to create a complex text layout. `NSLayoutManager` contains numerous classes for adding, removing, aligning, and otherwise working with NSTextContainer, which are covered more in depth in a later section.

NSTextStore

Each NSLayoutManager has an associated NSTextStorage that acts as a subclass of NSMutableAttributedString. Readers familiar with Core Text or Mac OS X text rendering might be familiar with an attributed string, which is used for storage of stylized text. An NSTextStorage provides an easy-to-interact-with wrapper for easily adding and removing attributes from text.

NSTextStorage can be used with setAttributes:range: to add new attributes to a string; for a list of attributes see Table 22.1. Polling the text for currently enabled attributes can be done using attributesAtIndex:effectiveRange:.

Table 22.1 **Available Text Attributes**

Attribute	Description
NSFontAttributeName	The font name for the text; defaults to Helvetica(Neue) 12.
NSParagraphStyleAttributeName	The paragraph style of the text; accepts NSParagraphStyle constants. Defaults to defaultParagraphStyle.
NSForegroundColorAttributeName	The color of the text lettering; accepts a UIColor, defaults to blackColor.
NSBackgroundColorAttributeName	The color of the background behind the text; accepts a UIColor. Defaults to nil, which is used for no color.
NSLigatureAttributeName	An NSNumber representing whether the text has ligatures turned on (1) or off (0); defaults to no ligatures.
NSKernAttributeName	An NSNumber which controls kerning. Although this property is available on iOS, values other than off (0) are not supported.
NSStrikethroughStyleAttributeName	An NSNumber representing whether the text is strikethrough (1) or nonstrikethrough (0); defaults to off.
NSUnderlineStyleAttributeName	An NSNumber representing whether the text is underlined (1) or nonunderlined (0); defaults to off.
NSStrokeColorAttributeName	A UIColor representing the text stroke coloring; defaults to nil, which uses the same color set in NSForegroundColorAttributeName.

Attribute	Description
NSStrokeWidthAttributeName	A floating NSNumber representing the width in percent of font point size. This is often used to create an outline effect. Defaults to 0 for no stroke. Negative values represent a stroke and fill, and positive values create a hollow stroke.
NSShadowAttributeName	The amount of shadow to be applied to the text; accepts constants from NSShadow and defaults to no shadow.
NSTextEffectAttributeName	The text effect; as of iOS 7 there is only one possible value other than nil for off, NSTextEffectLetterpressStyle.
NSAttachmentAttributeName	An NSTextAttachment, which is NSData represented by an UIImage; defaults to nil.
NSLinkAttributeName	An NSURL or NSString representing a link.
NSBaselineOffsetAttributeName	NSNumber containing a floating point value in points for a baseline offset; defaults to 0.
NSUnderlineColorAttributeName	A UIColor representing the color of the underline stroke; defaults to nil for same as foreground color.
NSStrikethroughColorAttributeName	A UIColor representing the color of the strikethrough stroke; defaults to nil for same as foreground color.
NSObliquenessAttributeName	An NSNumber floating-point value controlling the skew applied to glyphs. Defaults to 0 for no skew.
NSExpansionAttributeName	An NSNumber floating-point value controlling the expansion applied to glyphs. Defaults to 0 for no expansion.
NSWritingDirectionAttributeName	A value which accepts masking from NSWritingDirection and NSTextWritingDirection.
NSVerticalGlyphFormAttributeName	An NSNumber representing either horizontal text (0) or vertical text (1).

NSLayoutManagerDelegate

NSLayoutManager also has an associated delegate that can be used to handle how the text is rendered. One of the most useful sets of methods deals with the handling of line fragments that can be used to specify exactly how the line and paragraphs break. Additionally, methods are available when the text has finished rendering.

NSTextContainer

The NSTextContainer is another important new addition to iOS 7's TextKit. An NSTextContainer defines a region in which text is laid out; NSLayoutManagers discussed in the preceding section can control multiple NSTextContainers. NSTextContainers have support for number of lines, text wrapping, and resizing in a text view. Additional support for exclusion paths is discussed later in the section "Exclusion Paths."

Detecting Links Dynamically

Dynamic Link Detection is extremely easy to implement and provides a great user experience if the user is working with addresses, URLs, phone numbers, or dates in a text view. The easiest way to turn on these properties is through Interface Builder (shown in Figure 22.2).

Figure 22.2   Dynamic Link Detection controls in Xcode 6.

These properties can also be toggled on and off using code.

```
[textView setDataDetectorTypes: UIDataDetectorTypePhoneNumber |
➡UIDataDetectorTypeLink | UIDataDetectorTypeAddress |
➡UIDataDetectorTypeCalendarEvent];
```

TexKit added a new delegate method as part of UITextViewDelegate to intercept the launching of events. The following example detects the launch URL event on a URL and provides an alert to the user:

```
- (BOOL)textView:(UITextView *)textView shouldInteractWithURL:(NSURL
➡*)URL inRange:(NSRange)characterRange
{
```

```
toBeLaunchedURL = URL;

if([[URL absoluteString] hasPrefix:@"http://"])
{
    UIAlertView *alert = [[UIAlertView alloc]
    ➥initWithTitle:@"URL Launching" message:[NSString
    ➥stringWithFormat:@"About to launch %@", [URL
    ➥absoluteString]] delegate:self
    ➥cancelButtonTitle:@"Cancel"
    ➥otherButtonTitles:@"Launch", nil];

    [alert show];
    return NO;
}

return YES;
}
```

Detecting Hits

Hit detection has traditionally been complex to implement and often required for elaborate text-driven apps. TextKit added support for per-character hit detection. To support this functionality, a subclassed `UITextView` is created, called `ICFCustomTextView` in the sample project. The `UITextView` implements a `touchesBegan:` event method.

When a touch begins, the location in the view is captured and it is adjusted down the y axis by ten to line up with the text elements. A method is invoked on the `layoutManager` that is a property of the text view, `characterIndexForPoint: inTextContainer: fractionOf-DistanceBetweenInsertionPoints:`. This returns the index of the character that was selected.

After the character index has been determined, the beginning and end of the word that it is contained within are calculated by searching forward and backward for the next whitespace character. The full word is then displayed in a `UIAlertView` to the user.

```
- (void)touchesBegan:(NSSet *)touches withEvent:(UIEvent *)event
{
    UITouch *touch = [touches anyObject];
    CGPoint touchPoint = [touch locationInView:self];

    touchPoint.y -= 10;

    NSInteger characterIndex = [self.layoutManager
    ➥characterIndexForPoint:touchPoint
    ➥inTextContainer:self.textContainer
    ➥fractionOfDistanceBetweenInsertionPoints:0];
```

```objc
if(characterIndex != 0)
{
    NSRange start = [self.text
    ➥rangeOfCharacterFromSet:[NSCharacterSet
    ➥whitespaceAndNewlineCharacterSet]
    ➥options:NSBackwardsSearch range:NSMakeRange(0,characterIndex)];

    NSRange stop = [self.text rangeOfCharacterFromSet:
    ➥[NSCharacterSet whitespaceAndNewlineCharacterSet]
    ➥options:NSCaseInsensitiveSearch
    ➥range:NSMakeRange(characterIndex,self.text.length-
    ➥characterIndex)];

    int length =  stop.location - start.location;

    NSString *fullWord = [self.text
    ➥substringWithRange:NSMakeRange (start.location, length)];


    UIAlertView *alert = [[UIAlertView alloc]
    ➥initWithTitle:@"Selected Word"
    ➥message:fullWord
    ➥delegate:nil
    ➥cancelButtonTitle:@"Dismiss"
    ➥otherButtonTitles: nil];

    [alert show];
}

[super touchesBegan: touches withEvent: event];
}
```

Exclusion Paths

Exclusion Paths (shown in Figure 22.3) enable text to wrap around images or other objects that appear inline. TextKit added a simple property in order to add an exclusion path to any text container.

Figure 22.3   Text wrapping around a UIImage using iOS 7's exclusion paths.

To specify an exclusion path, a `UIBezierPath` representing the area to be excluded is first created. To set an exclusion path, an array of the avoided areas is passed to the `exclusion-Paths` property of a `textContainer`. The text container can be found as a property of the `UITextView`.

```
- (void)viewDidLoad
{
    [super viewDidLoad];

    UIBezierPath *circle = [UIBezierPath
    bezierPathWithOvalInRect:CGRectMake(110, 100, 100, 102)];

    UIImageView *imageView = [[UIImageView alloc]
    initWithFrame:CGRectMake(110, 110, 100, 102)];

    [imageView setImage: [UIImage imageNamed: @"DF.png"]];
    [imageView setContentMode:UIViewContentModeScaleToFill];
    [self.myTextView addSubview: imageView];

    self.myTextView.textContainer.exclusionPaths = @[circle];
}
```

Content Specific Highlighting

One of the most interesting features of TextKit is Content Specific Highlighting. Before iOS 7, using CoreText to modify the appearance of specific strings inside of a text view was elaborate and cumbersome. TextKit brings many improvements to rich text rendering and definition.

To work with custom attributed text, a subclass of an NSTextStorage is created, called ICFDynamicTextStorage in the sample project. This approach will enable the developer to set tokens for different attributed strings to be rendered per string encountered. A classwide NSMutableAttributedString is created, which will hold on to all the associated attributes for the displayed text.

```objc
- (id)init
{
    self = [super init];

    if (self)
    {
        backingStore = [[NSMutableAttributedString alloc] init];
    }

    return self;
}
```

A convenience method for returning the string is also created, as well as one for returning the attributes at an index.

```objc
- (NSString *)string
{
    return [backingStore string];
}

- (NSDictionary *)attributesAtIndex:(NSUInteger)location
➡effectiveRange:(NSRangePointer)range
{
    return [backingStore attributesAtIndex:location
        ➡effectiveRange:range];
}
```

The next four methods deal with the actual inputting and setting of attributes, from replacing the characters to making sure that text is being properly updated.

```objc
- (void)replaceCharactersInRange:(NSRange)range withString:(NSString
➡*)str
{
    [self beginEditing];
    [backingStore replaceCharactersInRange:range withString:str];
```

```
    [self edited:NSTextStorageEditedCharacters|
    ➥NSTextStorageEditedAttributes range:range
    ➥changeInLength:str.length - range.length];

    textNeedsUpdate = YES;
    [self endEditing];
}

- (void)setAttributes:(NSDictionary *)attrs range:(NSRange)range
{
    [self beginEditing];
    [backingStore setAttributes:attrs range:range];

    [self edited:NSTextStorageEditedAttributes range:range
    ➥changeInLength:0];

    [self endEditing];
}

- (void)performReplacementsForCharacterChangeInRange:
➥(NSRange)changedRange
{
    NSRange extendedRange = NSUnionRange(changedRange, [[self
    ➥string] lineRangeForRange:NSMakeRange(changedRange.location,
    ➥0)]);

    extendedRange = NSUnionRange(changedRange, [[self string]
    ➥lineRangeForRange:NSMakeRange(NSMaxRange(changedRange), 0)]);

    [self applyTokenAttributesToRange:extendedRange];
}

- (void)processEditing
{
    if(textNeedsUpdate)
    {
        textNeedsUpdate = NO;
        [self performReplacementsForCharacterChangeInRange:[self
        ➥editedRange]];
    }

    [super processEditing];
}
```

The last method in the subclassed `NSTextStore` applies the actual tokens that will be set using a property on the `NSTextStore` to the string. The tokens are passed as an `NSDictionary`, which defines the substring they should be applied for. When the substring is detected using the `enumerateSubstringsInRange:` method, the attribute is applied using the previous `addAttribute:range:` method. This system also allows for default tokens to be set when a specific attribute has not been set.

```
- (void)applyTokenAttributesToRange:(NSRange)searchRange
{
    NSDictionary *defaultAttributes = [self.tokens
    ➥objectForKey:defaultTokenName];

    [[self string] enumerateSubstringsInRange:searchRange
    ➥options:NSStringEnumerationByWords usingBlock:^(NSString
    ➥*substring, NSRange substringRange, NSRange enclosingRange,
    ➥BOOL *stop)
    {
        NSDictionary *attributesForToken = [self.tokens
        ➥objectForKey:substring];

        if(!attributesForToken)
        {
            attributesForToken = defaultAttributes;
        }

        [self addAttributes:attributesForToken
        ➥range:substringRange];

    }];
}
```

After the subclass of `NSTextStore` is created, modifying text itself becomes fairly trivial, the results of which are shown in Figure 22.4. A new instance of the customized text store is allocated and initialized, followed by a new instance of `NSLayoutManager`, and lastly an `NSTextContainer` is created. The text container is set to share its frame and bounds with the text view, and is then added to the `layoutManager`. The text store then adds the layout manager.

A new `NSTextView` is created and set to the frame of the view, and its text container is set to the previously created one. Next, the auto-resizing mask for the text view is configured to be scalable for screen sizes and other adjustments. Finally, scrolling and keyboard behavior for the text view are configured, and the text view is added as a subview of the main view.

The `tokens` property of the customized text field is used to set a dictionary of dictionaries for the attributes to be assigned to each substring encountered. The first example, `Mary`, will set the `NSForegroundColorAttributeName` attribute to red. A complete list of attributes was given earlier, in Table 22.1. The sample demonstrates multiple types of attributes on various keywords. The example for `was` shows how to add multiple attributes together using a custom font, color, and underlining the text. A default token is also set that specifies how text not specifically assigned will be displayed.

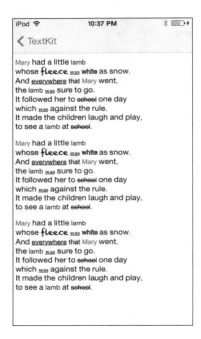

Figure 22.4   Content Specific Highlighting showing updated attributes for several keywords.

After the attributes have been set, some static text is added to the text view in the form of the poem "Mary Had a Little Lamb"; the resulting attributed text appears in Figure 22.4. Typing into the text view will update the attributes in real time and can be seen by typing out any of the substrings in which special attributes were configured.

```
- (void)viewDidLoad
{
    [super viewDidLoad];

    ICFDynamicTextStorage *textStorage = [[ICFDynamicTextStorage
    ➥alloc] init];

    NSLayoutManager *layoutManager = [[NSLayoutManager alloc] init];

    NSTextContainer *container = [[NSTextContainer alloc]
    ➥initWithSize:CGSizeMake(myTextView.frame.size.width,
    ➥CGFLOAT_MAX)];
```

```
container.widthTracksTextView = YES;
[layoutManager addTextContainer:container];
[textStorage addLayoutManager:layoutManager];

myTextView = [[UITextView alloc] initWithFrame:self.view.frame
➥textContainer:container];

myTextView.autoresizingMask = UIViewAutoresizingFlexibleHeight |
➥UIViewAutoresizingFlexibleWidth;

myTextView.scrollEnabled = YES;

myTextView.keyboardDismissMode =
UIScrollViewKeyboardDismissModeOnDrag;

[self.view addSubview:myTextView];

textStorage.tokens = @{ @"Mary":@{ NSForegroundColorAttributeName:
➥[UIColor redColor]},
➥@"lamb":@{ NSForegroundColorAttributeName:[UIColor blueColor]},
➥@"everywhere":@{ NSUnderlineStyleAttributeName:@1},
➥@"that":@{NSBackgroundColorAttributeName : [UIColor yellowColor]},
➥@"fleece":@{NSFontAttributeName:[UIFont
➥fontWithName:@"Chalkduster" size:14.0f]},
➥@"school":@{NSStrikethroughStyleAttributeName:@1},
➥@"white":@{NSStrokeWidthAttributeName:@5},
➥@"was":@{NSFontAttributeName:[UIFont fontWithName:@"Palatino-Bold"
➥size:10.0f], NSForegroundColorAttributeName:[UIColor purpleColor],
➥NSUnderlineStyleAttributeName:@1}, defaultTokenName:@{
➥NSForegroundColorAttributeName : [UIColor blackColor],
➥NSFontAttributeName: [UIFont systemFontOfSize:14.0f],
➥NSUnderlineStyleAttributeName : @0,
➥NSBackgroundColorAttributeName : [UIColor whiteColor],
➥NSStrikethroughStyleAttributeName : @0,
➥NSStrokeWidthAttributeName : @0}};

NSString *maryText = @"Mary had a little lamb\nwhose fleece was
➥white as snow.\nAnd everywhere that Mary went,\nthe lamb was sure
➥to go.\nIt followed her to school one day\nwhich was against the
➥rule.\nIt made the children laugh and play,\nto see a lamb at
➥school.";

[myTextView setText:[NSString stringWithFormat:@"%@\n\n%@\n\n%@",
➥maryText, maryText, maryText]];
}
```

Changing Font Settings with Dynamic Type

TextKit brings support for Dynamic Type, which enables the user to specify a font size at an OS level. Users can access the Dynamic Type controls under the General section of iOS 8's Settings. app (shown in Figure 22.5). When the user changes the preferred font size, the app will receive a notification named `UIContentSizeCategoryDidChangeNotification`. This notification should be monitored to handle updating the font size.

Figure 22.5   Changing the systemwide font size using Dynamic Type settings in iOS 7's Settings app.

```
[[NSNotificationCenter defaultCenter] addObserver:self
➥selector:@selector(preferredSizeDidChange:)
➥name:UIContentSizeCategoryDidChangeNotification object:nil];
```

To display text at the user's preferred font settings, the font should be set using one of the attributes from Font Text Styles, which are described in Table 22.2.

```
self.textLabel.font = [UIFont
➥preferredFontForTextStyle:UIFontTextStyleBody];
```

This returns a properly sized font based on the user settings.

Table 22.2   **Font Text Styles as Defined in iOS 7**

Attribute	Description
UIFontTextStyleHeadline1	A first-order headline
UIFontTextStyleHeadline2	A second-order headline
UIFontTextStyleBody	Body text
UIFontTextStyleSubheadline1	A first-order subheadline
UIFontTextStyleSubheadline2	A second-order subheadline
UIFontTextStyleFootnote	A footnote
UIFontTextStyleCaption1	A standard caption
UIFontTextStyleCaption2	An alternative caption

Summary

Text rendering on iOS is a deep and complex topic made vastly easier with the introduction of TextKit. This chapter merely broke the surface of what is possible with TextKit and text rendering on the iOS platform in general. Hopefully, it has created a topic not nearly as intimidating as text render has been in the past.

Several examples were explored in this chapter, from hit detection to working with attributed strings. In addition, the building blocks that make up text rendering objects should now be much clearer. Although text rendering is a vast topic, worthy of its own dedicated book, the information in this chapter should provide a strong foot forward.

Gesture Recognizers

What if an app needed a quick and easy way to handle taps, swipes, pinches, and rotations? Back in the Dark Ages (before the iPad was released), a developer had to subclass UIView, implement the touchesBegan:/touchesMoved:/touchesEnded: methods, and write custom logic to determine when any of these actions was taking place. It could take all day!

Apple introduced gesture recognizers to address this need with iOS 3.2 when the original iPad was released. UIGestureRecognizer is an abstract class that puts a common architecture around handling gestures. There are several concrete implementations to handle the everyday gestures that are commonly used, and even subclassing guidelines to create your own gestures using the same architecture. With these new classes, complex gesture handling can be implemented much more quickly than in the past.

Types of Gesture Recognizers

Gesture recognizers fall into two general categories, as defined by Apple:

- **Discrete:** Discrete gesture recognizers are intended to handle cases in which the interaction is quick and simple, like a tap. In that case, the app really needs to know only that the tap occurred, and then can complete the desired action.

- **Continuous:** Continuous gesture recognizers handle cases in which the interaction needs to keep getting information as the gesture proceeds, as in a pinch or rotation. In those cases, the app will likely require information during the interaction to handle UI changes. For example, it might need to know how far a user has pinched so that it can resize a view accordingly, or it might want to know how far a user has rotated her fingers and rotate a view to match.

Six predefined gesture recognizers are available, as listed in Table 23.1. They are versatile and can handle all the standard touch interactions that are familiar in iOS.

Table 23.1   **List of Built-In `UIGestureRecognizer` Subclasses**

Class Name	Type
UITapGestureRecognizer	Discrete
UIPinchGestureRecognizer	Continuous
UIPanGestureRecognizer	Continuous
UISwipeGestureRecognizer	Discrete
UIRotationGestureRecognizer	Continuous
UILongPressGestureRecognizer	Continuous

Basic Gesture Recognizer Usage

A basic gesture recognizer is simple to set up. Typically, a gesture recognizer would be set up in a view controller where there is visibility to the view of interest, and a logical place to put a method that can accomplish what is wanted. All that needs to be determined is what view the tap recognizer should belong to, and what method should be called for the recognizer.

```
UITapGestureRecognizer *tapRecognizer =
➥[[UITapGestureRecognizer alloc] initWithTarget:self
➥action:@selector(myGestureViewTapped:)];

[myGestureView addGestureRecognizer:tapRecognizer];
```

Some gesture recognizers will accept more parameters to refine how they act, but for the most part, only a view and a method are needed to get going. When the gesture has been recognized in the specified view, the method will get called with a reference to the gesture recognizer if desired.

Gesture recognizers can also be set up easily in a storyboard. To add a gesture recognizer, first find the desired recognizer type in the Object Library while viewing the storyboard. Drag the recognizer to the view that should receive and interpret touches for the gesture recognizer. When the recognizer is added to that view, it will appear in the bar for the view controller's scene. The gesture recognizer can then be configured like any other view in a storyboard, as shown in Figure 23.1. It can be assigned to a property, it can be assigned an action selector to call, or it can even be set up to trigger a segue.

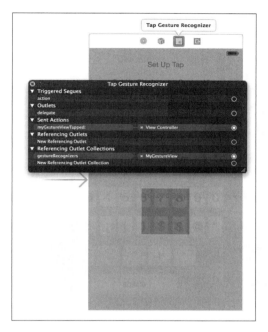

Figure 23.1   Example of a configured Tap Gesture Recognizer in a storyboard.

Introduction to the Sample App

The sample app for this chapter is called Gesture Playground. It has only one view, called myGestureView (shown in Figure 23.2), which will be manipulated by the gestures as they are introduced in the chapter. Tap the related button to configure the gesture recognizers for each example. Note that the sample project uses a storyboard with AutoLayout disabled; this is to make the examples simple and easy to understand and avoid any potential issues with layout changes to illustrate responding to gestures. To get started, open the project in Xcode.

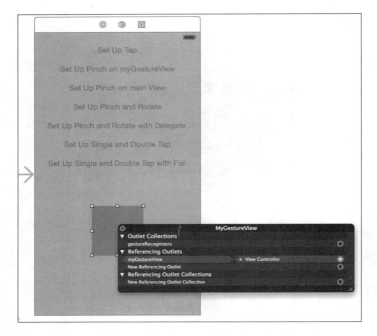

Figure 23.2   View of Gesture Playground's view controller in a storyboard.

Tap Recognizer in Action

The code to set up the tap gesture recognizer is in the `setUpTapGestureRecognizer:` method in the sample app's view controller. To execute that code, run the app and tap the button titled Set Up Tap. The method will first clear all gesture recognizers from the main view and `myGestureView`. Then a tap recognizer will be set up to call the `myGestureTapped:` method when a tap is recognized.

```
[self clearAllGestureRecognizers];

UITapGestureRecognizer *tapRecognizer =
➥[[UITapGestureRecognizer alloc] initWithTarget:self
                                   action:@selector(myGestureViewTapped:)];

[self.myGestureView addGestureRecognizer:tapRecognizer];
```

Because the tap gesture is a discrete gesture, the `myGestureViewTapped:` method will get called only after the gesture has been recognized. It will then present an alert:

```
- (void)myGestureViewTapped:(UIGestureRecognizer *)tapGestureRecognizer {
```

```
UIAlertController *alert =
➥[UIAlertController alertControllerWithTitle:@"Tap Received"
                                      message:@"Received tap in myGestureView"
                               preferredStyle:UIAlertControllerStyleAlert];

UIAlertAction *dismissAction =
➥[UIAlertAction actionWithTitle:@"OK, Thanks"
                          style:UIAlertActionStyleCancel
                        handler:^(UIAlertAction *action){
    [self dismissViewControllerAnimated:YES completion:nil];
}];

[alert addAction:dismissAction];

[self presentViewController:alert animated:YES completion:nil];
}
```

Run the project and tap anywhere inside the red view. An alert view will be presented, as shown in Figure 23.3.

Figure 23.3   Single tap received.

Try tapping around the outside of the view. Notice that the alert view does not get displayed unless a tap actually occurs in the view.

Tap Recognizer Versus Button

So why couldn't a button be used for that? It's quicker and easier, and could be set up in Interface Builder with no code! True. In a lot of cases, using a `UIButton` is the best approach. However, there are times when a tap recognizer is ideal. One example is when there are several input text fields that need to slide up and down with the keyboard, and you want to be able to tap anywhere to dismiss the keyboard. If you place all the fields in a `UIView`, a tap recognizer can be added to that view to easily dismiss the keyboard.

Pinch Recognizer in Action

A pinch recognizer can be used to handle the case in which the user puts two fingers on the screen and moves them closer together or farther apart. The change of distance between the fingers can then be used, for example, to adjust the size of a view or an image. In the sample app, tap Set Up Pinch on myGestureView to add a pinch gesture recognizer to the view. The method called will clear any existing gesture recognizers, and will then add a pinch gesture recognizer to myGestureView, and associate the myGestureViewSoloPinched: method as the target action for the gesture.

```
UIPinchGestureRecognizer *soloPinchRecognizer =
➥[[UIPinchGestureRecognizer alloc] initWithTarget:self
➥action:@selector(myGestureViewSoloPinched:)];

[myGestureView addGestureRecognizer:soloPinchRecognizer];
```

The method will have to inspect the pinch gesture recognizer to know how far a user has pinched. Happily, iOS will pass a reference to the gesture recognizer to the method, so an instance variable or property is not needed to store it. `UIPinchGestureRecognizer` instances also have a method called `scale`, which turns out to be perfect for setting up a scale affine transform on a view:

```
- (void)myGestureViewSoloPinched:(UIPinchGestureRecognizer *)
➥pinchGesture {
    CGFloat pinchScale = [pinchGesture scale];

    CGAffineTransform scaleTransform =
    ➥CGAffineTransformMakeScale(pinchScale, pinchScale);

    [myGestureView setTransform:scaleTransform];
}
```

Run the project, pinch in and out over the view, and note that it resizes with the pinch.

> **Note**
>
> To perform a two-finger pinch in the iOS Simulator, hold down the Option key and notice that two circles appear, which represent fingers. As the mouse pointer is moved, the fingers will get closer or farther apart. The center point between the fingers will be the center of the app's view. In Gesture Playground, this is a little inconvenient, because `myGestureView` is near the bottom of the screen. To reposition the center point, just hold down the Shift key while still holding the Option key and move the mouse pointer.

What if the view is small and hard to pinch? Add the gesture recognizer to the parent view, and it will pick up the pinch anywhere in that view. To see that approach working, tap the Set Up Pinch on main View button. That will clear all existing gesture recognizers, and will add the pinch gesture recognizer to the view controller's view so that pinches anywhere in the view will get picked up:

```
UIPinchGestureRecognizer *soloPinchRecognizer =
➡[[UIPinchGestureRecognizer alloc] initWithTarget:self
➡action:@selector(myGestureViewSoloPinched:)];

[[self view] addGestureRecognizer:soloPinchRecognizer];
```

Run the project and notice that pinches anywhere in the app will scale `myGestureView`. That is one of gesture recognizer's underrated features: the capability to easily decouple the touch action from the view to be affected. A touch can be detected anywhere in the app, and the touch data can be used or transformed to affect other views. To be more precise with this method, the touch location for the gestures can be examined using the `locationInView:` method, to determine whether it is close enough to the view to process.

Multiple Recognizers for a View

There are times when more than one recognizer will be needed on a view, for example, if the user wants to be able to scale and rotate `myGestureView` at the same time. To illustrate this, the sample app adds a rotation gesture recognizer to see how it interacts with a pinch gesture recognizer. Tap the Set Up Pinch and Rotate button, which will clear all existing gesture recognizers and then set up both the pinch recognizer and the rotation gesture recognizer:

```
UIPinchGestureRecognizer *pinchRecognizer =
➡[[UIPinchGestureRecognizer alloc] initWithTarget:self
➡action:@selector(myGestureViewPinched:)];

[myGestureView addGestureRecognizer:pinchRecognizer];

UIRotationGestureRecognizer *rotateRecognizer =
➡[[UIRotationGestureRecognizer alloc] initWithTarget:self
➡action:@selector(myGestureViewRotated:)];

[myGestureView addGestureRecognizer:rotateRecognizer];
```

Now, to handle both rotation and scaling at the same time, a new approach to build a concatenated affine transform to apply to `myGestureView` is needed. For that method to work, the
last and current scale and rotation factors will need to be stored so that nothing is lost between
gestures. Notice that these properties have been established in the view controller.

```
@property (nonatomic, assign) CGFloat scaleFactor;
@property (nonatomic, assign) CGFloat rotationFactor;
@property (nonatomic, assign) CGFloat currentScaleDelta;
@property (nonatomic, assign) CGFloat currentRotationDelta;
```

The `setUpPinchAndRotationGestureRecognizers:` method will initialize the `scaleFactor`
and `rotationFactor` to prevent flickering when the view is initially resized.

```
[self setScaleFactor:1.0];
[self setRotationFactor:0.0];
```

The `myGestureViewRotated:` method will handle the rotation recognizer, which conveniently
has a property called `rotation` to let you know how far the user has rotated his fingers:

```
- (void)myGestureViewRotated:(UIRotationGestureRecognizer *)
➥rotateGesture {
    CGFloat newRotateRadians = [rotateGesture rotation];

    [self updateViewTransformWithScaleDelta:0.0
    ➥andRotationDelta:newRotateRadians];
    if ([rotateGesture state] == UIGestureRecognizerStateEnded) {
        CGFloat saveRotation = [selfrotationFactor] +
        ➥newRotateRadians;
        [self setRotationFactor:saveRotation];
        [self setCurrentRotationDelta:0.0];
    }
}
```

This method will get the amount of rotation from the gesture recognizer, expressed in radians.
It will then call a custom method to create a scale and rotate affine transformation to apply to
the view. If the touch is ended, the method will calculate the last rotation amount based on
the current state and new rotation amount, and save it in the rotation factor property. Then
the method will clear the calculated rotation delta amount, which is used to keep the rotation
transformation from getting out of whack between touches. The method to create the scale and
rotate transformation looks like this:

```
- (void)updateViewTransformWithScaleDelta:(CGFloat)scaleDelta
➥andRotationDelta:(CGFloat)rotationDelta;
{
    if (rotationDelta != 0) {
        [self setCurrentRotationDelta:rotationDelta];
    }
    if (scaleDelta != 0) {
        [self setCurrentScaleDelta:scaleDelta];
```

```
    }
    CGFloat scaleAmount = [self scaleFactor]+[self currentScaleDelta];

    CGAffineTransform scaleTransform =
    ➥CGAffineTransformMakeScale(scaleAmount, scaleAmount);

    CGFloat rotationAmount =
    ➥[self rotationFactor]+[self currentRotationDelta];

    CGAffineTransform rotateTransform =
    ➥CGAffineTransformMakeRotation(rotationAmount);

    CGAffineTransform newTransform =
    ➥CGAffineTransformConcat(scaleTransform, rotateTransform);

    [myGestureView setTransform:newTransform];
}
```

This method will properly account for scale changes and rotation changes from touches. The method will check to see whether the amount of scale or rotation change is not equal to zero, since the gesture recognizer will return the scale or rotation as the amount of change from where the touch began. That amount is called the delta. Since the view should maintain its current state when a touch begins, the method cannot immediately apply the reported touch delta; rather, it must add the delta to the current state to prevent the view from jumping around.

Run Gesture Playground, touch with two fingers and rotate, and watch how the view turns. Also note that pinching still works, but that pinching and rotating at the same time does not. This is explained later in the chapter. First a bit more about how gesture recognizers handle touches.

Gesture Recognizers: Under the Hood

Now that basic gesture recognizers have been demonstrated in action and the first issue has been encountered with them, it is a good time to walk through, in a little more detail, how gesture recognizers work.

The first thing to understand is that gesture recognizers operate outside the normal view responder chain. The UIWindow will send touch events to gesture recognizers first, and they must indicate that they cannot handle the event in order for touches to get forwarded to the view responder chain by default.

Next, it is important to understand the basic sequence of events that takes place when an app is trying to determine whether a gesture has been recognized:

1. The window will send touch events to the gesture recognizer(s).

2. The gesture recognizer will enter the UIGestureRecognizerStatePossible state.

3. For discrete gestures, the gesture recognizer will determine whether the gesture is `UIGestureRecognizerStateRecognized` or `UIGestureRecognizerStateFailed`.

4. If it is `UIGestureRecognizerStateRecognized`, the gesture recognizer consumes that touch event and calls the delegate method specified.

5. If it is `UIGestureRecognizerStateFailed`, the gesture recognizer forwards the touch event back to the responder chain.

6. For continuous gestures, the gesture recognizer will determine whether the gesture is `UIGestureRecognizerStateBegan` or `UIGestureRecognizerStateFailed`.

7. If the gesture is `UIGestureRecognizerStateBegan`, the gesture recognizer consumes the touch events and calls the delegate method specified. It will then update to `UIGestureRecognizerStateChanged` every time there is a change in the gesture and keep calling the delegate method until the last touch ends, at which point it will become `UIGestureRecognizerStateEnded`. If the touch pattern no longer matches the expected gesture, it can change to `UIGestureRecognizerStateCancelled`.

8. If it is `UIGestureRecognizerStateFailed`, the gesture recognizer forwards the touch event(s) back to the responder chain.

Note that the time elapsed between `UIGestureRecognizerStatePossible` and `UIGestureRecognizerStateFailed` states can be significant and noticeable. If there is a gesture recognizer in the user interface that is experiencing an unexplained slowdown with touches, that is a good place to look. The best approach is to add logging into the gesture handling methods—log the method and state each time the method is called. Then, there will be a clear picture of the state transitions with time stamps from the logging so that it is clear where any delays are taking place.

Multiple Recognizers for a View: Redux

Now that the chapter has explained how the gesture recognizers receive and handle touches, it is clear that only one of the gesture recognizers is receiving and handling touches at a time. To get them both to handle touches simultaneously, there is a `UIGestureRecognizerDelegate` protocol that can be implemented to have a little more control over how touches are delivered to gesture recognizers. This protocol specifies three methods:

- **(BOOL) gestureRecognizerShouldBegin:(UIGestureRecognizer *) gestureRecognizer:** Use this method to indicate whether the gesture recognizer should transition from `UIGestureRecognizerStatePossible` to `UIGestureRecognizerStateBegan`, depending on the state of the application. If `YES` is returned, the gesture recognizer will proceed; otherwise, it will transition to `UIGestureRecognizerStateFailed`.

- **(BOOL)gestureRecognizer:(UIGestureRecognizer *)gestureRecognizer shouldReceiveTouch:(UITouch *)touch:** Use this method to indicate whether the gesture recognizer should receive a touch. This provides the opportunity to prevent a gesture recognizer from receiving a touch based on developer-defined criteria.

- **(BOOL)gestureRecognizer:(UIGestureRecognizer *)gestureRecognizer shouldRecognizeSimultaneouslyWithGestureRecognizer:(UIGestureRecognizer *)otherGestureRecognizer:** Use this method when there is more than one gesture recognizer that should simultaneously receive touches. Return YES to have everything operate simultaneously, or test the incoming gesture recognizers to decide whether they meet criteria for simultaneous handling.

The sample app implements the `shouldRecognizeSimultaneouslyWithGestureRecognizer:` method to enable the pinch and rotation gestures to be handled simultaneously:

```
- (BOOL)gestureRecognizer:(UIGestureRecognizer *)gestureRecognizer
➥shouldRecognizeSimultaneouslyWithGestureRecognizer:
(UIGestureRecognizer *)otherGestureRecognizer
{
    return YES;
}
```

To see this working, tap the Set Up Pinch and Rotate with Delegate button in the sample app. That method will set up the pinch and rotate gesture recognizers just as before, but will also set the delegates on them so that the `shouldRecognizeSimultaneouslyWithGesture-Recognizer:` method will get called.

```
UIPinchGestureRecognizer *pinchRecognizer =
➥[[UIPinchGestureRecognizer alloc] initWithTarget:self
➥action:@selector(myGestureViewPinched:)];

[pinchRecognizer setDelegate:self];
[[self view] addGestureRecognizer:pinchRecognizer];

UIRotationGestureRecognizer *rotateRecognizer =
➥[[UIRotationGestureRecognizer alloc] initWithTarget:self
➥action:@selector(myGestureViewRotated:)];

[rotateRecognizer setDelegate:self];
[[self view] addGestureRecognizer:rotateRecognizer];
```

Run Gesture Playground and touch with two fingers to pinch and rotate. The view will now resize and rotate smoothly (see Figure 23.4).

Figure 23.4   Simultaneously rotating and scaling.

Requiring Gesture Recognizer Failures

In some cases, a gesture recognizer needs to fail in order to meet an app's requirements. A great example is when a tap and a double tap need to work on the same view. By default, if a single-tap gesture recognizer and a double-tap gesture recognizer are attached to the same view, the single-tap recognizer will fire even if a double tap occurs—so both the single-tap and the double-tap target methods will get called. To see this in action in the sample app, tap the Set Up Single and Double Tap button. The called method will clear all existing gesture recognizers, and will set up and configure two tap gesture recognizers attached to myGestureView.

```
UITapGestureRecognizer *doubleTapRecognizer =
➥[[UITapGestureRecognizer alloc] initWithTarget:self
➥action:@selector(myGestureViewDoubleTapped:)];

[doubleTapRecognizer setNumberOfTapsRequired:2];
[myGestureView addGestureRecognizer:doubleTapRecognizer];

UITapGestureRecognizer *singleTapRecognizer =
➥[[UITapGestureRecognizer alloc] initWithTarget:self
➥action:@selector(myGestureViewTapped:)];

[myGestureView addGestureRecognizer:singleTapRecognizer];
```

Note that the handling methods now being called in the project are using `NSLog` statements for illustration instead of `UIAlertView`, which will block the user interface and prevent the double tap from working.

```
- (void)myGestureViewSingleTapped:(UIGestureRecognizer *)
➥tapGestureRecognizer {
    NSLog(@"Single Tap Received");
}


- (void)myGestureViewDoubleTapped:(UIGestureRecognizer *)
➥doubleTapGestureRecognizer {
    NSLog(@"Double Tap Received");
}
```

Both the single-tap and the double-tap methods get called with a double tap:

```
2014-08-04 14:00:45.299 GesturePlayground[38536:2398989] Single Tap Received
2014-08-04 14:00:45.476 GesturePlayground[38536:2398989] Double Tap Received
```

If that is not desired, the double-tap recognizer would need to fail before calling the single-tap target method. There is a method on `UIGestureRecognizer` called `requireGesture-RecognizerToFail`. To prevent both from firing, carry out these steps:

1. Set up the double-tap recognizer.

2. Set up the single-tap recognizer.

3. Call `requireGestureRecognizerToFail:` from the single-tap recognizer, passing the double-tap recognizer as the parameter.

To see this in action, tap the Set Up Single and Double Tap with Fail button in the sample app. That will set up the single- and double-tap gesture recognizers as before, but will also include the `requireGestureRecognizerToFail:` call for the single-tap gesture recognizer.

```
UITapGestureRecognizer *doubleTapRecognizer =
➥[[UITapGestureRecognizer alloc] initWithTarget:self
➥action:@selector(myGestureViewDoubleTapped:)];

[doubleTapRecognizer setNumberOfTapsRequired:2];
[myGestureView addGestureRecognizer:doubleTapRecognizer];

UITapGestureRecognizer *singleTapRecognizer =
➥[[UITapGestureRecognizer alloc] initWithTarget:self
➥action:@selector(myGestureViewTapped:)];

[singleTapRecognizer requireGestureRecognizerToFail:doubleTapRecognizer];

[myGestureView addGestureRecognizer:singleTapRecognizer];
```

Try it with a double tap first, and the single-tap method no longer fires on a double tap.

```
2014-08-04 14:03:39.137 GesturePlayground[38536:2398989] Double Tap Received
```

Custom `UIGestureRecognizer` Subclasses

When an app needs to recognize a gesture that falls outside of the standard gestures provided by Apple, `UIGestureRecognizer` needs to be subclassed. The first decision to be made is whether the custom recognizer should follow the discrete or continuous pattern. With that in mind, the subclass will need to implement the following methods:

```
- (void)reset;
- (void)touchesBegan:(NSSet *)touches withEvent:(UIEvent *)event;
- (void)touchesMoved:(NSSet *)touches withEvent:(UIEvent *)event;
- (void)touchesEnded:(NSSet *)touches withEvent:(UIEvent *)event;
- (void)touchesCancelled:(NSSet *)touches withEvent:(UIEvent *)event;
```

In the subclass, build logic in the `touchesBegan:`/`touchesMoved:`/`touchesEnded:` methods that recognize the gesture, and then update the subclass to the right state as the touches proceed. Remember to set the state to `UIGestureRecognizerStateFailed` as soon as possible to avoid UI delays, and to check the state in those methods to avoid doing any unnecessary logic. For example, if two touches are needed for the gesture, immediately fail in `touchesBegan:` if there are more or fewer touches. If the state is already `UIGestureRecognizerStateFailed`, return immediately from `touchesMoved:` and `touchesEnded:`.

In the reset method, update any instance variables used to track the gesture to their initial state so that the recognizer is ready to go with the next touch.

> **Note**
>
> For more detail on creating `UIGestureRecognizer` subclasses, check out Apple's Event Handling Guide for iOS: Gesture Recognizers at https://developer.apple.com/library/ios/documentation/EventHandling/Conceptual/EventHandlingiPhoneOS/GestureRecognizer_basics/GestureRecognizer_basics.html#//apple_ref/doc/uid/TP40009541-CH2-SW2. It has all the detail needed, and links to the relevant class references as well.

Summary

In this chapter, gesture recognizers were introduced, including the difference between a discrete and a continuous gesture recognizer, as were the six gesture recognizers that are available in iOS. This chapter walked through basic usage of a gesture recognizer, and then dived into some more advanced use cases with multiple gesture recognizers. Lastly, the concept of a custom gesture recognizer was introduced.

At this point, the reader should be comfortable creating and using the built-in gesture recognizers, and exploring some of the features that were not discussed (for example, how to handle a three-finger swipe). The reader should also understand the basics of how gesture recognizers work under the hood, and should be ready to attempt a custom subclass.

24

Accessing the Photo Library

All current iOS devices come with at least one camera capable of taking photos and videos. In addition, all iOS devices can sync photos from iTunes on a computer to the Photos app and organize them in albums. Before iOS 4, the only method for developers to access user photos was `UIImagePickerController`. This approach has some drawbacks; namely, only one photo can be selected at a time, and the developer has no control over the appearance of the UI. With the addition of the `AssetsLibrary` classes in iOS 4, Apple provided much more robust access to the user's photos, videos, albums, and events in an app. Although the `AssetsLibrary` classes were a big improvement over the `UIImagePickerController`, it was still difficult to navigate a large number of assets or get arbitrarily sized images with good performance. In addition, it was not simple (or in some cases possible) to manipulate the user's albums and maintain the images within an album.

To address these and other issues, Apple introduced the Photos framework with iOS 8. The Photos framework provides a robust, thread-safe way to access and administer the user's photo library. The Photos framework provides a method to retrieve arbitrarily sized versions of the images in the photo library, and provides a callback mechanism to notify a delegate when changes to the photo library have occurred. The Photos framework makes accessing photos in iCloud seamless as well; the same operations for accessing and updating the library work regardless of whether the photo is available locally on the device or remotely in iCloud.

The Sample App

The sample app, PhotoLibrary, is a minimal reproduction of some key parts of the iOS Photos app. It provides a tab bar to select between Photos and Albums. The Photos tab will display a collection view of all the images on the device, organized by moments. Tapping on a thumbnail will display a larger representation of the photo, and provide the opportunity to delete the photo from the device.

The Albums tab will display a table of the user-created albums available on the device, including the album name, number of photos, and a representative image. The user can add or remove albums from this view. Tapping an album will show thumbnails of all the photos in the album. Tapping a thumbnail will show a large representation of the photo.

Before running the sample app, prepare a test device by syncing some photos to it and taking some photos. That way, there will be photos in albums and the camera roll. If you use iCloud, turn on My Photo Stream as well.

> **Note**
>
> To use the Photos framework in an app, include `@import Photos;` in classes that need to access the Photos framework classes. This will automatically add the Photos framework to the project, and import the classes as needed.

The Photos Framework

The Photos framework consists of a group of classes to navigate and manage the collections, photos, and videos on the device. Here are some highlights:

- **PHPhotoLibrary:** This represents all the collections and assets on the device and iCloud. A shared instance (`[PHPhotoLibrary sharedPhotoLibrary]`) can be used to manage changes in a thread-safe way to the photo library, such as adding a new asset or album, or changing or removing an existing asset or album. In addition, the shared instance can be used to register an object as a listener for changes to the photo library, which can be used to keep the user interface in sync with asynchronous changes to the library.

- **PHAssetCollection:** This represents a group of photos and videos. It can be created locally on the device, can be synced from a photo album in iPhoto, can be the user's Camera Roll or Saved Photos album, or can be a smart album containing all photos that match a certain criteria (panoramas, for example). It provides methods for accessing assets in the group and getting information about the group. Asset collections can be organized in collection lists (`PHCollectionList`).

- **PHAsset:** This represents the metadata for a photo or video. It provides class methods to return fetch results to get assets with similar criteria, and provides instance methods with information about the asset, such as date, location, type, and orientation.

- **PHFetchResult:** This is a lightweight object that represents an array of assets or asset collections. When requesting assets or asset collections that match a given criteria, the class methods will return a fetch result. The fetch result will manage loading what is needed as requested instead of loading everything into memory at once, so it works very well for large collections of assets. The fetch result is also thread-safe, meaning that the count of objects will not change if changes to the underlying data occur. A class can register to be notified of changes to the photo library; and those changes, delivered in an instance of `PHFetchResultChangeDetails`, can be used to update a fetch result and any corresponding user interface.

- **PHImageManager:** The image manager handles asynchronously fetching and caching image data for an asset. This is especially useful for getting images that match a specific size, or for managing access to image data from iCloud. In addition, the photo library offers `PHCachingImageManager` to improve scrolling performance when viewing large numbers of assets in a table or collection view.

Using Asset Collections and Assets

Photos.app displays photos on the device organized by "moments"—or photos that took place on the same date in the same location. A moment is represented in the photo library by an instance of PHAssetCollection. Each image displayed for a moment is represented by an instance of PHAsset. User albums in Photos.app are also instances of PHAssetCollection, with images represented by PHAsset. Before accessing the asset collections and assets, an app needs to get the user's permission to access the photo library.

Permissions

The first time an app tries to access the photo library, the device asks the user for permission (as shown in Figure 24.1).

Figure 24.1   Access permission alert in the PhotoLibrary sample app.

To request permission, the app uses the requestAuthorization: class method on PHPhotoLibrary:

```
[PHPhotoLibrary requestAuthorization:^(PHAuthorizationStatus status) {
    if (status == PHAuthorizationStatusAuthorized) {
        [self loadAssetCollectionsForDisplay];
    } else {
```

```
        . . .
    }
}];
```

That method checks to see whether authorization has already been requested by the app. If not, it presents an alert to the user requesting permission to the photo library. After the user makes a selection, the user alert will occur only once every 24-hour period even if the app is deleted and reinstalled. To test responding to the user alert more than once a day, visit General, Reset in Settings.app, and select Reset Location & Privacy. That erases the system's memory of all location and privacy settings and requires responding to the user alert for all apps on the device.

If the user has already granted or denied permission, the alert will not be displayed again, and the user's selection will be returned. After the authorization status is known, the method calls the status handler block, passing in the current status. Note that the status handler can be called on a background thread, so be sure to switch to the main queue before updating the user interface.

If the user denies permission to access the photo library, the alert view presented explains to the user how to restore permission later if desired. To restore permissions, the user needs to navigate to the right spot in Settings.app (see Figure 24.2).

Figure 24.2   Settings.app: photo privacy.

When the user changes the setting, iOS kills the sample app so that it will launch again rather than coming out of the background and requiring an adjustment to the new privacy setting.

Asset Collections

When permission is granted, the app can now access the photo library to display moments, albums, and images. On the Photos tab in the sample app, the ICFPhotosCollectionViewController will get a list of the moments represented on the device with an instance of PHFetchResult in the loadAssetCollectionsForDisplay method:

```
PHFetchOptions *options = [[PHFetchOptions alloc] init];
options.sortDescriptors = @[[NSSortDescriptor sortDescriptorWithKey:@"startDate"
                                                           ascending:YES]];

self.collectionResult =
➡[PHAssetCollection fetchAssetCollectionsWithType:PHAssetCollectionTypeMoment
                                          subtype:PHAssetCollectionSubtypeAny
                                          options:options];
```

PHFetchResult can be used for both asset collections and assets. It acts like an NSArray, exposing methods such as objectAtIndex: and indexOfObject:, but it is smart enough to pull information about the results only when necessary. The method will then iterate over the moments from the fetch request, and store a fetch result instance in the property collection-AssetResults to get access to the assets in each moment.

```
self.collectionAssetResults =
[[NSMutableArray alloc] initWithCapacity:self.collectionResult.count];

for (PHAssetCollection *collection in self.collectionResult) {
    PHFetchResult *result = [PHAsset fetchAssetsInAssetCollection:collection
                                                          options:nil];
    [self.collectionAssetResults insertObject:result
    ➡atIndex:[self.collectionResult indexOfObject:collection]];
}
```

With the information available about the moments and assets, the view controller can now populate a collection view, showing a section header for each moment, and associated images in each section. For more information on collection views, refer to Chapter 21, "Collection Views." Determining the number of sections in the collection view is simple; the answer is just the count from the instance of PHFetchResult representing moments:

```
- (NSInteger)numberOfSectionsInCollectionView:(UICollectionView *)collectionView {
    return self.collectionResult.count;
}
```

Determining the number of items in a section requires looking up the fetch request for the assets in that section, and getting the count of results from it.

```
- (NSInteger)collectionView:(UICollectionView *)collectionView
    numberOfItemsInSection:(NSInteger)section {

    PHFetchResult *result =
    ➥(PHFetchResult *)[self.collectionAssetResults objectAtIndex:section];

    return result.count;
}
```

To display the dates and location information in the section header for a moment, the `collectionView:viewForSupplementaryElementOfKind:atIndexPath:` method gets the instance of `PHAssetCollection` representing the moment for the section indicated by the provided index path:

```
PHAssetCollection *moment = [self.collectionResult objectAtIndex:indexPath.section];

[headerView.titleLabel setText:
➥[NSString stringWithFormat:@"%@ - %@",
➥[self.momentDateFormatter stringFromDate:moment.startDate],
➥[self.momentDateFormatter stringFromDate:moment.endDate]]];

[headerView.subTitleLabel setText:moment.localizedTitle];
```

The method can then update the section header using the `startDate`, `endDate`, and `localizedTitle` properties from the `PHAssetCollection` instance to display the date range of the moment and the location of the moment (see Figure 24.3).

The Albums tab in the sample app displays any custom albums the user has added to the photo library in a table view, as shown in Figure 24.4. The list of albums is retrieved with a fetch result:

```
self.albumsFetchResult =
➥[PHAssetCollection fetchAssetCollectionsWithType:PHAssetCollectionTypeAlbum
                                subtype:PHAssetCollectionSubtypeAny
                                options:nil];
```

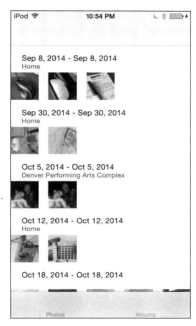

Figure 24.3   Moment Asset Collections in the PhotoLibrary sample app.

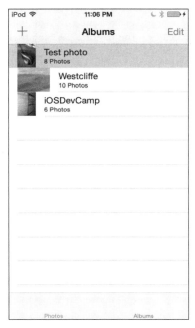

Figure 24.4   Albums in the PhotoLibrary sample app.

For each album in the table view, the `localizedTitle` is used to display the album name, and the count of assets in the album is determined using the `estimatedAssetCount` from the asset collection.

```
PHAssetCollection *album =
➡[self.albumsFetchResult objectAtIndex:indexPath.row];


[cell.textLabel setText:album.localizedTitle];


if (album.estimatedAssetCount != NSNotFound)
{
    NSString *albumPlural = album.estimatedAssetCount > 1 ? @"s" : @"";

    NSString *subTitle =
    ➡[NSString stringWithFormat:@"%lu Photo%@",
    ➡(unsigned long)album.estimatedAssetCount, albumPlural];

    [cell.detailTextLabel setText:subTitle];

} else
{
    [cell.detailTextLabel setText:@"-- empty --"];
}
```

When the user touches an album, the sample app will display all the assets for that album. Because the sample project uses storyboarding for navigation, a segue is set up from the table cell to the `ICFAlbumCollectionViewController`. The segue is named `showAlbum`. In `ICFAlbumCollectionViewController`, the `prepareForSegue:sender:` method sets up the destination view controller.

```
- (void)prepareForSegue:(UIStoryboardSegue *)segue sender:(id)sender {
    if ([segue.identifier isEqualToString:@"showAlbum"])
    {

        ICFAlbumCollectionViewController *controller =
        ➡(ICFAlbumCollectionViewController *)segue.destinationViewController;

        NSIndexPath *tappedPath = [self.tableView indexPathForSelectedRow];

        PHAssetCollection *tappedCollection =
        ➡[self.albumsFetchResult objectAtIndex:tappedPath.row];

        [controller setSelectedCollection:tappedCollection];
    }
}
```

The prepareForSegue:sender: method first checks that the segue's identifier is equal to showAlbum, since this method will be called for any segue set up for
ICFAlbumCollectionViewController. Then, it determines the index path for the tapped row
in the table, and uses the row to get the associated asset collection from the fetch result. It sets
the selected asset collection in the destination view controller, which will be used to display
the assets in the collection.

Assets

In the ICFPhotosCollectionViewController an asset needs to be accessed for each cell in
the collection view in order to display the asset's image. In collectionView:cellForItemAt-
IndexPath: the method will use the section of the indexPath to determine which fetch
result to look in for the asset, and then the row of the indexPath to get the specific asset.

```
PHFetchResult *result = self.collectionAssetResults[indexPath.section];
PHAsset *asset = result[indexPath.row];
```

The asset is metadata describing the image. An image representing the asset in a desired size
can be requested from the photo library. Since an image of the right size to display might not
be available immediately, it might be necessary to resize a local version or download a version
from iCloud. PHImageManager is designed to meet this need, and provide an image asynchronously to match what is needed for display. To request an image, provide a target size,
a content mode (see Chapter 20, "Working with Images and Filters," for more information
on content modes), options for the image fetching (PHImageRequestOptions), and a result
handler block. The method will return a PHImageRequestID, which can be used to cancel the
request.

```
__weak ICFPhotosCollectionViewCell *weakCell = cell;
PHImageManager *imageManager = [PHImageManager defaultManager];

PHImageRequestID requestID =
[imageManager requestImageForAsset:asset
                        targetSize:CGSizeMake(50, 50)
                       contentMode:PHImageContentModeAspectFill
                           options:nil
                     resultHandler:^(UIImage *result, NSDictionary *info){
                         [weakCell.assetImageView setImage:result];
                         [weakCell setNeedsLayout];
                     }];

cell.requestID = requestID;
```

The image manager will return a low-quality approximation of the image right away to the
resultHandler block if a local version is not available to the result handler (and will note
that the image is low quality by including the PHImageResultIsDegradedKey in the info
dictionary), and will call the result handler again with a higher-quality image when it is available. The result handler will be executed on the same queue that it was called on, so it is safe

to update the user interface without switching to the main queue if the request is made from the main queue. If the request is issued from a background queue, the synchronous property of PHImageRequestOptions can be set to YES to block the background queue until the request returns.

If the cell is scrolled off the screen before the image request can be fulfilled, the request can be cancelled in the prepareForReuse method of the cell:

```
- (void)prepareForReuse {
    self.assetImageView.image = nil;

    PHImageManager *imageManager = [PHImageManager defaultManager];
    [imageManager cancelImageRequest:self.requestID];
}
```

PHAsset instances are thread-safe, and can be passed around as needed. If the user taps a cell, a segue will fire to present a full-screen view of the asset.

```
- (void)prepareForSegue:(UIStoryboardSegue *)segue sender:(id)sender {
    if ([segue.identifier isEqualToString:@"showImage"]) {

        ICFAssetViewController *controller =
        ➡(ICFAssetViewController *)segue.destinationViewController;

        NSIndexPath *indexPath = [self.collectionView indexPathsForSelectedItems][0];
        PHFetchResult *result = self.collectionAssetResults[indexPath.section];
        controller.asset = result[indexPath.row];
    }
}
```

Then, the detail view (ICFAssetViewController) can request a full-screen image from the PHImageManager for display.

```
PHImageManager *imageManager = [PHImageManager defaultManager];
[imageManager requestImageForAsset:self.asset
                        targetSize:self.assetImageView.bounds.size
                       contentMode:PHImageContentModeAspectFit
                           options:nil
                     resultHandler:^(UIImage *result, NSDictionary *info){
                         [self.assetImageView setImage:result];
                         [self.assetImageView setNeedsLayout];
                     }];
```

Changes in the Photo Library

The photo library supports making changes to assets, asset collections, and collection lists in a robust, thread-safe manner. This includes adding, changing, or removing objects in the photo library. For assets, this can include not just adding a new asset or removing an existing asset, but also applying edits and filters to existing changes. The sample app illustrates adding and removing asset collections and assets; the same general approach applies to all photo library changes. To make a change to the photo library, an app needs to have the photo library object perform a change request, and then provide a listener to handle the changes after they are completed.

Asset Collection Changes

In the Albums tab, there is an add (+) button in the navigation bar. Tapping the add button will ask the user for the name of a new album, as shown in Figure 24.5.

Figure 24.5   Add Album in the PhotoLibrary sample app.

If the user selects Add Album, the action handler attempts to create an album with the name provided in the alert view.

```
UITextField *albumNameTextField = addAlbumAlertController.textFields.firstObject;
NSString *newAlbumName = albumNameTextField.text;
[[PHPhotoLibrary sharedPhotoLibrary] performChanges:^{
    [PHAssetCollectionChangeRequest
    ➥creationRequestForAssetCollectionWithTitle:newAlbumName];
} completionHandler:^(BOOL success, NSError *error) {
    if (!success) {
        NSLog(@"Error encountered adding album: %@",error.localizedDescription);
    }
}];
```

To add a new album, a change request is needed. There are change requests to handle creating new albums, changing existing albums, and deleting albums. The change request is passed to the photo library in a performChanges block, which will then respond with a completion-Handler indicating whether the changes were successfully made to the library. Similarly, the Edit button will enable the user to delete an album from the list of albums shown in the table view. In the tableView:commitEditingStyle:forRowAtIndexPath: method, the album for the selected row will be deleted.

```
if (editingStyle == UITableViewCellEditingStyleDelete) {

    PHAssetCollection *albumToBeDeleted =
    ➥[self.albumsFetchResult objectAtIndex:indexPath.row];

    [[PHPhotoLibrary sharedPhotoLibrary] performChanges:^{
        [PHAssetCollectionChangeRequest deleteAssetCollections:@[albumToBeDeleted]];
    } completionHandler:^(BOOL success, NSError *error) {
        if (!success) {
            NSLog(@"Error encountered adding album: %@",error.localizedDescription);
        }
    }];
}
```

Note that the completion handler does not provide any information about the actual changes completed; for that information, a view controller needs to register as an observer for the PHPhotoLibraryChangeObserver protocol.

```
[[PHPhotoLibrary sharedPhotoLibrary] registerChangeObserver:self];
```

Then, the photoLibraryDidChange method needs to be implemented. That method will receive an instance of PHChange, which can tell whether there are changes that affect any given fetch result, and if so can provide all the specific changes. For the album view, the method checks to see whether any of the albums in the fetch result are affected.

```
PHFetchResultChangeDetails *changesToFetchResult =
➥[changeInstance changeDetailsForFetchResult:self.albumsFetchResult];
```

If the fetch results were affected, they need to be updated to reflect the new state of the photo library. PHFetchResultChangeDetails has a simple way to accomplish this task; it provides both the before and the after views of the fetch result.

```
self.albumsFetchResult = [changesToFetchResult fetchResultAfterChanges];
```

Now that the fetch result is up-to-date, the change details can be used to update the table view so that it matches the fetch result. All the details needed to easily update a table view or collection view are provided.

```
if ([changesToFetchResult hasIncrementalChanges])
{
    [self.tableView beginUpdates];

    [[changesToFetchResult removedIndexes]
     ➡enumerateIndexesUsingBlock:^(NSUInteger idx, BOOL *stop) {

        NSIndexPath *indexPathToRemove =
        ➡[NSIndexPath indexPathForRow:idx inSection:0];

        [self.tableView deleteRowsAtIndexPaths:@[indexPathToRemove]
                         withRowAnimation:UITableViewRowAnimationAutomatic];
    }];

    [[changesToFetchResult insertedIndexes]
     ➡enumerateIndexesUsingBlock:^(NSUInteger idx, BOOL *stop) {

        NSIndexPath *indexPathToInsert =
        ➡[NSIndexPath indexPathForRow:idx inSection:0];

        [self.tableView insertRowsAtIndexPaths:@[indexPathToInsert]
                         withRowAnimation:UITableViewRowAnimationAutomatic];
    }];

    [self.tableView endUpdates];
}
```

The method checks to see whether the change details include incremental changes. If so, the method iterates over the removed indexes, creates an index path for each removed index, and deletes it from the table view with animation. Next, the method iterates over the inserted indexes, creates an index path for each added row, and inserts them into the table view with animation. The indexes are provided in the change details to support this pattern; note that the row deletions must take place first, or the indexes for additions and changes will not be correct. After the changes are complete, the table view animates all the changes and reflects the new state of the photo library.

Asset Changes

In the Albums tab in the sample app, select an album to view the assets in that album. The add button in the navigation bar will initiate the process of adding an image to the photo library, and adding that new image to the selected album. Tapping the add button will present a `UIImagePickerController` for the camera, so the sample app must be run on a device to test this feature. Note that an image can be added to the photo library from any external source; the image picker is just a convenient way to demonstrate the capability.

When the user takes a picture from the camera, the image is delivered to the picker's delegate method.

```
UIImage *selectedImage = [info objectForKey:UIImagePickerControllerOriginalImage];
```

To add the image to the photo library, a change request needs to be passed to the photo library in the `performChanges` block:

```
[[PHPhotoLibrary sharedPhotoLibrary] performChanges:^{

    PHAssetChangeRequest *addImageRequest =
    ➥ [PHAssetChangeRequest creationRequestForAssetFromImage:selectedImage];

    ...
} completionHandler:^(BOOL success, NSError *error) {
    if (!success) {
        NSLog(@"Error creating new asset: %@", error.localizedDescription);
    }
}];
```

Because the `PHAsset` representing the newly added image will not be available until the `photoLibraryDidChange:` method is called, how can the new image be added to the album? The answer is a placeholder object. The photo library can provide a placeholder object for new objects created in a change request so that those new objects can be used in the same change request.

```
PHObjectPlaceholder *addedImagePlaceholder =
➥ [addImageRequest placeholderForCreatedAsset];
```

The placeholder object can then be used to add the asset that is going to be created to the album:

```
PHAssetCollectionChangeRequest *addImageToAlbum =
➥ [PHAssetCollectionChangeRequest
➥ changeRequestForAssetCollection:self.selectedCollection];

[addImageToAlbum addAssets:@[addedImagePlaceholder]];
```

When the photo library has completed the changes, it calls the `photoLibraryDidChange:` delegate method on an arbitrary queue. After switching to the main queue, the method will check whether there are changes to the fetch result for the assets in the album.

```
PHFetchResultChangeDetails *changesToFetchResult =
➥[changeInstance changeDetailsForFetchResult:self.assetResult];
```

If there are changes, the method updates the fetch result and the table view:

```
if (changesToFetchResult)
{
    self.assetResult = [changesToFetchResult fetchResultAfterChanges];

    if ([changesToFetchResult hasIncrementalChanges]) {
        NSMutableArray *indexPathsToInsert = [[NSMutableArray alloc] init];

        [[changesToFetchResult insertedIndexes]
        ➥enumerateIndexesUsingBlock:^(NSUInteger idx, BOOL *stop) {

            NSIndexPath *indexPathToInsert =
            ➥[NSIndexPath indexPathForRow:idx inSection:0];

            [indexPathsToInsert addObject:indexPathToInsert];

        }];

        [self.collectionView insertItemsAtIndexPaths:indexPathsToInsert];
    }
}
```

The new cell in the collection view will be added with animation, and the new image will be displayed.

When the user taps on an image in the album view or in the moments view, the image will be displayed in a full-screen format in the `ICFAssetViewController`. There is a delete button in that view that allows the user to delete an asset from the photo library.

```
[[PHPhotoLibrary sharedPhotoLibrary] performChanges:^{
    [PHAssetChangeRequest deleteAssets:@[self.asset]];
} completionHandler:^(BOOL success, NSError *error) {
    if (success) {
        [self.navigationController popViewControllerAnimated:YES];
    } else {
        NSLog(@"Error deleting asset: %@",error.localizedDescription);
    }
}];
```

When the user taps the Delete button and the delete asset change request is performed, the photo library will present a confirmation alert, as shown in Figure 24.6. If the user selects Don't Allow, no action will be taken. If the user selects Delete, the asset will be deleted from the photo library, and any registered listeners will be notified.

Figure 24.6   Deleting a photo in the PhotoLibrary sample app.

Dealing with Photo Stream

Photo Stream is a photo-syncing feature that is part of Apple's iCloud service. When an iCloud user adds a photo to a Photo Stream–enabled device, that photo is instantly synced to all the user's other Photo Stream–enabled devices. For example, if the user has an iPhone, an iPad, and a Mac, and takes a photo on the iPhone, the photo will be visible immediately on the iPad (in the Photos app) and the Mac (in iPhoto or Aperture) with no additional effort required.

To use Photo Stream, the user needs to have an iCloud account. An iCloud account can be created free on an iOS device. Visit Settings, iCloud. Create a new account or enter iCloud account information. After the iCloud account information is entered on the device, Photo Stream can be turned on (see Figure 24.7).

When Photo Stream is enabled, moments are synced across devices automatically. No additional code is required in the sample app to display or handle moments from other devices. When requesting images for display from PHImageManager, options can be specified to either explicitly allow or prevent network access as desired.

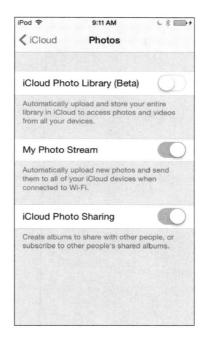

Figure 24.7   Settings: iCloud Photos.

Summary

This chapter explained how to access the photo library using the Photos framework introduced in iOS 8. It detailed the classes available to access the photo library, and showed how to handle permissions for the photo library. It covered how to work with the Photos framework classes to display images using the same organizational structures that Photos.app uses. This chapter discussed getting properly sized images asynchronously and over the network. Next, the chapter explored details of changing the photo library, including adding and deleting asset collections, and adding and deleting assets. Finally, this chapter explained how to enable iCloud Photo Stream to include remote photos in the photo library.

25

Passbook and PassKit

With iOS 6, Apple introduced a new standard app called Passbook, which is a place to keep and have easy access to a user's event tickets, traveling tickets, coupons, and store cards (like gift cards, prepaid cards, or rewards cards). Passbook is currently available only on iPhone and iPod touch devices, not on iPad devices.

Passbook has special access to the lock screen. If a user is within a geofence, defined by a location or set of locations listed in the pass, on a relevant date specified in a pass, the pass will be displayed on the lock screen so that the user can slide and open it directly in the Passbook app.

The Passbook app displays passes like a stack so that the user can see the top part of each pass. The top section contains a logo and colored background, and can contain some custom information. When a user taps on the top part of a pass, the pass will expand to display the entire pass, which can contain several areas of custom fields, a background graphic, and a barcode. The user can delete a pass when it is no longer needed. The Passbook app has support built in to leverage a Web service and push notifications to handle seamless updates to a pass already in Passbook.

Using Passbook requires building a "pass" in a prescribed format and delivering the pass to a user. The pass needs to be built somewhere other than the user's device, typically on a server, since it is a signed archive of files including icons and logos for display, a file with information about the pass, a signature file, and a manifest.

There are a few options available to deliver the pass to the user. Mail.app and Safari.app can recognize a pass and import it into Passbook, or a custom app can utilize PassKit to add a new pass or update an existing pass. For testing passes, the iOS Simulator can display a pass when it is dropped onto it.

PassKit is part of the iOS SDK that can be used by custom apps to import or update a pass in Passbook, check whether a pass is new or updated, and display some information about existing passes.

This chapter describes the design considerations relevant to different pass types, and how to build and test passes for Passbook. It demonstrates how to use PassKit to interact with passes from an app. Finally, it describes how Passbook can handle updates from a Web service.

The Sample App

The sample app is called Pass Test. It includes pre-signed sample passes for each pass type (see Figure 25.1). The user can add a new pass to Passbook in the app using PassKit, can simulate updating an existing pass with new information, can view the pass directly in Passbook, and can remove the pass from Passbook all from the app. The sample app is covered in more detail in the section "Interacting with Passes in an App."

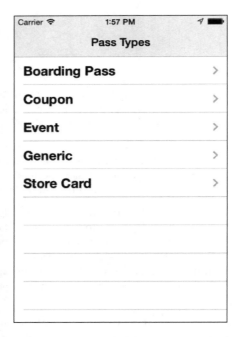

Figure 25.1   Pass Test sample app.

Designing the Pass

Before a pass can be sent to any users, the pass needs to be designed and configured. The pass provider needs to determine what type of pass should be used and how the pass should look. This includes figuring out what fields of information should be presented on the pass, where the fields should be placed, whether a barcode should be used, and what information will be provided to determine whether the pass should be displayed on the lock screen. An individual pass is actually a signed bundle of files, including some images, a JSON file called pass.json with information about the pass and display information, and a signature and manifest.

Pass Types

Apple has provided several standard pass types, each of which can be customized:

- **Boarding Pass:** A boarding pass is intended to cover travel situations, such as an airline boarding pass, a train ticket, a bus pass, a shuttle voucher, or any other ticket required to board a conveyance with a defined departure location and destination.

- **Coupon:** A coupon is a pass that handles a discount for a vendor. The coupon is designed to be flexible enough to handle a wide variety of permutations, such as percentage or dollar-off discounts, or discounts specific to a product or group of products, or no product at all, at a specific location, a group of locations, or any location for a vendor.

- **Event:** An event pass is a ticket for entry to any event, such as a theater production, movie, sporting event, or special museum event—anything with limited access granted by a ticket.

- **Store Card:** A store card pass is similar to a gift card, in that the user can buy a preset amount of money on the pass, display the pass to the vendor for payment, and have the payment amount decremented from the pass. The vendor might allow refilling the pass or might require the purchase of a new pass when the amount has been fully depleted. Store cards can also be used as reward or loyalty cards, in which points are collected with each purchase until a threshold is reached and a reward is given.

- **Generic:** A generic pass can be used for anything that does not fit into the prebuilt pass types, or where the prebuilt pass types are not sufficient. Generic passes include a thumbnail image so that they can be used for an organization-specific ID card like a gym membership card.

Each pass type has a specialized layout to be considered when the pass is being designed. Passes are divided into sections where fields of data can be presented: header, primary, secondary, auxiliary, and back. Passes can also use custom images in some instances. The following sections describe the layouts for each pass type.

Pass Layout—Boarding Pass

A boarding pass has the layout shown in Figure 25.2.

For a boarding pass, the departure location and destination are typically specified as the primary fields (a boarding pass can have up to two primary fields). Secondary and auxiliary fields are laid out beneath the primary fields. The footer image is optional.

Figure 25.2   Boarding pass layout.

Pass Layout—Coupon

A coupon pass has the layout shown in Figure 25.3.

Figure 25.3   Coupon pass layout.

A coupon can have only one primary field, and can optionally display a strip image behind the primary field. A coupon can have up to four total secondary and auxiliary fields.

Pass Layout—Event

An event pass has the layout shown in Figure 25.4.

Figure 25.4   Event pass layout.

An event pass can have only one primary field, and can optionally display a background image behind all the fields and the barcode. If provided, the background image is automatically cropped and blurred. An event can also optionally display a thumbnail image to the right of the primary and secondary fields.

Pass Layout—Generic

A generic pass has the layout shown in Figure 25.5.

Figure 25.5   Generic pass layout.

A generic pass can have only one primary field, and can optionally display a thumbnail image to the right of the primary field. Secondary and auxiliary fields are presented below the primary field.

Pass Layout—Store Card

A store card pass has the layout shown in Figure 25.6.

Figure 25.6   Store card pass layout.

A store card can have only one primary field, and can optionally display a strip image behind the primary field. A store card can have up to four total secondary and auxiliary fields, presented below the primary field.

Pass Presentation

Passes are presented to users in several situations outside Passbook, and it is important to understand which parts of the pass can be customized to handle that presentation. When a pass is distributed to a user via email, it looks like the screenshot displayed in Figure 25.7.

The image presented is icon.png from the pass bundle. The top line of text in blue is derived automatically from the type of pass as specified in the pass.json file, and the bottom line of text is the organization name specified in the pass.json file.

When the device is near a relevant location specified in the pass, or the date is a relevant date specified in the pass, the pass is visible on the device's lock screen much like a push notification, as shown in Figure 25.8. More information about this is available in the section "Building the Pass," in the "Pass Relevance Information" subsection.

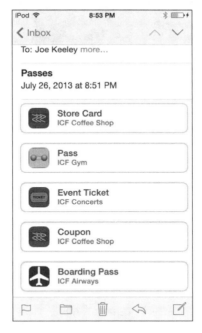

Figure 25.7   Passes distributed in email.

Figure 25.8   Pass displayed on the lock screen.

The icon image presented on the left of the notification is `icon.png` in the pass bundle. The top line of text is the organization name specified in the `pass.json` file, and the bottom line of text is the `relevantText` specified in the `pass.json` file, with the relevant locations.

Building the Pass

A pass will typically be built by an automated server. This section and the next section of the chapter describe building a pass manually so that the steps necessary are clear; automating the process would depend on the choice of server environment and is left as an exercise for the reader.

Several steps are required to build a pass. Apple recommends creating a folder to hold all the files required for an individual pass, for example, a folder called `Boarding Pass.raw`.

Place all the required and desired images in the pass folder. Passes support retina and nonretina versions of images using standard "@2x" and "@3x" naming syntax. The images that need to be provided are these:

- **`icon.png` (required):** A 29×29-pixel PNG image (and retina versions) will be displayed in any PassKit-capable app (such as Mail.app or Safari.app) when the app has detected a pass and is displaying the pass as something that can be used. The image is also displayed for the pass on the lock screen. The icon is automatically given rounded edges and a shine effect like an app icon.

- **`logo.png` (required):** A logo PNG image, with maximum dimensions of 160×50 pixels (and retina versions), is placed on the header of the pass in Passbook. Apple recommends using only an image in the logo, and recommends avoiding any stylized text in the logo. When the logo is presented, it will be presented with the standardized header (with customizable text) that will look uniform in Passbook.app.

- **`background.png` (optional, available only for event passes):** A PNG image with maximum dimensions of 180×220 pixels (and retina versions) can be specified for the entire background of the front of the pass. This image is automatically cropped and blurred.

- **`strip.png` (optional, available only for coupon, event, and store card passes):** A PNG image (and retina versions) can be specified to go behind the primary fields on the pass. The strip image has shine applied by default, which can be turned off. Maximum dimensions are 312×84 pixels for Event passes, 312×110 pixels for Coupons and Store Card passes with a square barcode, and 312×123 pixels for Coupons and Store Cards with a rectangular barcode.

- **`thumbnail.png` (optional, available only on event and generic passes):** A PNG image (and retina versions) can be displayed on the front of the pass. Apple recommends this for a person's image for a membership card, but it could also be used as a membership level indicator or graphical way of presenting pass data.

- **`footer.png` (optional, available only for boarding passes):** A PNG image (and retina versions) can be specified to go just above the barcode on the pass.

The majority of work building an individual pass is in creating the `pass.json` file. This file defines all the information for the pass, including unique identification of the pass, type of pass, relevance information, and layout and visual customizations for the pass in a JSON hash. Create a plain text file called `pass.json` in the pass folder, and prepare it with all the desired information for a pass.

> **Note**
>
> Refer to Chapter 9, "Working with and Parsing JSON," for more information on building a JSON hash. Note that you can unzip any existing pass and examine its `pass.json` file for a starting point.

Basic Pass Identification

The pass requires several fields to identify it, as shown in the following example from a pass:

```
"description" : "Event Ticket",
"formatVersion" : 1,
"passTypeIdentifier" : "pass.explore-systems.icfpasstest.event",
"serialNumber" : "12345",
"teamIdentifier" : "59Q54EHA9F",
"organizationName" : "ICF Concerts",
```

These are the required fields:

- **description (required):** A localizable string used by iOS accessibility to describe the pass.

- **formatVersion (required):** The Passbook format version, which must be the number 1 currently.

- **passTypeIdentifier (required):** An identifier, provided by Apple, for the pass type. See the section "Signing and Packaging the Pass," specifically the subsection "Creating the Pass Type ID," for more info on how to obtain a Pass Type ID.

- **serialNumber (required):** A unique identifier for the Pass Type ID. The combination of Pass Type ID and serial number makes an individual pass unique.

- **teamIdentifier (required):** A team identifier provided by Apple for the organization. It can be found in the Developer Member Center, under Organization Profile, in Company/ Organization ID.

- **organizationName (required):** A localizable string for the name of the organization providing the pass. This is displayed when the pass is presented in Mail.app on an iOS 6 or higher device, and when the pass is displayed on the lock screen as being relevant.

Pass Relevance Information

A pass can optionally supply relevance information, including locations that are relevant to the pass, and a date that is relevant to the pass as shown in this example:

```
"locations" : [
  {
    "latitude" : 39.749484,
    "longitude" : -104.917513,
    "relevantText" : "...is nearby, stop by for 20% off a coffee!"
  }
],
"relevantDate" : "2014h-10-20T19:30:00-08:00"
```

The relevance fields that can be used are these:

- **locations (optional):** An array of relevant location information. A location can have latitude, longitude, altitude, and relevantText. The relevantText will be displayed on the lock screen when the device is in proximity to a relevant location. The size of the radius used for the proximity check depends on the pass type.

- **relevantDate (optional):** An ISO 8601 date expressed as a string.

Different rules are applied depending on the pass type:

- **Boarding pass:** Uses a wide radius for the location check. Relevant if a location or date matches.

- **Coupon:** Uses a small radius for the location check and ignores the relevant date.

- **Event:** Uses a wide radius for the location check. Relevant if a location and date match.

- **Generic:** Uses a small radius for the location check. Relevant if a location and date match, or if a location matches and no date is provided.

- **Store card:** Uses a small radius for the location check and ignores the relevant date.

Barcode Identification

To display a barcode on the pass, provide a message, a barcode format, and a message encoding parameter. Optionally, provide an alternative text parameter that will display a human-readable version of the message.

```
"barcode" : {
  "message" : "123456789",
  "format" : "PKBarcodeFormatQR",
  "messageEncoding" : "iso-8859-1"
  "altText" : "123456789",
},
```

The following fields are used to display a barcode:

- **format (required):** A string representing a PassKit constant specifying the barcode format the barcode should be displayed in. Passbook currently supports QR (PKBarcodeFormatQR), PDF 417 (PKBarcodeFormatPDF417), and Aztec (PKBarcodeFormatAztec). PDF 417 is a rectangular barcode format, whereas QR and Aztec present square barcodes.

- **message (required):** A string message that will be encoded into a barcode.

- **messageEncoding (required):** A string representing the IANA character set used to convert the message from a string to data. Typically, iso-8859-1.

- **altText (optional):** Human-readable representation of the message encoded, which will be displayed near the barcode.

Pass Visual Appearance Information

A pass can customize the colors of the background, field values, and field labels, as well as the text displayed with the logo.

```
"logoText" : "ICF Concerts",
"foregroundColor" : "rgb(79, 16, 1)",
"backgroundColor" : "rgb(199, 80, 18)",
"labelColor" : "rgb(0,0,0)",
```

These are the fields that can be used to customize the appearance of the pass:

- **logoText (optional):** A localizable string, displayed in the header to the right of the logo image.

- **foregroundColor (optional):** A string specifying a CSS-style RGB color to be used for the field values on the pass.

- **backgroundColor (optional):** A string specifying a CSS-style RGB color to be used for the background of the pass. Ignored on an Event pass on which a background image is specified.

- **labelColor (optional):** A string specifying a CSS-style RGB color to be used for the field labels on the pass. Apple recommends using white to give passes a degree of uniformity.

- **suppressStripShine (optional):** A Boolean (true or false) indicating whether to suppress applying shine effects to a strip image (available only for a couple, event, or store pass). The default value is false, meaning shine effects are applied.

Pass Fields

Pass fields are specified in an element with a key indicating the type or style of pass; options are boardingPass, coupon, eventTicket, generic, and storeCard. Inside that element are additional elements that organize the fields on the pass.

```
"boardingPass" : {
  "transitType" : "PKTransitTypeAir",
  "headerFields" : [
      ...
  ],
  "primaryFields" : [
      ...
  ],
  "secondaryFields" : [
      ...
  ],
  "auxiliaryFields" : [
      ...
  ],
  "backFields" : [
```

```
      . . .
  ]
}
```

The fields that can convey pass-specific information are the following:

- **transitType (required for boarding pass, not allowed for other passes):** Identifies the type of transit for a boarding pass, using a string representing a pass kit constant. Choices are PKTransitTypeAir, PKTransitTypeTrain, PKTransitTypeBus, PKTransitTypeBoat, and PKTransitTypeGeneric. The pass will display an icon specific to the transit type.

- **headerFields (optional):** Header fields are displayed on the front of the pass at the very top. This section is also visible when the pass is in a stack, so it is important to be picky about what is shown here.

- **primaryFields (optional):** Primary fields are displayed on the front of the pass just below the header, and typically in a larger, more prominent font.

- **secondaryFields (optional):** Secondary fields are displayed on the front of the pass just below the primary fields, and typically in a normal font size.

- **auxiliaryFields (optional):** Auxiliary fields are displayed on the front of the pass just below the secondary fields, and typically in a smaller, less prominent font.

- **backFields (optional)** Back fields are displayed on the back of the pass.

Inside each of the fields elements is an array of fields. A field at minimum requires a key, value, and label.

```
{
  "key" : "seat",
  "label" : "Seat",
  "value" : "23B",
  "textAlignment" : "PKTextAlignmentRight"
}
```

For each field, the following information can be provided:

- **key (required):** The key must be a string identifying a field that is unique within the pass, for example, "seat".

- **value (required):** The value of the field, for example, "23B". The value can be a localizable string, a number, or a date in ISO 8601 format.

- **label (optional):** A localizable string label for the field.

- **textAlignment (optional):** A string representing a pass kit text alignment constant. Choices are PKTextAlignmentLeft, PKTextAlignmentCenter, PKTextAlignmentRight, PKTextAlignmentJustified, and PKTextAlignmentNatural.

- **changeMessage (optional):** A message describing the change to a field, for example, `"Changed to %@"`, where `%@` is replaced with the new value. This is described in more detail later in the chapter, in "Interacting with Passes in an App," in the subsection "Simulating Updating a Pass."

For a date and/or time field, a date style and time style can be specified. Both the date and the time style must be specified in order to display a date or time.

```
{
  "key" : "departuretime",
  "label" : "Depart",
  "value" : "2012-10-7T13:42:00-07:00",
  "dateStyle" : "PKDateStyleShort",
  "timeStyle" : "PKDateStyleShort",
  "isRelative" : false
},
```

The fields needed to specify a date and time are these:

- **dateStyle (optional):** Choices are PKDateStyleNone (corresponding to NSDateFormatterNoStyle), PKDateStyleShort (corresponding to NSDateFormatterShortStyle), PKDateStyleMedium (corresponding to NSDateFormatterMediumStyle), PKDateStyleLong (corresponding to NSDateFormatterLongStyle), and PKDateStyleFull (corresponding to NSDateFormatterFullStyle).

- **timeStyle (optional):** Choices are PKDateStyleNone (corresponding to NSDateFormatterNoStyle), PKDateStyleShort (corresponding to NSDateFormatterShortStyle), PKDateStyleMedium (corresponding to NSDateFormatterMediumStyle), PKDateStyleLong (corresponding to NSDateFormatterLongStyle), and PKDateStyleFull (corresponding to NSDateFormatterFullStyle).

- **isRelative (optional):** true displays as a relative date, false as an absolute date.

For a number, a currency code or number style can be specified.

```
{
  "key" : "maxValue",
  "label" : "Max Value",
  "value" : 1.50,
  "currencyCode" : "USD"
}
```

These are the fields that specify a number or currency style:

- **currencyCode (optional):** An ISO 4217 currency code, which will display the number as the currency represented by the code.

- **numberStyle (optional):** Choices are PKNumberStyleDecimal, PKNumberStylePercent, PKNumberStyleScientific, and PKNumberStyleSpellOut.

> **Tip**
>
> When constructing a pass.json file during development, test the JSON to confirm that it is valid. This can prevent lots of trial-and-error testing and frustration. Visit www.jslint.com and paste the JSON into the source area. Click the JSLint button and the site will validate the pasted JSON and highlight any errors. If it says, "JSON: good," the JSON is valid; otherwise, an error message will be presented.

After the pass.json file is ready and the other graphics are available, the pass can be signed and packaged for distribution.

Signing and Packaging the Pass

Passbook requires that passes be cryptographically signed to ensure that a pass was built by the provider and has not been modified in any way. To sign a pass, a Pass Type ID needs to be established in the iOS Provisioning Portal, and a pass signing certificate specific to the Pass Type ID needs to be generated. After the Pass Type ID and certificate are available, passes can be signed. For each unique pass instance a manifest file with checksums for each file in the pass needs to be built so that Passbook can verify each file.

Creating the Pass Type ID

The Pass Type ID identifies the type or class of pass that a provider wants to distribute. For example, if a provider wants to distribute a coupon and a rewards card, the provider would create two Pass Type IDs, one for the coupon and one for the rewards card. To create a Pass Type ID, visit the iOS Dev Center (https://developer.apple.com/devcenter/ios/index.action), and choose Certificates, Identifiers & Profiles in the menu titled iOS Developer Program on the right side of the screen. Click Identifiers and then the Pass Type IDs item in the left menu (see Figure 25.9).

Figure 25.9   iOS Provisioning Portal: Pass Type IDs.

To register a new Pass Type ID, click the button with the plus sign in the upper-right corner. A form to register a new Pass Type ID will be presented (see Figure 25.10).

Figure 25.10   iOS Provisioning Portal: register a Pass Type ID.

Specify a description and an identifier for the Pass Type ID. Apple recommends using a reverse DNS naming style for Pass Type IDs, and Apple requires that the Pass Type ID begin with the string "pass". Click the Continue button, and a confirmation screen will be presented, as shown in Figure 25.11.

Figure 25.11   iOS Provisioning Portal: confirm Pass Type ID.

Click the Register button to confirm the pass type settings and register the Pass Type ID. After the Pass Type ID has been registered, a certificate must be generated in order to sign passes with the new ID.

Creating the Pass Signing Certificate

To see whether a Pass Type ID has a certificate configured, click on the Pass Type ID in the list, and then click the Edit button. If a certificate has been created for the Pass Type ID, it will be displayed in the Production Certificates section. There will also be an option to create a new certificate for the Pass Type ID, as shown in Figure 25.12.

Click the Create Certificate button to start the certificate generation process. The iOS Provisioning Portal will present instructions to generate the certificate request (see Figure 25.13).

Figure 25.12   iOS Provisioning Portal: Pass Type ID list.

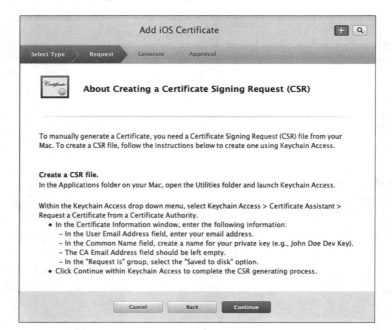

Figure 25.13   iOS Provisioning Portal: Pass Certificate Assistant, generating a Certificate Signing Request.

To generate a certificate request, leave the Pass Certificate Assistant open in your browser, and open Keychain Access (in Applications, Utilities). Select Keychain Access, Certificate Assistant, Request a Certificate from a Certificate Authority from the application menu. You will see the form shown in Figure 25.14.

Figure 25.14   Keychain Access Certificate Assistant.

Enter your email address and common name (typically your company name or entity name—it's safe to use whatever name you use for your Apple Developer account), and then select Saved to Disk. Click Continue, and specify where you would like the request saved. After that step is complete, return to the iOS Provisioning Portal and click Continue. The assistant will ask you to select the request that you just saved, as shown in Figure 25.15.

After you have selected your saved request, click Generate and your SSL certificate will be generated, as shown in Figure 25.16.

After your certificate has been generated, you need to download it so that you can use it to sign passes. Click the Download button to download your certificate. After it has successfully downloaded, you can click the Done button to dismiss the Certificate Assistant. Double-click the downloaded certificate file, and it will automatically be installed in Keychain Access. It should be visible in your list of certificates in Keychain Access, as shown in Figure 25.17. Click the triangle to confirm that your private key was delivered with the certificate.

Figure 25.15   iOS Provisioning Portal: Pass Certificate Assistant, submitting a Certificate Signing Request.

Figure 25.16   iOS Provisioning Portal: Pass Certificate Assistant, generating your pass certificate.

| ▼ ✉ Pass Type ID: pass.explore-systems.icfpasstest.example | certificate | Jul 26, 2014 9:31:00 PM | login |
| 🔑 Joe Keeley | private key | -- | login |

Figure 25.17   Keychain Access: pass certificate and private key.

To use the certificate for signing from the command line, it must be exported and converted to PEM format. Note that the certificate as displayed in Keychain Access actually contains a private key and a public key. The private key is what is used for signing the pass, and must be kept secret to prevent fraudulent signatures. The public key is used for external verification of the signature. To export the certificate, highlight it, right-click, and select Export; then select a destination for the file. Keychain Access will prompt for a password to protect the file—if it is to be used locally and deleted when done, it is acceptable to skip the password. If the file will be distributed at all, it is highly recommended to protect it with a strong password. Keychain Access will then export the private and public key into a file with a `.p12` extension. Execute the following command to extract the public key and save it in PEM format:

```
$ openssl pkcs12 -in BoardingPassCerts.p12 -clcerts -nokeys -out
➥boardcert.pem -passin pass:
```

Execute this command to extract the private key and save it in PEM format. Select a password to replace `mykeypassword`.

```
$ openssl pkcs12 -in BoardingPassCerts.p12 -nocerts -out boardkey.pem
➥-passin pass: -passout pass:mykeypassword
```

The last item needed to sign is the Apple Worldwide Developer Relations Certification Authority certificate. The certificate will already be available in Keychain Access (under Certificates) if Xcode has been used to build and deploy an app to a device (see Figure 25.18).

Figure 25.18   Keychain Access: Apple Worldwide Developer Relations Certification Authority certificate.

If that certificate is not visible in Keychain Access, download it from www.apple.com/certificateauthority/ and install it in Keychain Access. Right-click the certificate and select Export. Give the certificate a short name (like `AppleWWDRCert`), select PEM format, and save the certificate.

Creating the Manifest

A manifest file must be created for each individual pass. The manifest is a JSON file called `manifest.json`. It contains an entry for each file that makes up a pass with a corresponding SHA1 checksum. To create the manifest, create a new file in a text editor. Since the file represents a JSON array, it should start with an open bracket and end with a close bracket. For each file, put the file in quotation marks, add a colon, put the SHA1 checksum in quotation marks, and separate items with a comma. To get the SHA1 checksum for a file, perform the following command in a terminal window from the directory where the pass files exist:

```
$ openssl sha1 pass.json
SHA1(pass.json)= b636f7d021372a87ff2c130be752da49402d0d7f
```

The manifest file should look like this example when complete:

```
{
  "pass.json" : "09040451676851048cf65bcf2e299505f9eef89d",
  "icon.png" : "153cb22e12ac4b2b7e40d52a0665c7f6cda75bed",
  "icon@2x.png" : "7288a510b5b8354cff36752c0a8db6289aa7cbb3",
  "logo.png" : "8b1f3334c0afb2e973e815895033b266ab521af9",
  "logo@2x.png" : "dbbdb5dca9bc6f997e010ab5b73c63e485f22dae"
}
```

Signing and Packaging the Pass

The manifest file must be signed so that Passbook can validate the contents of the pass. To sign the manifest, use `openssl` from a terminal prompt. Specify the `certfile` as the Apple Worldwide Developer Relations certificate, the PEM version of the certificate created earlier as the signer, the PEM version of the key created earlier as the key, and the password set for the private key in place of `mykeypassword`.

```
$ openssl smime -binary -sign -certfile ../AppleWWDRCert.pem
➥-signer ../boardcert.pem -inkey ../boardkey.pem -in manifest.json
➥-out signature -outform DER -passin pass:mykeypassword
```

A file called `signature` will be created (`-out signature`). Any changes to any of the files listed in the manifest require updating the SSA signature for that file in the manifest and re-signing the manifest.

To package the pass, use the `zip` command from a terminal prompt, from the raw directory of pass files. Specify the destination file for the pass, and list the files to be included in the pass.

```
$ zip -r ../boarding_pass.pkpass manifest.json pass.json
➥signature icon.png icon@2x.png logo.png logo@2x.png footer.png
➥footer@2x.png
```

That will zip up all the files listed in an archive called `boarding_pass.pkpass` in the parent directory.

> **Note**
>
> Apple provides a tool called signpass with the Passbook information in the iOS Developer Portal. It comes in an Xcode project—just build the project and put the build product where it can be found in the terminal path. Then execute signpass, providing a pass directory, and it will automatically create and sign the manifest and package the pass in one step. It will utilize your keychain for all the needed certificates, so the steps to export all those are not needed during development. For example, `$ ./signpass -p Event.raw` will produce `Event.pkpass`.

Testing the Pass

To test the pass, drag and drop the file called `boarding_pass.pkpass` into the running Simulator. The Simulator will attempt to load the pass in Safari. If there is a problem with the pass, Safari will present an error message, as shown in Figure 25.19.

Safari will log any problems with the pass to the console. To find out what is wrong with the pass, open Applications, Utilities, Console and look for an error message, as shown in Figure 25.20.

Figure 25.19   Safari in iOS Simulator: error loading pass.

```
▼ 10:15:29 AM MobileSafari:
     Invalid data error reading card pass.explore-systems.icfpasstest.boardingpass/12345. Pass dictionary must contain key 'transitType'.

  10:15:29 AM MobileSafari: PassBook Pass download failed: The pass cannot be read because it isn't valid.
```

Figure 25.20   Console: displaying a pass error.

In this example, the error indicates that the pass must contain a key called transitType. This key is required for boarding passes, and is not allowed for any other types of passes. Ensure that there is a key called transitType inside the boardingPass section of pass.json, re-sign the pass, and drop it into the Simulator again to determine whether the error is fixed.

Be certain to tap Add to add the pass to Passbook in the Simulator, because not all pass errors are caught by just displaying the pass. There will be an animation when Add is tapped indicating that the pass has been added to Passbook. If that animation does not occur and the pass just fades away, there was an error with the pass and it will not be added to Passbook. Check the console for any additional errors.

Interacting with Passes in an App

Passes can exist completely outside the confines of an app—in fact, a custom app is not needed at all for the life cycle of a Pass. However, there are use cases in which a custom app is appropriate for getting new passes, handling updates to existing passes, and removing existing passes. The sample app demonstrates how to perform all these tasks.

Preparing the App

Several steps need to be completed to prepare the app to interact with Passbook. First ensure that `PassKit.framework` has been added to the project, and `@import PassKit;` has been added in any classes that need to use the PassKit classes.

Next, return to the iOS Provisioning Portal and click the App IDs item in the left menu. Click the button with a plus sign to create a new App ID, as shown in Figure 25.21.

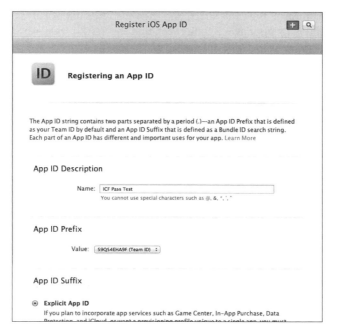

Figure 25.21   iOS Provisioning Portal: creating a new App ID.

The new app can be set to enable Passbook while it is being created, or can be updated to enable Passbook after it has been created. To enable Passbook for an existing App ID, click on the App ID on the list, and click the Edit button. Check the Enable Passes option. The iOS Provisioning Portal will present a dialog warning that any existing provisioning profiles created for the App ID must be regenerated in order to be enabled for passes, as shown in Figure 25.22.

Figure 25.22   iOS Provisioning Portal: App ID enabled for passes.

In Xcode, select the project, then the target, and then the Capabilities tab, as shown in Figure 25.23. Setting Passbook to On makes Xcode check that the PassKit framework is linked to the project, that the entitlements needed are configured correctly, and that the needed provisioning profiles are set up correctly.

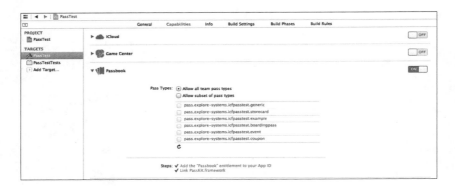

Figure 25.23   Xcode showing the Passbook section on the Capabilities tab.

> **Note**
>
> These steps to prepare the app are required only for running the app on a device. Interacting with Passbook works fine in the Simulator without these steps having been completed.

Now the app is set up to access passes in Passbook. The sample app includes samples of each type of pass in the main bundle for demonstration. Passes would typically not be distributed this way; rather, a pass would more likely be downloaded from a server after some information was provided about the pass recipient. To see how to programmatically interact with Passbook, start the sample app and tap any pass type (this example demonstrates the boarding pass). The app will check how many passes it can see in Passbook, and will determine whether the selected pass is already in Passbook (see Figure 25.24).

To get this information, the view controller needs to communicate with the pass library. For convenience, a property is set up to keep an instance of `PKPassLibrary`, which is instantiated in the `viewDidLoad` method.

```
- (void)viewDidLoad
{
    [super viewDidLoad];

    self.passLibrary = [[PKPassLibrary alloc] init];
    [self refreshPassStatusView];
}
```

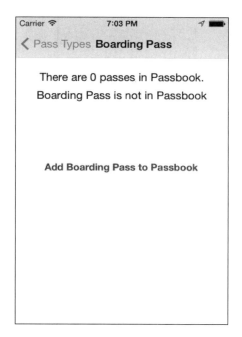

Figure 25.24   Pass Test sample app: boarding pass.

In the `refreshPassStatusView` method, the view controller first checks whether the pass library is available.

```
if (![PKPassLibrary isPassLibraryAvailable])
{
    [self.passInLabel setText:@"Pass Library not available."];
```

```
    [self.numPassesLabel setText:@""];
    [self.addButton setHidden:YES];
    [self.updateButton setHidden:YES];
    [self.showButton setHidden:YES];
    [self.deleteButton setHidden:YES];
    return;
}
```

If the pass library is not available, no further action can be taken, so the method updates the UI and hides all the buttons. If the pass library is available, the method gets the information from the passLibrary to update the UI. To determine how many passes are in the library, access the passes property on the passLibrary.

```
NSArray *passes = [self.passLibrary passes];

NSString *numPassesString =
➥[NSString stringWithFormat:
➥@"There are %d passes in Passbook.",[passes count]];

[self.numPassesLabel setText:numPassesString];
```

The passLibrary provides a method to access a specific pass using a pass type identifier and a pass serial number. This can be used to determine whether a specific pass is in the pass library.

```
PKPass *currentBoardingPass =
➥[self.passLibrary passWithPassTypeIdentifier:self.passIdentifier
                             serialNumber:self.passSerialNum];
```

If the pass is present in the library, currentBoardingPass will be a valid instance of PKPass; otherwise, it will be nil. The refreshPassStatusView method will check that and update the UI accordingly.

Adding a Pass

Tap the Add Boarding Pass to Passbook button, which will call the addPassTouched: method. This method will first load the pass from the main bundle (again, this would typically be loaded from an external source).

```
NSString *passPath =
➥[[NSBundle mainBundle] pathForResource:self.passFileName
                            ofType:@"pkpass"];

NSData *passData = [NSData dataWithContentsOfFile:passPath];

NSError *passError = nil;
PKPass *newPass = [[PKPass alloc]
➥initWithData:passData error:&passError];
```

PassKit will evaluate the pass data and return an error in `passError` if there is anything wrong with the pass. If the pass is valid and does not already exist in the pass library, the method will present a `PKAddPassesViewController`, which will display the pass as it will appear in Passbook, and manage adding it to the library based on whether the user chooses Add or Cancel (see Figure 25.25). Otherwise, the method will display an alert view with an appropriate error message.

```objc
if (!passError && ![self.passLibrary containsPass:newPass])
{
    PKAddPassesViewController *newPassVC =
    ➥[[PKAddPassesViewController alloc] initWithPass:newPass];

    [newPassVC setDelegate:self];

    [self presentViewController:newPassVC
                       animated:YES
                     completion:^(){}];

}
else
{
    NSString *passUpdateMessage = @"";

    if (passError)
    {

        passUpdateMessage =
        ➥[NSString stringWithFormat:@"Pass Error: %@",
        ➥[passError localizedDescription]];

    }
    else
    {
        passUpdateMessage = [NSString stringWithFormat:
        ➥@"Your %@ has already been added.", self.passTypeName];
    }

    UIAlertController *alertController =
    ➥[UIAlertController alertControllerWithTitle:@"Pass Not Added"
                                         message:passUpdateMessage
                                  preferredStyle:UIAlertControllerStyleAlert];

    [alertController addAction:
    ➥[UIAlertAction actionWithTitle:@"Dismiss"
                              style:UIAlertActionStyleCancel
                            handler:nil]];
```

```
    [self presentViewController:alertController
                       animated:YES
                     completion:nil];
}
```

Figure 25.25   Sample app displaying PassKit Add Passes View Controller.

After the user has chosen to add the pass, the `PKAddPassesViewController` will call the delegate method if a delegate is set.

```
- (void)addPassesViewControllerDidFinish:
➥(PKAddPassesViewController *)controller
{
    [self dismissViewControllerAnimated:YES completion:^{
        [self refreshPassStatusView];
    }];
}
```

The delegate is responsible for dismissing the `PKAddPassesViewController`. After it is dismissed, the UI is updated to reflect the addition of the pass, as shown in Figure 25.26.

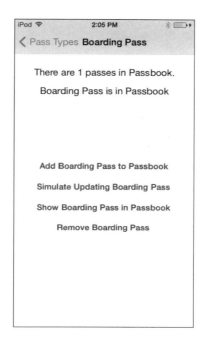

Figure 25.26   Pass Test sample app: boarding pass in the pass library.

> **Note**
>
> If there is a mismatch between your app's bundle ID and the pass ID (for example, com.myorg. mybundleid and pass.myorg.someotherid), the pass library will not be able to see the associated passes in the pass library, and will report there are zero passes available after a pass has been added (refer to Figure 25.24). If this is the case, in the Capabilities tab, select Allow Subset of Pass Types and check the passes that the app should be able to interact with.

Simulating Updating a Pass

Tap the Simulate Updating Boarding Pass button, which will call the `updatePassTouched` method. This method will first load the updated pass data from the main bundle (this is simulated in that the updated pass would typically be loaded from a server in response to a change), and then instantiate a `PKPass` object.

```
NSString *passName =
➡[NSString stringWithFormat:@"%@-Update",self.passFileName];

NSString *passPath =
➡[[NSBundle mainBundle] pathForResource:passName ofType:@"pkpass"];
```

```
NSData *passData = [NSData dataWithContentsOfFile:passPath];

NSError *passError = nil;

PKPass *updatedPass = [[PKPass alloc] initWithData:passData
                                        error:&passError];
```

The method will check whether there are any errors instantiating the pass, and whether the pass library already contains the pass. If there are no errors and the pass exists, it will replace the existing pass with the updated pass.

```
if (!passError && [self.passLibrary containsPass:updatedPass])
{

    BOOL updated = [self.passLibrary
    ➥replacePassWithPass:updatedPass];

    if (updated)
    {
        passUpdateMessage = [NSString stringWithFormat:
        ➥@"Your %@ has been updated.",self.passTypeName];

        passAlertTitle = @"Pass Updated";
    }
    else
    {
        passUpdateMessage = [NSString stringWithFormat:
        ➥@"Your %@ could not be updated.",self.passTypeName];

        passAlertTitle = @"Pass Not Updated";
    }

    UIAlertController *alertController =
    ➥[UIAlertController alertControllerWithTitle:passAlertTitle
                                    message:passUpdateMessage
                              preferredStyle:UIAlertControllerStyleAlert];

    [alertController addAction:
    ➥[UIAlertAction actionWithTitle:@"Dismiss"
                              style:UIAlertActionStyleCancel
                            handler:nil]];

    [self presentViewController:alertController
                      animated:YES
                    completion:nil];
}
```

The `replacePassWithPass:` method will indicate whether the pass was successfully updated, and an appropriate alert will be displayed to the user.

If the update is time sensitive and conveys critical information for the user to be aware of immediately, a `changeMessage` can be specified in the `pass.json` of the updated pass.

```
"headerFields" : [
  {
    "key" : "seat",
    "label" : "Seat",
    "value" : "14C",
    "textAlignment" : "PKTextAlignmentRight",
    "changeMessage" : "New Seat: %@"
  }
],
```

When a change message is specified, Passbook will display a notification to the user when the pass has been updated (as shown in Figure 25.27). The notification will display the icon included in the pass, the organization name specified in the pass, and a message. If `%@` is specified in the `changeMessage`, then the `changeMessage` specified will be presented in the notification to the user, and `%@` will be replaced with the new value of the field. If `%@` is not in the `changeMessage`, a generic message like `"Boarding Pass changed"` will be presented.

That notification will also remain in Notification Center until removed by the user.

Showing a Pass

To show an existing pass, tap on the Show Boarding Pass in Passbook button, which will call the `showPassTouched` method. Since PassKit does not support displaying a pass inside an app, the method needs to get the pass's public URL, and ask the application to open it. That will open the desired pass directly in Passbook.

```
PKPass *currentBoardingPass =
➡[self.passLibrary passWithPassTypeIdentifier:self.passIdentifier
                            serialNumber:self.passSerialNum];

if (currentBoardingPass)
{
    [[UIApplication sharedApplication]
    ➡openURL:[currentBoardingPass passURL]];
}
```

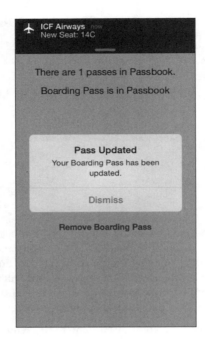

Figure 25.27   Pass change notification.

Removing a Pass

To remove a pass directly from the app, tap on the Remove Boarding Pass button, which will call the `deletePassTouched` method. The method will get the pass using the pass identifier and serial number, and remove it from Passbook.

```
PKPass *currentBoardingPass =
➡[self.passLibrary passWithPassTypeIdentifier:self.passIdentifier
                           serialNumber:self.passSerialNum];

if (currentBoardingPass)
{
    [self.passLibrary removePass:currentBoardingPass];

    [self refreshPassStatusView];

    NSString *passUpdateMessage =
    ➡[NSString stringWithFormat:@"Your %@ has been removed.",
    ➡self.passTypeName];
```

```
➥UIAlertController *alertController =
[UIAlertController alertControllerWithTitle:@"Pass Removed"
                                    message:passUpdateMessage
                             preferredStyle:UIAlertControllerStyleAlert];

[alertController addAction:
➥[UIAlertAction actionWithTitle:@"Dismiss"
                          style:UIAlertActionStyleCancel
                        handler:nil]];

[self presentViewController:alertController
                   animated:YES
                 completion:nil];
}
```

Updating Passes Automatically

One of the key features of Passbook is the capability to automatically update passes without the use of an app. This is an overview of the feature, since implementing it requires a server capable of building and updating passes and is beyond the scope of this chapter to fully illustrate.

If updating a pass will be supported, the `pass.json` needs to specify a `webServiceURL` and an `authenticationToken`. When the pass is first added, Passbook will call the `webServiceURL` to register the device and pass with the server, and will provide a push token for use in the next step.

When information related to a pass is updated on the server, the server needs to notify the device with the pass that an update is available. To do this, the server sends a push notification utilizing the push token received in the registration step to the device with the pass, and includes the pass type ID in the push.

> **Note**
> Refer to Chapter 10, "Notifications," for more information on sending push notifications.

After the device receives the push notification, Passbook will request a list of passes that have been changed from the server for the specified pass type ID and last updated tag. The server will respond with a list of serial numbers and a new last-updated tag.

The device will then iterate through the serial numbers, and request updated versions of passes from the server for each serial number. If the updated pass includes a `changeMessage` (described in more detail in the earlier section "Simulating Updating a Pass"), then Passbook will display a notification to the user for it.

Using this mechanism, a user's passes can be kept up-to-date with the latest information, and users can selectively be notified when critical, time-sensitive information is changed.

Summary

This chapter provided an in-depth look at Passbook. It covered what Passbook is and what types of passes are supported by Passbook. It explained how to design and build a pass, and the steps needed to sign and package an individual pass. The chapter demonstrated how to interact with passes and Passbook using PassKit from an app, and discussed how to use a Web server to keep passes up-to-date.

26

Debugging and Instruments

Unlike most of the other chapters in this book, this chapter has no associated sample code and no project. Throughout this book, the target has been implementing advanced features and functionality of the iOS SDKs. This chapter focuses on what to do when everything goes wrong. Debugging and performance tuning of any piece of software is a vital and sometimes overlooked step of development. Users expect an app to perform quickly, smoothly, consistently, and without errors or crashes. Regardless of the skill level of a developer, bugs will happen, crashes will be introduced, and performance won't be everything it can be. The material covered here will assist in developing software that gets the most out of the system and performs to the highest possible standards.

Introduction to Debugging

"If debugging is the process of removing bugs,
then programming must be the process of putting them in."

Edsger W. Dijkstra

Computers are complex—so complex that few, if any, people understand how they work on all levels. Very few developers understand programming in binary or assembly, even though that is what the machine itself understands. This complexity means that things will go wrong even if everything is seemingly done correctly. Bugs relating to issues, such as race conditions and thread safety, are hard to plan for and can be even harder to troubleshoot.

When we leverage the technology provided by the debugger, the difficulty of debugging software becomes drastically easier. From using custom breakpoints to parameters such as NSZombies, most of the hard work of debugging can be turned into a quick task. Debugging, like any other discipline, takes time and practice; always try to figure out the solution yourself before turning for help. The difference between solving a problem and looking up a solution makes all the difference for growing as a developer.

The First Computer Bug

In 1947, the first computers were making their rounds through large corporations, universities, and government institutes. Grace Murray Hopper was working on one of these early systems at Harvard University, a Mark II Aiken Relay Calculator. On September 9, 1947, the machine began to exhibit problems and the engineers investigated. What they found was surprising but not entirely unexpected when computers were large machines taking up entire rooms. A simple household moth had become trapped between the points of Relay #70 in Panel F of the Mark II Aiken Relay Calculator. The moth was preventing the relay from functioning as expected, and the machine was quite literally debugged. The engineers knew they had a piece of history and they preserved the moth with a piece of tape and the handwritten note, "First actual case of bug being found" (see Figure 26.1). Today, the first computer bug can be found at the Naval Surface Warfare Center Computer Museum at Dahlgren, Virginia.

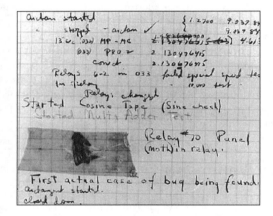

Figure 26.1   The first ever computer bug removed from a Mark II Aiken Relay Calculator in 1947.

Debugging Basics with Xcode

Like most modern IDEs, Xcode has a debugger built into it, LLDB. Computers execute code very quickly, so quickly that it is nearly impossible to see all the steps as they are happening. This is where a debugger comes in handy; it enables the developer to slow down the execution of code and inspect elements as they change. The debug view might initially be hidden, but it can be accessed with the center view button, as shown in Figure 26.2. The debugger is available only when an app is being executed from within Xcode.

Figure 26.2   Accessing the debugger area in Xcode is done through the lower view area.

The debug area (see Figure 26.3) consists of three primary parts. On the left side is the variable view, which is used to inspect detail information about the objects currently within the scope of memory. The right side is composed of the console, which also contains the debugger prompt. On the top of the view lies the debugging command bar for interacting with the debugger.

Figure 26.3   The debug area.

The debugger will, by default, automatically show whenever an exception is encountered. The developer can pause the current execution and bring up the debugger via the Pause button in the debugging toolbar.

It is often possible, if the debugger has stopped at an exception, to be able to continue past the exception. This can be achieved by using the Resume button in the toolbar. The toolbar also affords several other useful commands. On the toolbar, from left to right, the Step Over command will move to the next line of execution while remaining paused. The Step Into command will move into a new method or function that the debugger is currently stopped on. Likewise, the Step Out Of button will move back outside of the current method or function.

Additionally, from the debugger toolbar each thread in execution can be inspected, showing the stack trace. The stack trace will provide the sequence of events leading up to the current point in execution. This same information can be accessed with the Debug Navigator, which can be accessed from the leftmost pane of the Xcode window, shown in Figure 26.4.

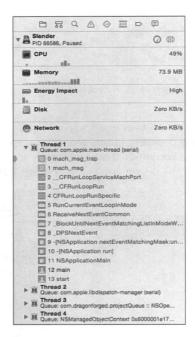

Figure 26.4   The Debug Navigator showing a backtrace across several threads.

Breakpoints

Most developers begin their adventures into debugging by printing log statements to the console to get an insight into how the code is executing or behaving. This is likely because printing to the console is part of the initial Hello World program for many languages. Log statements are very useful but they are very limited in their functionality. Breakpoints inform the debugger that the code being executed should be halted to allow for more thorough debugging and inspection. To create a new breakpoint, click the line number where the code should pause. A blue indicator will appear, representing a new breakpoint; to remove the breakpoint, drag the blue indicator off the line number bar. To temporarily disable a breakpoint, toggle it off by clicking on it, and the breakpoint will become a light transparent blue.

After a breakpoint has been tripped, the execution of code will pause. The variable view will populate with all the in-scope variables and the stack trace will show the path of methods and calls that lead to the breakpoint. Calls that are in code written by the developer will appear in black, and system calls appear in a lighter gray. The developer can click through the stack trace to show the line of code that was responsible for calling the following item (see Figure 26.5).

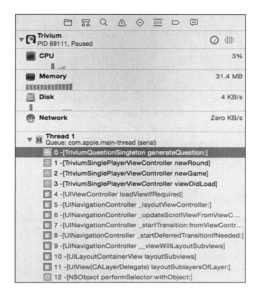

Figure 26.5   A common stack trace. The code is frozen at item 0 in the method `generateQuestion:`. The events that lead to this method can also be seen, from `viewDidLoad` to `newGame` to `newRound`. The lighter gray methods are system calls.

Customizing Breakpoints

Breakpoints can be customized to change the conditions under which they are triggered. Right-clicking a breakpoint will reveal the edit view shown in Figure 26.6. The first property that can be customized is adding a condition for the breakpoint, such as `x == 0`. This can be useful when the breakpoint should be fired only under certain circumstances, such as x being equal to 0.

Figure 26.6   Customizing a breakpoint.

The developer might also have a need to ignore the breakpoint the first several times it is hit. For example, a bug might present itself only after a line of code is executed a certain number of times, and this can remove the need for continuously clicking the Continue button.

Breakpoints can also have actions attached to them, such as running an AppleScript, executing a debugger command, performing a shell command, logging a message, or even playing a sound. Playing a sound can be particularly useful as an audio indicator of an event happening, such as a network call or a Core Data merge. Under certain conditions, such as playing audio, the developer might not want to pause the code execution during the breakpoint. If the preferred action is to log a message or play a sound without pausing, the Automatically Continue after Evaluating Actions option can be enabled.

Symbolic and Exception Breakpoints

In addition to user-set breakpoints, there are two types of breakpoints that can be enabled. These are done through the Breakpoint Navigator found in the left pane of the Xcode window.

Symbolic breakpoints can be used to catch all instances of a method or a function being run. For example, to log every instance of `imageNamed:` being called, a new symbolic breakpoint can be created for the symbol `+[UIImage imageNamed:]`. Figure 26.7 shows a symbolic breakpoint that will log each use of `imageNamed:` by playing a sound.

Figure 26.7   A symbolic breakpoint that will play a sound and continue every time a new image is created using the method `imageNamed:`.

Exception breakpoints work very much like symbolic breakpoints except that they are thrown whenever any exception occurs. Often, setting a global exception breakpoint will provide a better stack trace than is typically provided by a crash. This is because the stack trace is provided based on the breakpoint, whereas a crash can be a result of an exception but does not necessarily point back to the root cause. It is considered by many developers to be best practice to always keep a global exception breakpoint on while debugging.

Breakpoint Scope

You can also set the scope of a breakpoint (see Figure 26.8) by right-clicking on a breakpoint in the Breakpoint Navigator. The available scope options are project, workspace, and user. In addition to specifying a scope, the user also has the option of creating a shared breakpoint. A shared breakpoint is helpful when working on a project with multiple developers across a version control system in which it is important that breakpoints are turned on for all users. Additionally, users can enable breakpoints as user breakpoints that will be active on all new projects they create.

Figure 26.8   Setting up various breakpoints' scope, including user and shared breakpoints, in Xcode.

Working with the Debugger

Xcode features a modern robust debugger, LLDB. The debugger can be accessed anytime code execution is currently paused. An `lldb` prompt will appear at the bottom of the console window. Although the debugger is a very large and complex system, there are several commands that are relevant for the iOS developer.

The first command to turn to when in doubt is the `help` or `h` command. The `help` command will print a root-level help menu, and `help` followed by any command will print information specific to that command.

The most common debugger commands that will be required by an iOS developer are `p` or `print` and `po` or `print object`. The `print` command will print the value of a scalar expression, such as `x + y`, or structs, such as `CGRect`. With the `print` command, it is also possible to change the value of variables while in the debugger.

```
(lldb) p scaleStage2
(float) $0 = 0.600019991
(lldb) p scaleStage2 = 5.25
(float) $1 = 5.25
(lldb) p scaleStage2
(float) $2 = 5.25
```

The print object (po) command will ask an objective-C object to print its description. For example, to see the contents of a memory address, you can type the following command into the lldb prompt:

```
(lldb) po 0x7c025990
<UIImageView: 0x7c025990; frame = (0 0; 320 480); opaque = NO;
►autoresize = RM+BM; userInteractionEnabled = NO; layer = <CALayer: 0x7c025ad0>>
```

Alternatively, an object name can be used, such as this:

```
(lldb) po backgroundView
<UIImageView: 0x7c025990; frame = (0 0; 320 480); opaque = NO;
►autoresize = RM+BM; userInteractionEnabled = NO; layer = <CALayer: 0x7c025ad0>>
```

The list command can be helpful as well. list will print the code surrounding the current breakpoint line. In addition, list takes the parameter of +/- x to specify lines before or after the breakpoint in which to display.

There are times when it is required for a developer in the process of debugging a method or function to override the return value or provide an early return. This can be done using the return x command. For example, typing return 0 followed by continuing will simulate the code returning successfully at the breakpoint.

The backtrace command, or bt, can be used to print the current backtrace to the console. Although this can be helpful for debugging, this information is typically available in a user-friendlier format in the Debug Navigator.

In addition to these commands, the basic toolbar commands can be executed from the debugger prompt, which is often easier than navigating to the very small button in the toolbar. step or s will move to the next line of code in execution. continue or c will continue past the breakpoint and resume executing code. fin will continue until the end of the method, a useful command that does not have a toolbar equivalent. Finally, kill will terminate the program.

LLDB is a powerful tool that can provide a tremendous amount of power and flexibility to debugging. To read more about what can be done in LLDB, see the official documentation at http://llvm.org/docs/.

Instruments

"Instruments" collectively refers to the dozens of profiling and analyzing tools that come bundled with Xcode. Table 26.1 shows a list of instrument bundles. Although the exact details and behaviors of these instruments warrant a book in and of itself, the basics of how to read and interact with instruments is enough to cover the vast majority of what will be needed by the ordinary iOS developer.

Table 26.1   **Instruments Provided in Xcode and Their Functionality**

Instrument	Description
Allocations	Measures heap memory usage by tracking allocations.
Leaks	Measures general memory usage, checks for leaked memory, and provides statistics on object allocations.
Activity Monitor	Monitors system activity, including CPU, memory, disk, network, and statistics.
Zombies	Measures general memory usage while focusing on the detection of over-released "zombie" objects. Also provides statistics on object allocations by class, as well as memory address histories for all active allocations.
Time Profiler	Performs low-overhead time-based sampling of processes running on the system's CPU.
System Trace	Provides information about system behavior by showing when threads are scheduled and showing all their transitions from user into system code.
Automation	Executes a script that simulates UI interaction for an iOS application launched from Instruments.
File Activity	Monitors file and directory activity, including file open/close calls, file permission modifications, directory creation, file moves, etc.
Core Data	Traces Core Data filesystem activity, including fetches, cache misses, and saves.
Energy Diagnostics	Provides diagnostics regarding energy usage, as well as basic on/off state of major device components.
Network	Analyzes the usage of TCP/IP and UDP/IP connections.
System Usage	Records I/O system activity related to files, sockets, and shared memory for a single process launched via instruments.
Core Animation	Monitors graphic performance and CPU usage of processes using Core Animation.
OpenGL ES Driver	Measures OpenGL ES graphics performance, as well as CPU usage of a process.
OpenGL ES Analysis	Measures and analyzes OpenGL ES activity to detect OpenGL ES correctness and performance problems. It also offers recommendations for addressing these problems.
Cocoa Layout	Observe and debug changes to `NSLayoutConstraint` objects to help debug layout constraint bugs.
Counters	Collect performance monitor counter events using time- or event-based sampling methods.
Dispatch	Monitors and measures dispatch queue activity and block invocations with duration.

Instrument	Description
Multicore	Measures multicore performance, including thread states, dispatch queues, and block usage.
UI Recorder	Allows the developer to capture user interaction and play it back later.
Sudden Termination	Analyzes sudden termination of a target process, reporting backtraces for file system accesses.

Note

It is important to realize that not all instruments are available under certain circumstances. For example, the Core Data instrument is available only when running on the simulator, and the Network instrument is available only while running on a physical device.

The Instruments Interface

To access the instruments interface in Xcode, select the build target, either a simulator or a device, and select the Profile option from the Product menu. A new window (see Figure 26.9) will appear, enabling the user to select the type of instrument he would like to run. After an option is selected, additional items can be added to it from the library (see Figure 26.10).

The instruments interface itself consists of several sections that will vary depending on the exact instrument you are running.

On the top toolbar of the Instruments window, various controls are present, such as those to pause, record, and restart the execution of the current target. Additionally, new targets can be selected from all running processes. The user also has control of setting an inspection range of any instrument that will filter items that do not occur between the left and right markers.

The instruments app will also save each run of the app so that changes to performance can quickly be compared to each other. The user can also add new instruments from the library in order to combine multiple tests. The left view, which can be toggled from the view menu, contains settings specific to the selected instrument. The bottom view will contain detailed information about the test being run, such as the Call Tree or Statistics; these also vary depending on the instrument selected. The last view is the right extended information view; this view will often contain the backtrace for the selected item in the center view.

Figure 26.9   Selecting instruments to run after running an app in profile mode.

Figure 26.10   The basic instruments interface, shown running the Allocations tool.

Most base-level objects found in the center or right view can be double-clicked to provide additional information, such as the referencing section of code.

In the following sections, two of the most common instruments are examined. The first, Time Profiler, is used by developers to determine which code within an app is taking the most time to execute. By analyzing the time each line of code takes to run, the developer is able to provide optimizations and enhancements to that code to increase the overall speed and performance of the app. The second instrument set that is examined consists of the Leaks and Allocation toolsets. These enable developers to analyze how memory is being used in their app, as well as easily find memory leaks and overreleases.

Exploring Instruments: The Time Profiler

The Time Profiler provides line-level information about the speed at which code is being executed. There are many bottlenecks that can cause an app to perform slowly, from waiting for a network call to finish to reading and writing from storage too often. However, a very common cause of performance issues and one of the easiest to address is the overuse of the CPU. Time Profile provides the developer with information about the execution time resulting from various calls, which in turn enables the developer to focus on problem areas of the app and provide performance improvements.

Time Profiler can be selected from the list of instrument templates and can be run on either the simulator or the device. When you are profiling CPU usage, it is important to remember that the device is typically much slower than the simulator, and users will not be running software on the simulator.

Time Profiler being run on an app with high CPU usage is shown in Figure 26.11. The top section in purple represents percentage of CPU used; dragging the cursor over the time bar will reveal the exact CPU usage percentage. The call tree reports that 99.6% of the process time is spent in Main Thread, and if that information is expanded/dropped, 99.1% of the time is spent in `main()` itself. This information is not entirely helpful on the surface, because an Objective-C app should be spending a considerable amount of its time in `main()`, but it does let the developer know that there is very high CPU usage, at some points at 100%.

To retrieve more useful information from the Time Profiler, the first thing that should be done is inverting the call tree, which is a check box in the Time Profiler settings (see Figure 26.11, right side). Instead of grouping time spent from the top down, it will group from the base functions up. In addition to inverting the call tree, it can be helpful to check off the box for Hide System Libraries. Although system library calls might be taking up a considerable amount of processing time, they can often be traced back to the developer's code itself. Viewing system calls can also be helpful for troubleshooting more difficult issues. Depending on whether the code base is using Objective-C only, it might also be helpful to use the Show Obj-C Only option.

Figure 26.11   Running the Time Profiler instrument on an app with high CPU usage.

After the proper configurations have been made, what is left is a list of calls that the developer has specifically made and the amount of CPU time they are taking up. The best-practice approach is to optimize from the largest usage to the least, because often fixing a larger issue will cascade and fix a number of the smaller issues as well. To get more information on the code in question, double-click on the item that will be investigated in the call tree. This will reveal a code inspector that is broken down by line with annotations indicating the amount of processor time used relative to the method, as shown in Figure 26.12.

> Note
>
> The code cannot be edited using the instruments code inspector; however, clicking on the Xcode icon (shown in Figure 26.12) will open the code in Xcode.

Although Time Profiler is not smart enough to make recommendations on how to optimize the code that is running slowly, it will point the developer in the right direction. Not every piece of code can be optimized, but equipped with the line numbers and the exact overhead required to run them, the challenge is greatly reduced.

Figure 26.12   Inspecting Time Profiler information at a line-by-line level.

> **Tip**
>
> Using the inspection range settings in instruments is useful for pinpointing exact spikes or sections of time to be investigated. The controls are used to mark the beginning and end of the inspect range on a timeline.

Exploring Instruments: Leaks

The Leaks instrument, and by close association the Allocations instrument, gives the developer a tremendous amount of insight into finding and resolving memory-related issues. It can assist in finding overuse of memory, leaks, retain cycles, and other memory-related issues. With the popularization of Automatic Reference Counting (ARC), the Leaks and Allocation tools are slowly falling from their previous grace; however, they can still offer tremendous benefits to the developer. Additionally, when ARC does fail to properly handle a memory issue, Instruments is the first place to look for the problem.

The Leaks instrument can be launched from the Instrument Selector window in the same fashion as the Time Profiler. When Leaks is launched, it will automatically also include the Allocations instrument, both of which can be run on the device and the simulator. In Figure 26.13, a poorly performing app is profiled, resulting in an increasing memory footprint, as indicated by the growing graph under the Allocations section. Additionally, several leaks have been detected, as indicated by the red bars in the Leaks section. Given enough time, these issues will likely result in the app running out of memory and crashing.

Figure 26.13   Running the Leaks and Allocation instruments against a project with memory leaks.

Although memory issues can also be debugged using the call tree grouping as shown in the section "Exploring Instruments: The Time Profiler," it is sometimes more useful to look at the Statistics or Leaks presentation of information. To see the leaks, which are often the cause of increasing memory usage, select the Leaks instruments from the upper left. In this sample project shown in Figure 26.14, there are numerous leaks of a UIImage object.

Instruments will attempt to group leaks into identical backtraces; however, the system is not perfect and leaks being caused by the same problem might appear more than once in the list. Best practice calls for resolving the highest number of leaks first and then running the profiler again. To trace the leak back to a section of code, the left view needs to be exposed. This is done with the view controller in the title bar of the Instruments window. Selecting a leak will reveal the backtrace to that event. Double-clicking the nonsystem-responsible call (typically shown in black text) will reveal the code in which the leak has occurred.

Figure 26.14   Investigating a large number of UIImage leaks from a sample project with a growing memory footprint.

There might be times when the memory footprint of an app grows to unacceptable levels but no leaks are present. This is caused by the app using more memory than is available. To troubleshoot this information, select the Allocations instrument and view the call tree. The same approach to inverting the call tree, hiding system libraries, and showing only Obj-C from the Time Profiler section might be helpful here. In Figure 26.15, 19.30MB of memory is being allocated in cellForRowAtIndexPath:, which causes the app to run poorly. Double-clicking this object will reveal a code inspector that will pinpoint which lines are using the most memory, which will provide guidance in the areas to troubleshoot.

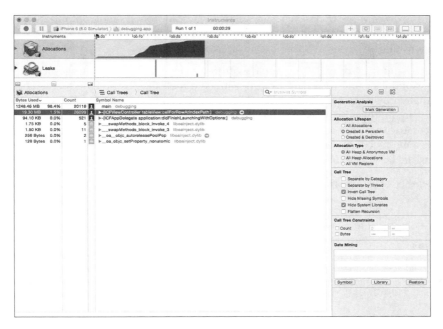

Figure 26.15   Investigating an Allocations call tree that shows a very large amount of memory being used in `cellForRowAtIndexPath:`.

Going Further with Instruments

Instruments is a highly explorable tool. After a developer has an understanding of the basic functionality and controls, the majority of instruments become very easy to deduce. Apple continues to aggressively improve on and push for developers to leverage instruments. At this point, there are tools to troubleshoot just about everything an app does, from Core Data to battery statistics, and there are even tools to help optimize animations in both Core Animation and OpenGL ES. To learn more about a particular instrument, visit Apple's online documentation at http://developer.apple.com/library/mac/#documentation/DeveloperTools/Conceptual/InstrumentsUserGuide/Introduction/Introduction.html.

Summary

This chapter, unlike most of the other chapters in this book, did not cover a sample project or demonstrate the proper usage of a new framework. Instead, it provided something more valuable, an introduction to debugging and code optimization. Debugging, in and of itself, is a huge topic that is worthy of not just one book but several books. We hope that this chapter has provided a jumping-off point for a lifelong passion of squeezing the most out of code and hunting down those tricky bugs. A developer who can troubleshoot, optimize, and debug quickly and effectually is a developer who never has to worry about finding work or being of value to a team.

Instruments and the Xcode IDE are Apple's gift to developers. Not too long ago, IDEs cost thousands of dollars and were hard to work with, and tools like Instruments were nonexistent. When Apple provided Xcode to everyone free, it was groundbreaking. Over the years, they have continued to improve the tools that developers use to create software on their platforms. They do this because they care about the quality of software that third-party developers are writing. It has become the obligation of all iOS developers to ensure that they are using the tools and providing the best possible software they can.

Index